Evaluation

Evaluation

Obtaining and Interpreting Data
3rd Edition

Edited by
**Jim Hinojosa, PhD, OT, FAOTA;
Paula Kramer, PhD, OTR, FAOTA; and
Patricia Crist, PhD, OTR, FAOTA**

Foreword by
Wendy J. Coster, PhD, OTR/L, FAOTA

The American
Occupational Therapy
Association, Inc.

AOTA Centennial Vision Statement

We envision that occupational therapy is a powerful, widely recognized, science-driven, and evidence-based profession with a globally connected and diverse workforce meeting society's occupational needs.

AOTA Mission Statement

The American Occupational Therapy Association advances the quality, availability, use, and support of occupational therapy through standard-setting, advocacy, education, and research on behalf of its members and the public.

AOTA Staff

Frederick P. Somers, *Executive Director*
Christopher M. Bluhm, *Chief Operating Officer*

Chris Davis, *Director, AOTA Press*
Ashley Hofmann, *Development/Production Editor*
Victoria Davis, *Editorial Assistant*

Beth Ledford, *Director, Marketing and Member Communications*
Emily Harlow, *Technology Marketing Specialist*
Jennifer Folden, *Marketing Specialist*

American Occupational Therapy Association, Inc.
4720 Montgomery Lane
PO Box 31220
Bethesda, MD 20814
Phone: 301-652-AOTA (2682)
TDD: 800-377-8555
Fax: 301-652-7711
www.aota.org

To order: 1-877-404-AOTA or store.aota.org

Disclaimers

This publication is designed to provided accurate and authoritative information in regard to the subject matter covered. It is sold or distributed with the understanding that the publisher is not engaged in rendering legal, accounting, or other professional service. If legal advice or other expert assistance is required, the services of a competent professional person should be sought.
—*From the Declaration of Principles jointly adopted by the American Bar Association and a Committee of Publishers and Associations*

It is the objective of the American Occupational Therapy Association to be a forum for free expression and interchange of ideas. The opinions expressed by the contributors to this work are their own and not necessarily those of the American Occupational Therapy Association.

ISBN: 978-1-56900-291-9

Library of Congress Control Number: 2010920897

Cover Design by Debra Naylor, Naylor Design, Inc., Washington, DC
Composition by Maryland Composition, Laurel, MD
Printed by Automated Graphic Services, Inc., White Plains, MD

We dedicate this book to all who are evaluated by occupational therapists and to those who have evaluated us. Evaluation promotes learning something new about the people we serve and ourselves.

We are very grateful to have the love and support of the following people, who continually help us learn about ourselves:

Steven A. Smith
David L. Hunt
Andrew L. K. Hunt
Billy E. Hickerson
Esther Mae Daetz

Contents

List of Figures, Tables, Boxes, Case Examples, and Appendixes Used in This Publication

Figures

Tables

Boxes

Case Examples

Appendixes

Acknowledgments

We are very proud of the illustrious group of people involved in this project. We extend our heartfelt thanks to all the contributing authors who worked diligently to share their thoughts and ideas in a way that would be useful to students, occupational therapists, and occupational therapy assistants. Also, we offer a special thank you to the spouses, significant others, and families who have supported them during the writing process. We know how grueling it can be!

On every project, there are particular people who stand out for their contributions. On this project, we acknowledge Chris Davis, Director; Ashley Hofmann, Development/Production Editor; and Victoria Davis, Editorial Assistant of AOTA Press, who have guided this project and been supportive throughout. We are always grateful to our colleagues at New York University, University of the Sciences in Philadelphia, and Duquesne University, who stimulate our thoughts and help shape our perspective.

Finally, we could not have undertaken this project without the love and caring of our families and significant others. They will always be the center of our lives.

Contributors

Rebecca Austill-Clausen, MS, OTR/L, FAOTA
President
Austill's Rehabilitation Services, Inc.
Austill's Services, Inc.
Exton, PA

Julie D. Bass-Haugen, PhD, OTR/L, FAOTA
Professor
Department of Occupational Science and Occupational Therapy
College of St. Catherine
St. Paul, MN

Jane Case-Smith, EdD, OTR/L, FAOTA
Professor and Chairperson
Division of Occupational Therapy
School of Allied Medical Professions
Ohio State University
Columbus

Denise Chisholm, PhD, OTR/L, FAOTA
Associate Professor and Vice Chairperson
Department of Occupational Therapy
School of Health and Rehabilitation Sciences
University of Pittsburgh

Michelle E. Cohen, PhD
Associate Professor
Departments of Occupational Therapy and Physical Therapy
Associate Dean of Research
Samson College of Health Science
University of the Sciences in Philadelphia

Patricia Crist, PhD, OTR FAOTA
Chairperson and Professor
Department of Occupational Therapy
Rangos School of Health Sciences
Duquesne University
Pittsburgh

Lou Ann Griswold, PhD, OTR/L, FAOTA
Associate Professor
Department of Occupational Therapy
School of Health and Human Services
University of New Hampshire
Durham

Carol Haertlein Sells, PhD, OT, FAOTA
Professor
Occupational Therapy
College of Health Sciences
University of Wisconsin–Milwaukee

Jim Hinojosa, PhD, OT, FAOTA
Professor
Department of Occupational Therapy
Steinhardt School of Culture, Education, and Human Development
New York University

Pamalyn J. Kearney, MS, OTR/L
Assistant Professor
Department of Occupational Therapy
Samson College of Health Science
University of the Sciences in Philadelphia

Paula Kramer, PhD, OTR, FAOTA
Professor and Chair
Department of Occupational Therapy
Samson College of Health Science
University of the Sciences in Philadelphia

Penny L. Kyler, ScD, OT, FAOTA
Public Health Analyst, Genetics Services Branch
Maternal and Child Health Bureau
Health Resources and Services Administration
U.S. Department of Health and Human Services

Aimee J. Luebben, EdD, OTR, FAOTA
Professor
Occupational Therapy Program
School of Nursing and Health Professions
University of Southern Indiana
Evansville

Jaime Phillip Muñoz, PhD, OTR/L, FAOTA
Associate Professor
Department of Occupational Therapy
Rangos School of Health Sciences
Duquesne University
Pittsburgh

Charlotte Brasic Royeen, PhD, OTR, FAOTA
Dean
Edward and Margaret Doisy College of Health Sciences
St. Louis University

Fern Silverman, EdD, OTR/L
Assistant Professor
Department of Occupational Therapy
Temple University
Philadelphia

Virginia Carroll Stoffel, PhD, OT, BCMH, FAOTA
Associate Professor, Graduate Coordinator, and Chair
Department of Occupational Therapy
University of Wisconsin–Milwaukee

Foreword

From my very first days as an occupational therapist, I have wrestled with the challenges of evaluation. It always seemed like the thorniest—and therefore the most interesting—part of the clinical process. How does one go about developing a clear understanding of a client's current situation? What questions should be asked? How and when is the best time to ask those questions? Which tools will be best to construct an accurate portrait of his or her situation—and what information should I use to select the best tools? How do I know when the "picture" I have created of a client's situation is accurate, and how will I know when I've headed down the wrong path?

As I wrestled with these questions, I came to appreciate the extent to which the decisions we make during evaluation shape the rest of our work with the client. Since then I have come to realize that evaluation is key to how a profession defines itself, both to its practitioners and to the consumers of its services. What we examine and how we do so does as much or more to define who we are than the actual interventions we provide. This is because the evaluation process defines "the problem" as occupational therapists perceive it, and this definition then guides our decisions about what will follow during intervention.

There have been periods in occupational therapy history when our evaluations did not communicate effectively our core concern with occupational performance. This was the situation when I entered practice in the early 1970s. One of my responsibilities at the time was to conduct evaluations of kindergartners in Boston public schools who were having a difficult time in the classroom and to make recommendations to their teachers about how best to help them. The formal tools I had available were a small set of standardized developmental tests, which I dutifully administered and scored as I had been trained. However, when it came time to make recommendations to the teachers, I faced a dilemma: The scores from the tests did not readily connect to the problems I had observed in the classroom, and they provided little obvious guidance about what to do to help the children.

Trombly (1993), among others, described the disconnect that occurred in this period when clients were referred to occupational therapy because of problems in daily function, but the evaluation focused almost exclusively on identifying component deficits (*impairments* in the language of the *International Classification of Functioning, Disability and Health [ICF]*; World Health Organization [WHO], 2001). Not surprisingly, interventions also tended to focus on changing discrete body functions. The end result, Trombly noted, was that clients were left confused about how their evaluation and treatment related to their daily problems in living, and they were confused about the purpose and value of occupational therapy.

Trombly (1993), Christiansen and Baum (1991), and Kielhofner (1985) were among early advocates for a shift to what Trombly called "top-down" evaluation (in contrast to "bottom-up" evaluation), referred to in this text as *outcome-focused evaluation*. The key difference between the two approaches is what drives or directs the inquiry process. *Bottom-up evaluation* starts with an examination of factors at the body function or body structure level of analysis (e.g., as determined by a standard protocol) and uses this information to propose an explanation of the person's difficulties with daily life. In contrast, *top-down evaluation* begins with a detailed analysis of the person's priority occupational performance problems. This analysis leads to hypotheses about which factors are most likely giving rise to those difficulties, and these hypotheses are then tested through subsequent steps of the evaluation process. The final goal of the process is to determine which factors can be changed through intervention and which factors must be taken into account in order to design an intervention that best matches the person's strengths, limitations, and current context.

The difference between these two approaches may not appear profound when described on paper. However, the differences in practice are quite significant. In particular, the shift toward a top-down or outcome-focused approach stimulated development of new measures that were better designed to assess occupational performance or, in *ICF* (WHO, 2001) terms, to measure *activity* and *participation*. Prior to this period there were almost no standardized assessments that occupational therapists could use for that first, key step of the evaluation process. This also meant that there were limited instruments available that could measure the effect of occupational therapy in improving the person's activity performance and participation in home, school, work, or community life.

The development of new measures designed to support the profession's evaluation needs is a significant advance. Like most advances, however, it also presents challenges. In particular, it is important for therapists conducting evaluations to be prepared to make their own independent assessment of the merits of available instruments for their current purpose and to be able to articulate the rationale for and to defend their choices. We work with very diverse client groups in very diverse settings, and it is unlikely that any instrument has been systematically tested across all of them. Thus, there may be limited evidence on whether the score from a given assessment tool is likely to be a valid indicator of a particular client's status. Rather than rely on blanket statements in a manual or in a research article that the assessment is "reliable and valid," occupational therapists must be able to appraise the evidence themselves to make an informed decision. We must also be able to distinguish and communicate what an instrument's score does—and does not—mean.

The current *Occupational Therapy Practice Framework: Domain and Process, 2nd Edition* (American Occupational Therapy Association, 2008) reflects the profession's renewed focus on occupational performance, the outcome of the earlier efforts to reshape the evaluation process. However, as the editors of this text note, it does not provide a detailed guide to conducting an evaluation. Without such a guide, it can be easy to get derailed by the significant external forces that also influence our practice such as tradition, payer or institutional requirements, or time constraints. Thus, one of the most important contributions of this text is to fill in the necessary details that will guide an evaluation process that is effective and truly helpful for the client as well as congruent with occupational therapy's focus and philosophy.

—Wendy J. Coster, PhD, OTR/L, FAOTA
Professor and Chairperson
Department of Occupational Therapy
Acting Chairperson
Department of Physical Therapy and Athletic Training
College of Health and Rehabilitation Sciences, Sargent College
Boston University

References

American Occupational Therapy Association. (2008). Occupational therapy practice framework (2nd ed.). *American Journal of Occupational Therapy, 62,* 625–683.

Christiansen, C. C., & Baum, C. A. (Eds.). (1991). *Occupational therapy: Overcoming human performance deficits.* Thorofare, NJ: Slack.

Trombly, C. A. (1993). Anticipating the future: Assessment of occupational function. *American Journal of Occupational Therapy, 47,* 253–257.

Kielhofner, G. (Ed.). (1985). *A Model of Human Occupation: Theory and application.* Baltimore: Williams & Wilkins.

World Health Organization. (2001). *International classification of functioning, disability and health, short version.* Geneva: Author.

Preface

In 1994 the American Occupational Therapy Association's (AOTA's) Commission on Practice requested the first edition of this book to address the importance of the evaluation process. Time passes, and the profession has continued to grow. During the past 5 years, AOTA's documents have changed; philosophies have changed; evaluation tools have dramatically expanded; and the knowledge, skills, and demand for evidence to provide a comprehensive evaluation has increased. Recently, AOTA adopted the *Occupational Therapy Practice Framework: Domain and Process, 2nd Edition* (AOTA, 2008) and revised standards of practice (AOTA, 2005a, 2005b). The Accreditation Council for Occupational Therapy Education® (ACOTE®) adopted revised *Standards for an Accredited Educational Program for the Occupational Therapist* (2007a, 2007b) for master's and doctoral entry-level programs. The profession's move to the postbaccalaureate entry level for the occupational therapist also has mandated increased depth and breadth in the area of evaluation.

Evaluation promotes a greater understanding of the people occupational therapy serves. It is the foundation of occupational therapy practice and provides evidence to guide "best practices." This third edition reflects current knowledge and best practices in occupational therapy relative to evaluation and assessment. The book presents a comprehensive view of the evaluative process. The depth of information reflects the needs of professionals and the level of content required in postbaccalaureate education. The focus is on the role of the occupational therapist as an evaluator with discussion regarding assessment support provided by the occupational therapy assistant. In this book, authors discuss the various aspects of a comprehensive evaluation, including screening, evaluation, reassessment, and re-evaluation. Evaluation is presented as part of the total scheme of practice and as a means of supporting the efficacy for interventions.

In this text, the authors focus on how the occupational therapist's understanding of human occupation influences evaluation. Within this context, the authors have reaffirmed the importance of understanding the person as an occupational being. This includes the role of culture and the potential of test bias when assessments are not culturally sensitive. Authors explore the roles and influences of the examiner on assessment and evaluation. The authors also acknowledge the critical importance of understanding the psychometric properties of assessments and the need to interpret assessment data so that it is applicable to practice. Further, the authors explore how an occupational therapist uses evaluation data to determine intervention effectiveness.

Our intention with this revision is to provide the profession with a much-needed comprehensive book on the occupational therapy evaluation process. The expansion of this text in breadth and depth reflects contemporary evaluation approaches. Most important, the authors discuss the important influence that evaluation practices have on occupational therapy practice. As therapists, we need to constantly keep best practice in mind and think about what the current practice environment wants an evaluation to be as well as what we believe a comprehensive evaluation should be.

—Jim Hinojosa, PhD, OT, FAOTA
Paula Kramer, PhD, OTR, FAOTA
Patricia Crist, PhD, OTR FAOTA

References

Accreditation Council for Occupational Therapy Education. (2007a). Accreditation standards for a doctoral-degree-level educational program for the occupational therapist. *American Journal of Occupational Therapy, 61,* 641–651.

Accreditation Council for Occupational Therapy Education. (2007b). Accreditation standards for a master's-degree-level educational program for the occupational therapist. *American Journal of Occupational Therapy, 61,* 652–661.

American Occupational Therapy Association. (2005a) Standards for continuing competence. *American Journal of Occupational Therapy, 59,* 661–662.

American Occupational Therapy Association. (2005b). Standards of practice for occupational therapy. *American Journal of Occupational Therapy, 59,* 663–665.

American Occupational Therapy Association. (2008). Occupational therapy practice framework: Domain and process (2nd ed.). *American Journal of Occupational Therapy, 62,* 625–683.

Evaluation: Where Do We Begin?

Jim Hinojosa, PhD, OT, FAOTA
Paula Kramer, PhD, OTR, FAOTA
Patricia Crist, PhD, OTR, FAOTA

Overview

Clinical reasoning is central to the process of evaluation. In their professional lives, occupational therapists engage in constant reflection, making choice after choice about which pieces of information are important, which are missing, and how to obtain the information needed to reach an effective decision. Effective decisions in the evaluation phase lead to a clear intervention plan and, eventually, to improved client outcomes. Aggregating client evaluation information for program evaluation and outcomes studies ultimately leads to sound decisions regarding the overall effectiveness of intervention programs.

After defining the evaluation-related terms used in this book and discussing how evaluation and assessment fit within the context of several important documents, this chapter outlines the responsibilities of occupational therapists in the evaluation process. This chapter also discusses the influence of evaluation data on intervention planning and implementation, describes clinical decision making in the evaluation process, and notes external influences on the evaluation process. Finally, this chapter provides brief descriptions of some other important concepts in occupational therapy evaluation, including accountable evaluation, evidence-based evaluation, and outcome-focused evaluation.

Importance of Evaluation in Occupational Therapy

Although occupational therapists have always recognized the importance of evaluation, they have used the evaluation process and associated terms inconsistently. In addition, therapists have been guided by the question, "What information do I need to determine if there is a need for intervention?" without giving sufficient attention to the optimal way of obtaining the necessary information. Such a lack of attention to getting the best information possible can lead to an evaluation process that looks meaningful (i.e., is valid) but has low quality (i.e., has low reliability). The emphasis on treatment strategies over evaluation in the occupational therapy literature is reflected in practice. The profession now needs to revisit the concept and practice of occupational therapy evaluation to better ascertain and describe the client's need for interventions, the results of intervention, and program outcomes.

Occupational therapy textbooks that discuss evaluation usually focus on the use of specific assessment tools and provide extensive overviews of proper administration of the tools and guidance in interpreting their specific findings. These descriptions of the assessments, however, do not address how occupational therapists should use the tools to obtain a full perspective of the client and guide occupational therapy practice. This volume provides a broad and comprehensive exploration of the evaluation process, contributing to the process of clinical reasoning. It provides professional knowledge and skills underpinning competent decision making in selecting and delivering quality evaluation approaches.

Definitions of Terms Used in This Book

Screening, evaluation, and *assessment* are terms that have distinct definitions. Using these terms interchangeably can cause confusion. In this book the following definitions are used:

- *Screening* refers to the process of reviewing available data, observing a client, or administering screening instruments to identify a person's (or a population's) potential strengths and limitations and the need for further assessment. Screening results should never be the evaluative basis for diagnostics, intervention planning, or monitoring.
- *Evaluation* refers to the comprehensive process of obtaining and interpreting the data necessary to understand the person, system, or situation. Evaluation requires synthesis of all data obtained, analytic interpretation of that data, reflective clinical reasoning, and consideration of occupational performance and contextual factors. Evaluation reports document the evaluation process, synthesize all findings, and state results and recommendations including the need for intervention. Evaluation reports may also describe potential changes to the intervention plan or summarize the client's performance abilities and limitations at the time of termination from current service.
- *Reevaluation* refers to a formal comprehensive review of a client, system, or situation at some point after the initial evaluation. It may identify any need to modify the intervention plan or change the intervention ap-

proaches. Reevaluation may or may not include the use of tools or instruments for assessment. When standardized tools are not used, clinical reasoning and judgment direct intervention decisions that are made as part of the reevaluation process.

- *Assessment* refers to a specific tool, instrument, or systematic interaction (e.g., observation, interview protocol) used to collect occupational profile and occupational performance areas during the evaluation process. Assessments, which vary from basic to complex, are component parts of the evaluation process.
- *Reassessment* refers to the ongoing process of reviewing client performance at any time other than at initial evaluation as an ongoing ("formative") or termination-of-intervention ("summative") measure of intervention change. Reassessment may include the use of standardized or non-standardized assessment tools. It is used to determine whether the intervention is effective or whether an intervention plan needs to be modified, and it contributes to reevaluation decision making. Use of the same tool during reassessment allows the detection of changes more easily; when this is not appropriate, a new tool that measures the same construct or performance may be selected.

The consistent use of terms can help the occupational therapy profession communicate internally with greater efficacy. In turn, this will increase occupational therapists' understanding of the evaluation and assessment processes and broaden the body of knowledge in this area. It is important to note that many professions continue to use these terms interchangeably and that some define *evaluation* and *assessment* differently than we have defined them here.

Foundational Documents for Evaluation in Occupational Therapy

Occupational therapy evaluation has changed over the years, and the profession currently embraces several core constructs. First, the importance of occupation as a component of health and performance is a key concept to address in a comprehensive evaluation. Meaningful, successful occupations are grounded in the person's ability to function. The focus of a comprehensive evaluation is identifying the client's strengths, skills, weaknesses, and limitations. Client-centeredness is an essential component of the evaluation process, to the extent that it is possible. Because evaluation is directed toward deciding what the therapist will do with the client, the client must be embraced as an essential part of the evaluation process. These core constructs are at the heart of several key documents that have important implications for occupational therapy evaluation.

Occupational Therapy Practice Framework: Domain and Process

The *Occupational Therapy Practice Framework: Domain and Process, 2nd Edition* (*Framework–II*; American Occupational Therapy Association [AOTA], 2008), describes the occupational therapy process as having three steps: evaluation, intervention, and outcomes. The discussion of the evaluation process in the *Framework–II* includes the occupational profile and analysis of occupational performance, two important components of an occupational therapy evaluation.

The *Framework–II* does not identify screening as a step in the evaluation process, but screening does take place in standard practice. In our view, one key element of the evaluation process is screening. The result of a screening provides guidance and direction to the therapist about needs for additional evaluation, and screening data assist the therapist in choosing appropriate assessments for a comprehensive evaluation. Further, screening data provides direction for the selection of a theory-based guide for intervention.

The occupational profile presented in the *Framework–II* is based on the fundamental philosophical belief in the importance of human occupation and client-centered care. It is a summary of occupational history, patterns of daily living, interests, values, and needs (AOTA, 2008) and thus provides a perspective that should always be part of the occupational therapy evaluation and intervention. Additionally, an important point recognized in the *Framework–II* is that "the occupational therapist's knowledge and skills, as well as theoretical principles and available evidence, guide his or her clinical reasoning for the selection and application of various theories and frames of reference throughout the evaluation process" (AOTA, 2008, p. 649). However, missing from the *Framework–II*'s discussion of evaluation is a consideration of real-world practicality. In some settings, there may not be enough time to compile a thorough occupational profile as the *Framework–II* describes it. In this book, we propose that the occupational profile is a process and that it may be most useful when used over time, throughout both the evaluation and treatment phases of intervention, rather than purely as an evaluation tool.

In the *Framework–II*, the analysis of occupational performance is

> the step in the evaluation process during which the client's assets, problems, or potential problems are more specifically identified. Actual performance is often observed in context to identify what supports performance and what hinders performance. Performance skills, performance patterns, context or contexts, activity demands, and client factors are all considered, but only selected aspects may be specifically assessed. (AOTA, 2008, p. 646)

Although the *Framework–II* emphasizes the importance of such analysis, the manner in which it is carried out is not clarified. In a comprehensive evaluation, an occupational therapist must use multiple assessments, including standardized and nonstandardized tools, to have sufficient data to plan intervention. The ideas in this book are built on the principle that in best practice the therapist uses multiple tools when evaluating a client, always considering the client's occupational history and goals. Without describing the use of additional assessment tools, the outline provided in the *Framework–II* may not be comprehensive or broad enough to guide an entry-level therapist through completing a thorough evaluation (Gutman, Mortera, Hinojosa, & Kramer, 2007).

Scope-of-Practice Documents

Professional associations, legislative acts, and common practice generally define the scope of practice. The purpose of a scope of practice is to define both the parameters of a profession and what practitioners do on a day-to-day basis. Scope-of-practice documents lay out accepted evaluations and interventions for the profession (AOTA, 2010; Buning et al., 2004; Clark, Polichino, & Jackson, 2004; Moyers & Dale, 2007). Furthermore, they define the parameters for decision making, thereby setting limits on practice. Legislative action, such as state practice acts, may accept the profession's identification of its own boundaries or establish boundaries for the profession, including the qualifications required to practice. Most state licensure acts put some specific limitations on the areas in which occupational therapists can practice, and some establish that particular areas of practice are not exclusive to occupational therapy.

Common practice also serves to determine the scope of practice of a profession. Some roles were accepted practice for occupational therapists in the past, but not for today's occupational therapists; consequently, these roles are no longer considered part of the occupational therapy scope of practice. In many settings, the roles and functions of occupational therapists are consistent with accepted practice for the profession, although roles may be modified in other settings. For example, in some hospital settings, morning activities of daily living (ADLs) are handled by nursing staff; therefore, the occupational therapist may not evaluate bedside ADL functions. In this type of situation, the setting influences the scope of practice of occupational therapy. Regardless of the external influences, demands, or standards, the professional never abdicates the ethical responsibility for delivering quality intervention reflecting clinical reasoning.

AOTA's official scope-of-practice document (2010) specifies what an occupational therapist should evaluate but does not discuss the process of evaluation or the specific tools that occupational therapists might select. It clearly identifies that occupational therapists evaluate factors affecting ADLs, instrumental activities of daily living (IADLs), education, work, play, leisure, and social participation, including

- Client factors, including body functions (e.g., neuromuscular, sensory, visual, perceptual, cognitive) and body structures (e.g., cardiovascular, digestive, integumentary, genitourinary systems);
- Habits, routines, roles, and behavior patterns;
- Cultural, physical, environmental, social, and spiritual contexts and activity demands that affect performance; and
- Performance skills, including motor, process, and communication/interaction skills. (AOTA, 2010)

The Guide to Occupational Therapy Practice (Moyers & Dale, 2007) describes the occupational therapy evaluation process consistent with the *Framework*. Moyers and Dale define *evaluation* as developing an occupational profile and analyzing occupational performance. The analysis of occupational performance is to gain an understanding of a person's ability to complete ADLs, IADLS, education, work, play, leisure, and social participation. The analysis requires an examination "among performance skills and patterns, contexts and environment, general activity demands, and client factors" (Moyers & Dale, 2007, p. 23). When the evaluation is complete, the occupational therapist develops an occupational performance statement based on all the collected data. This occupational performance statement has six elements or areas of focus:

1. Intervention focus on occupational performance in prioritized areas of occupation
2. Intervention focus on prioritized activities within the areas of occupation
3. Occupational performance skills (motor, cognitive, communication, and interaction) as demanded by prioritized activities
4. Occupational performance patterns (roles, habits, rituals, and routines)
5. Person factors (body structure and function, spirituality, beliefs, and values)
6. Contextual and environmental supports and barriers (cultural, physical, social, personal, temporal, or virtual). (Moyers & Dale, 2007, p. 30)

Although *The Guide to Occupational Therapy Practice* describes the important aspects of an occupational therapy evaluation, it does not address how theoretical perspectives can influence evaluation or intervention. Occupational therapists use a wide range of theoretical perspectives that determine their approach to intervention.

Standards of Practice for Occupational Therapy

One of AOTA's most important responsibilities to society and to the profession is to establish practice standards. *Practice standards* define the minimum requirements for performance and quality of care by occupational therapists and occupational therapy assistants. They provide minimal levels of performance to guide daily practice in all settings. Employers, clients, peers, and the general public use these standards to assess the appropriateness and quality of services received. Any performance or quality of care below these standards is incompetent practice.

The occupational therapy assistant participates in the evaluation process under the direction of the occupational therapist (AOTA, 2005c). The supervising therapist may delegate aspects of specific assessments to be administered by the occupational therapy assistant. Both the therapist and the assistant have a shared responsibility to ensure that the occupational therapy assistant is competent enough to administer the specific tool assigned. Although the process may be collaborative, the supervising therapist is ultimately responsible for selecting specific assessments, initiating and completing the evaluation, interpreting the data, and developing the intervention plan (AOTA, 2005c).

The AOTA Representative Assembly regularly revises and updates the standards for the occupational therapy profession. *Standards of Practice for*

Occupational Therapy (AOTA, 2005c) provides occupational therapists and occupational therapy assistants with guidelines for fulfilling their day-to-day responsibilities within the scope of occupational therapy practice. It is the professional responsibility of each occupational therapist and occupational therapy assistant to show and maintain compliance with AOTA's current *Standards of Practice for Occupational Therapy* (2005c) and *Standards for Continuing Competence* (AOTA, 2005b).

The current *Standards of Practice for Occupational Therapy* (2005c) have one standard related to screening, evaluation, and reevaluation (see Box 1.1). Using ideas from the American Counseling Association (2005) and the Council for Exceptional Children (2004), we propose the following changes (on pages 8 and 9) to the current standards, expanding them to ensure competent performance of assessment and evaluation:

Box 1.1. AOTA Standards of Practice for Occupational Therapy: Standard II: Screening, Evaluation, and Reevaluation

1. An occupational therapist accepts and responds to referrals in compliance with state laws or other regulatory requirements.
2. An occupational therapist, in collaboration with the client, evaluates the client's ability to participate in daily life activities by considering the client's capacities, the activities, and the environments in which these activities occur.
3. An occupational therapist initiates and directs the screening, evaluation, and reevaluation process and analyzes and interprets the data in accordance with law, regulatory requirements, and AOTA documents.
4. An occupational therapy assistant contributes to the screening, evaluation, and reevaluation process by implementing delegated assessments and by providing verbal and written reports of observations and client capacities to the occupational therapist in accordance with law, regulatory requirements, and AOTA documents.
5. An occupational therapy practitioner follows defined protocols when standardized assessments are used.
6. An occupational therapist completes and documents occupational therapy evaluation results. An occupational therapy assistant contributes to the documentation of evaluation results. An occupational therapy practitioner abides by the time frames, formats, and standards established by practice settings, government agencies, external accreditation programs, payers, and AOTA documents.
7. An occupational therapy practitioner communicates screening, evaluation, and reevaluation results within the boundaries of client confidentiality to the appropriate person, group, or organization.
8. An occupational therapist recommends additional consultations or refers clients to appropriate resources when the needs of the client can best be served by the expertise of other professionals or services.
9. An occupational therapy practitioner educates current and potential referral sources about the scope of occupational therapy services and the process of initiating occupational therapy services.

Screening

1. An occupational therapist initiates and directs the screening process in accordance with law, regulatory requirements, and AOTA documents.
2. An occupational therapist observes a potential client, reviews available records, or administers screening instruments to identify a person or population's potential strengths and limitations and the need for an evaluation.
3. An occupational therapy assistant contributes to the screening process by implementing delegated assessments and providing oral and written reports of observations and client capacities to the occupational therapist in accordance with law, regulatory requirements, and AOTA documents.
4. An occupational therapist is responsible for communicating the results of the screening to the client and other appropriate people, groups, or organizations, making referrals when appropriate.

Evaluation

1. An occupational therapist is responsible for choosing appropriate tools for the evaluation of the client. Therapists select assessments that do not discriminate against people because of race, color, creed, culture, gender, language preference, religion, national origin, age, political practices, family or social background, sexual orientation, or disability status.
2. An occupational therapist uses only the assessments for which he or she has appropriate knowledge, expertise, and skills and is competent in administering. An occupational therapist never allows unqualified people under his or her supervision to administer tests for which they do not have appropriate training and experience.
3. An occupational therapist, in collaboration with the client, evaluates the client's ability to participate in daily life activities by considering the client's capacities and activities and the environments in which these activities occur.
4. An occupational therapy assistant contributes to the evaluation process by administering delegated assessments in accordance with law, regulatory requirements, and AOTA documents. He or she must be competent in administering any test or assessment he or she uses.
5. An occupational therapist explains, before administering any assessment, the purpose of the evaluation. Furthermore, the therapist outlines the purpose of each assessment and explicitly states how the results will be used.
6. An occupational therapist and an occupational therapy assistant administer assessments in the manner in which they were intended. When administering a standardized assessment, an occupational therapist and occupational therapy assistant follow established protocols.
7. An occupational therapist interprets assessment results in the manner intended by the developer or publisher of each assessment.

8. An occupational therapist is responsible for the appropriate scoring, interpretation, and use of assessment instruments.

9. An occupational therapist ensures the accuracy and appropriateness of the evaluation summary. The therapist completes evaluation summaries within the time frames, formats, and standards established by the professional practice settings, government agencies, external accreditation programs, and third-party payers. Evaluation summaries reflect the guidelines for assessment interpretation provided by the developers or publishers of the assessment tools used.

10. An occupational therapist writes an evaluation report that explicitly reflects a synthesis of all data obtained, analytic interpretation of that data, reflective clinical reasoning, and consideration of contextual factors. Evaluation reports document the evaluation process, synthesize all findings, and state results and recommendations, including the need for initiation of or changes in intervention.

11. An occupational therapist and occupational therapy assistant respect the boundaries of client confidentiality. They maintain the confidentiality of information, except when information is released with specific written consent and within statutory confidentiality requirements.

Occupational Therapy Code of Ethics

Occupational therapists and occupational therapy assistants must abide by the *Occupational Therapy Code of Ethics* (AOTA, 2005a), which AOTA is currently revising. The revised document, the *AOTA Occupational Therapy Code of Ethics and Ethics Standards (2009)*, is reported to be an "aspirational guide to professional conduct...tailored to address ethical trends of the profession in education, research and practice" (AOTA, 2009). The draft version of the document can be found at http://www.aota.org/Practitioners/Ethics/Docs.aspx. In this chapter, we will discuss the key ethical principles that are referred to in the *Code of Ethics* (AOTA, 2005a, 2009) as they relate to evaluation practices. During the evaluation process, multiple issues may arise that create ethical dilemmas for the therapist; these issues are discussed in-depth in Chapter 14. Many of the principles in the Code relate to the evaluation process; however, we review only three key ethical principles in this chapter: beneficence, autonomy and confidentiality, and nonmaleficence.

Beneficence

Beneficence is the ethical principle that a professional shall demonstrate concern for the well-being and safety of clients and should not put the client at risk for harm. All tests have biases, and therapists must recognize the biases in the assessment tools they use. Biases can occur because of gender, educational level, socioeconomic background, ethnic background, cultural background, geographic environment, or medical status. Because occupational therapists are concerned with a person's everyday life and the performance of daily tasks, they need information about the person and his or her background and culture to select a tool appropriate to that particular person as a whole, rather than merely matched superficially to his or her age or diagnosis. For example, if a therapist receives a referral to evaluate a person with right hemiplegia, the therapist first needs to find out about the person's age, gender, culture, and other factors that influence the client in order to gain a better understanding of the types of occupations in which the client engages. It would also help to find out about the client's personal interests and goals. On the basis of this information, the therapist can choose an appropriate assessment tool that accurately reflects the client's performance.

No single assessment tool should be the basis for determining a problem area. The use of multiple tools helps therapists to avoid test bias and gives a more accurate picture of variations that may occur in a client's performance. Therapists frequently find that a combination of standardized and nonstandardized instruments, combined with observations and clinical judgment, provides a reasonably accurate overall portrait of a client's strengths and limitations.

Additionally, when writing an evaluation report, the therapist must take care to ensure that data in the report are accurate. Further, conclusions made by the therapist in the report should be directed toward helping the client, rather than labeling the client in a way that is harmful.

Autonomy and Confidentiality

The principle of *autonomy and confidentiality* addresses the client's rights and the occupational therapist's and occupational therapy assistant's responsibility to respect the client and keep the client's information private. Practitioners must protect the confidential nature of information obtained from a client during the screening and evaluation process. The Health Insurance Portability and Accountability Act of 1996 (Pub. L. 104–191) further reinforces confidentiality protections. All information gathered during the evaluation process is confidential.

In most cases, the evaluation process is not complete until the findings have been written up in an evaluation report or evaluation summary. These reports should be concise yet comprehensive and should include only honest and accurate information. Evaluation data should be interpreted using a theoretical framework and the therapist's knowledge and expertise in working with a population with characteristics akin to the client's. Interpretation of evaluation data should include both the strengths and limitations of the client. If the interpretation of the data only labels and categorizes clients with specific deficits, clients will be identified by their limitations rather than their potential. Such information may follow clients well into the future and may have significant consequences for their lives, including the influencing they are given and the services they receive. It is important to present a comprehensive picture of the client, including positive findings as well as findings that require intervention. Therapists should also be careful not to overinterpret data or suggest results that may still be inconclusive. In addition, it is important that occupational therapy evaluation summaries reflect the domain of concern of occupational therapy and identify strengths and limitations related to the client's occupational performance.

Nonmaleficence

The ethical principle of *nonmaleficence* refers to the importance of not doing harm to the client. In all aspects of evaluating a client, therapists must ensure that no harm is done. Therapists must be careful with the selection of assessments and how they are used. Standardized and nonstandardized assessments are designed for specific uses, such as with specific populations or age groups, with people who share particular backgrounds, or with people fluent in the language of the tool. When therapists use an assessment with clients whose characteristics differ from those of the intended testing population, the results may not be comparable or even valid, and areas identified as deficits may not actually be deficits.

Entry-level occupational therapists cannot be expected to be competent in all the assessments that occupational therapists use. However, it is imperative that therapists be competent in the administration and interpretation of an assessment before using it with a client. To achieve such competency, therapists need to read about the evaluation, understand its unique purpose and use, understand the psychometric properties involved, know whether or not it requires the use of standardized procedures, have adequate knowledge and skills to perform these procedures, and be able to interpret results.

Some assessments are not designed for use by entry-level occupational therapists. These tools may require certification, post-professional continuing education, or even an additional academic degree. Examples of advanced-level assessment tools include the *Sensory Integration and Praxis Tests* (Ayres, 1989) and the *Assessment of Motor and Process Skills* (Fisher, 1992). Therapists often choose to receive post-professional education to develop the skills and competencies necessary to use specialized assessment tools. It is a professional responsibility to ensure that one has the necessary skills and underlying knowledge before using and interpreting specialized tools. Furthermore, it is essential that therapists accurately represent to clients their qualifications to administer these assessments. When therapists use specialized tests that are more frequently associated with other disciplines, they have the additional challenge and responsibility to make sure that their use of the instruments addresses the domain of concern of occupational therapy. Chapter 3 discusses the identification and selection of assessment tools in greater detail.

Accredited Educational Programs for the Occupational Therapist

Professional-level education prepares occupational therapists and occupational therapy assistants for their therapeutic responsibilities. According to recent accreditation standards for occupational therapists (Accreditation Council for Occupational Therapy Education [ACOTE], 2007b), occupational therapy students are required to learn to select, administer, and interpret standardized and nonstandardized tests and assessments, in addition to be able to make skilled observations, take relevant histories, and interview clients and family members. The many skills needed to perform these tasks are honed during therapists' educational and professional experience.

The role of the occupational therapy assistant in the evaluation process is to obtain data to share with the occupational therapist. The occupational therapy assistant may use a variety of standardized and nonstandardized assessments, done under the supervision of and in collaboration with the occupational therapist (ACOTE, 2007a).

In addition, recent accreditation standards for occupational therapists (ACOTE, 2007b) state that it is the role of the occupational therapist to select appropriate assessment tools for screening and evaluation of clients, use standardized formats for the administration of those tools, and interpret the evaluation data. The occupational therapist is responsible for considering potential areas of bias in an evaluation, interpreting standardized assessments based on an understanding of psychometric data, and relating the interpretation of evaluation data to professional standards and theoretical perspectives. Both occupational therapists and occupational therapy assistants may document screening and evaluation services.

There are some inconsistencies between recent accreditation standards for occupational therapists and occupational therapy assistants (ACOTE, 2007a, 2007b) and official documents of the American Occupational Therapy Association. The accreditation standards specifically discuss the role of both occupational therapists and occupational therapy assistants in the screening process, an area that is omitted from the *Framework–II*. Additionally, the accreditation standards (ACOTE, 2007a) are the only documents that specifically mention that the occupational therapist supervises and collaborates with the occupational therapy assistant in the screening and evaluation process.

International Classification of Functioning, Disability and Health

The World Health Organization (WHO) has worked diligently to facilitate the use of common language regarding disability across countries and cultures. In the most current revision to the *International Classification of Functioning, Disability and Health* (ICF; WHO, 2001), the WHO sought to change the lexicon from a medically oriented disease and disability model to one that focuses on a social model of health and participation (Hinojosa, Kramer, Royeen, & Luebben, 2003). This model is well suited to occupational therapy and valuable because it uses concepts consistent with the profession in a way that can be readily understood by a general audience.

The *ICF* provides parameters for gaining a comprehensive understanding of the person in two areas: (1) functioning and disability, which includes the two components of body structure and function, activity, and participation, and (2) contextual factors, which includes environmental factors and personal factors (WHO, 2001). One of the intended applications of the *ICF* is "as a clinical tool—in needs assessment, matching treatments with specific conditions, vocational assessment, rehabilitation and outcome evaluation" (p. 5). It is important to note that an evaluation consistent with *ICF* principles has a broad perspective, including an exploration of the interaction between the person and context. Additionally, the *ICF* proposes that a person may need a comprehensive evaluation to understand his or her needs and abilities (WHO, 2001).

Responsibilities of Occupational Therapists in Evaluation

Effective evaluators have a comprehensive knowledge of the domain of concern of the profession, human development and individual variation, statistics, and tests and measurements and an understanding of the concepts of activities and occupation. Additionally, therapists have to be skilled in interacting with clients to elicit information and judge their performance and the quality of their response. Therapists need to be competent in administering a broad repertoire of assessment tools and understand the principles of tests and measurements. When using a specific assessment tool, therapists should know its strengths and limitations, psychometric properties, and applicability to specific situations. Finally, when interpreting the results of the evaluation, therapists need to put the data within the context of the individual's personal view of his or her life, environment, and chosen occupations.

Therapists also need to understand the circumstances of the evaluation and how these influence the selection of assessment tools. These circumstances include the time and space available for testing, the service delivery model, the purpose of the evaluation, and other evaluations being administered to the individual. On the basis of their knowledge of psychometrics and an understanding of the individual, therapists decide which assessments will be reliable and valid, whether subjective and objective data are needed, whether standardized and nonstandardized tools will be used, and which tools will be most relevant within the context of the evaluation. Therapists also need to have the expertise and skills to administer the chosen assessments and, once the assessments have been administered, to interpret the data.

Data interpretation involves combining data from various sources and determining which data are important and how the data fit, both with the domain of concern of occupational therapy and with the role of occupational therapy within the setting. Therapists must then document their findings in a format that is appropriate to the setting and that makes points clearly and concisely so that everyone involved can understand the issues. In addition to documenting the evaluation, therapists often need to convey the findings to the client, his or her family or caregivers, and other professionals. This communication should be clear and accurate, appropriate to the audience, and conducive to providing the best services for the client within and between provider groups and agencies.

Influence of Evaluation on Intervention Planning

Once occupational therapists have completed a screening, they decide how to proceed with the evaluation and what tools will be most appropriate for the setting and the data being sought. The tools used in the evaluation process will affect the intervention process and approach. Sometimes, therapists know what theory or frame of reference would be appropriate for the client just by reading a chart or interviewing a client. Other times, there is limited information available to help determine which theoretical approach would be the best to follow. In such cases, therapists begin by deciding, in collaboration with the client and his or her family, how to approach evaluation. Theoretical considerations in evaluation and intervention planning are discussed in detail in Chapter 2.

During the process of evaluation, occupational therapists continually review the assessment data and make decisions and judgments based on this information. The process is intensive and dynamic, requiring constant thinking and decision making as the client completes each assessment. As the therapist reviews the data from each assessment, he or she decides how to proceed. Each decision leads to another set of choices, such as whether to implement another assessment, until the therapist has gathered enough information to draw conclusions. For the experienced therapist, clinical decision making flows smoothly and indubitably; however, the entry-level therapist typically has little time for the extended reflection initially required for such decision making. The entry-level therapist needs to become familiar with a wide variety of tools and the strengths and limitations of each tool. He or she must then develop skills in using these tools to become a competent evaluator. Although current practice may not provide much time for the development of such expertise, it is a professional responsibility that should not depend on the clinical setting and its constraints.

Other clinical constraints influence clinical decision making during evaluation. Practice settings typically allow little time for evaluation and, at times, third-party payers or certain settings such as schools prescribe the assessment tools to be used. In addition, an institution may have a set protocol for evaluation that is required for every client, regardless of his or her individual needs. In such situations, the therapist's evaluation decisions are significantly influenced by outside factors, decreasing the autonomy of the professional. It is imperative that therapists develop their skills and competence so that they can adequately justify their actions and decisions in evaluations. Once they have obtained skills and competence, therapists will need to develop evidence-based research to substantiate their method's evaluation processes. This topic is discussed in Chapter 15.

Other Concerns in Occupational Therapy Evaluation

The occupational therapy evaluation process is influenced by a number of factors beyond the assessment, administration of the assessment, and the interpretation of results. Other factors include the form and content of the evaluation report, accountability questions, and the degree to which the report is evidence-based or outcome-focused. When a team-based approach is used, evaluations might not be done by a single individual.

Evaluation Report

Because the purpose of the report is to communicate information to others, therapists need to know the target audience when constructing the report. The client may need a report that is written with an educational focus, a physician may need medical data presented in a very succinct manner, and a third-party payer may require documentation to show that the situation meets the criteria for reimbursement. Thus, more than one summary may need to be written for the same client. Regardless of audience, it is often prudent to avoid using jargon and complex language. Reports should be proofread carefully to ensure that there are no misspellings, grammatical errors, or awkward sentences that may be unclear to readers. Finally, formal reports, particularly those going outside the institution, should be formatted and typed in a professional style; the report is often the first impression therapists make and therefore must be presented in a professional manner. Likewise, therapists must ensure that documentation is accurate, legally defensible, unalterable by others, and secure.

Accountable Evaluation

Accountable evaluation starts with using an evaluation process or choosing specific tools that are acceptable to other professionals, consumers, and third-party payers. These tools or processes are defensible in terms of professional standards and best practice, and they reflect the domain of concern of the profession. Full accountability requires that an evaluation provide an accurate assessment of the client's performance, skills, and deficits, combined with his or her personal needs and goals, in a manner that is generally acceptable in the context of that person's life.

Evidence-Based Evaluation

The evaluation process must be tailored to the individual needs of the client. Evidence-based evaluation requires sufficient facts about the client, the assessment tools, and the evaluation process to support appropriate decision making. Using a reflective process, occupational therapists consider what the particular client needs and explores the literature for guidance about best practice. The literature can help therapists identify the assessment tools often used in the relevant type of situation, the value and rigor of those tools, and how this information is applicable to the particular client. As part of this process, therapists are required to scrutinize their own clinical experiences and integrate them with information gleaned from the literature regarding the assessment tools, client characteristics, and context of the evaluation. This reflective process results in a well-thought-out plan for evaluation.

Outcome-Focused Evaluation

Outcome-focused evaluation is the process of evaluating clients based on their desired outcomes. This process requires therapists to use reverse thinking and to begin with the clients' identified needs, desires, and limitations. Once clients have identified their preferred outcomes of treatment (through an interview or an occupational profile), therapists need to determine what type of evaluation and intervention will facilitate the achievement of those desired outcomes. Clients' desired outcomes guide therapists' judgment during evaluation and throughout treatment.

Another type of outcome evaluation can take place before discharge from occupational therapy services. Therapists identify the client's levels of performance at the beginning and again at the end of the intervention process relative to the stated expectations at the beginning of intervention. Not only do therapists consider whether or not the desired outcomes were reached, but careful reflection is also required to determine whether the initial goals were realistic and whether the process used was effective enough to achieve the desired results. At the end of this process, therapists may determine that different tools should be used either for initial evaluation in the future or for determining outcome performance.

Team Approach

Team approaches are commonly used in treatment. Often, occupational therapy evaluation reports are part of a larger comprehensive team evaluation. Sharing hypotheses with the team may provide an enhanced view of the client. Each member of the team contributes a different perspective on the individual, and information gained from the collaborative process can provide a more complete picture of the client's abilities and disabilities. The team should discuss which assessments each member will use and the purpose of each assessment to ensure that unnecessary duplication is avoided and that assessments provide complementary data regarding the client's abilities and disabilities. In addition, it is helpful for team members to keep their findings and interpretations confidential until all members have completed their evaluations; when multiple professionals evaluate the individual, it can be helpful for each to come to his or her own conclusions individually before the team meets collectively. This strategy can prevent one member from being swayed by the hypotheses of another, helping the team avoid an inaccurate conclusion. This strategy can also help the team identify variations in the client's performance from one evaluation session to another.

External Influences on the Evaluation Process

At times, the type or focus of the evaluation is determined externally. The institution may require that an evaluation include one or more specific assessments; for example, a hospital may require that all clients on their inpatient unit be evaluated using the Bay Area Functional Performance Evaluation (Williams & Bloomer, 1987). Alternatively, a service delivery model may require that the evaluation have a specific focus; for example, a school system typically requires an evaluation with a focus on educational relevancy or a screening to provide early identification of students with potential learning difficulties. In other circumstances, a referral may suggest or require a specific type of evaluation, such as a referral for occupational therapy following joint replacement surgery. Regardless of whether occupational therapists have a choice in the evaluation process or the tools used, they have a professional responsibility to make sure that the overall evaluation meets the needs of the client, reflects the domain of concern of occupational therapy, and is relevant to the programming and intervention services that will be offered.

Another important influence on the type and focus of evaluation is the client. It is incumbent upon the therapist to listen to the client and respond appropriately. The client may have specific concerns or expectations; for example, a client may want to be independent in bathing and toileting but is content to receive help with dressing. In this case, the therapist has two options: to evaluate and address only the performance areas of concern to the client, or to educate the client about how identified areas might be improved or enhanced through therapy. Clients always have the right to refuse evaluation or intervention. They also have the right to know the outcomes of specific assessments, so therapists should review the results with clients and answer any questions they may have.

Informed clients often bring their own concerns, ideas, and expectations about what the evaluation process will include and what outcomes they expect. Therapists may agree with the client's perspective, or they may have differing views about what the evaluation should entail. It is critical that therapists involve the client and consider his or her point of view. Open discussion about the evaluation process, the use of the results, and the concerns of both parties can be a big step forward in developing a rapport that will serve as the basis for a positive therapeutic relationship. Therapists can inform clients that therapists likely cannot interpret the specific results from an assessment session immediately because they need time to consider the meaning of overall assessment results first. Through a collaborative process, therapists and clients work toward reaching a consensus on the evaluation, its focus, and what it will include. Forthright discussion and willingness to consider each other's perspectives enable mutual trust to develop, and an open, trusting relationship established during evaluation can serve as the foundation for future intervention.

Focus and Content of This Book

The focus of this book is the evaluation and assessment of people seeking occupational therapy services. Although the authors mention specific assessment tools and processes in some chapters to illustrate their points, no chapter presents or reviews the use of specific assessment tools or evaluations with specific populations. Professionals are responsible for choosing the appropriate tools from all those available to provide the data they need to make sound clinical judgments. One goal of this book is to explore evaluation as a vehicle for determining the need for intervention and for developing or changing intervention plans. This book will not deal with the complex topic of non–client-related

evaluations that occupational therapists engage in, such as systems evaluations, facilities evaluations, or outcomes assessments. However, systematic and
well-planned evaluation that is congruent with the goals of each occupational
therapy program provides valuable data for these other very important types
of evaluation as well.

A critical element of this book is its emphasis on the process of evaluation rather than on the tools for evaluation. An understanding of the entire
evaluation process will help occupational therapists better determine the need
for intervention, establish an appropriate treatment plan, and determine the
results of intervention. Moreover, the ongoing process provides therapists with
an understanding of when and how to modify the intervention plan on the basis of ongoing clinical reasoning and monitoring of intervention effectiveness.
Collaboration with the client is essential to ensure that the intervention has the
desired effect of enabling him or her to engage in meaningful occupation. Once
they thoroughly understand the various concepts foundational to evaluation,
therapists are in a better position to choose the most appropriate assessment
tools for the situation at hand.

Chapter 2 continues the discussion of the general theoretical issues in evaluation begun in this chapter. It describes the philosophical basis of evaluation
and its relationship to occupational therapy theory and, in particular, to frames
of reference. It also provides an overview of the evaluation process. Chapters 3
through 6 center on the use of assessment tools throughout the evaluation process: Chapter 3 provides a process for identifying and selecting assessments to
use in practice, Chapter 4 discusses evaluation issues in today's complex practice environment, Chapter 5 discusses the use of evaluation in the intervention
planning process, and Chapter 6 discusses the administration of evaluation and
assessment. Chapter 7 explores the influence of context on the client and the
evaluation process. Subsequent chapters discuss the use of nonstandardized tools
(Chapter 8); the psychometrics of standardized assessments, including reliability
and validity (Chapter 9); and the scoring and interpretation of assessment results
(Chapter 10). Chapter 11 presents discussions of the critical areas of data interpretation and documentation of evaluation results. Chapter 12 investigates reassessment and reevaluation in depth. Evaluation issues with special populations
are addressed in Chapter 13, and the ethical implications of evaluation are out-
lined in Chapter 14. Chapter 15 discusses the use of evaluation data to support
evidence-based practice, and Chapter 16 describes other uses of evaluation data,
including outcomes measurement, research, and program development.

Conclusion

Evaluation is a primary aspect of the occupational therapy process. Although
there are many ways of conceptualizing practice, occupational therapists generally approach the evaluation of clients by starting with an assessment of an aspect of the profession's domain of concern. Comprehensive evaluation requires
that occupational therapists assess all aspects of the domain of concern as they

relate to the individual client. In the occupational therapist's role as an evaluator, he or she must comply with AOTA's current standards of practice, the *Code of Ethics*, and sound professional judgment. The occupational therapy assistant participates in the evaluation process under the direction of the occupational therapist.

The process of evaluation is complex and challenging. It requires both knowledge and skill on the part of the therapist. Basic academic education provides a core understanding of evaluation in general; however, this is just the beginning. To gain proficiency in evaluation, occupational therapists must continually learn new assessment tools, develop mastery of a wide variety of assessment tools, reflect on the relevancy of generally used assessment tools, understand the various roles that the client plays in the evaluation process, and examine the literature regarding all aspects of evaluation. This text provides the foundational knowledge on evaluation to competently engage in test and measurement processes as an occupational therapist.

Questions

1. Explain why an occupational therapist should not develop an intervention plan based on screening data alone.
2. What is the difference between reassessment and reevaluation? Why is it important to differentiate between these two concepts?
3. The authors state that a supervising therapist may delegate specific assessments to be administered by an occupational therapy assistant. How would a therapist justify the delegation of this responsibility?
4. How would the current AOTA standards of practice influence your conceptualization and administration of an evaluation?
5. Identify the consistencies and inconsistencies in the various documents regarding the role and activities associated with occupational therapy evaluation discussed in this chapter.
6. Examine the occupational profile and analysis of occupational performance. Describe how you would use this as part of an evaluation. What critical elements would you add to make it a comprehensive evaluation?
7. Identify the basic characteristics and benefits of a good evaluation program.
8. What are the potential problems or challenges that arise when a practitioner does not implement evaluation for individuals, the system, or setting?

References

Accreditation Council for Occupational Therapy Education. (2007a). Accreditation standards for a doctoral-degree-level educational program for the occupational therapist. *American Journal of Occupational Therapy, 61,* 641–651.

Accreditation Council for Occupational Therapy Education. (2007b). Accreditation standards for a master's-degree-level educational program for the occupational therapist. *American Journal of Occupational Therapy, 61,* 652–661.

American Counseling Association. (2005). *ACA code of ethics*. Retrieved July 22, 2009, from http://www.counseling.org/Resources/CodeOfEthics/TP/Home/CT2.aspx

American Occupational Therapy Association. (2005a). Occupational therapy code of ethics (2005). *American Journal of Occupational Therapy, 59*, 639–642.

American Occupational Therapy Association. (2005b). Standards for continuing competence. *American Journal of Occupational Therapy, 59*, 661–662.

American Occupational Therapy Association. (2005c). Standards of practice for occupational therapy. *American Journal of Occupational Therapy, 59*, 663–665.

American Occupational Therapy Association. (2008). Occupational therapy practice framework: Domain and process (2nd ed.). *American Journal of Occupational Therapy, 62*, 625–683.

American Occupational Therapy Association. (2009). *Draft AOTA occupational therapy code of ethics and ethics standards*. Retrieved October 1, 2009, from http://www.aota.org/Practitioners/Ethics/Docs.aspx

American Occupational Therapy Association. (2010). Scope of practice. *American Journal of Occupational Therapy, 64*.

Ayres, A. J. (1989). *Sensory Integration and Praxis Tests*. Los Angeles: Western Psychological Services.

Buning, M. E., Hammel, J., Angelo, J., Schmeler, M., Doster, S., Voelkerding, K., et al. (2004). Assistive technology within occupational therapy practice. *American Journal of Occupational Therapy, 58*, 678–680.

Clark, G. F., Polichino, J., & Jackson, L. (2004). Occupational therapy services in early intervention and school-based programs. *American Journal of Occupational Therapy, 58*, 681–685.

Council for Exceptional Children. (2004). *Assessment system standards*. Retrieved July 22, 2009, from http://www.cec.sped.org/Content/NavigationMenu/ProfessionalDevelopment/ProfessionalStandards/Assessment_System_Standards.htm

Fisher, A. G. (1992). *Assessment of Motor and Process Skills* (rev. ed.) [Unpublished test manual]. Fort Collins: Colorado State University, Department of Occupational Therapy.

Gutman, S. A., Mortera, M. H., Hinojosa, J., & Kramer, P. (2007). Revision of the *Occupational Therapy Practice Framework*. *American Journal of Occupational Therapy, 61*, 119–126.

Health Insurance Portability and Accountability Act of 1996, Pub. L. 104–191, 45 C.F.R. § 160, 164. Retrieved October 27, 2004, from http://www.hhs.gov/ocr/hipaa/

Hinojosa, J., Kramer, P., Royeen, C. B., & Luebben, A. (2003). The core concept of occupation. In P. Kramer, J. Hinojosa, & C. B. Royeen (Eds.), *Perspectives in human occupation: Participation in life* (pp. 1–17). Philadelphia: Lippincott Williams & Wilkins.

Moyers, P., & Dale, L. (2007). *The guide to occupational therapy practice* (2nd ed.). Bethesda, MD: AOTA Press.

Williams, S. L., & Bloomer, J. (1987). *Bay Area Functional Performance Evaluation administration and scoring manual* (2nd ed.). Palo Alto, CA: Consulting Psychologist Press.

World Health Organization. (2001). *International classification of functioning, disability and health*. Geneva: Author.

Philosophical and Theoretical Influences on Evaluation

Paula Kramer, PhD, OTR, FAOTA
Jim Hinojosa, PhD, OT, FAOTA

Overview

Each occupational therapist has a set of philosophical assumptions and beliefs based in part on those of the profession; in part on personal experiences, especially those gained during his or her professional career; and acquired through education. These assumptions and beliefs influence the way a therapist performs evaluation, the assessments he or she chooses, the theories he or she uses, and the approaches he or she takes to intervention. Some therapists follow particular models, others use distinct paradigms, and still others use specific frames of reference. In all of these perspectives, evaluation is an essential part of practice. This chapter focuses on the links among philosophy, theory, and practice as they influence evaluation and provides an overview of the evaluation process.

Philosophical Influences on Evaluation

The profession of occupational therapy has philosophical beliefs that influence what occupational therapists and occupational therapy assistants consider important and that guide their actions. These philosophical beliefs collectively form the unique philosophical foundations of the profession. Therefore, occupational therapy's philosophical beliefs have a strong influence on therapists' actions, including how they perform evaluation and provide intervention. The following foundational beliefs for occupational therapy were first attributed to William Rush Dunton, Jr., in a retrospective article (American Occupational Therapy Association, 1967):

- Occupation is as necessary to life as food and drink.
- Every human being should have both physical and mental occupation.
- All should have occupations that they enjoy or hobbies—at least two, one outdoor and one indoor.
- Sick minds, sick bodies, and sick souls may be healed through occupation.

Although a variety of authors have updated these basic beliefs (e.g., Kielhofner, 2009; Mosey, 1986), the core is still the same: Occupation is necessary to a healthy, meaningful life (Baum & Christiansen, 2005; Kielhofner, 2009).

One conceptualization of the profession's philosophy (Mosey, 1996) reflects this philosophy in terms of its view of the person and his or her rights. Occupational therapists and occupational therapy assistants believe that a person

- Has the right to a meaningful existence;
- Is influenced by the biological and social nature of the human species;
- Can be understood only within the context of family, friends, community, and cultural group membership;
- Has the need to participate in a variety of social roles and to have periodic relief from participation;
- Has the right to seek his or her potential through personal choice within the context of accepted social constraints; and
- Is able to reach his or her potential through purposeful interaction with the human and nonhuman environments.

Occupational therapists thus believe that clients have the right to make choices and to be active participants in the therapeutic process. The importance of the client's collaboration in the evaluation process is discussed throughout this book. Evaluation begins with the person and considers his or her life experiences, life roles, interests and occupations, age, cultural background, and situational context. The client's own view of what is important and his or her own perceived strengths and limitations are essential to the evaluation process in occupational therapy. Throughout evaluation, a therapist must take into consideration the multiple factors that influence intervention outcomes for an individual client. The first and most important factor is the needs of the particular client and the desired outcomes of that person and his or her family (Law, 1998).

Additionally, occupational therapists have strong beliefs about the importance of occupations and activities, including that people are naturally active beings (i.e., have an occupational nature) and that occupation is necessary to society and culture. Kielhofner (2009) proposed that occupation is a basic need for people, a source of meaning in their lives, and a domain of human behavior. These constructs influence the way occupational therapists look at people, the way they evaluate clients, and the areas in which they intervene. Thus, an occupational therapy evaluation always considers the person's

- Biological and individual development,
- Cultural and social context,

- Relationship with family and significant others,
- Engagement in meaningful occupations,
- Quality of occupational performance, and
- Unique occupations in relation to their physical and psychological development.

An individual therapist is further influenced by his or her own personal beliefs, values, and biases, which are separate from the beliefs and values of the profession. These beliefs, values, and biases influence the therapist's choice of assessment tools and interpretation of the results. For example, if a therapist believes that sensorimotor development is one of the most critical aspects of child development, then the therapist will include a sensorimotor assessment as part of a pediatric evaluation.

Basic philosophical beliefs influence the way an occupational therapist performs an evaluation. A therapist operationalizes his or her beliefs, values, and biases when evaluating clients. We propose the following six principles as best reflecting the philosophy of the occupational therapy profession regarding evaluation and as being fundamental to an effective evaluation process:

1. Evaluation, in the form of screening, starts when the occupational therapist first receives information about the client or population and continues until the client is discharged from therapy.
2. Evaluation of a client always considers his or her perspective as well as those of the family, significant others, and caregivers.
3. Specific meaningful information about the client or population is best acquired through the use of assessments.
4. Assessments have potential biases that may influence their usefulness and appropriateness with clients, groups of people, or populations, and therapists must be alert for the effects of biases on assessment results.
5. Contextual factors may influence a client's performance on assessments.
6. The therapist continually gathers information about the client during intervention through reassessment.

The following sections discuss how these principles influence the evaluation process.

Evaluation Starts With Receipt of First Information

When the occupational therapist first makes contact with a potential client, the evaluation process has begun. The first step of the evaluation process is to screen the client using data collected from observations, referral information, and knowledge of the possible sequelae of the client's diagnosis. If occupational therapy services are needed, the process continues with a thorough review of available data to determine the most appropriate assessments for use in that particular situation. Once the therapist selects assessments, the formal evaluation begins. The administration of assessments and the data collected are part of a dynamic interactive process between the therapist and the client. Both parties shape the evaluation through their input, interaction, and responses to each other and to the assessments or activities. Although the therapist may start with a formalized assessment, the process is fluid and may take many different directions.

A therapist spends much effort evaluating his or her clients, striving to do so effectively and efficiently to obtain all the information necessary with optimal reliability and validity. The formal evaluation provides a baseline measurement of the client's performance. Using this baseline, with ongoing reassessment, the therapist determines the client's specific needs for intervention and continually observes whether the client is making progress and if a change in programming is needed. Thus, once an initial evaluation is done, reassessment takes place throughout the intervention. At regular intervals, reevaluations are conducted to ensure that the intervention plan is meeting the identified goals.

This overview of evaluation emphasizes that evaluation begins with the first contact the practitioner has with the client and continues until the client is discharged from therapy. The evaluation summary should include a comprehensive description of the person's occupational roles, client factors, performance skills, performance patterns, context and environment, and activity demands that influence his or her occupational performance. The occupational therapy philosophy provides a continual underpinning for practice, making the profession's contribution to society unique. This philosophy defines who the occupational therapist is and what his or her focus is. It guides a therapist's practice, identifying what is important to him or her, what he or she will assess, and how he or she will intervene.

Consideration of the Perspective of the Client, the Family, Significant Others, and Caregivers

The evaluation process must include the client's perspective and reflect his or her desired outcomes for intervention to the degree possible. Additional sources of data may include information from the family, significant others, or caregivers. A client cannot be evaluated in isolation, however, and it is important in a client-centered approach to consider the client's wishes regarding the involvement of family members, significant others, and caregivers. These individuals are an additional source of data who may give the therapist another perspective on the client and his or her ability to engage in meaningful activities. The therapist interprets information from these sources using clinical reasoning and judgment to gain a total picture of the client.

The documented evaluation should include a comprehensive picture of the client's occupational roles, client factors, performance skills, performance patterns, context and environment, and activity demands that influence a person's occupational performance. Written evaluations need to be sufficiently complete to provide others with all important information about the total person, his or her lifestyle, and the occupations and activities that are important to him or her. Evaluation summaries should not discuss just one client factor, performance skill, performance pattern, or contextual factor that influence a person's occupational performance and should reflect the client's strengths as well as any limitations. Occupational therapy evaluation narratives should reflect the values of the profession in providing an integrated snapshot of the person's life. Reassessments throughout the intervention process should capture the focus of intervention and the functional changes that occur as the intervention progresses. Reassessment data may be gathered routinely through a variety of sources, including family members, significant others, and other professionals who interact with the client. The goal of intervention—progress toward meaningful, relevant goals—will be reflected in the data about the client's daily life activities.

Client or Population Assessment

The data collected from assessments are specific to the client or population and offer insight into who the client is, what occupations are important to the client, and what the client's performance skills are. Data collected from assessments are personalized, reflecting the fact that no two persons have the same strengths, needs, or expected outcomes from intervention. For a population, assessments offer a greater understanding of its members as a group, its unique characteristics that identify it as a population, the health needs and life patterns of the group, and the specific activities in which members engage. Assessments and the interpretation of that data should also provide some insight into the activity needs of the population and the supports needed to participate in society. Some characteristics may be common across groups, but the data also will reflect the unique identity of each group, including differing values, strengths, limitations, and performance goals.

The data that an occupational therapist collects should be within the occupational therapy scope of practice and should shed light on how to facilitate engagement in personally meaningful activities and occupations that will fulfill life roles. Once a therapist interprets the data, the therapist may find that he or she needs more information from additional assessments or from other professionals and team members.

Assessment Biases

Assessments have potential biases that may influence their applicability, usefulness, and appropriateness with selected groups of people. All assessments have some degree of bias. The most obvious biases are based on culture, gender, age, lifestyle, health status, geographic area, and socioeconomic status. With standardized assessments, the bias may result from the use of a homogeneous population when standardizing the tool. It also may come from certain items that are specific to one cultural group or gender or to a particular region of the country.

Another type of bias is personal or examiner bias, resulting from personal beliefs or feelings of the evaluator that are conscious or unconscious (Goldyne, 2007; King-Thomas, 1987). One type of examiner bias is based on expectations. If the client is wearing soiled clothes, for example, the examiner may expect that he or she will not do well on the evaluation, and his or her unconscious actions or attitudes may influence the results. Everyone has some prejudices but may not be aware of them and how they affect the way they view others. Although it is difficult to acknowledge and explore one's own prejudices, it is important to do so to prevent them from interfering with one's professional judgment (Campinha-Bacote, 2003; Jeffreys, 2006).

Additionally, an occupational therapist may have preconceived notions about client characteristics based on his or her professional background and experiences. When a therapist reads a diagnosis in a chart, for example, he or she may expect to see certain characteristics that may or may not be present. A therapist needs to be aware of what he or she is actually observing to guard against being deceived by expectations. Although reading a chart and becoming familiar with the client's history are part of good practice, a therapist needs to avoid letting that information influence his or her own data gathering and conclusions.

Influence of Contextual Factors on Assessment Performance

Occupational therapy is concerned with the functional performance of the person in his or her daily life, including not only what the person can or cannot do, but also how he or she functions within the context of his or her environment. When using assessments, a therapist must think about the physical, social, cultural, and temporal influences of the context on the client's performance. A therapist must also examine potential contextual supports for and barriers to the person's performance (Dunn, Brown, & Youngstrom, 2003). As Dunn and her colleagues noted, a person reacts to contextual variables in unique ways. For one person, background music might be distracting, whereas for another it might be relaxing. A group setting for one young adult might be stimulating and for another might contribute to social anxiety. When interpreting data from assessments, the therapist must consider whether contextual factors affected the client's performance.

Ongoing Data Gathering Through Reassessment

The occupational therapist or occupational therapy assistant continually monitors the client's responses to intervention and gathers data about any changes in behaviors or performance. The ongoing reassessment that continues throughout intervention is less formalized than the initial evaluation. Data from a variety of sources are used to ascertain whether the intervention is working toward achieving the established short-term goals. Progress is identified by comparing the baseline evaluation data against any ongoing reassessment data obtained. Significant others and other professionals may provide valuable reassessment data. The principle of reassessment requires that the occupational therapist and the occupational therapy assistant continually reflect on what happens during the intervention and identify changes in the client's behaviors or performance skills. When an occupational therapist and occupational therapy assistant determine that reassessment data indicate that the intervention program needs to be changed or modified, the therapist and therapy assistant should engage in a collaborative discussion to modify the plan.

Use of Theory in Evaluation

In addition to an understanding of the influence of philosophical beliefs on the evaluation process, it is critical to explore the effect of theory on this process. Philosophical beliefs guide, to some extent, those theories that are applicable to or appropriate for the profession to use. The theories that an occupational therapist chooses to guide practice must be congruent with the philosophical perspective of the profession.

Theories are a collection of concepts, definitions, and postulates that help professionals make predictions about relationships between events. *Concepts* are labels describing phenomena that have been observed; the meanings of concepts are their definitions. The stated relationships between two or more concepts are *postulates* (Kramer & Hinojosa, 2010). The person or people who develop a theory identify and define the concepts and state the postulates, thus determining the scope and parameters of the theory. A theory organizes information and explains the relationships between ideas and observed events in a logical, understandable manner. A theory is encapsulated, in that it links the various concepts, definitions, and principles in a coherent way around a central theme or organizing principle. Theories are critical to the foundation of any type of intervention, and therefore are basic to evaluation.

Ideally, a wide variety of assessment tools would be developed based on the theories relevant to occupational therapy. An occupational therapist could choose assessments for an evaluation on the basis of the theory that was applicable to the client, and the tool would fit with the therapist's concern for the client or contextual factors that influence the client's occupational performance. In reality, some assessments focus on specific areas that fit neatly with the theories and philosophical beliefs important to occupational therapy, whereas many others relate to the profession's concerns but were developed using other theoretical orientations. An occupational therapist has the challenge of selecting assessment tools and interpreting the information they provide so that it is consistent with his or her own professional concerns and beliefs. For example, the Bruininks–Oseretsky Test of Motor Proficiency (Bruininks & Bruininks, 2005) was developed for use in special education. An occupational therapist, however, uses this tool because it gives a good picture of gross and fine motor skills and bilateral integration and balance, especially with older children. An occupational therapist would feel comfortable using this tool because it is consistent with his or her philosophical perspectives.

Although theory is important in the choice of assessment tools, other factors also influence which assessment tools are used. Some assessments are used because they are popular. Others assessments are used because other professions value them. Some are used because they are standardized, and standardized data are required by certain settings. Some are used because an institution, regulations, or a particular service delivery model require that they be used. Under these circumstances, the occupational therapist has the additional responsibility to translate the assessment results into the domain of concern of the profession.

The application of theory to practice is a complex process. The therapist is obliged to take ideas that are abstract and apply them at a level at which they can be used functionally. There are several acceptable ways of conceptualizing occupational therapy practice. In each of these, evaluation is an important component and serves as the basis for intervention. Some of the more common conceptualizations are frames of reference (Bruce & Borg, 2002; Kramer & Hinojosa, 2010; Mosey, 1970, 1996), models (Reed & Sanderson, 1999), conceptual models of practice (Ikiugu, 2007; Kielhofner, 2008), and occupation-based frameworks for practice (Baum & Christiansen, 2005). All of these vehicles allow a therapist to use theory as the basis for his or her evaluations and interventions. In this book, we use frames of reference as the way of conceptualizing practice to illustrate the evaluative process.

A frame of reference is an acceptable vehicle for organizing theoretical material in occupational therapy and translating it into practice through a functional perspective. A *frame of reference* provides a linking structure between theory and practice (Kramer & Hinojosa, 2010; Mosey, 1996) and draws from one or more theories to provide a basis for what will occur throughout the intervention process. Based on the theoretical information, a frame of reference addresses specific behaviors or physical signs that are considered functional and specific behaviors or physical signs that are considered dysfunctional (Mosey, 1992, 1996). A therapist often uses more than one frame of reference to address a client's distinctive therapeutic needs.

Inherent within a theoretical perspective or frame of reference may be a *top-down approach*, which looks first at the person's occupations; a *bottom-up approach*, which looks first at the components of tasks that are interfering with performance; or a *contextual approach*, which looks at the contextual effects on performance. The theory and the available assessment tools that are consistent with the theory then help to define the evaluation process. The therapist's personal predilections should not guide the choice of assessment tools. Many more assessment tools are component-driven than driven by occupations or contextual issues. Regardless of whether the therapist selects a top-down, bottom-up, or contextual approach, it is incumbent on him or her to explore all of these areas to gain a comprehensive view of the client. One perspective is generally primary during the intervention process, but effective intervention usually combines all three approaches.

Choosing the Frame of Reference

Theory and practice need to be continually linked. Screening provides the first opportunity to decide which theory or theories will guide practice with a particular individual. If the screening provides enough information to decide on a theoretical approach, then the evaluation is theory-based; however, if the screening does not yield sufficient information to choose a theoretical approach, then the therapist uses specific tools to gain more information about the client and determine an appropriate theoretical approach. Occupational therapy intervention should always be based on the use of theory.

Screening Stage

Screening plays a critical role in the choices that a therapist makes in evaluating the client. Data from the screening process have an ongoing effect on the evaluation and intervention process. Sometimes, just by reading a chart or interviewing a client, a therapist knows what theory or frame of reference is appropriate for the client. When a therapist determines during a screening that a specific frame of reference is appropriate, he or she proceeds to administer assessments that are consistent with that frame of reference. For example, if a therapist screens a file of a young man with a hand injury to his nondominant hand due to a fracture following a fall from his bicycle, the therapist may decide to use a biomechanical frame of reference. On the basis of this decision, the therapist proceeds to administer assessment tools consistent with this approach (e.g., range of motion, manual muscle testing).

When a frame of reference is not immediately apparent, a therapist can use specific screening tools or data collection strategies to gather more information about the client and his or her needs. The purpose of *screening* is to obtain an overview of the person's needs, strengths, limitations, and environment. It is not meant to be a comprehensive evaluation. Screening may involve an observation of the client, a chart review, medical and developmental history, information gained from the family or care providers, or data gathered by other professionals involved with the client (Collier, 1991). The following are examples of standardized and nonstandardized screening tools that can help the therapist identify an appropriate frame of reference: the Denver II Developmental Screening Test (Frankenberg et al., 1991), the Ayres Clinical Observations of Neuromuscular Integration (Ayres, 1976), the Family Observation Guide (Hinojosa & Kramer, 2008), the Activity Configuration (Mosey, 1986), the Interest Checklist (Matsutsuyu, 1969), the Occupational History (Moorehead, 1969), the Autonomic Nervous System Inventory (Farber, 1982), and the Functional Status Questionnaire (Jette et al., 1986). A screening is usually complete when the therapist has enough information to decide whether the client needs to receive occupational therapy services and to determine an appropriate frame of reference or intervention approach if services are required.

The screening data provide the therapist with a preliminary picture of the client and a potential view of what occupational therapy might offer. While reflecting on the screening data, the therapist decides whether the needs of the client relate to the domain of concern of occupational therapy and, if so, how to proceed with the evaluation using the tools that will be most appropriate for the setting and for obtaining the data needed. If the therapist decides that occupational therapy is not necessary, the client is discharged from occupational therapy and, if indicated, referred by the therapist to another service.

Assessment Stage

When selecting the assessments to use in the comprehensive evaluation, there are three possible scenarios (Figure 2.1): (1) The therapist has enough information from the screening to choose a frame of reference to guide evaluation and intervention; (2) the therapist needs to use an exploratory approach to determine which way to proceed in evaluating the client; or (3) the therapist with expertise decides, given the client's specific problems, that he or she must use an idiosyncratic approach to evaluation.

The therapist chooses assessment tools that will identify the presence of functional and dysfunctional behaviors and physical signs as described by the frame of reference selected. Some frames of reference are associated with specific assessment tools; with others, it is up to the therapist to determine which tool will best be able to identify the presence of the behaviors or physical signs. The same theories should underlie both the assessment tools and the treatment approach to ensure that they are congruent.

Clear Choice of a Frame of Reference

When a clear theoretical approach is evident from the screening data, the occupational therapist chooses an assessment tool based on that approach (Figure

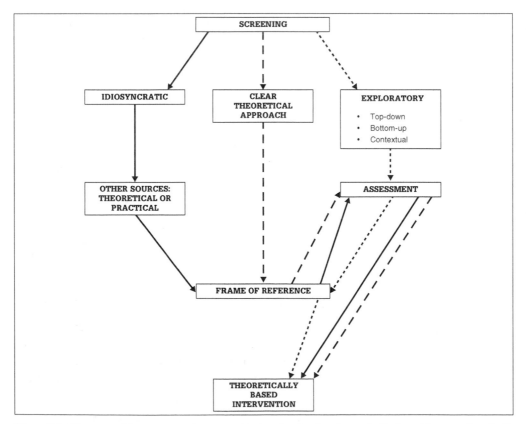

Figure 2.1. Diagram of three approaches to evaluation that lead to theoretically based intervention. Individual approaches are presented in Figure 2.2, which shows a clear choice of a frame of reference (the long dashed line in this figure), and Figure 2.3, which shows exploratory (the small dashed line in this figure).

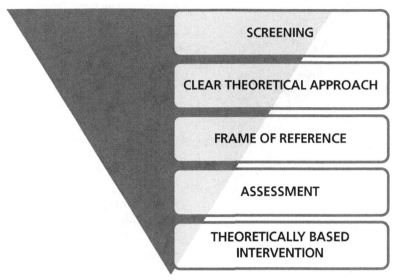

Figure 2.2. Occupational therapy process when presented with a clear choice of a frame of reference.

2.2). Many frames of reference or theoretical approaches are associated with one or more assessment tools that are consistent with that theoretical perspective (see Case Example 2.1).

● ● ● ● ● ●

Case Example 2.1. A Clear Choice of a Frame of Reference

Sharon was a 16-month-old who had high tone (distal) in both upper extremities and severely delayed developmental milestones. Her diagnosis was cerebral palsy with spasticity. A review of Sharon's medical chart provided the therapist with extensive information. The therapist also observed Sharon for a period of time and then held her, finding low proximal tone and high distal tone. After this screening, the therapist selected a postural control approach with handling and decided to use the neurodevelopmental frame of reference (Barthel, 2010). During the assessment, along with a more extended observation of Sharon's ability to interact with toys and other aspects of her environment, the therapist used the Alberta Infant Motor Scale (Piper & Darrah, 1994) to assess Sharon's gross motor abilities. Once the therapist determined the specific delays, she could proceed to develop a plan for intervention.

● ● ● ● ● ●

Exploratory Approach to Evaluation

After the screening, if the therapist does not have a clear theoretical direction for how to proceed in the evaluation process, he or she might consider taking an exploratory approach. This broad approach to evaluation includes, if possible, a more in-depth interview of the client to determine specific personal goals

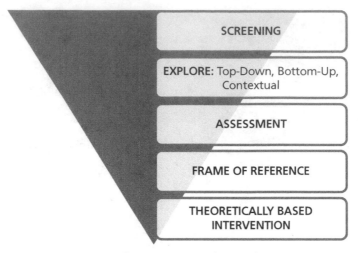

Figure 2.3. Exploratory approach to evaluation.

and to explore physical, psychosocial, and environmental issues (and their component parts) that may prevent those goals from being met. It is essential to understand the client's perspective on why these goals cannot be met at this time. Within the exploratory approach, the therapist may start in many places: from the top down, by exploring the client's meaningful occupations; from the bottom up, by exploring the underlying components of meaningful tasks; or from a contextual perspective, by exploring environmental issues (Hinojosa & Kramer, 1998; Ideishi, 2003; Weinstock-Zlotnick & Hinojosa, 2004). The therapist's intent is to understand the client and the identified problems and to determine a theoretical approach or frame of reference for intervention (Figure 2.3; Case Examples 2.2, 2.3, and 2.4).

● ● ● ● ● ●

Case Example 2.2. A Top-Down Approach

Joe, age 48, was 1 week post–cerebrovascular accident and was medically stable. He was referred to occupational therapy for a complete evaluation and potential intervention. The therapist read the medical documentation as part of the screening process and met with Joe. Joe's concerns and the data the therapist collected from the screening directed the therapist to focus on activities of daily living (ADLs). Her evaluation explored Joe's ability to feed, bathe, toilet, and dress himself. Through functional activities and specific assessments, including the Canadian Occupational Performance Measure (Law, Baptiste, Carswell, McColl, Polatajko, & Pollock, 1998) and the Performance Assessment of Self-Care Skills–Revised (Rogers & Holm, 1994), the therapist determined that Joe had a problem with the performance area of ADLs. She evaluated specific components of his performance (i.e., bottom-up approach), such as manual muscle testing and range of motion, to gain more information about how a body structure deficit might be affecting this area of occupation. Then, with consideration to the context, she was able to develop a plan for intervention.

● ● ● ● ● ●

Case Example 2.3. A Bottom-Up Approach

Mariko, age 4, was referred to occupational therapy because of suspected developmental delay. After reading the referral documentation and getting an overview of the child as a person through a discussion with her care providers, the occupational therapist decided to assess her gross and fine motor skills, muscle tone, movement patterns, and manipulation skills using a standardized assessment, the Miller Assessment for Preschoolers (MAP; Miller, 1993). Once the therapist identified those components of performance that were interfering with Mariko's functional abilities through clinical observation and the data obtained from the MAP, the therapist ascertained which areas of occupation were affected. Following this, and considering the context, the therapist was able to develop a plan for intervention.

● ● ● ● ● ●

Case Example 2.4. A Contextual Approach

Muhammad, age 72, was recovering from an aneurysm that had resulted in mild motor deficits. He was referred to occupational therapy for an ADL evaluation before being admitted to a skilled nursing facility. After reading the referral documentation, the occupational therapist decided to assess Muhammad's performance of ADLs, considering in the process both his wants and what he would need to do in the skilled nursing facility. The therapist interviewed Muhammad and observed the skilled nursing facility. She found that before his hospitalization Muhammad lived alone and that he now was fearful of returning to his apartment. Given his age and lifestyle, along with his newly acquired disability, he felt that he would be more comfortable in the skilled nursing facility, which had an assisted living residence to which he could move if his condition improved. He chose this particular setting because he believed that it was respectful of his cultural background and that he would feel comfortable with the people there. The therapist used the data from the assessment of the context as the background for the assessment of the areas of occupation and the components of performance. On the basis of all the data, the therapist was able to develop an intervention plan for Muhammad that focused on developing his ability to function within the skilled nursing facility with the potential of an eventual move to a less-restrictive environment.

● ● ● ● ● ●

Although a therapist might begin an evaluation with one approach, a comprehensive evaluation requires the therapist to continually analyze the data and to consider all approaches—top-down, bottom-up, and contextual—before a comprehensive evaluation is complete. The therapist's clinical reasoning skills may lead him or her to determine that a change in focus is warranted to address the issues that arise from the individual client. On the basis of the data he or she has collected, the therapist selects an appropriate theoretical perspective to guide intervention.

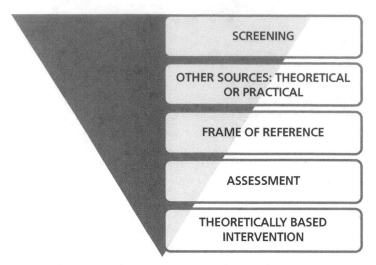

Figure 2.4. Idiosyncratic approach to evaluation.

Idiosyncratic Approach

An occupational therapist with advanced knowledge and expertise sometimes screens a client whose data are unique. The presenting picture of such clients is not consistent with known frames of reference or traditional problems seen in occupational therapy. When a therapist moves into nontraditional or emerging areas of practice, develops a new program area, or begins work with a new population not generally seen in occupational therapy, he or she may encounter such clients. This situation also may occur when new phenomena are seen in a clinical environment, such as postpolio syndrome or the aging process in extended life. The type of evaluation process needed for such clients is referred to here as *idiosyncratic* (Case Example 2.5). Rather than starting with traditional assessments, the therapist may need to look to other areas of study for theoretical perspectives to use as a basis for developing an appropriate theoretical base to guide intervention. Once the theoretical base is articulated, it provides the foundation for selecting appropriate assessment tools for the evaluation of these clients. In some cases, other professions and disciplines have already dealt with this problem or have theories that relate to this problem that allow the occupational therapist to combine that knowledge with the unique view of occupational therapy (Figure 2.4). This type of evaluation is complex and should not be the role or responsibility of the novice therapist.

● ● ● ● ● ●

Case Example 2.5. An Idiosyncratic Approach

Jane, age 16 and obese, was having difficulty relating to her peer group, resulting in depression, social isolation, and acting-out behaviors. She had been receiving ongoing psychological help for 3 years and had been involved in an occupational therapy group, but she showed little response and stopped receiving treatment. Jane was referred again to occupational therapy to try a different approach involving exploration of Jane's self-image and obesity to promote more appropriate social behaviors. Because there is no articulated frame of reference identified with working with adolescent obesity, the therapist needed to search for theoretical information outside occupational therapy. The therapist explored literature on lifestyle reengineering, cognitive–behavioral therapy, and theories related to locus of control. Once the therapist identified particular constructs that might relate to the client, he proceeded to identify tools that would provide information to develop a plan for intervention. Although the therapist was not using occupational therapy literature or tools, he was able to develop an idiosyncratic approach to providing occupational therapy evaluation of this client. Once the therapist chose a frame of reference, he explored the evaluation data to determine appropriate goals for the client. These goals were the foundation of the treatment plan.

● ● ● ● ● ●

Although the idiosyncratic approach sounds different and complex, occupational therapists have addressed unique client issues in this way for years. When occupational therapists first started working with clients with HIV/ AIDS, postpolio syndrome, and autism spectrum disorders, they used an idiosyncratic approach to evaluation.

Theory in Intervention Planning and Implementation

Throughout the course of evaluation, an occupational therapist interprets data and draws conclusions. This reasoning process is ongoing throughout the evaluation process. Once the evaluation is complete, the therapist has a wealth of information to use in developing an intervention plan. If he or she has not already chosen a particular frame of reference, at this time the therapist chooses a theoretical approach to lay the foundation for the development of goals and creation of a comprehensive intervention plan for the client. When planning the intervention, the therapist is generally heavily influenced by the context of care and payers for services. However, the therapist must ensure that the evaluation completed is consistent with the frame of reference he or she has chosen, as he or she must develop goals and interventions based only on the data he or she has gathered. Additionally, the therapist has to weigh that the needs of the client, the therapist's professional responsibilities, and the ethics of his or her actions are consistent with the requirements of the setting and the availability of payment.

An enormous amount of information is collected during the evaluation of a client, and its scope and complexity can be overwhelming. The therapist's goal is to synthesize the data and interpret them to develop appropriate goals consistent with the frames of reference or guidelines for intervention. A therapist often uses more than one frame of reference to address a client's distinctive therapeutic needs. Interpretation of evaluation data requires that a therapist bring all the findings together to create a profile of the person as an occupational being in his or her life context. With this visualization of the client, the therapist conscientiously selects key long- and short-term goals that reflect an integration and synthesis of all the evaluation data and, when possible, the needs and aspirations of the client. The goals should be realistic, functional, and achievable, based on clear baseline data. Finally, the number of goals should be limited to major goals that are reasonable given the intervention approach and the frequency of sessions. We recommend that a therapist develop no more than six long-term goals. When using more than one frame of reference, each frame of reference should have at least one long-term goal.

The initial evaluation is complete when the therapist writes the evaluation summary. An evaluation summary is important to both the client and the third-party payer. Reports should be a documentation of findings and not a lecture on the selected frame of reference. Evaluation reports should be concise and provide a sound argument for occupational therapy services based on the synthesis of the evaluation data. Test scores should be provided to support the therapist's interpretations. A therapist should be careful not to overinterpret data and should check all scores for accuracy. Reports should include clear descriptions of baseline data that describe a client's behaviors and performance deficits. Hinojosa and Foto (2004) described the importance of evaluation summaries for communicating information in a succinct and effective manner. They suggested that all evaluation summaries avoid jargon and be proofread for misspellings, grammatical errors, and awkward sentences. They described a comprehensive evaluation summary as one that

- Identifies key information considered when preparing the report, including client age, diagnosis, and referral information;
- Lists all tests administered and reports how they were administered;
- Identifies factors influencing the client's performance;
- Records actual test scores and interpretation of the data, disclosing any concerns about cultural issues or test bias;
- Presents a clear description of the client's performance and behaviors;
- Reports findings that provide an objective baseline of the client's performance deficits and abilities; and
- Documents baseline data that provide a clear picture of the client's overall functional level and that can be used to assess the efficacy of the intervention plan.

Therapist Perspectives, Theory, and Practice

Other factors important throughout the evaluation process are the occupational therapist's skills and his or her perspective. Each person acquires a different set of skills based on what he or she has been formally and informally taught, what he or she has learned, what his or her experiences have been, and who he or she is. Although most occupational therapists have been taught a consistent body of knowledge, it may have been presented from different orientations and organized in different manners. For example, all professional educational programs base their content on the standards for an accredited educational program for the occupational therapist (Accreditation Council for Occupational Therapy Education, 2007a, 2007b); however, this content may be taught using different orientations and emphasizing different areas. Some programs may focus on specific treatment techniques, whereas others may accent the clinical reasoning process. In addition, although occupational therapists may be taught the same content, individual differences mean that therapists learn and interpret material differently. Depending on individual experiences and training, a therapist may identify a favorite frame of reference that he or she prefers to use more frequently.

Finally, the therapist's practice setting also influences the choice of frame of reference. For example, some frames of reference may be impossible to implement within a home-based, school-based, or community setting or hospital. While all of the factors mentioned may influence the choice of a frame of reference, the client's needs should be given primary consideration.

Conclusion

Occupational therapy is based in philosophy; therefore, the process of evaluation has a strong philosophical basis, and each assessment combines a philosophical basis with a theoretical orientation. In choosing assessments, a therapist needs to be aware of the theoretical orientation of each assessment and its consistency with the philosophy of occupational therapy. The assessment tools used must be consistent with the needs of the client and the frame of reference that the therapist will use to guide intervention. The evaluation process is complex and requires clinical reasoning so the therapist can adequately identify the needs and concerns of the client and the areas that require intervention.

Questions

1. Identify three personal philosophical beliefs about human development and performance. Are they consistent with those found in this chapter? In what ways are they similar or different?
2. When would it be most appropriate to include a significant other in the evaluation process? What factors might preclude involving the significant other in this process?
3. Reflect on an experience in which you were evaluated. Can you identify any biases (positive or negative) that you experienced or sensed during the evaluation that might have affected the outcome? Do you think that you have any biases that might affect your ability to evaluate another person?
4. The authors purport that theory should influence the choice of an assessment tool. Identify two assessment tools, and then identify the theories, frames of reference, or models of practice that provide the foundation for these tools.

5. Explain the difference between a top-down approach and a bottom-up approach to evaluation. In what ways are they similar, and in what ways are they different?

References

Accreditation Council for Occupational Therapy Education. (2007a). Accreditation standards for a doctoral-degree-level educational program for the occupational therapist. *American Journal of Occupational Therapy, 61,* 641–651.

Accreditation Council for Occupational Therapy Education. (2007b). Accreditation standards for a master's-degree-level educational program for the occupational therapist. *American Journal of Occupational Therapy, 61,* 652–661.

American Occupational Therapy Association. (1967). Presidents of the American Occupational Therapy Association (1917–1967). *American Journal of Occupational Therapy, 21,* 290–298.

Ayres, A. J. (1976, March). *Clinical observations of neuromuscular integration: Administration of the Southern California Sensory Integration Tests* [Certification course]. Conference sponsored by the Center for the Study of Sensory Integrative Dysfunction, Valhalla, NY.

Barthel, K. A. (2010). A frame of reference for neuro-developmental treatment. In P. Kramer & J. Hinojosa (Eds.), *Frames of reference for pediatric occupational therapy* (3rd ed., pp 187–233). Baltimore: Lippincott Williams & Wilkins.

Baum, C. M., & Christiansen, C. (2005). Person–Environment–Occupation–Performance: An occupation-based framework for practice. In C. Christiansen, C. M. Baum, & J. Bass-Haugen (Eds.), *Occupational therapy: Performance, participation, and well-being* (3rd ed., pp. 243–266). Thorofare, NJ: Slack.

Bruce, M. A., & Borg, B. (2002). *Psychosocial frames of reference: Core for occupation-based practice* (3rd ed.). Thorofare, NJ: Slack.

Bruininks, R., & Bruininks, B. (2005). *Bruininks–Oseretsky Test of Motor Proficiency* (2nd ed.). Circle Pines, MN: AGS Publishing.

Campinha-Bacote, J. (2003). *The process of cultural competence in the delivery of healthcare services: A culturally competent model of care.* Cincinnati, OH: Transcultural C.A.R.E. Associates.

Collier, T. (1991). The screening process. In W. Dunn (Ed.), *Pediatric occupational therapy: Facilitating effective service provision* (pp. 11–33). Thorofare, NJ: Slack.

Dunn, W., Brown, C., & Youngstrom, M. J. (2003). Ecological model of occupation. In P. Kramer, J. Hinojosa, & C. B. Royeen (Eds.), *Perspectives in human occupation: Participation in life* (pp. 222–263). Baltimore: Lippincott Williams & Wilkins.

Farber, S. D. (1982). Neurorehabilitation evaluation concepts. In S. D. Farber (Ed.), *Neurorehabilitation: A multisensory approach* (pp. 107–114). Philadelphia: W. B. Saunders.

Frankenberg, W. K., Dodds, J., Archer, P., Bresnick, B., Maschka, P., Edelman, N., et al. (1991). *The Denver II Developmental Screening Test.* Denver, CO: Denver Developmental Materials.

Goldyne, A. J. (2007). Minimizing the influence of unconscious bias in evaluations: A practical guide. *Journal of the American Academy of Psychiatry Law, 35,* 60–66.

Hinojosa, J., & Foto, M. (2004, December). Occupational therapy documentation for reimbursement. *Sensory Integration Special Interest Section Quarterly, 27,* 1–3.

Hinojosa, J., & Kramer, P. (1998). Evaluation—Where do we begin? In J. Hinojosa & P. Kramer (Eds.), *Occupational therapy evaluation: Obtaining and interpreting data* (pp. 1–15). Bethesda, MD: American Occupational Therapy Association.

Hinojosa, J., & Kramer, P. (2008). Integrating children with disabilities into family play. In D. L. Parham & L. S. Fazio (Eds.), *Play in occupational therapy for children* (2nd ed., pp. 321–334). St. Louis, MO: Mosby-Year Book.

Ideishi, R. I. (2003). The influence of occupation on assessment and treatment. In P. Kramer, J. Hinojosa, & C. B. Royeen (Eds.), *Perspectives in human occupation: Participation in life* (pp. 278–296). Baltimore: Lippincott Williams & Wilkins.

Ikiugu, M. N. (2007). *Psychosocial conceptual practice models in occupational therapy: Building, adaptive capacity.* St. Louis, MO: Elsevier/Mosby.

Jeffreys, M. R. (2006). *Teaching cultural competence in nursing and health care: Inquiry, action, and innovation.* New York: Springer.

Jette, A. M., Davis, A. R., Cleary, P. D., Calkins, D. R., Ruberstein, L. V., Fink, A., et al. (1986). The Functional Status Questionnaire: Reliability and validity when used in primary care. *Journal of General Internal Medicine, 1,* 143–149.

Kielhofner, G. (2008). *Model of Human Occupation: Theory and application* (4th ed.). Baltimore: Lippincott Williams & Wilkins.

Kielhofner, G. (2009). *Conceptual foundations of occupational therapy practice* (4th ed.). Philadelphia: F. A. Davis.

King-Thomas, L. J. (1987). Responsibilities of the examiner. In L. J. King-Thomas & B. J. Hacker (Eds.), *The therapist's guide to pediatric assessment* (pp. 11–18). Boston: Brown & Company.

Kramer, P., & Hinojosa, J. (2010). *Frames of reference for pediatric occupational therapy* (3rd ed.). Baltimore: Lippincott Williams & Wilkins.

Law, M. (1998). Client-centered occupational therapy. In M. Law (Ed.), *Client-centered occupational therapy* (pp. 1–18). Thorofare, NJ: Slack.

Law, M., Baptiste, S., Carswell, A., McColl, M. A., Polatajko, H., & Pollock, N. (1998). *Canadian Occupational Performance Measure* (3rd ed.). Ottawa, Ontario: CAOT Publications.

Matsutsuyu, J. (1969). The Interest Checklist. *American Journal of Occupational Therapy, 23,* 323–328.

Miller, L. J. (1993). *Miller Assessment for Preschoolers.* San Antonio, TX: Psychological Corporation.

Moorehead, L. M. (1969). The occupational history. *American Journal of Occupational Therapy, 23,* 329–336.

Mosey, A. C. (1970). *Three frames of reference for mental health.* Thorofare, NJ: Slack.

Mosey, A. C. (1986). *Psychosocial components of occupational therapy.* New York: Raven Press.

Mosey, A. C. (1992). *Applied scientific inquiry in the health professions: An epistemological orientation.* Rockville, MD: American Occupational Therapy Association.

Mosey, A. C. (1996). *Applied scientific inquiry in the health professions: An epistemological orientation* (2nd ed.). Bethesda, MD: American Occupational Therapy Association.

Piper, M. C., & Darrah, J. (1994). Alberta Infant Motor Scale: Construction of a motor assessment tool for the developing infant. In M. C. Piper & J. Darrah (Eds.), *Motor assessment of the developing infant* (pp. 25–35). Philadelphia: W. B. Saunders.

Reed, K. L., & Sanderson, S. N. (1999). *Concepts of occupational therapy* (4th ed.). Philadelphia: Lippincott Williams & Wilkins.

Rogers, J. C., & Holm, M. B. (1994). *Performance Assessment of Self-Care Skills–Revised* (PASS; Version 3.1). [Unpublished functional performance test]. Pittsburgh, PA: University of Pittsburgh.

Weinstock-Zlotnick, G., & Hinojosa, J. (2004). The Issue Is—Bottom-up or top-down evaluation: Is one better than the other? *American Journal of Occupational Therapy, 58,* 594–599.

3

● ● ● ● ●

Assessment Identification
and Selection

●

Julie D. Bass-Haugen, PhD, OTR/L, FAOTA

Overview

This chapter introduces a process for identifying and selecting assessments for use in occupational therapy practice. Major sources of information on assessments in occupational therapy and other disciplines are identified. This chapter also includes a summary of assessment criteria and a discussion of various practical and ethical issues related to the use of assessments.

Introduction

Identifying and selecting the best assessments for evaluation are important steps in the occupational therapy process. Using a formal process to choose assessments is one of the best mechanisms for ensuring that the outcome of an evaluation and intervention is efficient and effective and that the use of an assessment is fair (American Psychological Association, Joint Committee on Testing Practices, 2004).

Identifying assessments that meet the purpose of the evaluation process requires a methodical approach that includes knowing what you are looking for, where to look, and how to look. Many strategies and tools can help in this process, and selecting a specific assessment requires a careful examination of existing tools and instruments. This examination includes determining the strengths and weaknesses of the assessment in terms of specific criteria and finding a recommendation about how the assessment should be used in a particular setting.

Occupational therapists need to be cautious and rigorous when selecting assessments for a client. Therapists should not simply use what is currently available in the setting. They must be confident that the specific assessment is appropriate for assessing the client. When they decide that they need to adapt an existing assessment or develop an instrument, they need to follow sound test construction design to ensure the credibility of the instrument. If these guidelines are not followed, the use of an adapted or developed assessment instrument is not best practice in occupational therapy. In addition, it may jeopardize the professional standing of occupational therapy when it is used.

Identifying Assessments

Identifying assessments that meet the needs of an evaluation involves the following three steps:

1. Determining the need for a specific assessment in the evaluation process
2. Locating and examining information about existing assessments that describes their intended purpose, characteristics, quality, and use in evaluation
3. Identifying a few assessments that seem to match the practice need and drawing up a plan to analyze and compare them in a more deliberate manner. This last step results in the selection of a specific assessment for the evaluation process.

Describing the Need for an Assessment

In almost every practice setting, there comes a time when a therapist needs to select an assessment as part of an evaluation process. Before reviewing available assessments, the therapist must begin with some reflection on the overall need for an assessment in a particular situation. Therapists should consider several broad areas of needs:

- A description of the overall need for an assessment and the characteristics of interest and importance
- The intended uses for the assessment
- The population of clients to be evaluated using this assessment
- The qualifications or characteristics of the user of the assessment
- Other practical considerations.

Characteristics of Interest and Importance in the Assessment

There are several approaches to describing the characteristics or traits of interest and importance in an assessment. Several chapters in this text and others have introduced ideas to help therapists reflect on the characteristics and purposes of evaluation. The person–environment–occupation and other occupational therapy practice models have received increasing attention in the literature as organizing frameworks for evaluation. Conceptual, practice, and health models (Reed & Sanderson, 1999) provide alternative approaches to identifying the focus of occupational therapy evaluation. Finally, classification systems like the *International Classification of Functioning, Disability and Health* (*ICF;* World Health Organization [WHO], 2001) aim to propose an international language that is helpful in describing individual status.

Person–environment–occupation models (Baum & Christiansen, 2005; Dunn, Brown, & Youngstrom, 2003; Kielhofner, 2008; Law et al., 1996; Mathiowetz & Bass-Haugen, 1994; Trombly, 1995) and other occupational therapy practice models provide an important foundation for identifying different factors that a therapist must consider when selecting an assessment. The characteristics of interest and importance in an assessment generally include a description of the person's characteristics, the contextual and environmental characteristics, and the person's occupations or occupational performance. Person–environment–occupation models and occupational therapy practice models also provide the necessary terminology for accessing the literature and may suggest related terms or keywords found in other sources. For example, a therapist might be interested in measuring performance in daily living activities for a given client in a given situation. One person–environment–occupation model might include the concept of activities of daily living (ADLs) in its description. A review of this model and other models might indicate that a group of terms—self-care, daily living skills, self-maintenance, and functional performance—are also used to describe those occupations that are basic components of everyday life.

Conceptual and practice perspectives also provide guidelines for evaluation. Occupational therapy uses concepts, models, theories, and frames of reference to describe ideas that influence the conceptual and practice foundations of the profession. Individual therapists, and most practice settings, adopt beliefs or perspectives that guide clinical reasoning and the occupational therapy process. Regardless of the perspective adopted, therapists must always remember that the unique contribution of occupational therapy is occupational performance (Baum & Law, 1997).

Conceptual and practice perspectives may originate either outside occupational therapy or within the domain of occupational therapy. Reed and Sanderson (1999) described 10 models of health commonly used in occupational therapy practice: biomedical, biopsychosocial, chronicity, holistic, milieu, health education and prevention, health development, wellness, normality, and rehabilitation. Numerous models of occupational therapy also have been described and may be organized by domains of concern (Reed & Sanderson, 1999) that include adaptation, context/ecology, occupation/activity, occupational performance and competence, development, prevention, productivity, play/leisure, sensorimotor, cognitive, psychosocial, and professional development. For example, a therapist may be interested in evaluating the biomechanical characteristics (a sensorimotor domain of concern) that support or limit a person's occupational performance after a hand injury. An examination of this perspective on performance may lead to assessments related to joint range of motion and physical endurance.

Classification systems provide another option for describing the characteristics measured by an assessment. The *ICF* (WHO, 2001) has become an important tool for characterizing people and the environments in which they live. The primary classification areas of the *ICF* are body structure, body function, activity, participation, and contextual factors of the person and environment. For example, an occupational therapist who needs to assess support systems for occupational performance might find it helpful to look at the subcategories under "Support and Relationships" in the *ICF*. Other classification systems used by occupational therapy practitioners include the *Occupational Therapy Practice Framework: Domain and Process, 2nd Edition* (*Framework–II*; American Occupational Therapy Association [AOTA], 2008). The National Center for Medical Rehabilitation Research (1993, 2006) and the Institute of Medicine (Committee on Assessing Rehabilitation Science and Engineering, Division of Health Sciences Policy, Institute of Medicine, 1997) have introduced alternative classifications and models to characterize the complex characteristics of the person–environment–occupation relationship. Enacting any one of these systems in practice guides the therapist's assessment, focusing the identification and selection process.

Intended Purposes or Uses for the Assessment

After identifying the characteristics of interest and importance, the next step in describing the need for an assessment is determining the intended purposes or uses of the assessment. Initially, it may help to think about the purposes or uses in words that depict a specific situation. For example, one therapist might need an assessment of functional and community mobility for the purpose of discharge planning with a client. In another scenario, an occupational therapy researcher might need an assessment of executive cognitive function to support theory development in Alzheimer's research.

A broad summary of the intended purposes or uses of an assessment will help to identify the need in a given situation (Dunn, 2005). Three purposes of assessments are often described in the literature: description, decision making, and theory building. Assessments used for description clarify and define a person's current needs or performance abilities. If an assessment is needed for decision making, the purpose may be to select interventions, predict future performance, or demonstrate outcomes of services, along with an array of other decisions based on assessment and evaluation results. Theory-building assessments may be part of larger research agendas that support development of the occupational therapy and occupational science knowledge base.

When the intended purpose or use of an assessment involves decision making, the therapist should consider the nature of the decisions that will be made using the assessment (Law, King, & Russell, 2005). In some situations, the results of assessment may be part of decisions that greatly affect people's lives. In occupational therapy, the outcomes of evaluation may contribute to decisions about where a person should live, the driving status of an older person, classroom placement for a child, qualification for specific services, the ability to return to work after an injury, or an individual's need for guardianship.

In such cases, it is critical to uphold high standards for selecting assessments (Plake, 2002).

Description of Populations/Clients

Along with identifying the personal characteristics of interest in the evaluation process, it is also important to describe the general population of clients who will be evaluated. The population may be described in terms of age, certain demographic characteristics, clinical conditions, special needs, or some combination of these. This step in defining the needs for a practice setting is necessary because most assessments have been developed for specific populations. When trying to locate assessments, information on the characteristics of the population or functional performance to be evaluated will help to identify more targeted assessments.

User Qualifications

When examining the need for an assessment in a specific setting, it is important to consider the qualifications of the therapist(s) who will be using the assessment. Users of occupational therapy evaluations have four primary responsibilities: administration, scoring, interpretation, and reporting. These responsibilities may be carried out by one person or by different people who contribute to the evaluation process. Several questions can be asked to clarify the qualifications of the user(s):

- What is the training and educational background of the therapist(s) with respect to the assessments?
- What is the experience of the therapist(s) in the specific evaluation area?
- What level of expertise do the therapist(s) have in administration, scoring, and interpretation in general, as well as specific to the selected assessment?
- What professional standards have been established for evaluation in this area?
- What resources are available to obtain additional training in these assessments, if needed?

Some professional associations and test publishers have specific standards related to user qualifications for assessments (College of Occupational Therapists of Ontario, 2007; Turner, DeMers, Fox, & Reed, 2001). These should be referred to when describing the qualifications of therapists in a specific setting.

Practical Considerations

The practical needs of the setting in which the assessment will be administered must be considered. The format, cost, and time available for an assessment all contribute to defining the practical characteristics that must be taken into consideration during the selection of an assessment. The available options for the format of an assessment may include observation or performance-based tests, self-reporting, and written or oral questionnaires. The assessment may not cost anything, requiring only the permission of the author. On the other hand, some assessments may require the purchase of the test itself and an ongoing budget for the training of test users or the acquisition of test booklets, assessment kits, and software. The time required for the overall evaluation process also must be considered. Some assessments can be completed in a single session, but other assessments include an extensive battery of subtests to obtain a complete picture of a person's performance.

Locating Existing Assessments That Meet Current Needs

The description of the need for an assessment, as discussed above, should be documented and should guide the strategies used for the next step: locating existing assessments that meet this need. Several strategies are available for locating information on assessments relevant to occupational therapy. One strategy is to consider disciplines or professions that may have an interest in measuring the identified characteristics. Naturally, occupational therapy and occupational science are the first areas to investigate. *OT Search* (a database available through the American Occupational Therapy Foundation), *OTseeker* (an Internet site and database that focuses on evidence-based practice in occupational therapy), occupational therapy sourcebooks (e.g., Asher, 2007; Hemphill-Pearson, 2008; Law, Baum, & Dunn, 2005; Mulligan, 2003; Paul & Orchanian, 2003), and textbooks in occupational therapy are important tools for finding occupational therapy assessments. Psychology, education, and medicine are secondary areas that may have assessments relevant to occupational therapy. A second strategy is to consider the sources of information on assessments themselves. Libraries have reference books (e.g., *Mental Measurement Yearbook* [Geisinger, Spies, Carlson, & Plake, 2007]), databases (e.g., *Health and Psychosocial Instruments* [HaPI] from Behavioral Management Database Services), journals, textbooks, and other materials that can help locate and critique assessments. The Internet has a wide array of sites that provide information on assessment tools (American Psychological Association, 2009). There are also publishers who specialize in tests and assessments and have developed reputations for marketing measurement tools with a certain focus. A third strategy is to use professional connections and networks to keep abreast of changes in assessment and evaluation; these may include professional associations, government agencies, professional colleagues, and experts in the field. A good identification strategy includes using more than one resource to compare independent reviews.

Reed and Sanderson (1999) reported that more than 300 assessments are used in occupational therapy practice. Despite this large number, it is critical that occupational therapists explore sources outside occupational therapy and occupational science. These sources of information have been described by various authors (Asher, 2007; Hemphill-Pearson, 2008; Law, Baum, & Dunn, 2005; Mulligan, 2003; Paul & Orchanian, 2003). Furthermore, Reed and Sanderson (1999) described knowledge resources for occupational therapy as including biological sciences, social sciences, humanities and the arts, applied sciences (medicine, nursing, physical therapy, social work, and speech pathology), engineering and technology, orthotics and prosthetics, business and management, government, and vocational rehabilitation. The *Occupational Competence Model* (Polatajko, 1992) also suggested searching within disciplines relevant to

- The person (i.e., psychology, biology, kinesiology/human movement, philosophy, human ethnology),
- The environment (i.e., architecture, forestry, ecology, geography, sociology, political science, economics, social policy), and
- An occupation's interaction with the person or environment or both (i.e., career development, leisure studies, psychology of play, sports psychology, anthropology, archeology, human geography, human ecology, sociology).

Identifying Major Databases or Resources To Locate Assessments

Numerous databases or resources may be helpful in locating assessments. Box 3.1 provides a summary of the most common resources in occupational therapy, psy-

---

Box 3.1. Sources of Information for Assessments

Occupational Therapy
Assessments in occupational therapy mental health: An integrative approach (2nd ed.; Hemphill-Pearson, 2008)
Measuring occupational performance: Supporting best practice in occupational therapy (2nd ed.; Law, Baum, & Dunn, 2005)
Occupational therapy assessment tools: An annotated index (3rd ed.; Asher, 2007)
Occupational therapy evaluation for children: A pocket guide (Mulligan, 2003)
OT Search (American Occupational Therapy Foundation; http://www1.aota.org/otsearch)
OTseeker (http://www.otseeker.com/)
Pocket guide to assessment in occupational therapy (Paul & Orchanian, 2003)

Psychology
Measures for psychological assessment: A guide to 3,000 original sources and their applications (Chun, Cobb, & French, 1975)
Mental Measurements Yearbook (http://buros.unl.edu/buros/jsp/search.jsp)
Psychware sourcebook (Krug, 1987)
PsycInfo (http://www.apa.org/psycinfo/)

Education
ERIC/AE Digest (www.ericdigests.org/1996-1/test.htm)
Test collection (2nd ed.; Educational Testing Service, 1993)
The Test Locator (www.ets.org/testcoll/)

Medicine/Rehabilitation
CINAHL (http://www.ebscohost.com/cinahl/)
Cochrane Library (www.cochrane.org/)
Health and Psychosocial Instruments (HAPI; www.ovid.com/site/catalog/DataBase/866.jsp)
Medline (http://medline.cos.com/)

chology, education, and medicine. In most disciplines, reference books or databases contain lists and brief descriptions of tests and assessments for relevant domains. These reference books and databases are important tools for obtaining both general and specific information on existing assessments. The information provided often includes a description of the assessment, the publisher, supporting research studies, measurement characteristics, and critiques by experts in the field. These resources are helpful for both novice and experienced practitioners who want an efficient and effective way of obtaining key information on assessments. Therapists unfamiliar with these sources of information should initially consult a reference librarian to access them. Some institutions have medical libraries with reference librarians to assist with information location and access. Most academic libraries provide instructions, guides, and Web site addresses that are helpful for a new user of these sources. The freedom to access information will change rapidly in the future with general access through search engines such as Google Scholar.

Analyzing the Quality of an Assessment: Formal Method Assessment

A search for existing assessments may often lead to several matches that meet the needs of a specific situation. The next stage in the selection process is to analyze the overall quality of each assessment using standards and criteria associated with good measurement tools. The *Standards for Educational and Psychological Testing* (American Educational Research Association, American Psychological Association, & National Council on Measurement in Education, 1999) provide guidelines for evaluating the quality of tests and testing practices. While it may be difficult for occupational therapists to meet all of these guidelines, they present a model toward which the profession should strive. Most assessment ratings, or critique forms and guidelines, are similar to or based on these standards (Bass-Haugen, 1989; Law, 2008; Reed & Sanderson, 1999; Tickle-Degnen, 2008). The standards include four parts:

1. Technical standards for test construction and evaluation
2. Professional standards for test use
3. Standards for particular applications (including a section on testing people with handicapping conditions)
4. Standards for administrative procedures (including scoring and interpretation).

Assessment analysis begins with the acquisition of available documentation on the assessment. Several resources should be obtained prior to beginning a critique of an assessment: the technical manual (if available), published summaries and critiques of the assessment, and published research on the assessment. Documentation of the resources used to analyze the quality of an assessment is important because the quality and utility of an assessment may change over time as it is developed further. An assessment may not be selected at one point in time because of its overall quality; however, it may later evolve into an assessment that meets specific needs of the evaluation and may become the most appropriate assessment available.

A formal method of analysis involves two primary steps: (1) a description of the assessment as it relates to practice needs and (2) the evaluation of the overall quality of the assessment (see Figure 3.1). The description of the assessment includes the characteristics of interest and importance, the purpose, the population/clients, user qualifications, and practical considerations. The evaluation of the overall quality of the assessment requires the examination of

- The technical manual,
- The method of assessment development and administration,
- Scoring and scales and norms used for interpretation,
- Reliability evidence, and
- Validity evidence.

The *Standards for Educational and Psychological Testing* (American Educational Research Association, American Psychological Association, & National Council on Measurement in Education, 1999) and other guidelines provide specific criteria for each of these analysis areas. For example, the National Center for Education Statistics (Department of Education, National Center for Education Statistics, 2002) states that the development of an assessment must abide by an explicit set of specifications. These specifications must be clearly documented so that the development of the assessment can be replicated. Examples of specifications include the purpose of the assessment, the domain/constructs, the framework for the format, the number of items, time requirements, the context, participant characteristics, psychometric properties, the administration, scoring procedures, and the reporting of results. Testing standards are especially important when high-stakes decisions are made on the basis of the assessment. For such uses, especially in educational settings, it is critical that the assessment be evaluated in terms of the alignment to test specifications, the opportunity to learn, freedom from bias and sensitive situations, developmental appropriateness, score consistency and reliability, and appropriateness of mastery-level cut points (Plake, 2002).

Therapists should make good use of expert critiques to complete an analysis of an assessment, evaluate technical standards, and determine proper and improper use. Sourcebooks and critical reviews in the literature provide expert critiques of commonly used assessments. These critiques summarize the quality of an assessment in key areas and provide recommendations on how the assessment should be used in practice. Tracking the dates of published critiques and more recent studies can give the practitioner an indication of an assessment's stage of development and how the assessment has been used in practice, theory development, and outcomes research.

Completion of formal analyses of several assessments can help the practitioner identify the best assessment for a given situation or setting. It also makes the therapist aware of the appropriate uses for an assessment and the caution that must be taken, given its limitations. These types of summary statements and recommendations about an assessment should be incorporated into the information given during the evaluation process and shared in appropriate ways with both the health care team and the client.

		Sources of Information
Assessment Name & Publication Information		
Characteristic		
Purpose		
Population/Clients		
User Qualifications		
Practical Considerations		
Technical Manual		
Development & Administration		
Scores, Scales, & Norms		
Reliability		
Validity		
Characteristics & Summary		
Recommendations & Comments		
Critique		

Figure 3.1. Worksheet for a formal method for analyzing assessment.

Ethical Issues Related to Selection and Use of Assessments

Ethical dilemmas occur at every stage of the evaluation process, which is why professional associations adopt and enforce codes of ethics and standards of practice that guide evaluation and practice (AOTA, 2005a, 2005b). Three ethical issues will be noted here as they relate to the selection and use of assessments. Other responsibilities and values related to ethics and best practice in evaluation are described in other chapters of this text.

One pertinent ethical issue relates to the unauthorized use of published and copyrighted assessments. In the past, it was common practice in many health care and education settings to simply copy test manuals and test scoring forms from original publications. However, that is usually a violation of copyright law. Therefore, it is the responsibility of the assessment user to purchase published assessments directly from the publisher. If an assessment is copyrighted but is not available through a publisher, the user must contact the author and obtain permission in writing to use the assessment (American Psychological Association, 2009).

A second ethical issue relates to the selection of assessments that may not be a good match with the qualifications of the assessment users. Some organizations (Association for Assessment in Counseling and Education, 2003) provide specific criteria on the qualifications of test users, including knowledge and skills in the following areas:

- Professional practice and relevant theory supporting an assessment
- Testing theory
- Measurement concepts and statistics
- Ability to review, select, and administer appropriate assessments
- Administration and scoring in relation to specific assessment's purposes
- Impact of diversity on accuracy
- Responsible use of assessments and evaluation in diagnosing, predicting future ends, and planning interventions.

If the current qualifications of the therapist are not adequate for a given assessment, several options may be considered. Therapists can obtain and maintain the additional knowledge and skills required to use the assessment. Sometimes qualifications include earned academic degrees, professional credentials, or certification to administer a specific assessment. Alternatively, another assessment with similar characteristics and fewer user restrictions may be chosen, or the assessment may be used only for limited purposes (e.g., screening), with clearly identified cautions against misuse and as part of a larger evaluation process.

A third ethical dilemma arises when no existing assessments are found in the literature for the needs in a specific practice setting. Unfortunately, a common practice is to "do your own thing" and create or adapt an assessment that seems to fit the situation. Routinely adopting this approach can set in motion dangerous practices for administering, scoring, and interpreting assessments. Adapting a standardized assessment will not yield a standard score and may not give the user appropriate information. Keep in mind that assessment and evaluation are powerful tools that either support or refute occupational therapy outcomes, occupational therapy recommendations to clients and other professionals, and the credibility of occupational therapy practice in the larger health care, social services, and educational systems in which practitioners work. The creation or use of "homegrown" assessments, or the adaptation of existing assessments, should be rare in occupational therapy practice and should be accompanied by disclaimers that warn others against inappropriate application and caution interpretation of the results. It is important that major decisions and recommendations regarding clients are never based on these types of assessments alone.

Conclusion

Assessment identification and selection is an important component of the evaluation process. It is a critical step in the effort to ensure that the results of evaluation are accurate and that the outcomes of interventions are effective and efficient. This chapter introduced a three-stage process for selecting assessments, including reflection on the needs in practice, identification of existing assessments that meet those needs, and critical analysis to evaluate the strengths and limitations of assessments and to determine the best assessment for a given situation. Using a formal method to identify and select assessments is one of the best ways to develop confidence in the assessments chosen for evaluation and to gain a professional reputation for excellence in evaluation.

Questions

1. When planning an assessment for a particular client with a stroke, what parameters would you use to choose an assessment? What parameters would be different if the client was a 3-year-old child with Down syndrome? How does setting or context influence assessment selection?
2. Three purposes of assessment are description, decision making, and theory building. Explain each of these and how they relate to occupational therapy. Go to an online assessment database, select a performance area, and find three appropriate tools for use with an adolescent client.
3. What are the ethical issues related to creating your own assessment method to meet a particular situation? How could you avoid this ethical dilemma?
4. A therapist has suggested that you use a particular assessment for an evaluation. How would you analyze the quality of this assessment? How would you handle the situation if you determined that it was not a quality assessment?

References

American Educational Research Association, American Psychological Association, & National Council on Measurement in Education. (1999). *Standards for educational and psychological testing.* Washington, DC: Authors.

American Occupational Therapy Association. (2005a). Occupational therapy code of ethics (2005). *American Journal of Occupational Therapy, 59,* 639–642.

American Occupational Therapy Association. (2005b). Standards of practice for occupational therapy. *American Journal of Occupational Therapy, 59,* 663–665.

American Occupational Therapy Association. (2008). Occupational therapy practice framework: Domain and process (2nd ed.). *American Journal of Occupational Therapy, 62,* 625–683.

American Psychological Association, Joint Committee on Testing Practices. (2004). *Code of fair testing practices in education.* Washington, DC: Author. Retrieved July 6, 2009, from http://www.apa.org/science/fairtestcode.html

American Psychological Association. (2009). FAQ/Finding information about psychological tests. *Testing and Assessment.* Retrieved June 19, 2009, from http://www.apa.org/science/faq-findtests.html

Asher, I. E. (Ed.). (2007). *Occupational therapy assessment tools: An annotated index* (3rd ed.). Bethesda, MD: AOTA Press.

Association for Assessment in Counseling and Education. (2003). *Standards for qualifications of test users.* Alexandria, VA: Author. Retrieved July 21, 2009, from http://www.theaaceonline.com/standards.pdf

Bass-Haugen, J. (1989, October). *Identifying and critiquing measurement tools in clinical practice.* Pre-conference institute at the annual meeting of the Minnesota Occupational Therapy Association, Minneapolis.

Baum, C. M., & Christiansen, C. H. (2005). Person–environment–occupation performance occupation-based framework for practice. In C. H. Christiansen, C. M. Baum, & J. Bass-Haugen (Eds.), *Occupational therapy: Performance, participation, and well-being* (3rd ed., pp. 242–266). Thorofare, NJ: Slack.

Baum, C. M., & Law, M. (1997). Occupational therapy practice: Focusing on occupational performance. *American Journal of Occupational Therapy, 51,* 277–288.

Chun, K.-T., Cobb, S., & French, J.R.P. (1975). *Measures for psychological assessment: A guide to 3,000 original sources and their applications.* Ann Arbor, MI: Survey Research Center, Institute for Social Research.

College of Occupational Therapists of Ontario. (2007). *Standards for occupational therapy assessments.* Retrieved July 6, 2009, from http://www.coto.org/pdf/Standards_for_Occupational_Therapy_Assessments.pdf

Committee on Assessing Rehabilitation Science and Engineering, Division of Health Sciences Policy, Institute of Medicine. E. N. Brandt & A. M. Pope (Eds.). (1997). *Enabling America: Assessing the role of rehabilitation science and engineering.* Washington, DC: National Academy Press.

Department of Education, National Center for Education Statistics. (2002). *NCES statistical standards.* Retrieved July 21, 2009, from http://nces.ed.gov/statprog/2002/stdtoc.asp

Dunn, W. (2005). Measurement issues and practices. In M. Law, C. Baum, & W. Dunn (Eds.), *Measuring occupational performance: Supporting best practice in occupational therapy* (2nd ed., pp. 21–32). Thorofare, NJ: Slack.

Dunn, W., Brown, C., & Youngstrom, M. J. (2003). The ecology of human performance: A framework for considering the effect of context. In P. Kramer, J. Hinojosa, & C. B. Royeen (Eds.), *Perspectives in human occupation: Participation in life* (pp. 21–32). Baltimore: Lippincott Williams & Wilkins.

Educational Testing Service, Test Collection. (1993). *The ETS test collection catalog* (2nd ed.). Phoenix, AZ: Oryx Press.

Geisinger, K. F., Spies, R. A., Carlson, J. F., & Plake, B. S. (2007). *Mental measurements yearbook* (17th ed.). Lincoln, NE: Buros Institute of Mental Measurements.

Hemphill-Pearson, B. (2008). *Assessments in occupational therapy mental health: An integrative approach* (2nd ed.). Thorofare, NJ: Slack.

Kielhofner, G. (2008). *Model of human occupation: Theory and application* (4th ed.). Baltimore: Lippincott Williams & Wilkins.

Krug, S. E. (1987). *Psychware sourcebook*. Kansas City, MO: Test Corporation of America.

Law, M. (2008). Appendix F: Outcome Measures Rating Form Guidelines. In M. Law & J. MacDermid (Eds.), *Evidence-based rehabilitation: A guide to practice* (2nd ed., pp. 381–386). Thorofare, NJ: Slack.

Law, M., Baum, C., & Dunn, W. (Eds.). (2005). *Measuring occupational performance: Supporting best practice in occupational therapy* (2nd ed.). Thorofare, NJ: Slack.

Law, M., Cooper, B. A., Strong, S., Stewart, D., Rigby, P., & Letts, L. (1996). The person–environment–occupation model: A transactive approach to occupational performance. *Canadian Journal of Occupational Therapy, 63*, 9–23.

Law, M., King, G., & Russell, D. (2005). Guiding therapist decisions about measuring outcomes in occupational therapy. In M. Law, C. Baum, & W. Dunn (Eds.), *Measuring occupational performance: Supporting best practice in occupational therapy* (2nd ed., pp. 33–44). Thorofare, NJ: Slack.

Mathiowetz, V., & Bass-Haugen, J. (1994). Motor behavior research: Implications for therapeutic approaches to central nervous system dysfunction. *American Journal of Occupational Therapy, 48*, 733–745.

Mulligan, S. (2003). *Occupational therapy evaluation for children: A pocket guide*. Philadelphia: Lippincott Williams & Wilkins.

National Center for Medical Rehabilitation Research. (1993). *Research plan for the National Center for Rehabilitation Research* (NIH Publication No. 93-3509). Washington, DC: U.S. Government Printing Office.

National Center for Medical Rehabilitation Research. (2006). *National Center for Medical Rehabilitation Research NICHD: Report to the NACHHD Council, January 2006*. Washington, DC: U.S. Government Printing Office. Retrieved July 21, 2009, from http://www.nichd.nih.gov/publications/pubs_details.cfm?from=&pubs_id=5049

Paul, S., & Orchanian, D. (2003). *Pocket guide to assessment in occupational therapy*. Clifton Park, NY: Delmar.

Plake, B. (2002). Evaluating the technical quality of educational tests used for high-stake decisions. *Measurement and Evaluation in Counseling and Development, 35*, 144–152.

Polatajko, H. (1992). Naming and framing occupational therapy: A lecture dedicated to the life of Nancy B. *Canadian Journal of Occupational Therapy, 59*, 189–199.

Reed, K. L., & Sanderson, S. N. (1999). *Concepts of occupational therapy* (4th ed.). Baltimore: Lippincott Williams & Wilkins.

Tickle-Degnen, L. (2008). Communicating evidence to clients, managers, and funders. In M. Law (Ed.), *Evidence-based rehabilitation: A guide to practice* (2nd ed., pp. 263–295). Thorofare, NJ: Slack.

Trombly, C. (1995). Occupation: Purposefulness and meaningfulness as therapeutic mechanisms (Eleanor Clarke Slagle Lecture). *American Journal of Occupational Therapy, 49*, 960–972.

Turner, S. M., DeMers, S. T., Fox, H. R., & Reed, G. M. (2001). APA's guidelines for test user qualifications: An executive summary. *American Psychologist, 56*, 1099–1113.

World Health Organization. (2001). *International classification of functioning, disability and health*. Geneva: Author.

Practical Aspects of the
Evaluation Process

Denise Chisholm, PhD, OTR/L, FAOTA
Rebecca Austill-Clausen, MS, OTR/L, FAOTA

Overview

The increased demands of today's practice environments require that an occupational therapist perform evaluations more effectively and efficiently. Evaluation is a complex process that guides occupational therapy intervention and, as such, is an essential component of providing quality services. Many practical considerations facilitate efficacy and efficiency of the evaluation process. This chapter outlines useful information for the occupational therapist to use as he or she strives to evaluate clients in a manner that comprehensively focuses on the priority issues using quality assessments in the shortest amount of time. Unfortunately, there is no magic recipe, but if the occupational therapist has a working knowledge of the basic aspects of the evaluation process, he or she can identify strategies that maximize efficacy and efficiency. This chapter discusses the essential aspects of the evaluation process, including referral and screening, assessments, environment, time, teamwork, materials, documentation, accountability, occupational therapy assistants, and professional development. Most important considerations are applicable across practice environments. However, when appropriate, specific information related to the unique aspects of specific occupational therapy practice settings is provided.

Referral

The evaluation process for the majority of practice settings includes a referral. However, referral procedures vary based on state laws and the regulatory requirements of the facility and/or practice setting. An occupational therapist needs to accept and respond to referrals in compliance with state laws and regulatory codes. Therefore, the occupational therapist must be familiar with and have a working knowledge of the laws and regulatory codes that affect practice and understand the interpretation of the rules. Often, the definitions and rules are different for direct services versus indirect services, consultation, and screening. For example, in Pennsylvania a referral is not required for an evaluation; Act 140 of 1982: Occupational Therapy Practice (Commonwealth of Pennsylvania, 2008) states

> An occupational therapist may enter a case for the purposes of providing indirect services, consultation, evaluating an individual as to the need for services. ... Implementation of direct occupational therapy to an individual for a specific medical condition shall be based on a referral from a licensed physician, licensed optometrist or a licensed podiatrist. (Section 14, Practice and Referral, pg. 9)

An occupational therapist needs to make sure he or she has access to and knows the current rules, because laws and regulations change, and changes in other laws affect current laws. For example, Pennsylvania changed part of Section 14 of Act 140 of 1982, as revised in 2008 (Commonwealth of Pennsylvania, 1982, 2008), adding certified registered nurse practitioners and physician assistants to the list of professionals who may refer patients for occupational therapy services in that state. Similar licensure changes have occurred in other states as well.

A therapist must be familiar with the laws and regulations of the state where he or she practices. While examining the laws, rules, and regulations, a therapist should identify those sections related to the evaluation process (i.e., referral, evaluation, screening, occupational therapy assistants, supervision). Often, due to the complexity of the language, it is helpful to discuss these documents with colleagues, including those within the facility and those in the same or similar practice settings. The goal is to have a working knowledge of the content of these documents. In addition, a therapist must establish a system for obtaining updates and revisions. When a therapist has a question or is unsure about the content, he or she should address questions to the boards or agencies overseeing the laws and regulations. Sometimes the state and national professional organizations also can help clarify issues.

A *referral* is usually a written order from a licensed physician. State laws also may address oral orders (i.e., if and when a referral in the form of an oral order can be accepted) and identify other professionals from whom an occupational therapist can accept a referral (e.g., licensed optometrist, licensed podiatrist, certified registered nurse, physician assistant). A therapist needs to read the referral form and associated documentation carefully, making sure to address all pertinent areas of the form during the evaluation process. A therapist also needs to ensure that the professional ordering services understands the unique focus of occupational therapy. It is the responsibility of the occupational therapist to ensure that referral sources understand that the focus of occupational therapy services is on *occupations*; that is, the "activities that people engage in throughout their daily lives to fulfill their time and give life meaning" (Hinojosa & Kramer, 1997, p. 865). Referrals should reflect the services being ordered. When they do not, the therapist needs to identify education opportunities and implement strategies to facilitate the appropriate ordering of services.

In pediatric practice settings, the child's parent or guardian must give permission for an occupational therapy evaluation. In the educational setting, a referral usually addresses education issues. The state rules and regulations may differentiate between the need for services to address an educational issue versus a medical need and may not require a referral to address problems related to educational issues. In the educational setting, in addition to determining whether a referral is required, it is important to confirm that the parent or guardian signed a form giving permission to evaluate prior to initiating the evaluation.

Screening

Many practice settings (e.g., acute care, skilled nursing, long-term care facilities) typically include screening prior to or as a component of the evaluation process. Screening determines the need for further evaluation. Typically, the screening of a potential client is not a reimbursable service, so a therapist must carefully consider the amount of time and effort dedicated to screening. Screening can be a highly valuable service because it can generate referrals for clients in need of reimbursable occupational therapy evaluation and intervention. Screening methods should be as efficient as possible. A therapist needs to determine the reasonable or approved time frame for the completion of the screening of a potential client for that practice setting or facility. Many facilities have a guideline of approximately one unit of service (15 minutes). If the process of reviewing available data, observing the client, or administering a screening instrument to determine the need for further evaluation takes longer than 15 minutes for a client, then it is likely that the therapist needs a referral for occupational therapy services to comprehensively evaluate the client.

State laws and regulatory codes may address screening, so it is essential that an occupational therapist know what the rules are in his or her state. Every occupational therapy program should have available a copy of or quick access to the current state laws and regulatory requirements applicable to the facility and practice setting.

Assessments

There are many assessments available to a therapist; the difficulty is finding the best one(s) for the situation and client. The specific assessments—the tools, instruments, or systematic interactions (e.g., observation, interview protocol) used in the evaluation process—need to address occupational therapy's unique focus on occupational performance or address the factors that support occupational performance. The occupational therapist selects assessments on the basis of the demographic and clinical characteristics of the practice setting and occupational performance needs of the client population. Before a therapist selects an assessment, he or she needs to identify and understand implications related to the type of setting (e.g., school system, acute care, rehabilitation), diagnoses and ages of clients, placement or discharge destination, and reimbursement sources. On the basis of the demographic and clinical characteristics, the occupational therapist considers and prioritizes the relevant areas of occupation, client factors (e.g., body functions, body structures), performance skills and patterns, and environmental factors relevant to the client population. From this data, the therapist identifies the potential assessments that measure the occupational performance needs of the typical client; the therapist can then use this list to determine which assessment to use with a specific client. To reduce the list of potential assessments, the occupational therapist should carefully analyze each assessment, considering the following:

- Psychometric integrity (i.e., test–retest and interrater reliability and internal consistency; face, criterion-related, construct, and content validity)
- Theoretical perspective basis of the assessment
- Clinical population (i.e., age, diagnosis, abilities, limitations)
- Setting
- Degree of measurable objective data obtained
- Costs associated with using the assessment (i.e., purchase, training, maintenance, and use; environmental requirements related to both use and maintenance)
- Time issues (i.e., training and administration, including setup and cleanup; documentation of results)
- Client perception of the assessment
- Utility in conjunction with the assessments used by other disciplines on the team.

Later in this chapter, we will address specific considerations related to issues of time and documentation. The most effective method of selecting assessments is to involve multiple therapists. It should not be the sole responsibility of one therapist.

Completing an evaluation inventory and analysis can provide valuable information about the assessments available. In analyzing the evaluation process of a practice, the occupational therapist should identify the demographic and clinical characteristics of the practice setting and client population. Next, he or she should consider the typical problem areas of the client population and identify the evaluation process most often used. This would include specific assessments, as well as other options and assessments a therapist might use in this type of evaluation process. It is the responsibility of the therapist to check whether the most current edition of an assessment is available. Once the list is complete, he or she considers issues that support or limit using the best evaluation options and assessments in this practice and revises the list to provide evaluations that reflect best practices. The inventory ends when the therapist establishes a system for completing an evaluation inventory and analysis on an annual basis.

Selecting the Assessment

The process for selecting the most appropriate assessment for a particular client becomes more intuitive and efficient with increased clinical experience. However, both novice and expert therapists can benefit from using assessment resources. A valuable resource that connects a therapist to other therapists in his or her practice area(s) is the American Occupational Therapy Association's (AOTA) Special Interest Sections (SISs). The SIS *Quarterly* newsletters and discussion forums are a resource for identifying assessments in practice areas (i.e., Developmental Disabilities, Early Intervention and School, Gerontology, Home and Community Health, Mental Health, Physical Disabilities, Sensory Integration, Technology, Work and Industry). Additionally, AOTA offers publications (e.g., *American Journal of Occupational Therapy*, *OT Practice*) and an extensive collection of products (e.g., assessments, books, CDs, DVDs) that a therapist can easily search by topic (e.g., assessment and evaluation, low vision, mental health, pediatrics) or keyword (e.g., assessment, cognition, early intervention). The third edition of *Occupational Therapy Assessment Tools* (Asher, 2008), which contains profiles of nearly 400 instruments, is useful to a therapist choosing appropriate assessments for clinical practice or research purposes. Two other additional resources that are useful in choosing evaluation tools are *Occupational Therapy Evaluation for Children: A Pocket Guide* (Mulligan, 2003) and *Occupational Therapy Evaluation for Adults: A Pocket Guide* (Neistadt, 2000).

Occupational therapy and occupational therapy assistant programs are also excellent resources when exploring and choosing assessments. Faculty can be a great resource because they are generally willing to assist their students, alumni, and clinical educators with clinical issues, including investigating assessments. The program may have a wide range of assessments available to examine. Additionally, the faculty may be familiar with the psychometric integrity of the assessments and be able to assist with the interpretation. In addition, faculty are able to connect a therapist with a network of professional resources.

It is helpful to have a summary of available assessments. One effective way of doing this is to create user-friendly one-page handouts on typically used assessments. Include the complete reference for the assessment, format, purpose (what it is intended to measure), population(s), length of time for administration, setup and testing criteria, required materials, psychometric properties (reliability and validity), scoring, and helpful hints or considerations for administration. Finally, a summary chart of preferred assessments or a chart of assessments used to evaluate a specific area (e.g., basic activities of daily living, strength, fine motor skills) will guide new therapists and students in the selection of the most appropriate assessment for a client.

Learning the Assessment Tool

Reading the assessment manual is crucial to successfully administering and appropriately using the instrument in practice. It is beneficial for the therapist to read and reread the assessment manual and relevant literature (i.e., research articles) and analyze and discuss the information to understand the utility of the instrument for the practice setting. During the investigation of assessments, a therapist needs to determine the purpose of the assessment: What do the authors of the assessment state that the instrument measures? What are the clinical and research uses of the results? Ensuring that the theoretical approach of the assessment matches the theoretical approach of the practice setting and facility is important. Additionally, the population(s) the instrument was developed for and the population(s) the instrument will be administered to in the clinical or research setting need to match.

A therapist not only needs to review the psychometric information but also needs to understand the reliability and validity of the assessment. Just because an instrument is published and the authors report good psychometric integrity does not necessarily mean that it actually has good psychometric integrity. A therapist needs to know how repeatable or consistent the assessment is *(reliability)*, that is, the degree to which the instrument yields the same results or measures the same way each time it is administered under the same condition with the same population. In addition, a therapist needs to assess whether the assessment measures the specific concept it is intended to measure and whether the conclusions, inferences, or propositions are correct *(validity)*. A therapist should use resources to interpret and better understand the psychometric integrity of the assessment.

An effective method of learning about the psychometric integrity of assessments is to establish a journal club in your department, facility, or school that reviews publications related to assessments. The journal club can include staff members and students. It is important to designate specific meetings to address the evaluation process. For example, if the journal club meets monthly, consider having 4 out of the 12 meetings address evaluation. The article(s) selected can address the evaluation of particular diagnostic categories (e.g., stroke, brain injury, developmental disabilities) related to client population, or they can address a particular assessment. The journal club builds the evidence-based skills of those participating. While participating in the journal club, the participants should not merely read and repeat what the author reports but discuss and interpret the psychometric properties of the assessments. Students can be significant contributors to and facilitators of this process.

Another consideration is the format of the assessment. Assessment formats range from interviews to paper-and-pencil tests, from performance-based tasks to computerized tests. A therapist needs to consider which format is best for the population and practice setting. Additionally, the therapist must consider which format best measures occupational performance or the components that support the client's occupational performance. Although performance-based measures may take a therapist more time to administer, these measures may also yield objective data related to occupational performance. When choosing an assessment, the therapist needs to consider both the quality and quantity of measurable objective data.

The therapist must be knowledgeable of the time it takes to administer the assessment. This is particularly important when evaluating younger children or people with low endurance or cognitive limitations. The therapist also must consider the amount of time required to set up and clean up the assessment, and the time needed to score and interpret the assessment. Ideally, the assessment gives the therapist the best objective and useful information in the shortest amount of time. There are other time considerations to consider, including the amount of time required for both formal and informal training, depending on the requirements of the assessment.

Occupational therapy staff at most facilities or practice settings have identified assessments appropriate for their clinical population(s). The facility should have the most recent edition of each assessment. This is particularly important for pediatric assessments that periodically revise normative data for age and skill comparisons. If an outdated version of the assessment is used, the results will not be considered an accurate measure of the child's skills. The facility also should have an established method for obtaining and maintaining literature and resources relevant to using the assessment. For example, a staff member or pair of staff members can provide a staff development session on the updates or revisions and evidence related to a specific assessment. An evidence-based library of assessments relevant to the practice of the department can be created and maintained (i.e., updated at least annually). Evidence-based activities are great learning assignments for students during fieldwork experiences. As a rule, assessments that obtain objective, clearly defined, quantifiable data are most effective to include in the evaluation process for all populations; however, they are critical in a school-based program, where the initial evaluation helps to determine placement decisions.

The process of creating an evidence-based library of the assessments used in your clinical practice or at your work site begins by identifying an appropriate organizational structure. The information could be organized by type of assessment (e.g., performance-based, interview, questionnaire), the domain addressed by the assessment (e.g., areas of occupation, body functions and body structures, environmental factors), or age group for which the assessment is designed (e.g., 0–3 years of age, 3–7 years of age, 7–12 years of age, adult). Establish a system for adding new evidence related to the evaluation process and assessments to your library.

Assessment Environment

A therapist must carefully consider the environment when selecting appropriate assessments for a facility and when administering the assessments in clinical practice. *Environment* includes both physical and emotional factors. Physical factors include space, seating, sound, temperature, people, and tasks, and the emotional factors involve both the client and therapist.

The therapist must consider the size and type of space needed and available for administration of the assessment. He or she also must take into account the type and amount of objects and materials needed and available. Additionally, the arrangement of the objects and materials, including seating, is important. Does the therapist need a large space so the client can perform gross motor movements? Does the therapist need to seat the client across from him or her at an appropriately sized table? The therapist needs to know the environmental requirements of the assessment and identify the optimal environment for administering the assessment. Often, the therapist must modify the clinical setting to create the most favorable environment for the administration of the assessment. Additionally, if the clinical environment does not match the environmental requirements of the assessment, the therapist needs to determine whether modification is permissible, that is, if the therapist administers the assessment in an alternate or modified environment, will it result in skewed data and invalidate the results of the evaluation?

The therapist also must attend to the temperature and sound of the environment. The client's perception and needs should be the determining factor in adjusting temperature and monitoring sound. Eliminating excess noise and distractions is optimal for administering most, if not all, assessments, but is paramount when conducting a pediatric evaluation.

The location of the evaluation is dependent on the type of practice setting. In many practice settings, the evaluation process usually occurs in a small room. Ideally, the therapist conducts an evaluation in a private, or at least semiprivate, location to support the client's best performance. The therapist should avoid environments where other people (e.g., practitioners, clients, parents, teachers) are in the area or passing through the area. The therapist often has to be creative in selecting an evaluation location. For example, a therapist who works in the school environment may use the hallways, cafeteria (ideally not during lunch because of the excessive noise, unless specifically addressing feeding issues), gymnasium, playground, auditorium stage, or classrooms not in use, whereas clinical practice settings may have specified areas for evaluation.

The number of people present and their roles can affect the evaluation process and the client's performance. In these busy environments, the therapist might not obtain the client's best or optimal performance. If available, the therapist should consider the use of a two-way mirror that allows parents (or others) an opportunity to observe the child (or the client) during the evaluation process without creating undue distractions. Unfortunately, this setup is typically only available in pediatric outpatient or hospital settings.

If a parent or caregiver is present during the evaluation, it may be helpful to ask him or her to leave the room temporarily to observe the client interacting independently with the environment. It is important to receive parental and caregiver input when evaluating children because parents and caregivers are integral components of the evaluation process.

An occupational therapist who works in a client's home has special challenges. For example, a therapist who works in early intervention or with seniors often needs to evaluate the client in his or her home. If possible, the therapist should request clarification of the evaluation site location prior to conducting the evaluation. The home environment may have many variations that can both positively and negatively affect the evaluation process. Administering assessments in the home requires more spontaneous decision making and flexibility because a therapist does not have the opportunity to preplan or familiarize with the environment prior to the evaluation session.

A therapist also needs to consider the tasks or items required by the assessment and their relationship with the environment. How complex are the tasks? Are there time limits and restrictions? Are the tasks highly structured or loosely organized? Do the tasks require a serious atmosphere or encourage a playful mood? Is there a social dimension to the tasks? If so, is it more cooperative or competitive? The therapist must consider the order in which the assessment tasks or items are administered. First and foremost, the therapist must refer to the assessment manual to determine whether there is a standardized format for the administration of the tasks. If the assessment specifies the order, the therapist must adhere to it so that the results are valid. If the order is flexible, then the occupational therapist must determine the most favorable order for the client while taking into account the environmental constraints.

In addition to the physical factors of the environment, special consideration must be given to the emotional factors—the mood of both the client and the therapist. The therapist cannot control the mood of the client; however, a therapist can promote and facilitate desired affective behaviors. Effective communication strategies are a key element to this endeavor. An occupational therapist, as a health care professional, may need to modify his or her natural communication style and learn more effective communication techniques. The challenge is that the therapist needs to change communication styles depending on the needs and styles of the client. The therapist's clinical effectiveness in the evaluation process is directly related to his or her communication skills. The therapist can learn communication techniques and incorporate effective techniques into his or her style through ongoing self-evaluation, practice, and feedback. Remember, all communication has a nonverbal message (i.e., how does the therapist convey the information?) in addition to the verbal message (i.e., how does the therapist give the information?). Preparing the client and his or her family members or significant others for the evaluation is essential.

The Emotional Environment

The initial contact with the client at the start of the evaluation session is critical in creating a therapeutic atmosphere. That atmosphere communicates trust and caring. The therapist must make sure to provide a thorough user-friendly orientation to both occupational therapy services and the evaluation process. A client must understand what a therapist is going to do and what the therapist expects him or her to do. A client may be more involved and invested in the process if he or she understands how the services and evaluation connect with his or her health goals.

Regardless of the practice setting, occupational therapists tend to use a lot of therapy jargon. The therapist needs to transform the medical and therapy terminology used during the evaluation process into user-friendly language for clients and their families. For example, therapists working in an educational setting should use parent-friendly language. Words such as *proprioception, vestibular, sensory integration, sensory processing,* and *kinesthetic* need to be clearly defined using plain, nonmedical language. Clear, plain language will ensure that parents and team members (i.e., teachers, school administrators) understand what the therapist says or writes. The therapist needs to accept that "preparing the client" (including the family) is an ongoing process and that it is the therapist's responsibility to do so to provide high-quality, individualized services.

The mood of the occupational therapist—that is, "our" mood—is the other half of the emotional factor of the environment. Our mood is the therapist's temperament and how he or she conveys it and how it influences communication with a client. Our mood can facilitate or hinder desired affective behaviors of the client. The therapist needs to be aware of his or her mood, the message he or she is conveying through his or her mood, and the effect it has on the therapeutic relationship. Mood is interrelated with communication techniques, and the same ongoing process of self-evaluation, practice, and feedback applies for incorporating effective techniques into one's interpersonal style.

Time

The occupational therapist needs to consider time-related factors as well, including the time requirements for responding to the referral for an evaluation, the time it takes to administer the assessment, and the time needed to become proficient in documenting the evaluation results. In the majority of today's practice settings, time demands are many, so efficiency is essential.

The occupational therapist needs to complete the evaluation process in a timely manner. Doing so requires that the occupational therapist knows the "time" rules (i.e., state laws and regulatory codes, facility/setting policies) for evaluations. The timeline for the evaluation process varies by practice setting and facility. The occupational therapist may have 24 hours to respond to and complete the evaluation of a client in an intensive care unit, whereas the timeline for a client in another unit (e.g., acute, skilled, rehabilitation) in another facility or practice setting may be within 48 hours, 3 working days, or 1 week. In early intervention (0–2 years), preschool (ages 3–5 years), and school-based (ages 6–21 years) services, there is a 60-calendar-day timeline for all initial evaluations to be completed and for the interdisciplinary team meeting to be held (Jackson, 2008).

The evaluation process is typically completed in one session; however, it may be acceptable or typical in some settings for it to take more than one session. Facilities may have a policy regarding the time allotted for the completion of the evaluation. The policy of one facility may be for the evaluation to be completed within a 45-minute session, whereas the policy of another facility may allow up to 1.5 hours for the completion of an evaluation. Additionally, facilities may have policies regarding the time allotted for the occupational therapist to interpret and document the assessment data and develop and document objective and measurable goals that address targeted outcomes. The documentation format affects the time needed. The time needed to complete electronic documentation may be different from the time needed to complete a written narrative or to dictate the evaluation findings.

There are also "time" differences within formats. The electronic documentation procedure at one facility may be more or less time intensive than that at another facility. A therapist must consider both the hands-on time for administering the assessments and the time for documentation when determining total time needed for the evaluation. For example, the hands-on component of a pediatric evaluation takes approximately 1.5 hours, including parental consultation time, followed by documentation time of approximately 1.5 hours, for an average total of 3 hours per evaluation. However, some pediatric evaluations may extend to 4 or 5 hours, depending on the complexity of the assessments.

A therapist also needs to know the rules and regulations regarding reevaluation. What is the time frame for reassessment and reevaluation of the plan relative to achieving targeted outcomes? The time frame may vary from weekly to monthly to every 6 months or annually, depending on the practice setting (e.g., early intervention evaluations are completed yearly with reviews every 6 months). The occupational therapist needs to be aware that the laws, regulations, and facility policies change, sometimes frequently, so being up-to-date on the rules that affect one's practice is essential. As previously stated, the therapist needs to have a working knowledge of the current state laws, regulatory requirements, and facility policies relevant to his or her practice setting. It is important to consider all of these time factors when determining the evaluation time needed in the schedule of an occupational therapist and when coordinating the schedules of occupational therapists and occupational therapy assistants in a department.

Teamwork

A therapist always needs to remember that he or she is part of a team. The occupational therapist does not work with the client in isolation, but as one member of a team where each member contributes unique services but all focus on maximizing the health and wellness of the client. Team members may include a physician, nurse, physical therapist, speech–language pathologist, audiologist, psychologist, recreational therapist, dietitian, respiratory therapist, neurologist, and/or other specialized physicians. In schools, the team typically includes a teacher, guidance counselor, principal, and director of special education.

Communication

Central to the team and a member of the team is the client and his or her family (e.g., parent, guardian, spouse, adult child). The communication skills addressed earlier apply not only to interactions with the client and family but also to interactions with all of the team members. A therapist needs to ensure that all members of the team understand the unique focus of occupational therapy and its relevance to the services provided or overseen. No matter how indirect or brief the interaction, everyone the therapist comes in contact with professionally should understand that the focus of occupational therapy services is on occupation. Each team member needs to know the unique contributions that the other team members add to the comprehensive evaluation of the client. An occupational therapist needs to ensure that the evaluation process, including the assessment(s) administered, focuses on the client's occupational performance and the underlying factors that affect performance. The evaluation documentation also needs to reflect the unique focus of occupational therapy. Additionally, communication with team members by e-mail, phone, or in writing during the evaluation process is essential for completion of a comprehensive evaluation.

Materials

The occupational therapist needs to determine the materials needed to complete the evaluation. These include general materials in addition to those that are specifically required by an assessment. Typically, a list of required equipment and supplies for each assessment is in the assessment manual. The more occupation-based the assessment, the more likely the materials will reflect "real world" materials (i.e., materials available in people's homes and for purchase in local retail stores). Examples of these materials include dishes, pots and pans, clothing, banking forms, job applications, and medication bottles. Additionally, clients often have their own "materials" for occupation-based assessments (e.g., hygiene supplies, clothing, medications). There also may be materials used in the evaluation process that are not assessment-specific, such as paper, pencil, pen, clipboard, watch or stopwatch, tape measure, and magnifying glass. When conducting an evaluation in a pediatric practice setting, additional materials important for the occupational therapist to have available include a desk and chair (child-size for younger children), therapy mat, midsize therapy ball, a variety of sizes of writing implements (e.g., crayons, pencils, markers, colored pencils), pencil grips, sensory items (e.g., Koosh™ balls, sand, rice, dry beans), paper (construction, lined, unlined), manipulatives (e.g., stress balls, sand, beans, small objects), and scissors (child-sized, right- and left-handed, easy grip).

A therapist should organize evaluation materials for the most efficient access and use. In a practice where there are a number of therapists using the same assessments, careful thought must be given to methods for the storage and maintenance of the assessment materials. As with all equipment and supplies, it is beneficial to have an established system for determining who currently has the assessment and its associated materials, how the assessment and materials are maintained, and who is responsible for monitoring the system. Often, evaluation equipment is stored in plastic bins, canvas or lightweight portable bags, or rolling upright small suitcases. For a therapist working in home settings or schools, where equipment must travel from site to site, lightweight portable file boxes work well to keep files and materials organized in a car trunk. Two ways of organizing supplies are alphabetically by days of the week and by different colors for each school or program site. Tickler systems using accordion file folders organized by monthly dates (1–31 days), Excel spreadsheets, and book or cell phone calendars are all helpful in keeping track of evaluation due dates and requirements. General and organizational supplies and storage containers are available at many retail, sporting goods, discount, and office supply stores.

Documentation

Whenever a therapist provides a skilled service to a client, he or she must document the services provided. A well-written and comprehensive evaluation report is essential, because it articulates the rationale for providing occupational therapy services and connects the services to the client's outcomes. The occupational therapist needs to know and understand the state laws and regulatory requirements of the practice setting and the facility policies regarding documentation. A therapist needs to be mindful of the type of practice setting, service model, and theoretical perspective of the facility when writing evaluation reports. Knowing the focus of the practice setting is important, because it directs the focus and language of the report. Hospital-based and outpatient settings are typically more medically driven, whereas community- and school-based settings may focus on social, family, and education issues.

An occupational therapist who provides early intervention services needs to know whether the services in his or her state are medical-based or education-based, because the service model in early intervention varies from state to state. Early intervention services are both family-driven and family-focused; thus, the family is the prime service model and the early intervention evaluation should concentrate on issues that affect both the child and the family (Nanof & Schefkind, 2008). A therapist who evaluates preschool children (ages 3 to 5 years) will generally administer the assessments in a preschool setting, although occasionally he or she may administer them in the child's home. At this point, the family moves from being the primary area of concentration to a secondary service area. The family always remains important, but when writing the evaluation report, it is vital to recognize this shift of evaluation and service philosophy, because the evaluation content now focuses primarily on educational issues; family issues become secondary.

When a therapist evaluates a school-age child (ages 6 to 21 years), he or she focuses on facilitating educational access to the school environment. An appropriate evaluation for a school needs to address how the student can successfully access the educational environment (Individuals With Disabilities Education Improvement Act, Pub. L. 108–446). Parental input is always important, because parents are vital members of the team. Concentration on school-based issues remains the top priority when providing school-based evaluations. A therapist might provide supplemental school services in addition to education-based programs. A therapist should get clarification from the school-based work site program supervisor regarding the roles of private outpatient and medical-based services before completing an evaluation.

Recommendations, including frequency and duration of services, also are dependent upon the type of practice setting. In a pediatric practice setting, it is helpful to begin by asking the work site supervisor about

- The service philosophy regarding treatment frequency;
- Consultation in addition to direct service;
- Involvement of professionals external to the practice setting;
- Parental involvement;
- Team members and their collaborative roles;
- Potential use of instructional aides; and
- The need for nurses if dealing with a child's medical condition, assistive devices, and supplemental equipment and training needs.

All of these areas are important to understand before writing the evaluation report and providing recommendations. It often is confusing for parents to receive concurrently a report from a medical-based outpatient facility and another report from a school-based program. Both sites have differing service philosophies, and billing practices and legal mandates need to be explained clearly to the parents and team when determining service needs for the child. Having a clear understanding of the roles and responsibilities of the evaluating occupational therapist before the evaluation is completed helps make the process smooth and manageable.

The *Guidelines for Occupational Therapy Documentation* (AOTA, 2008) is a good resource for determining what information to include in an evaluation report. According to the AOTA guidelines, an evaluation report should include the referral source, a description of the client's occupational profile, an analysis of occupational performance and those factors that support or inhibit performance, and potential areas of occupation and occupational performance that would be the focus of intervention and outcomes.

A therapist should consider the people reading the evaluation reports. The readers likely include a range of health professionals on the team (e.g., physician, nurse, physical therapist, speech–language pathologist, audiologist, psychologist, recreational therapist, dietitian, respiratory therapist, neurologist, other specialized physicians); in school-based practice, readers also would include numerous education staff (e.g., teacher, guidance counselor, principal, director of special education). Other readers are the client and family. Another important reader in most practice settings is the reimbursement source. Each reader reviews the evaluation document from his or her perspective, looking for elements relevant to his or her role in the client's services.

A therapist needs to make sure that the report addresses the content the readers expect to see in an occupational therapy evaluation. The challenge for the therapist is to complete evaluation documentation in the most efficient yet comprehensive manner. The therapist needs to read his or her documentation through the eyes of those reading it—people who are not occupational therapists. Consider how they interpret the information. Just because the report information seems clear to a therapist and likely clear to other occupational therapists does not mean that the information is understandable to other readers of the report. For example, health and education services use many acronyms. Either avoid the use of acronyms, or clearly define acronyms. Also, avoid or clearly define medical or educational jargon.

Accountability

The occupational therapist is responsible for the services he or she provides. *Accountability* includes promoting and maintaining high standards of conduct (AOTA, 2005b). Practical considerations related to accountability apply to a range of professional behaviors including, but not limited to, honesty, communication, competence, confidentiality, and reimbursement (AOTA, 2005a, 2006). A therapist must understand his or her strengths and limitations and needs to be truthful about individual professional competencies (i.e., does he or she have the training and proficiency required to perform the assessments included in the evaluation process?).

The occupational therapy evaluation may reveal needs of the client that are not within the scope of occupational therapy practice or the expertise of the therapist. If so, and when appropriate, a therapist needs to refer clients to other health care providers. The evaluation report must accurately describe the quality and the quantity of the services provided. The therapist must inform the client truthfully of the results of the evaluation and the risks and benefits associated with the recommendations.

Effective communication is an important professional behavior. A therapist needs to be truthful in all aspects of communication, including written, oral, and electronic forms of communication. Effective communication includes honest statements; adherence to applicable laws, guidelines, and regulations; accurate documentation; and avoidance of biased or derogatory language. Competence includes not only a therapist's current level of skill but also maintaining and increasing competence. A therapist needs to ensure that he or she has the appropriate education and training before incorporating new assessments into practice.

Confidentiality

Information obtained during or associated with the evaluation process is protected information, and as such, a therapist must maintain the confidentiality of the information. A therapist must maintain the confidentiality of all oral, written, electronic, augmentative, and nonverbal communication as required by the Health Insurance Portability and Accountability Act of 1996 Privacy Rule (HIPAA, Pub. L. 104–191) and the Family Educational Rights and Privacy Act of 1974 (FERPA, 20 U.S.C. § 1232g), also known as the Buckley

Amendment. A pediatric therapist must be mindful that privacy rules prohibit him or her from communicating with professionals outside the immediate service agency unless a parent has given specific written permission to allow it. A therapist always should consult with a supervisor regarding privacy restrictions before initiating communication with other professionals who may be familiar with a client the therapist is evaluating.

It is important to maintain the privacy of clients by keeping names on files covered if the files are on a desk in the office or on a table in the clinic. A therapist working in pediatric and home care practice may transport client files in his or her own car. These confidential files must be protected by being concealed and locked in the vehicle. Use only initials in the subject line of an e-mail rather than the client's full name. Delete electronic files by following your work site's privacy procedures. Consider privacy rules when responding to or acknowledging clients both within and outside the therapy setting. It is helpful to ask clients during the evaluation session how they would like to be recognized (or not recognized) when seen outside therapy. For example, some older children do not like their therapists to acknowledge them when they are with their peers.

The Therapist's Responsibility

A therapist needs to ensure that the evaluation services provided are fair and equitable and the fee for an evaluation is reasonable and commensurate with the service performed. Accountability includes being responsible for one's time. A therapist needs to keep track of evaluation time, including direct "hands-on" time and indirect documentation time. Depending on the practice setting, a therapist also may be required to keep track of the time spent in consultation with parents, family, and team members, as well as the travel time associated with an evaluation. A therapist should record his or her time daily, typically in 5- to 15-minute increments. Submitting paperwork, including the paperwork associated with billing, is a critical issue for which a therapist is accountable. Paperwork may need to be submitted daily, weekly, or monthly. No matter the time requirement, a therapist should submit paperwork on time. There are federal, state, and agency or facility rules regarding the length of time copies of client records, including evaluation reports and associated time and billing reports, must be retained. The typical standard for retaining records is a minimum of 3 years; however, a therapist should confirm the appropriate length of time to retain records with the work site supervisor and follow the procedures accordingly. Although this chapter focuses on the evaluation process, the practical considerations associated with accountability relate to services across the occupational therapy process, not just the evaluation.

In addition to being accountable for the services provided, a therapist also is accountable for understanding his or her employment role. There are essentially two reimbursement models of services: employee and independent contractor. The Internal Revenue Service has very specific rules regarding these two reimbursement models (Department of the Treasury, Internal Revenue

Service, 2006). Essentially, employees receive a salary and benefits and work a prescribed number of hours each week, whereas independent contractors determine their own schedule. They have flexibility regarding their caseload and traditionally receive a higher hourly reimbursement rate than an employee because the independent contractor is responsible for his or her own benefits and tax payments. In each reimbursement scenario, it is important that a therapist be clear about how he or she is being reimbursed for services. A therapist must know and understand the implications if being paid by the hour for direct and indirect time providing occupational therapy services or if being paid a flat sum for an all-inclusive evaluation session.

Another employment consideration is reimbursement for travel. This is an important issue, particularly in pediatric and home care practice settings. Clarify travel reimbursement before you engage in the evaluation process. Typically, a therapist is not reimbursed for travel when he or she drives to and from a home because this type of travel is considered commuting to and from the work site. Occasionally, and most often with independent contracting situations, travel time or mileage may be reimbursed if a therapist is driving between evaluation sessions on the same day and for the same agency. A therapist in practice settings requiring travel to and from multiple work sites should keep track of travel time by using a travel log (available at most office supply stores).

A therapist who works as an independent contractor should consult with a certified public accountant to assist with appropriate tax and expense filing requirements. Independent contractors should also ask about the availability, type, and number of assessments available for use; on-site equipment and supplies; evaluation formats and content requirements; mentoring for evaluation education and training; and documentation requirements. Independent contractors may be responsible for purchasing and maintaining assessments, whereas in the employee service model, the facility generally provides all the required materials for the evaluation process. The answers to these questions can help determine the most appropriate employment reimbursement model for you.

Occupational Therapy Assistants

Occupational therapy assistants are valuable members of the team. An occupational therapist and occupational therapy assistant must know the role of each and their contribution to each component of the occupational therapy process, including some aspects of the evaluation. The AOTA *Standards of Practice for Occupational Therapy* states that "an occupational therapy assistant contributes by implementing delegated assessments and by providing verbal and written reports of observations and client capacities to the occupational therapists in accordance with law, regulatory requirements, and AOTA documents" (AOTA, 2005b, p. 664). As previously stated, an occupational therapist and occupational therapy assistant need to know and adhere to the state laws and regulatory requirements of the facility and practice setting, including rules governing the involvement of occupational therapy assistants in the evaluation process and the supervision requirements for occupational therapy assistants.

Professional Development

A great first step in professional development is finding a mentor. Mentors are invaluable, especially for entry-level occupational therapists or therapists new to a practice setting. A mentor can assist a therapist in identifying strategies to obtain education and training in the evaluation process, including education and training related to the administration of specific assessments. The strategies may include review of evaluation guidelines appropriate for the practice setting and facility and opportunities to observe the evaluation process. A mentor may not and does not need to have expertise in the administration of a specialized evaluation, such as sensory processing evaluations, that a therapist wants or needs to learn; however, a mentor can connect a therapist with other occupational therapists with expertise in that area. Mentors also can provide support for managing clients with challenging behaviors during the evaluation process. There are many times during a therapist's career that it is appropriate to request mentorship, including when a therapist is entry level; when a therapist is transitioning to a new practice setting, facility, or agency; and when a therapist is learning a new evaluation process or assessment. Mentoring is effective in enhancing a therapist's knowledge and skills. Remember that mentoring is a win-win situation—both the person being mentored and the mentor grow professionally.

Being a member of AOTA and the state occupational therapy association and being certified by the National Board for Certification in Occupational Therapy (NBCOT) can help facilitate high-quality professional services throughout a career as an occupational therapist. Maintaining involvement with these dynamic associations can spearhead lifelong professional development, stimulation, and camaraderie. Be an active member of these professional associations, and use the resources they have available. For example, a therapist working in a pediatric practice should join the AOTA Early Intervention and School SIS, including the Early Intervention and School discussion forum on OTConnections (http://otconnections.aota.org/). The discussion forum is a great place to post evaluation and assessment questions. These forums give therapists the opportunity to receive feedback from therapists across the country and are a great resource for finding a mentor and connecting with experts in the field. A therapist can attend national and state education events, including annual conferences that typically offer presentations in all practice areas and workshops for specialized content areas. Reduced registration rates are a typical benefit for association members. AOTA offers a range of continuing education opportunities for its members, including continuing education articles, conference session Webcasts, online and self-paced clinical courses, and a variety of publications. These resources address a variety of practice areas and issues, including topics related to the evaluation process. A therapist also can consider pursuing specialty certifications in a practice area.

All therapists should be active, participating members in their national and state occupational therapy associations. Participation includes attending educational events related to the evaluation process and submitting proposals for presentations. Some possible proposals are for a poster on a specific assessment, presentations on a comparison of assessments, or a case study of a client's evaluation process.

Conclusion

The goal of the occupational therapist is to provide high-quality evaluation services in the most effective and efficient manner. To do so, a therapist must be aware of the current laws and regulatory requirements of the practice area and specific facility policies. A therapist also should seek out and use professional resources to enhance competence in performing evaluations. A therapist with an understanding of the practical aspects associated with the evaluation process likely will be better able to identify and implement strategies to maximize proficiency in providing evaluation services.

Questions

1. What would you do if you had questions regarding a rule or regulation related to a referral for an occupational therapy evaluation?
2. What specific steps would you include in the identification, selection, and analysis of assessment tools? What resources are available to assist you in identifying, selecting, and analyzing potential assessments for your practice setting?
3. What teaching methods would you use to assure you are competent in administering, scoring, and documenting the results of a new assessment? What strategies would you implement on an ongoing basis to maintain current knowledge about the assessment?
4. Identify two positive features and two negative features of the physical environment that affect the evaluation process. How can you improve the physical environment?
5. What can you do to positively influence the emotional environment during the evaluation process?
6. How would you describe the unique focus of occupational therapy in the evaluation process and its relevance to the services provided in client care? How would your description of the occupational therapy evaluation process change when speaking with a nurse, a physical therapist, a teacher, or a family member?
7. Identify at least three readers of your evaluation report and the content each reader expects to see in it. Review an occupational therapy evaluation report through the eyes of those reading it. What is an aspect of the documentation that could be changed to make the information more understandable to the readers of the report?

References

American Occupational Therapy Association. (2005a). Occupational therapy code of ethics (2005). *American Journal of Occupational Therapy, 59,* 639–642.

American Occupational Therapy Association. (2005b). Standards of practice for occupational therapy. *American Journal of Occupational Therapy, 59,* 663–665.

American Occupational Therapy Association. (2006). Guidelines to the Occupational Therapy Code of Ethics. *American Journal of Occupational Therapy, 60,* 652–658.

American Occupational Therapy Association. (2008). Guidelines for occupational therapy documentation. *American Journal of Occupational Therapy, 62,* 199–204.

Asher, I. E. (Ed.). (2008). *Occupational therapy assessment tools: An annotated index* (3rd ed.). Bethesda, MD: AOTA Press.

Commonwealth of Pennsylvania. (1982). *Act 140 of 1982: Occupational Therapy Practice Act.* Harrisburg: Author.

Commonwealth of Pennsylvania. (2008). *Act 140 of 1982: Occupational Therapy Practice Act revision.* Harrisburg: Author.

Department of the Treasury, Internal Revenue Service. (2006, November). *Determination of worker status for purposes of federal employment taxes and income tax withholding* (Form SS-8). Washington, DC: Author.

Family Educational Rights and Privacy Act of 1974, Pub. L. 93–380, 20 U.S.C. §1232g, 34 C.F.R. Part 99.

Health Insurance Portability and Accountability Act of 1996, Pub. L. 104–191, 45 C.F.R. §§160, 164.

Hinojosa, J., & Kramer, P. (1997). Fundamental concepts of occupational therapy: Occupation, purposeful activity, and function. *American Journal of Occupational Therapy, 51,* 864–866.

Individuals With Disabilities Education Improvement Act (IDEA) of 2004, Pub. L. 108–446, 20 U.S.C. §1400 *et seq.*

Jackson, L. (Ed.). (2008). *The new IDEA: An occupational therapy toolkit* (2nd ed.). Bethesda, MD: AOTA Press.

Mulligan, S. (2003). *Occupational therapy evaluation for children: A pocket guide.* Philadelphia: Lippincott Williams & Wilkins.

Nanof, T., & Schefkind, S. (2008, April). *IDEA overview and early intervention practice.* Paper presented at the AOTA Annual Conference & Expo, Long Beach, CA.

Neistadt, M. E. (2000). *Occupational therapy evaluation for adults: A pocket guide.* Baltimore: Lippincott Williams & Wilkins.

5

●　●　●　●　●

Evaluation in the Intervention
Planning Process

●

Lou Ann Griswold, PhD, OTR/L, FAOTA

Overview

The occupational therapist strives to enhance a client's occupational performance and participation in activities that are important to him or her. Knowing where to begin and how best to support a client is determined through evaluation. The evaluation process answers many of the questions an occupational therapist has about a client and is the essential first step that enables him or her to plan intervention. Evaluation guides the therapist in considering what is important to the client and establishes a baseline for performance against which the effectiveness of intervention can be measured. This chapter describes how evaluation informs decision making from the first contact with a client through intervention to the point of discharge. Several case examples illustrate the relation between evaluation and intervention.

An emphasis on occupation when sharing evaluation information with clients and professional colleagues promotes client-centered care. Further, the focus on occupation informs others about the contributions of occupational therapy to improving the client's quality of life. Assessment options are introduced in the context of intervention planning, particularly the purpose of the assessment and the intended use of the information gathered. The case examples allow for examination of the pragmatic issues determined by the context of the setting that influence evaluation and intervention. The chapter concludes by encouraging therapists to continue to update their knowledge and skills in assessment tools and their administration.

The Evaluation Process

Evaluation refers to the entire process of gathering information. Neistadt (2000) described evaluation as an ongoing thought process during which a therapist continues to talk with a client, observe his or her performance and reactions, and interpret all information gathered. One might logically assume that evaluation precedes intervention. The *Occupational Therapy Practice Framework: Domain and Process, 2nd Edition* (*Framework–II*; American Occupational Therapy Association [AOTA], 2008b) identifies evaluation as the first phase in occupational therapy practice. In reality, the evaluation process of gathering information about a client continues throughout all phases of occupational therapy practice. The purpose and timing of the evaluation determines the type of data collected and the assessment instruments or measures used and ultimately assists in decision making regarding occupational therapy services and intervention (Ideishi, 2003; Weinstock-Zlotnick & Hinojosa, 2004). Evaluation leads into intervention, beginning with planning and continuing through implementation and review of the client's progress. Evaluation also is connected clearly to outcomes; it is through the information-gathering processes during evaluation that outcomes are identified; these outcomes are then reevaluated at the conclusion of therapy.

Evaluation Phase Leading to Intervention Planning

Getting to know the client as a person is a critical step in any evaluation process (AOTA, 2008b; Brown, 2009; Fisher, 2009; Hocking, 2001; Mulligan, 2003; Neistadt, 2000; Trombly Latham, 2008). Identifying the activities the client likes to do currently, enjoyed doing in the past, and would like to do in the future enables the therapist to know what is important to the person. Learning the client's history gives the therapist information about patterns of behavior and strengths or interests that might be useful in therapy. Understanding the client as an occupational being and the occupations that are important to him or her will focus intervention and identify goals that are meaningful to the client (Brown, 2009). Knowing the client as an occupational being also has been found to enable a therapist to predict more accurately the outcome of occupational therapy intervention (Simmons, Crepeau, & White, 2000). At times, family members provide information to enable the therapist to understand the client, especially when working with children (Mulligan, 2003) but often with clients of all ages (Fisher, 2009).

During evaluation, an occupational therapist strives to identify the client's roles, strengths, needs, and goals and the context in which he or she lives, works, and plays. Evaluation is central to identifying desired outcomes and developing a plan for intervention. Knowing the occupational roles of the client indicates what the client values and suggests possible tasks that are important to support the identified roles. A therapist then can explore which tasks are easy and which are difficult for the client to perform. Learning the client's perception of how the environment supports or hinders his or her roles and tasks further enables the therapist to understand more about the person and his or her natural contexts. After gathering information, the therapist helps the client identify his or her priorities and goals for occupational therapy. The following case example illustrates these points; Jean, the occupational therapist, has received a referral from her team members in a community mental health center.

● ● ● ● ● ●

Case Example 5.1. Jean and Tonya

Jean, an occupational therapist, worked in a community outpatient mental health center. **Tonya** sought help through the mental health center because she was feeling "depressed and alone." Tonya identified her primary role at this time as a mother of two toddlers. She listed the tasks that supported this role as preparing snacks and meals, cleaning, playing, and supporting and fostering the children's development. Tonya felt that she was not doing these tasks well; for example, she often started to prepare a meal but then became distracted and changed her plans. She stated that the meals she prepared were not nutritionally complete and that her house was "forever a mess." She stated that she did not feel she really played with the children, but rather only watched them. Tonya had wanted to have children and stay at home with them while they were young, but now she felt isolated. She said that she was not as motivated to keep up with the housework and meal preparation as she would like. Tonya acknowledged that she had little enthusiasm to perform the activities she knew were important to her as a mother. Tonya was married, but her husband was out of town 4 days a week for work. She and her family lived on the outskirts of a small town.

Jean learned that Tonya was in drama clubs during high school and college and enjoyed that period of her life. Further exploration revealed that Tonya liked not only the acting but also the energy level she felt when in contact with large groups of people. Tonya recalled that in college her grades improved as the pressures of a theater production increased. Before her children were born, Tonya worked as a kindergarten teacher, where she felt she was able to use her artistic talents in many ways to promote her students' development.

Jean listened as Tonya talked about her past, present, and dreams for the future. Tonya said that she would like to be around other people but did not want to be employed while her children were young. She stated she wanted to feel that she was "doing something worthwhile with her life." She also wanted to do a better job caring for her children's daily needs and to "have fun with them."

● ● ● ● ● ●

Throughout this stage of the evaluation, Jean gathered an occupational profile of Tonya (AOTA, 2008b). Occupational therapists may conduct an informal interview with a client to obtain an occupational profile (as Jean did with Tonya), or they may use assessment protocols to determine how a client spends his or her time, values given occupational roles and routines, engages in interests, and obtains feelings of competence. Two assessment instruments used to gather such data are the Canadian Occupational Performance Measure (COPM; Law, Baptiste, Carswell, McColl, Polatajko, & Pollock, 2005) and the Occupational Performance History Interview (OPHI–II; Kielhofner et al., 1998). The COPM gathers specific information regarding the occupations the client wants or needs to do and his or her perception of his or her performance of and satisfaction with these occupations. The OPHI–II provides a more expansive occupational profile.

Jean decided to evaluate Tonya's occupational performance (AOTA, 2008b) and identified Tonya's desired outcomes for intervention. She also considered Tonya's age, culture, disability, and supports. She used her clinical reasoning and decided that she needed a specific measurement of occupational performance. As suggested by Trombly Latham (2008) and Fisher (2009), Jean observed Tonya engaging in occupational tasks to assess occupational performance. The therapist might observe a client performing an occupational task that is important to him or her. Jean and Tonya decided that it might be informative to have Jean observe Tonya complete a simple cooking task. Jean could do this using her own observational skills or a standardized assessment tool such as the Assessment of Motor and Process Skills (AMPS; Fisher, 2003).

As indicated by the client's performance, the therapist then determines whether further evaluation is needed to assess specific client factors, environmental contexts, or activity demands (AOTA, 2008b; Fisher, 2009; Trombly Latham, 2008). Only the aspects necessary to more thoroughly understand the client's performance need to be assessed. For some clients, assessing the environmental context of the place of employment might be relevant. For example, visiting a job site would enable the therapist to determine the challenges and supports within that environment. The therapist might consider any physical, social, and cultural aspects of the environment that might be supporting or hindering a client's performance. In other situations, assessing client factors such as range of motion or strength might help to determine any underlying causes of problems in occupational performance. Assessing activity demands, including the objects used in occupational tasks and the required actions, timing, and sequencing of actions to use these objects, also might be informative (AOTA, 2008b). It is up to the therapist to determine whether the assessment of any of these areas will be helpful in better understanding the client and his or her occupational performance. These areas would be assessed using observation or specific assessment tools or measures as appropriate.

In Tonya's case, Jean determined that she needed more information about how Tonya spent her time each day—the temporal dimension of context. She asked Tonya to keep a log of all activities and tasks that she engaged in for a 7-day period. Jean interpreted all of the evaluation information that she had gathered from the interview and Tonya's activity log and reviewed it with Tonya.

Once all the relevant information has been gathered, the therapist interprets all of the results and identifies the client's strengths and weaknesses (AOTA, 2008b). The therapist then shares his or her hypotheses about the client's abilities with the client, and together they establish goals that will lead to the client's desired outcomes. Jean learned that Tonya was motivated to carry out her role as a mother and that she had the motor and process skills to do these tasks. These were Tonya's strengths. Through a review of Tonya's activity log, Jean determined that Tonya engaged in many activities throughout the week that she felt she had to do but did not enjoy doing. Jean noted that Tonya engaged in very few activities that were enjoyable to her. She reported that Tonya had trouble focusing her attention on any given task. She hypothesized that the environment in which Tonya lived was not conducive to her need for contact with others, particularly adults. She also hypothesized that Tonya was frustrated by not using her talents. Jean shared her conclusions with Tonya, who agreed with them and said that she would like to have more contact with other adults and to become involved in drama in some way again. These were Tonya's desired outcomes. Jean and Tonya then identified goals that would enable Tonya to reach her desired outcomes.

Using the model of human occupation (Kielhofner, 2009), Jean focused on Tonya's role as a mother and the importance of this role in her life. Moreover, Tonya had a great desire to interact with adults, which relates to her volitional subsystem. By working with Tonya to help fulfill an occupational role that was important to her—that of mother—and her desire to interact with adults in a meaningful and creative way, Jean provided Tonya with activities that were critically important to her life.

Reassessment Throughout the Intervention Process

The evaluation process ends and intervention planning begins with setting goals and the therapist's selection of a theoretical perspective that will guide the evaluation and intervention processes. Choosing a specific theoretical perspective or several congruent perspectives directs the selection of the assessment tools and specific intervention strategies to address identified problem areas gathered during the occupational profile. The intervention process consists of three steps: planning, implementation, and review (AOTA, 2008b). The evaluation process continues throughout intervention, in the form of reassessment, as a therapist monitors a client's responses and modifies the intervention as needed. Because of this explicit link between evaluation and intervention, it is helpful to consider how evaluation informs each step of the intervention process.

Planning Phase of Intervention

Evaluation is tied most closely to planning intervention. An intervention plan draws on the information from assessments during the evaluation phase and includes the client's desired outcomes of therapy, appropriate goals and objectives for therapy, the intervention approach to be used, and details of service delivery (AOTA, 2008b). As illustrated in the example of Tonya and Jean, an occupational therapist bases the intervention plan on the client's desired outcomes that focus on occupational goals that support participation in meaningful life activities (AOTA, 2008b; Brown, 2009; Hinojosa, Kramer, Royeen, & Luebben, 2003). Desired outcomes vary in nature and specificity across clients.

Examples of desired outcomes for clients at different ages and with different types of disabilities and needs include the following:

- To prepare a simple lunch of a sandwich and cold beverage
- To meet the demands associated with the role of grandmother
- To adapt to new social expectations at the playground
- To feel emotionally ready to return to work and interact socially with peers.

The intervention plan takes into account what is important to the client and his or her current level of occupational performance, as well as supporting assessment data on client factors, environmental contexts, and task demands. Using all of this information, the therapist selects a theoretical perspective or frame of reference to guide the intervention. The therapist decides whether it is more appropriate to take a skill acquisition approach, facilitating the (re) learning of skills, such as manipulating small objects or regulating impulsive behaviors (Kaplan, 2010), or a restorative approach to establish or restore underlying abilities such as muscle strength or skilled movement (Bass-Haugen, Mathiowetz, & Flinn, 2008). Alternatively, the therapist might choose to take a compensatory approach and adapt tasks or modify the environment to promote more successful engagement in occupations (Brown, 2009; Fisher, 2009).

The therapist should share his or her knowledge and evidence regarding the different intervention options with the client. In collaboration with the client, the therapist should determine the best approach to obtain the identified goals and create a plan for intervention. The therapist uses clinical reasoning, professional experiences, selected theoretical perspective, and evidence-based research to determine reasonable and appropriate objectives and methods to reach the desired outcomes.

Implementation Phase of Intervention

As the occupational therapist and occupational therapy assistant work with a client to implement an intervention plan, they engage in ongoing reassessment to ensure that therapy is meaningful and effectively facilitating progress toward the established goals and objectives. As an occupational therapist implements services, he or she continually seeks new activities to promote the client's progress. Activities that are relevant and meaningful to the client have been shown to be more effective in helping him or her reach the established goals (Mastos, Miller, Eliasson, & Imms, 2007; Phipps & Richardson, 2007). The occupational therapist selects activities identified during the evaluation phase as meaningful and relevant to the client. Monitoring the client's affective response to activities and approaches used during therapy enables an occupational therapist to determine the meaning that these hold for the person (Park, 2008; Price, 2009). Such monitoring and ongoing reassessment keep the intervention client-centered.

An occupational therapist, with the assistance of an occupational therapy assistant, formally reevaluates a client's performance and progress throughout intervention to modify the intervention plan (Radomski, 2008; Stewart, 2005; Tickle-

Degnan, 2009). A review of ongoing observations and formal assessment data can redirect an occupational therapist's decision making and services. An occupational therapist may observe poor performance during a therapy activity, leading to a change in intervention focus or additional formal reevaluation that, in turn, redirects intervention. As the review of progress occurs, the therapist moves into the review phase of intervention.

Monitoring Progress: The Review Phase of Intervention

Review of the client's response and results from intervention occurs continually. The occupational therapist and occupational therapy assistant gather more information and modify their intervention plan as needed. Review time may be built into the intervention plan if allowed by the pragmatic constraints that influence practice. The time frame may be after a certain number of visits or at set intervals (such as weekly or monthly), often determined by reimbursement guidelines. During these reviews, the desired outcomes, goals, and measurable objectives of the occupational therapy intervention plan form the basis for determining the effectiveness of the intervention. The initial assessment measures may be repeated to determine change in occupational performance, which is important for the therapist to consider when choosing the assessments to use in the initial evaluation. Comparison of assessment data over time enables the therapist and client to objectively measure progress and determine whether therapy should continue or whether the client should be discharged. The therapist and client work together to modify the intervention plan as needed for continued therapy. Review of the intervention may also facilitate a referral to another professional colleague.

Using Evaluation for Intervention Planning

Two case examples illustrate very different types of evaluation approaches that address the client's occupational goals. The assessments differ for the two cases because of differing types of data most relevant to the clients' occupational goals and the resulting intervention planning, implementation, and progress review.

● ● ● ● ● ●

Case Example 5.2. Joan and Mr. Muñiz

Joan worked as an occupational therapist at a home-based rehabilitation program. She was allowed four visits to see her client, Mr. Muñiz, including time for evaluation and intervention. **Mr. Muñiz** had had a cerebrovascular accident and had already received 2 months of inpatient occupational therapy services. Joan knew that evaluation was essential to enable her to know what to focus on in intervention; however, she was also very aware that she had limited time to spend with her client and wanted to move into intervention as quickly as possible. She received documentation on Mr. Muñiz from the inpatient rehabilitation setting where he had received services most recently.

The documentation Joan received enabled her to more quickly establish a therapeutic rapport with Mr. Muñiz. She used the assessment data provided by the previous occupational therapist and did not need to repeat the same assessments. She also knew the client's interests, concerns, abilities, and needs from this documentation. Joan built on her existing knowledge of Mr. Muñiz and directed her attention to how he was doing at home, an area not addressed during inpatient rehabilitation. Thus, Joan focused her evaluation on Mr. Muñiz's current needs and began intervention almost immediately.

Joan spent the first 10 minutes of her home visit talking with Mr. Muñiz and his wife. She quickly learned through her informal interview that Mr. Muñiz wanted to make his own coffee in the morning, tend his rose garden, and grill meat for family meals. Although he was not independent in all personal activities of daily living, Mr. and Mrs. Muñiz agreed that the routine they had worked out met his needs, and Mrs. Muñiz felt comfortable assisting him. As part of her evaluation, Joan determined that she wanted to assess Mr. Muñiz's occupational performance, activity demands, and the environmental context by observing him performing tasks that were important to him. She decided to use the AMPS (Fisher, 2003), a standardized assessment instrument, to determine the effort, efficiency, and safety that Mr. Muñiz exhibited during familiar instrumental activities of daily living. For the assessment, she and Mr. Muñiz chose AMPS tasks that directly related to his desired outcomes. Joan observed him potting a plant and making a pot of coffee.

● ● ● ● ● ●

From this assessment, including the discussion with Mr. and Mrs. Muñiz and observing his task performance, Joan gathered a great deal of information about Mr. Muñiz's abilities and needs. She determined that further assessing Mr. Muñiz's specific physical or cognitive skills would not help her plan or implement intervention or review progress. Joan followed Mr. Muñiz's desires and interests in goal setting and planning. Aware of his abilities and his stage of recovery, Joan decided to use a compensatory approach to support Mr. Muñiz's performance in his desired occupations. At the conclusion of her first visit, Joan was ready to begin intervention by making suggestions for modifying Mr. Muñiz's environment in the kitchen and adapting the task demands in his garden area. Joan blended evaluation and intervention into the first of her four sessions with Mr. Muñiz.

Joan repeated the AMPS at the end of the intervention period to provide a standardized measure of the progress that Mr. Muñiz had made. Another measure of effectiveness of occupational therapy intervention was Mr. Muñiz's reported improved participation in the three occupations that he had identified as being important. By using a client-centered approach, Joan was able to help Mr. Muñiz meet his goals of making his own coffee, tending to his roses, and grilling for his family.

● ● ● ● ● ●

Case Example 5.3. Danielle and Pierre

Danielle, an occupational therapist, took a slightly different approach during evaluation. Danielle was working with **Pierre,** a plumber, as a client. Pierre was eager to return to work after sustaining an on-the-job injury to his left hand. He had a tendon repair and was referred for occupational therapy by his orthopedic surgeon. Because of the nature of the injury, Pierre's insurance preapproved eight sessions.

Danielle began her first session by interviewing Pierre to get to know his job requirements and leisure interests. She learned about the types of hand movements that Pierre needed to do on his job and looked at the tools and materials he used on the job. She also found out that Pierre bowled regularly with friends and built model trains at home. Pierre said that he could still bowl with his right hand, but was not able to use his left hand to work on his trains.

● ● ● ● ● ●

Although building trains was important to him, Pierre was most concerned about returning to work. Danielle observed Pierre using his plumbing tools; she knew that limited range of motion and limited strength in his left hand were the underlying causes of his difficulty with occupational performance in his work setting. Danielle knew that her intervention approach would be one of remediation of hand function to support Pierre's job performance and enable him to perform other activities that were important to him. Danielle selected a biomechanical frame of reference to guide Pierre's evaluation and intervention (Flinn, Jackson, McLaughlin Gray, & Zemke, 2008). Thus, assessment focused on measuring range of motion and grip strength in Pierre's left hand, because these would be important in monitoring his progress toward his occupational performance goals supporting his roles as plumber, bowler, and builder of model trains.

Intervention Planning in the Case Examples

In both case examples, the occupational therapists focused on the occupational interests and desires of the clients. Joan had preliminary information about her client, so she did not have to spend as much time collecting information for an occupational profile as Danielle. However, Joan did need to do some assessments because the focus of her services was different from that of the occupational therapy services her client had received previously. Joan needed to observe Mr. Muñiz as he engaged in occupations that were important to him now that he was home so that she could determine the extent to which compensatory skills were needed. Joan consciously decided not to further assess Mr. Muñiz's abilities around muscle tone, movement, or cognition; information from these types of assessments would not have helped her plan for intervention.

Danielle selected a biomechanical frame of reference and began her evaluation by gathering information to construct an occupational profile of Pierre before assessing motor abilities and skills. She did this efficiently, spending only a short time observing Pierre work with his tools and assessing his occupational performance. Consistent with the biomechanical frame of reference, Danielle focused her assessment on the client factors she knew were the underlying cause of Pierre's inability to engage in work routines.

These two case examples illustrate that there is no single right way to complete an evaluation. The process varies based on the client, the information available from other sources, and information gathered during the initial steps of the evaluation process. The pragmatics of service delivery (particularly the number of visits allowed by third-party payers) influence what a therapist can do. Joan's services to Mr. Muñiz were limited to a short period of time; however, her evaluation was appropriate, and she was able to begin intervention immediately.

Documentation of Evaluation Results

The evaluation phase concludes with the documentation of results and the reporting of recommendations. Documentation should include all information that is relevant and important in addressing the initial purpose of the evaluation. The assessment data reported also should be framed by occupation, the focus of occupational therapy services. The purpose of the evaluation may have been clearly stated in the referral to occupational therapy. For example, Eric, a student in an elementary school setting, was referred for occupational therapy evaluation "to determine if he has sensory processing difficulties that are interfering with his ability to attend in the classroom." In this case, the occupational therapist would ensure that he or she answered this question in the evaluation report. The occupational role of student is implied and easily enables the therapist to talk about occupation.

In some cases, the therapist needs to frame the assessment in terms of the client's occupation and the client's ability to function. If, for example, the referral for Pierre had read "evaluate and treat: post-tendon injury and surgical repair," Danielle would need to document how the hand injury hindered Pierre's performance in occupations that were meaningful to him. Because of the nature of the referral, she also would need to document the underlying client factors of range of motion and strength in Pierre's hand and to relate these factors to his occupational performance.

Occupational therapy evaluation results provide valuable information about the client that will be informative to other professional colleagues, particularly when planning for discharge. Often the occupational therapist is the professional who is best able to determine how independently and safely a person can perform activities and occupations, information essential in determining discharge readiness and recommendations. Consequently, occupational therapy evaluation reports should be written clearly so that other professionals can easily understand the types of assessment used, the findings, and the interpretation of those findings that relate to occupational performance and subsequent goals and recommendations. Appendix 5.A of this chapter provides one example of an evaluation report template based on the AOTA *Guidelines for Documentation of Occupational Therapy* (2008a). The report template leads the occupational therapist through reporting evaluation findings to planning intervention in the Recommendations section. Appendix 5.B illustrates using this template for Pierre, the case example discussed earlier.

Although a facility often determines the format for evaluation reports, most reports conclude with recommendations. The recommendations usually include the broad goals for intervention and the approach to use during therapy and may include details of services to be provided. For example, Joan might recommend that Mr. Muñiz receive three more occupational therapy visits in which the therapist uses a compensatory approach to modify the demands of tasks and Mr. Muñiz's environment to support his safety and independence in performing instrumental activities of daily living at home.

Even if therapy is not warranted, the report should include recommendations (in the form of suggestions) that address the reason for referral. For example, Eric's referral was "to determine if he has sensory processing difficulties that are interfering with his ability to attend in the classroom." If the therapist does not find that Eric has sensory processing difficulties and finds no reason for his difficulty in class that warrants occupational therapy services, the therapist still might offer suggestions to enhance Eric's ability to pay attention during class. The therapist might suggest moving Eric to a location in the classroom with fewer distractions or suggest that the teacher be sure he has Eric's attention before giving instructions. Suggestions might also include a referral to another professional—for example, to a speech–language pathologist—to confirm hearing acuity and processing, which also may influence Eric's attention span in class. These suggestions become a form of consultation. The recipients of the evaluation report (in this case, Eric's parents and teachers) receive a written report of the evaluation findings and some guidance regarding how to proceed.

All client information, when written, serves as a permanent record of the client's abilities and progress made during intervention. An evaluation report documents the present performance level and the client's desired outcomes and goals, which can inform others who work with the client in the future. Such information is especially helpful for clients who are transferred from one facility or type of care to another. In the continuum of health care used in the United States, it is not unusual for a client to receive services in several different facilities or different departments within one facility. Information gathered during evaluation often goes into the client's chart for future use by other occupational therapists and professionals in subsequent settings. An occupational therapist at the receiving facility could use and build on previous assessments so that clients do not have to repeat assessments, ensuring that the therapist at the receiving facility not lose valuable intervention time during a client's limited length of stay and rehabilitation time. Confirming the client's desired outcomes and goals can be done efficiently at the onset of services, helping to establish a therapeutic relationship with the client and keep services client-centered. The therapist then can begin intervention almost immediately and can continue to gather more evaluation data throughout intervention. The example of Joan and Mr. Muñiz illustrates good use of information from another facility.

Types of Assessment Data

Several assessment strategies were presented in the three client examples in this chapter. As Chapter 6 discusses, assessment instruments vary in their specific purpose and how they are used to obtain, score, and interpret gathered information. Occupational therapists need to be aware of assessment options and choose a procedure that provides a good match with the intended use of the assessment results (Tickle-Degnen, 2009). It is important that therapists select assessments on the basis of the initial information gathered in a screening (e.g., occupational profile) rather than on the therapist's own comfort or familiarity with limited assessments. Assessment procedures chosen with the individual client in mind are more likely to result in client-centered practice. Further, assessments may be selected based on the frame of reference a therapist selects to use with the client. A therapist may need to seek out new assessments to address clients' evaluation needs.

An occupational therapist can use assessment instruments to gather information during all steps of the evaluation process. Knowing the type of data needed and the purpose of each assessment is essential in choosing the most appropriate tool for a specific client. A therapist uses assessments to gather information about a client's occupational history, interests, and roles. Other assessments provide guidelines for observing occupational performance. Still others focus on client factors, context, or activity demands. Instruments vary in procedure, the type of data obtained, and usefulness.

Some assessments provide *quantitative* information, such as a numeric score from a norm-referenced standardized assessment tool, which is useful when comparing a client's performance with people similar in age, disability, ethnicity, culture, or other relevant characteristic. Other assessments are *qualitative,* providing descriptive information about a client; his or her perception of abilities, needs, values, and interests; or any other area of focus. Qualitative assessments include interviews with the client, family members, or others who spend time with the client; observations of performance; and interactions with the environment.

The quantitative data gathered from standardized assessments and the qualitative information gathered from assessments offer different types of information to therapists, clients, and team members. To select the tool that best meets the identified purpose, it is essential to know the purpose of the assessment, administration procedures, type of data obtained, and how the information may be used. The therapist's knowledge and skills in administering a given assessment also will influence what instrument is used.

Standardized assessments provide objective data that can help identify or determine levels of dysfunction. A test of this type also can be used to predict performance in a related task or overall functional ability. Results from a standardized test may vary in their usefulness in planning an intervention program. Repeating a standardized assessment tool can document changes over time and provide data for evidence-based research (Mulligan, 2003). Standardized assessment tools have specific procedures for administration and scoring that therapists must follow to obtain reliable and valid results. These assessments are limited because they often measure performance in unnatural conditions (unless occupational performance in a natural environment is the condition of testing). More typically, standardized assessments require the client to perform tasks outside a meaningful context. Examples include stacking 1-inch cubes, sorting cards or objects, squeezing a dynamometer, or determining correct change in a simulated purchasing task. The results may help the therapist better understand the client and his or her abilities, but the therapist then needs to transfer the results to a context and relate the findings to occupational performance. Many standardized assessments require extensive education or training to learn how to administer the assessment tasks, score them, and interpret the data, to ensure that the data they provide are reliable.

Norm-referenced assessments provide scores that can be compared to the scores of a specific reference group—the *normative group.* The normative group might be children of a certain age or people with a given disability or condition. Knowing the normative group is important when selecting an appropriate assessment instrument. A test that was normed on a small group of people or a homogeneous group might not be relevant for the client being assessed. Norm-referenced assessments are used to determine the severity of identified delays or dysfunction and to evaluate change at a later time (Richardson, 2005). Norm-referenced assessments may be helpful in identifying intervention goals specific to the skills assessed, but they may not be particularly helpful in guiding other aspects of intervention planning. Normative data do not necessarily give the therapist a picture of the whole person.

Criterion-referenced assessments compare a client's performance to a set of criteria rather than to the performance of other people (Richardson, 2005). The criteria identify the tasks that a client can or cannot do or evaluate the quality of performance. Criteria also may include information about the amount of assistance needed or the approach the client uses to complete a task. Criterion-referenced assessments and observations are useful in guiding intervention planning, enabling the therapist to identify the client's skill level and build on his or her abilities and strengths in intervention (Richardson, 2005).

An *ipsative and nonstandardized assessment* enables the therapist to understand how a client performs a task, often in the usual performance context. Nonstandardized assessments allow flexibility in the task and environment when assessing a client's performance. During nonstandardized assessments, a therapist may interview the client or a family member or observe the client engaging in an occupational task. Interviews provide the primary means of obtaining an occupational profile of a client and allow the therapist to understand the client's perspective on problems in occupational performance. Interviews also provide an opportunity to establish therapeutic rapport with the client. Interviews may be informal and conversational in nature or may be formal and structured using an assessment protocol.

Observations may be structured or natural. In structured observation, the therapist sets up the environment to elicit certain behaviors and skills. For example, a therapist may want to observe how a child performs during typical preschool activities, so the therapist might ask the child to color and cut out a picture to provide opportunity to observe the child's fine motor skills. In a natural observation, the therapist observes the child in a preschool class during regular schoolwork activities that may include coloring and cutting. Observation in a natural context enables the therapist to consider how the physical and social environments support or hinder a client's performance. Observations can be especially helpful in planning intervention because they provide the therapist with an understanding of how the person performs identified tasks. When observation is done in the environment in which the client typically needs to perform these tasks, the therapist also can consider how the demands of the task and the context influence performance and include adaptations when intervention planning.

Observations are often not standardized. The limitations of nonstandardized assessments include inconsistency and subjectivity of the information gathered and potential bias in observing and interpreting the results. Nonstandardized assessments also lack reliability and validity to support the conclusions that therapists draw from the assessment data (Mulligan, 2003). While a nonstandardized evaluation is better than no evaluation at all, a therapist using nonstandardized assessments must be careful in reporting the outcome from these assessments as definitive and may choose to do more than one assessment of a specific problem to confirm or reinforce findings.

Standardized observations provide a therapist with information to support intervention planning and can reliably be used as a measure of progress. Few natural context observation-based assessments are standardized. The Assessment of Motor and Process Skills (AMPS; Fisher, 2003) evaluates personal and instrumental activities of daily living for ages 3 years through adulthood. The Árnadóttir OT-ADL Neurobehavioral Evaluation (A-ONE; Árnadóttir, 1999) and the Functional Independence Measure (FIM™; Uniform Data System for Medical Rehabilitation, 1997) frequently are used to assess personal activities of daily living. The WeeFIM II (Uniform Data System for Medical Rehabilitation, 2004–2006) is similar to the FIM and assesses personal activities of daily living for children. The School Assessment of Motor and Process Skills (School AMPS; Fisher, Bryze, Hume, & Griswold, 2007) assesses children's performance of schoolwork tasks. The Evaluation of Social Interaction (ESI; Fisher & Griswold, 2009) and the Assessment of Communication and Interaction Skills (ACIS; Forsyth, Lai, & Kielhofner, 1999) assess social interaction skills.

Using a variety of methods and tools for assessment provides a range of data to inform an evaluation that is appropriate to the needs of the client. A therapist draws from different quantitative and qualitative methods depending on the questions he or she has about a client. Being aware of the options for assessment and learning new tools is part of a therapist's ongoing professional responsibility.

The following example illustrates an occupational therapist's use of two types of assessments: norm-referenced and a standardized observation. The occupational therapist deliberately chose the assessments she used and carefully considered the information they provided. Each type of assessment provided different information to help the therapist gain a complete understanding of the client's abilities and challenges. The therapist used clinical reasoning to interpret all of the findings and to consider intervention.

● ● ● ● ● ●

Case Example 5.4. Luke and Crystal

Luke, a 10-year-old fifth grader, was referred to occupational therapy by his teacher and the school's special education referral team. Luke had received occupational therapy services as a preschooler for motor skills, particularly fine motor development. Occupational therapy was discontinued when he entered kindergarten because assessments indicated that his motor development was within age range. At the beginning of second grade, Luke was diagnosed with a language-based learning disability and has received speech and language therapy and help with reading since that time. Luke's fifth-grade teacher was concerned because Luke is not getting his work done in a timely manner. She reported that he frequently does only half of the required writing, with illegible, sloppy handwriting. She wondered if his difficulty with written work is because of fine motor and handwriting issues in addition to his learning disability, which could be affecting his spelling. Because of Luke's history of fine motor difficulty in preschool and now handwriting difficulty, the team asked for the occupational therapist to assess his fine motor skills as they relate to education.

Crystal, the occupational therapist, talked with Luke's teacher and learned that he has difficulty with all writing tasks and that his problem is more pronounced when he needs to write several paragraphs. Crystal learned that Luke also does not complete most classroom projects in a timely manner and that the end product is usually incomplete and sloppily done. Crystal found out that Luke finishes his math work, most of which is done in a math workbook. Crystal's focus was not on how well Luke was performing academically but on Luke's performance of his schoolwork tasks—on occupation.

● ● ● ● ● ●

On the basis of her conversation with Luke's teacher, Crystal arranged to observe Luke during a science activity in which he and the other students would be graphing results from an experiment and writing up the results in paragraph form—both tasks that would be challenging for Luke. During the observation, Crystal noted that Luke made several trips to gather paper, ruler, and pencils needed to complete the two tasks. His materials were on top of one another within his workspace, making it difficult for him to locate certain materials when he needed them. Luke paused for long periods during each task.

He also played with his ruler and pencils, at one point putting a pencil through a hole in the ruler and spinning the ruler around. Another student sitting near him cued him to get back to work. He then worked quickly and wrote without keeping his writing in between the lines on the paper. Crystal noted that Luke held his pencil with a mature grasp and easily manipulated his pencil and other materials in his hands. Crystal concluded that Luke's difficulty in writing was not due to fine motor skills but rather to inefficiently using time, space, and materials related to the schoolwork tasks.

Crystal had learned how to score her observations using the School AMPS (Fisher et al., 2007). After using the criteria to score the observations, Crystal entered the scores into the School AMPS software program to obtain a school motor performance measure of 2.1 logits and a school process performance measure of 0.03 logits. The motor performance measure indicated that Luke demonstrated little effort in using tools and materials. The process performance measure indicated that he was inefficient when organizing time, space, and materials. Transformation of the two performance measures revealed that Luke's motor performance was in the average range when compared to his same-age peers but that his process performance was significantly below that of his peers, with standardized z scores of -1.0 for motor performance and -2.4 for process performance. Standardized scores would be familiar to other team members and would help them to understand Luke's performance in relation to other students of the same age.

Crystal knew that the special education team and Luke's teacher would expect her to have assessed his fine motor and visual–motor skills, factors that support handwriting. Although she did not believe they were issues for Luke, she reasoned that specific assessments in these areas would be relatively quick to do, would enable her to rule out these areas of concern, and would provide information expected by the team. Crystal chose the fine motor control tasks on the Bruininks–Oseretsky Test of Motor Proficiency (BOT–2; Bruininks & Bruininks, 2005) and the Beery–Buktenica Developmental Test of Visual–Motor Integration (Beery–Buktenica VMI; Beery, Buktenica, & Beery, 2004). Both are standardized assessments. As Crystal had already determined during the observation, Luke's fine motor skills were in the average range, with a z score of -1.2 as measured by the BOT–2. On the Beery–Buktenica VMI, Luke's standard score was 99 and was in the 47th percentile. The results from these two standardized assessments confirmed the clinical reasoning of Crystal's observation of Luke in the classroom.

Crystal shared her findings with the team and reported that Luke demonstrated fine motor and visual–motor skills to support his handwriting. Luke's scores on the standardized assessments supported her interpretation. Crystal emphasized that Luke did have difficulty completing his schoolwork tasks because of inefficiency in gathering materials and organizing his time. Her recommendations to support Luke in the classroom resulted from her observation of his work during schoolwork tasks, the context in which he typically did these tasks. Crystal will use her observations and problem solve with the teacher to find ways to make gathering tools and materials less challenging for Luke. Crystal will work with Luke on strategies to keep his desktop more organized as he works. All three will develop a plan to help Luke begin working more quickly and sustain work behaviors throughout a task. Because Crystal was able to use a standardized assessment of her observations, she will be able to document changes in Luke's performance when she observes him later in the school year.

The example of Luke and Crystal enables us to consider the use of two types of assessments: a criterion-referenced assessment and norm-referenced assessment. The School AMPS is a criterion-referenced assessment based on observation in a natural context. This particular assessment allowed Crystal to generate a baseline performance measure (a number) to which to compare Luke's performance in the future. Crystal's observation of Luke in the classroom provided her with a wealth of information to consider his needs and options for occupational therapy services. The norm-referenced assessments on fine motor and visual–motor skills were helpful to rule out difficulty in these areas. If Luke had difficulty on these two assessments, the standardized results would have informed Crystal of weaknesses in these areas but would not have helped her know what to do for intervention. In this example, if Crystal had limited her evaluation to the norm-referenced tests only, the results would have led her to logically conclude that Luke did not need occupational therapy services. Fortunately, Crystal observed Luke doing tasks that he needed to do in school, and she saw difficulties that occupational therapy could address. In Luke's case, occupational therapy will play an important role to support his schoolwork performance.

Evaluation in Context: Pragmatic Issues of Evaluation

Although the focus of evaluation is on the client, options are often limited by the pragmatic constraints on practice, including reimbursement implications determined by federal policies, facility procedures, and resources in the community where the client lives, as well as the occupational therapist's own attributes (Neistadt, 2000).

Reimbursement Implications

The time many occupational therapists spend on evaluation is constrained by federal, insurance, or facility policies guiding reimbursement (seen in the case examples of Mr. Muñiz and Pierre). In some cases, an occupational therapist may have only half an hour for evaluation. In other situations, the facility will be reimbursed only if the therapist engages in intervention during the first visit with a client, thus limiting the amount of formal evaluation time, as with Mr. Muñiz (Neistadt, 2000). When evaluation time is limited, a therapist must rely more on screening techniques. A *screening* is a preliminary assessment process that is used to determine whether a problem exists. Results of a screening are not sufficient for intervention planning but may indicate the need for more extensive evaluation (Neistadt, 2000; Radomski, 2008; Richardson, 2005). A screening can include observation of the client, review of a client's medical records, or administration of a standardized assessment tool designed as a screening instrument (Mulligan, 2003; Richardson, 2005). A therapist can blend some direct measures of occupations and findings from assessments directly into intervention goals. Thus, the transition from evaluation to intervention is nearly seamless, leading to time efficiencies. For instance, in the case of Mr. Muñiz, Joan discovered during an interview that he wanted to tend to his rose garden (occupational profile). Joan used the potting-a-plant task (AMPS) as part of her evaluation. Consequently, at the end of the evaluation, Joan had observed performance in the desired task (i.e., gardening) and knew how to help Mr. Muñiz. Her findings and goals were enhanced by using the AMPS scores.

Because of reimbursement constraints, it is imperative that the occupational therapist is clear about the purpose of evaluation and the usefulness of the information gathered for decision making. The therapist needs to ensure that he or she is gathering information that is useful and relevant to the desired purpose. Knowing the potential use of evaluation data and the type of information that is relevant to address clients' needs will enable therapists to gather the essential information more quickly. In the case examples of Mr. Muñiz and Pierre, the therapists began their evaluations by getting to know the clients as people and learning what was important to them so that services could focus on the clients' goals and support their occupational interests and performance. From there, the therapists were quick to determine what other assessment data would enable them to plan and monitor intervention. Both therapists chose assessments with a specific purpose in mind.

Facility Procedures

Each facility has its own way of conducting business. Professionals work together in a variety of ways to gather evaluation information and provide services to clients. The working relationship or type of teamwork that the facility subscribes to influences how the occupational therapist works with colleagues who are simultaneously gathering evaluation data. Teams might be multidisciplinary, interdisciplinary, or transdisciplinary in nature. Coordinating efforts always proves to be efficient, informative, and cost-effective. Clearly identifying each professional's domain of focus and services may help to determine the purpose of their respective evaluations, regardless of the type of team used in a facility. Some evaluation information may be universally desired, and team members can determine who is in the best position to gather that information and share it with the team. Having one professional gather information for the rest of the team reflects client-centered thinking, because the client has to give information or perform similar assessment tasks only once.

The type of setting and the mission and philosophy of the facility, the composition of professionals, and the complexity of clients' needs often determine how professionals coordinate their efforts for evaluation and intervention (Case-Smith, 2005). In medical settings and frequently in mental health practice, each professional on a multidisciplinary team typically gathers his or her own assessment data and then shares results with other team members (Case-Smith, 2005; Cohn, 2009). This team model may result in an overlap of assessments performed. In some rehabilitation settings and in many pediatric settings, professionals work as an interdisciplinary team, collaborating in the assessment process. Team members determine the type of assessment data needed and how each member will contribute to the process. They share their respective evaluation results and develop an integrated intervention plan (Cohn, 2009). When a team has worked together in a facility over time, each professional knows the team expectations and focuses on discipline-specific information. An occupational therapist usually acquires information to complete an occupational profile and focuses on how a disability affects the client's occupational performance; other team members may gather specific client factor information. There are two major reasons for a team evaluation: (1) The team evaluation maximizes the specific information needed to coordinate intervention, and (2) the team evaluation reduces cost inefficiencies created by duplicate assessments of the same performance or behaviors.

Transdisciplinary teams are commonly seen in early intervention programs for infants and young children (Case-Smith, 2005; Mulligan, 2003), but they also may be used in other areas of practice. In this model, team members have a stable relationship from working together over time and have shared knowledge and skills, enabling them to observe and record assessment results for one another. With a transdisciplinary team, professional boundaries are blurred and expertise is shared so that assessment and intervention services are integrated and often done by one person (Case-Smith, 2005). Transdisciplinary teams may use an "arena" assessment to conduct an evaluation: One person presents assessment tasks, and each professional consults and gathers respective information (Case-Smith, 2005). Transdisciplinary team members share knowledge with the one member designated to provide intervention services.

Community Resources

Communities vary greatly in the options and natural supports available to citizens. Natural community supports include health care options, religious supports, employment and volunteer opportunities, and leisure and social networks. Communities with senior citizen centers may have a cadre of volunteers who provide supports to older adults to enable them to live longer in their home environment. Knowing the availability of natural supports for all community members helps a therapist ensure that clients are at the right level of independence and, prior to discharge, have access to supports to help ensure their safety and well-being. Knowing the community options for discharge helps a therapist anticipate goals for clients and make decisions regarding assessment foci. For example, knowing that Meals On Wheels is available for a client might enable the therapist to focus on other aspects of instrumental activities of daily living. When a therapist evaluates a client living in a community that is unfamiliar to the therapist, an environmental assessment might be helpful to identify the broader community resources.

Therapist Attributes

Pragmatically, a therapist's own knowledge and experience naturally limit what he or she does during an evaluation. Staying abreast of new models of practice and frames of reference, as well as the implications of new perspectives for evaluation and intervention, enables therapists to reflect current professional thinking. Reviewing and critiquing evidence related to how best to evaluate or intervene with a given condition for a client informs therapists of the best practice known to date (Tickle-Degnen, 2009). In addition, knowing a range of assessment instruments enables a therapist to practice in a client-centered manner; learning new assessment instruments should be part of a therapist's ongoing professional competence objectives.

Learning a New Assessment Procedure

Learning is a process that requires time and practice, and learning a new assessment procedure or instrument is no exception. Some assessment tools require specific education and certification processes. For example, the Sensory Integration and Praxis Tests (Ayres, 1989) and the AMPS (Fisher, 2003) both require that therapists take a course, practice using the assessment, and then demonstrate standardized use or calibration of scoring. Other assessment tools, such as the Sensory Profile (Dunn, 1999), the Occupational Performance History Interview–II (Kielhofner et al., 1998), and the Canadian Occupational Performance Measure (Law et al., 2005), require the therapist to study and practice the assessment according to procedures described in the assessment manual to accurately administer, score, and interpret the results.

In all cases, an occupational therapist learning a new assessment instrument should know the purpose of the assessment and the type of information it will provide. He or she should have read the instrument manual and know, before using the instrument with a client, how to administer, score, and interpret the results. Practice in administering the assessment is essential to competence in its use. Some assessments require standardized administration, meaning that the therapist must use very specific directions and responses during administration. Giving too much or too little information or doing the assessment tasks incorrectly, including not giving instructions as described in the assessment manual, can influence the client's response and invalidate the results. Other assessments do not require specific wording in directions given to the client, but the manual provides parameters for client instructions.

When learning a new assessment, a single reading of a manual is never sufficient, even for experienced therapists. Tests that have standardized administration may require the therapist to create note cards or other prompts to help remind him or her of what to do next or what to observe while assessing. The therapist needs to imagine using the assessment instrument, then practice using it, possibly without another person present. Some instruments have objects to present to a client, such as blocks, small toys, or pegs and a pegboard. Therapists may need to know which side of the client to sit on, because this may affect test administration. Once the therapist is comfortable with the assessment instrument's items, their order of presentation, and the scoring of a client's performance, he or she should practice giving the instrument to another person with the same characteristics as the population for whom the assessment was intended. This practice person may be a friend or colleague, but therapists learning a new tool must anticipate a response from someone who might be less able. Therapists should be prepared to provide certain types of support as appropriate. For example, the assessment manual may have specific guidelines to follow when a person makes an error; therapists need to know in advance what constitutes an error. Some assessments end when a person has made a certain number of errors, so therapists should know when to end the test.

Learning a new instrument can be daunting. However, the rewards of learning and using a new assessment protocol are worth every minute of preparation, further increasing the accuracy of the assessment findings and ensuring that the therapist is competent in administering and interpreting the assessment. Finally, comfort with the assessment focuses the evaluation and, ultimately, intervention. The result is a valid, ethical, fair evaluation process leading to increased confidence and reliability in outcomes.

New assessments will continue to be developed as the profession evolves. The influence of the *Framework–II* (AOTA, 2008b) and the focus on observing occupational performance will generate new protocols that highlight what occupational therapists do best—evaluate and promote occupational performance and engagement in occupation. Therapists will have many opportunities to learn new assessments throughout their careers, to stay current in practice, and to provide the quality services that they want to offer to clients.

Therapeutic Use of Self During Evaluation

Regardless of the type of assessment used and the constraints on evaluation and practice, the occupational therapist should always consider how he or she is influencing the evaluation process. The value of establishing a positive working relationship with clients has been important to occupational therapists throughout the profession's history (Peloquin, 2003). Use of one's own personal and professional attributes, termed *therapeutic use of self*, promotes collaboration with a client. Attributes of a therapeutic relationship include being honest and open with the client and being empathic to and respectful of his or her situation (Peloquin, 2003; Price, 2009). When an occupational therapist possesses and uses these qualities, a client feels more comfortable fully participating in the evaluation and intervention process. A client will talk more easily about likes and dislikes and what is important to him or her. Through asking the right questions of a client, actively listening to the client's responses, and responding in a sensitive manner, therapists use themselves as agents of change (Price, 2009).

Many clients and family members are anxious about the condition that brought the client to occupational therapy (Price, 2009). A client might be apprehensive about what led to the hospitalization or referral for occupational therapy. A client also may be concerned about what the therapist will conclude about his or her ability to perform meaningful activities in the future. To promote a positive working relationship and obtain the most accurate results in an evaluation, the therapist needs to remain empathic and respectful to help clients feel comfortable and safe (Price, 2009). Establishing a positive relationship with the client helps establish rapport and a sense of trust that will better enable the client to fully invest in the planning and implementation of occupational therapy services. Getting to know the client as a person—asking about the person's history, what he or she enjoys doing, what is important to him or her, and what his or her personal goals are—is an essential step in the evaluation process and provides an opportunity for the therapist to use himself or herself as a therapeutic tool. When gathering information about the client as a person, the therapist can ask questions that help the client make connections between his or her past, present, and future. Through active listening, the therapist can identify potential activities that are meaningful to the client and may enable the client to participate in valued occupations in the future.

A therapist uses therapeutic use of self continually throughout the evaluation process as he or she and the client determine what occupation is of greatest concern and what tasks the therapist might observe the client perform. If the task is difficult for the client to perform successfully, the experience will likely trigger frustration, sadness, anger, or despair. The therapist must be ready to support the client as appropriate. Poor performance may lead to a goal and motivation for therapy; it also may be the point at which the therapist needs to help the client consider other options in his or her life and find meaning in new activities. Using one's self in this way, as a medium of therapy, is considered the "art of therapy" and is just as important as the theoretical and technical knowledge and skills that therapists possess (Peloquin, 2003).

Conclusion

Evaluation provides the foundational information on which occupational therapy services are built. The process begins by getting to know the client as a person and understanding the occupations that are important to him or her. The occupational therapist examines the client's occupational performance in tasks that are relevant, important, and challenging to the client. The therapist may determine that further assessment of client factors, context, or task demands would help plan intervention. The evaluation process is as long or short as necessary to enable the therapist to plan and implement appropriate occupational therapy services. Many methods can provide information that might be interesting; however, a longer evaluation is not necessarily a better one. The therapist must determine the salient information to answer the questions posed by the referral that address the client's need to participate in meaningful life experiences. A sound evaluation process leads to informed planning and intervention services.

Questions

1. The author describes how evaluation leads to intervention planning in the case example of Jean and Tonya. What other assessments might you have used with Tonya?
2. Can you think of some additional types of interventions that Jean might have developed for Tonya based on the information provided? Are there other areas on which you would have focused?
3. Reflect on a case with which you are familiar. When reviewing interventions to consider making changes, what kind of information would have made you consider changing the intervention plan? Identify specific data that you wanted to gather before changing the plan with the client in the case you chose.
4. In the example of Joan and Mr. Muñiz, how might the evaluation (and possibly the intervention) have been different if the number of visits had not been limited?
5. Think about a case with which you are familiar. What were the critical elements that needed to be included in the documentation to justify occupational therapy intervention in that setting?
6. In the case example of Jean and Tonya, what are strategies Jean might have used to develop a therapeutic rapport with Tonya that supported occupational therapy intervention?
7. Consider a case example of your own. What other types of evaluation questions might you ask to enhance the focus of evaluation and intervention on occupation? What assessment tools or methods would help you glean the desired information?

References

American Occupational Therapy Association. (2008a). Guidelines for documentation of occupational therapy. *American Journal of Occupational Therapy, 62,* 684–690.

American Occupational Therapy Association. (2008b). Occupational therapy practice framework: Domain and process (2nd ed.). *American Journal of Occupational Therapy, 62,* 625–683.

Árnadóttir, G. (1999). Evaluation and intervention with complex perceptual impairment. In C. Unsworth (Ed.), *Cognitive and perceptual dysfunction: A clinical reasoning approach to evaluation and intervention* (pp. 393–454). Philadelphia: F. A. Davis.

Ayres, A. J. (1989). *Sensory Integration and Praxis Tests.* Los Angeles: Western Psychological Services.

Bass-Haugen, J., Mathiowetz, V., & Flinn, N. (2008). Optimizing motor behavior using the occupational therapy task-oriented approach. In M. V. Radomski & C. A. Trombly Latham

(Eds.), *Occupational therapy for physical dysfunction* (6th ed., pp. 598–617). Philadelphia: Lippincott Williams & Wilkins.

Beery, K. E., Buktenica, N. A., & Beery, N. A. (2004). *The Beery–Buktenica Developmental Test of Visual–Motor Integration* (5th ed.). Minneapolis, MN: Pearson.

Brown, C. (2009). Functional assessment and intervention in occupational therapy. *Psychiatric Rehabilitation Journal, 32,* 162–170.

Bruininks, R. H., & Bruininks, B. D. (2005). *Bruininks–Oseretsky Test of Motor Proficiency* (2nd ed.). Circle Pines, MN: AGS Publishing.

Case-Smith, J. (2005). Teaming. In J. Case-Smith (Ed.), *Occupational therapy for children* (5th ed., pp. 32–52). St. Louis, MO: Mosby/Elsevier.

Cohn, E. S. (2009). Team interaction models and team communication. In E. B. Crepeau, E. S. Cohn, & B.A.B. Schell (Eds.), *Willard and Spackman's occupational therapy* (11th ed., pp. 396–402). Philadelphia: Lippincott Williams & Wilkins.

Dunn, W. (1999). *Sensory Profile: User's manual.* San Antonio, TX: Psychological Corporation.

Fisher, A. G. (2003). *Assessment of Motor and Process Skills* (5th ed.). Fort Collins, CO: Three Star Press.

Fisher, A. G. (2009). *Occupational therapy intervention process model: A model for planning and implementing top-down, client-centered, and occupation-based interventions.* Fort Collins, CO: Three Star Press.

Fisher, A. G., Bryze, K., Hume, V., & Griswold, L. A. (2007). *School Assessment of Motor and Process Skills.* Fort Collins, CO: Three Star Press.

Fisher, A. G., & Griswold, L. A. (2009). *Evaluation of Social Interaction.* Fort Collins, CO: Three Star Press.

Flinn, N. A., Jackson, J., McLaughlin Gray, J., & Zemke, R. (2008). Optimizing abilities and capacities: Range of motion, strength, and endurance. In M. V. Radomski & C. A. Trombly Latham (Eds.), *Occupational therapy for physical dysfunction* (6th ed., pp. 573–597). Philadelphia: Lippincott Williams & Wilkins.

Forsyth, K., Lai, J. S., & Kielhofner, G. (1999). The Assessment of Communication and Interaction Skills (ACIS): Measurement properties. *British Journal of Occupational Therapy, 62,* 69–74.

Hinojosa, J., Kramer, P., Royeen, C. B., & Luebben, A. (2003). Core concept of occupation. In P. Kramer, J. Hinojosa, & C. B. Royeen (Eds.), *Perspectives in human occupation: Participation in life* (pp. 1–17). Philadelphia: Lippincott Williams & Wilkins.

Hocking, C. (2001). Implementing occupation-based assessment. *American Journal of Occupational Therapy, 55,* 436–469.

Ideishi, R. I. (2003). Influence of occupation on assessment and treatment. In P. Kramer, J. Hinojosa, & C. B. Royeen (Eds.), *Perspectives in human occupation: Participation in life* (pp. 278–296). Philadelphia: Lippincott Williams & Wilkins.

Kaplan, M. (2010). A frame of reference for motor acquisition. In P. Kramer & J. Hinojosa (Eds.), *Frames of reference for pediatric occupational therapy* (3rd ed., pp. 390–424). Philadelphia: Lippincott Williams & Wilkins.

Kielhofner, G. (2009). Model of human occupation. In G. Kielhofner (Ed.), *Conceptual foundations of occupational therapy* (3rd ed., pp. 147–174). Philadelphia: F. A. Davis.

Kielhofner, G., Mallinson, T., Crawford, C., Nowak, M., Rigby, M., Henry, A., et al. (1998). *A user's guide to the Occupational Performance History Interview–II* (OPHI–II; Version 2.0). Chicago: Model of Human Occupation Clearinghouse, Department of Occupational Therapy, College of Applied Health Sciences, University of Illinois.

Law, M., Baptiste, S., Carswell, A., McColl, M. A., Polatajko, H., & Pollock, N. (2005). *The Canadian Occupational Performance Measure* (4th ed.). Toronto, Canada: CAOT Publications.

Mastos, M., Miller, K., Eliasson, A. C., & Imms, C. (2007). Goal-directed training: Linking theories of treatment to clinical practice for improved functional activities in daily life. *Clinical Rehabilitation, 21,* 47–55.

Mulligan, S. (2003). *Occupational therapy evaluation for children: A pocket guide.* Philadelphia: Lippincott Williams & Wilkins.

Neistadt, M. E. (2000). *Occupational therapy evaluation for adults: A pocket guide.* Philadelphia: Lippincott Williams & Wilkins.

Park, M. (2008). Making scenes. *Medical Anthropology Quarterly, 22,* 234–256.

Peloquin, S. M. (2003). The therapeutic relationship: Manifestations and challenges in occupational therapy. In E. B. Crepeau, E. S. Cohn, & B.A.B. Schell (Eds.), *Willard and Spackman's occupational therapy* (10th ed., pp. 157–170). Philadelphia: Lippincott Williams & Wilkins.

Phipps, S., and Richardson, P. (2007). Occupational therapy outcomes for clients with traumatic brain injury and stroke using the Canadian Occupational Performance Measure. *American Journal of Occupational Therapy, 61,* 328–334.

Price, P. (2009). The therapeutic relationship. In E. B. Crepeau, E. S. Cohn, & B.A.B. Schell (Eds.), *Willard and Spackman's occupational therapy* (11th ed., pp. 328–341). Philadelphia: Lippincott Williams & Wilkins.

Radomski, M. V. (2008). Planning, guiding, and documenting practice. In M. V. Radomski & C. A. Trombly Latham (Eds.), *Occupational therapy for physical dysfunction* (6th ed., pp. 40–64). Philadelphia: Lippincott Williams & Wilkins.

Richardson, P. K. (2005). Use of standardized tests in pediatric practice. In J. Case-Smith (Ed.), *Occupational therapy for children* (5th ed., pp. 246–275). St. Louis, MO: Mosby/Elsevier.

Simmons, D. C., Crepeau, E. B., & White, B. P. (2000). The predictive power of narrative data in occupational therapy evaluation. *American Journal of Occupational Therapy, 54,* 471–476.

Stewart, K. B. (2005). Purposes, processes, and methods of evaluation. In J. Case-Smith (Ed.), *Occupational therapy for children* (5th ed., pp. 218–240). St. Louis, MO: Mosby/Elsevier.

Tickle-Degnen, L. (2009). Evidence-based practices: Using available evidence to inform practice. In E. B. Crepeau, E. S. Cohn, & B.A.B. Schell (Eds.), *Willard and Spackman's occupational therapy* (11th ed., pp. 291–302). Philadelphia: Lippincott Williams & Wilkins.

Trombly Latham, C. A. (2008). Conceptual framework for practice. In M. V. Radomski & C. A. Trombly Latham (Eds.), *Occupational therapy for physical dysfunction* (6th ed., pp. 1–20). Philadelphia: Lippincott Williams & Wilkins.

Uniform Data System for Medical Rehabilitation. (1997). *Guide for the uniform data set for medical rehabilitation* (Adult FIM™; Version 5.1). Buffalo: State University of New York.

Uniform Data System for Medical Rehabilitation. (2004–2006). *WeeFIM II.* Amherst, NY: Author.

Weinstock-Zlotnick, G., & Hinojosa, J. (2004). Bottom-up or top-down evaluation: Is one better than the other? *American Journal of Occupational Therapy, 58,* 594–599.

Appendix 5.A. Occupational Therapy Evaluation Report Template

Facility/Agency Name

Occupational Therapy Evaluation Report

Name: (Client's full name) _____ Date of Birth: _____

ID #: (Given by facility/agency) _____ Date of Evaluation: _____

Primary Diagnosis: (If known) _____ Age: _____

Reason for Referral

Include the referral source, reason for referral, and the presenting primary concern(s). Identify the evaluation procedures and tools used and a brief notation regarding the purpose of the procedure and/or tools used.

Occupational Profile

Include information about the client's current living situation, employment status, and leisure activities. For each area, discuss the context (social and physical environment), satisfaction level, internalized role, and regular or necessary tasks performed that support the role. Discuss history if it provides information about the client's ability to adapt to the presenting situation. Identify the client's self-identified strengths, limitations, goals, and priorities.

Evaluation Results

Results may be organized in a variety of formats. Often the information in this section is organized by the assessment tool, by the evaluation procedure used, or by areas of occupation. Specific numeric findings often are included in an appendix.

Interpretation

This section provides a synthesis and summary of the evaluation results reported above. The interpretation may be what busy colleagues read first (or at all), so it should provide a complete overview of the evaluation findings and lead into recommendations in the following section.

Recommendations

Recommendations for occupational therapy services, if warranted, should include suggestions for the focus of intervention, intervention approach, and service delivery model, often with suggested frequency and duration of services. The recommendations should address the reason for referral and reflect the client's goals and priorities noted early in the report.

Appendix 5.B. Example of Occupational Therapy Evaluation Report

Facility/Agency Name

Occupational Therapy Evaluation Report

Name: Pierre Sample

ID #: 77007

Primary Diagnosis: Limited function, post injury and surgery of flexor pollicis longus

Date of Birth: November 25, 1986

Date of Evaluation: January 31, 2010

Age: 23 years

Reason for Referral

Pierre was referred by A-1 Hand Surgery, Inc., 5 weeks post surgical repair of flexor pollicis longus in his left hand, surgical restrictions removed. The injury was sustained on the job when equipment crushed his hand while he was working as a plumber. Presenting problems include limited range of motion and strength in his left hand, resulting in limited use. Evaluation included gathering information from Pierre regarding difficulties in task performance, observation of his performance during tasks he reported he needed for his job, and goniometric measurements, as well as evaluation of grip strength and body functions required for hand use.

Occupational Profile

Pierre reported that he lives with his girlfriend, who does most of the meal preparation and is willing to do household chores that he typically does until his hand function returns. Pierre works for a local plumbing company where he primarily installs pipes and heating systems in new home construction. He described his primary job tasks to be drilling holes, cutting and fitting pipes, and soldering. He usually works with one other plumber when he goes out to a job site. Pierre enjoys his job and is working toward advancing his status. He said that his boss is holding his job for him. In addition to work, Pierre reported that he is an avid bowler and bowls two to three times a week for a social outlet. Pierre stated that he can continue bowling as he does this with his uninjured right hand. He also builds model trains, which he began doing with his father when he was a young boy. His trains have been shown in many public events, particularly around the holidays. Pierre expressed concern regarding his inability to pinch the tiny train parts with his left hand. He reported that after experiences of recovering from past sports injuries in high school, he knows he needs to do his exercises and is eager to begin therapy. His goals are to return to work and to resume building model trains.

Evaluation Results

Evaluation of left thumb range of motion indicated moderate limitation. AROM for thumb MP was 30° and thumb IP 55°. Secondary to prolonged immobility, lumbrical strength for digits 2 through 4 was MMT score of 3, limiting grasp and pinch. Functionally, he is unable to pick up objects smaller than 3 inches in size. Evaluation of strength for flexor pollicis longus was manual muscle testing score of 2. Dynamometer results indicated a left grasp of 70 pounds. Secondary to AROM limitation, pinch strength was not evaluated. Sensory evaluation noted no deficits in sensory functioning.

Interpretation

Pierre has limited range of motion and strength in left hand flexors and thumb adduction and opposition. He is currently unable to oppose and achieve forceful thumb flexion to pinch and pick up objects less than 3 inches in diameter and has functional issues with grasp. His limited hand function affects his return to work as a plumber because he needs his left hand to grasp and support copper pipe of 1-inch diameter. His leisure activity of building trains is also compromised. He is able to perform personal activities of daily living with adaptation, and he is independent with necessary instrumental activities of daily living. Pierre's goals of returning to work and engaging in all leisure activities are realistic. He is motivated to participate in occupational therapy to achieve his goals.

Recommendations

Outpatient occupational therapy services are recommended to address left hand function, post surgical repair of flexor pollicis longus and intrinsic muscle weakness, to meet the goal of grasping and manipulating tools and materials, as required to return to work. Services include 8 sessions over a 4-week period of time and a home exercise program. Adapted handles on work tools will enable return to work prior to and facilitate full range of motion and strength.

—Danielle Exemplar, MS, OTR/L
    Occupational Therapist

Administration of Evaluation and Assessments

Michelle E. Cohen, PhD
Jim Hinojosa, PhD, OT, FAOTA
Paula Kramer, PhD, OTR, FAOTA

Overview

This chapter discusses the key issues that a therapist needs to consider when administering and interpreting an assessment. We begin the chapter by detailing concerns regarding specific categories of assessment tools, followed by a discussion of general principles that guide the administration of standardized and nonstandardized assessments, including environmental considerations and sources of error in testing. We conclude with a brief description of the influence of assessments on intervention.

Categories of Assessment Tools With Standardized Protocols

The purpose of an evaluation is to obtain useful information about the client and his or her life situation. Occupational therapists use data from assessments to identify a client's strengths and limitations and develop an appropriate intervention plan. The first step in the evaluation process is selecting the most appropriate assessment tools. We strongly recommend that an occupational therapist use standardized assessment tools whenever possible. Standardized assessments, when administered in the recommended manner, provide reliable and valid data. Most standardized assessments are appropriate for reevaluation because the therapist can compare the retest scores, performance measures, or behavioral indicators to identify changes in a client's performance. A therapist should read the literature regarding the specific standardized tools he or she is using or planning to use because it will increase the therapist's knowledge about the tool, including its advantages and limitations. Further, knowledge about the specific instrument and its standardization determine whether the therapist can use the tool as part of a reevaluation.

Standardized tools have established procedures or protocols. These procedures ensure that all clients who undergo evaluation using a particular tool have consistent testing experiences. Following standardized procedures when administering the instrument is necessary to obtain reportable, valid results. Many standardized instruments have specific processes for data analysis. The common forms of standardized tests are normative, criterion-referenced, and ipsative.

Normative Assessments

A test developer designs a *normative assessment* from data from research conducted on a specific sample of people (the *normative group*). Often, the normative group is the "normal" population, or *normed sample*. Data from a normed sample forms a probability distribution shaped like a bell curve, with the scores of a majority of the people clustered in the center. When a therapist obtains data about a client from a normative assessment, the therapist can compare the client's performance against the normed sample. When the standardization sample is a group of people who are typical, the therapist compares the person's scores, behaviors, or performance against the group's scores, behaviors, or performance. When a developer designs a test for a group with a specific disability, the standardization often describes how the person with a disability performs relative to both the normal sample and other people with the specific disability. It is critical that the therapist understand to whom the client is being compared and explicitly states this information in the evaluation summary report.

The therapist must consider the psychometric integrity and potential limitations of a standardized assessment when interpreting data. *Psychometrics* includes the reliability and validity of the test, the sample size and demographics of the normed sample, and the standard error of measurement. All of these are important for judging how valuable the data from the tool will be in understanding the client's abilities and limitations.

Reliability measures the consistency of the results an assessment provides, whereas *validity* measures how true the measure is to the underlying theory and concepts. Reliability is necessary but not sufficient to determine psychometric integrity. A measure can be reliable but not valid, but a valid measure will provide reliable assessments. A reliable measure is relatively free of measurement error. Reliability estimates can range from 0 to 1.00. Generally, a score of ≥0.70 indicates that a measure is reliable (Fleiss, 1981; Nunnally, 1967). Scores of >0.80 have excellent reliability. There is no single score or system to determine an assessment's validity; therefore, there is no one score or value that one can use to determine a measure's validity. In reality, many of the assessment tools an occupational therapist uses do not meet these standards. However, the assessment selected may be the only available instrument or the best instrument available for the purpose. See Chapter 9 for a more complete discussion of psychometric concepts.

When the psychometric integrity of an assessment is less than desirable, a therapist needs to consider whether there is another tool available for this population that has better psychometric data. If there is one, the therapist should explore using it. Sometimes, however, a therapist decides on a particular assessment with lower psychometric integrity. When a therapist makes this decision, he or she should be clear about why he or she has made this choice. Greater familiarity with an assessment is not a good justification for choosing an assessment with less psychometric integrity. But sometimes, the only assessment available for testing a specific factor is one with weak psychometric integrity; in such cases, the therapist should report in the evaluation summary the limitations of the assessment. Some normative assessments frequently used by occupational therapists are the Mini-Mental State Exam (Folstein, Folstein, McHugh, & Fanjiang, 2001), the Sensory Integration and Praxis Tests (SIPT; Ayres, 1989), the Lowenstein Occupational Therapy Cognitive Assessment (LOTCA; Itzkovich, Elazar, Averbuch, Katz, & Rahmani, 1990), and the Assessment of Motor and Process Skills (AMPS; Fisher, 2003).

Criterion-Referenced Assessments

Criterion-referenced assessments measure how well a person performs against a set of criteria rather than against another person. The developer of a criterion-referenced instrument selects items that reflect mastery of the area of concern or content. If the area of concern is reading, for example, a teacher might develop a test based on the components required to demonstrate mastery of reading. The development of a test based on a particular criterion begins with the construction of a table of specifications that lists the indicators associated with each component specification. If a test developer wanted to develop an instrument to assess the ability to dress oneself, for example, he or she would begin by identifying the component aspects of dressing (i.e., selecting clothes, putting on a shirt, putting on pants or a skirt, putting on socks, putting on shoes). Generally, a criterion-referenced test provides an established score that reflects mastery. A person's performance on a criterion-referenced test is how well the person performs against the set score for mastery. A criterion-based test does not compare scores, behaviors, or performances to a norm; instead, the focus is on the mastery of the area of interest.

Sometimes a test developer selects criteria for a criterion-referenced assessment for which normative information is available. When using a criterion-referenced test, the therapist cannot use information about the normal range of the criteria as a basis for comparing the client's performance against the known norm. Comparing criterion-referenced data with normative-referenced data is like comparing apples to oranges. Criterion-referenced data are based on mastery; normative-referenced data are based on performance as it relates to a normative sample, as described above. A criterion-referenced test cannot become a normative test just because normative data are available. Criterion-referenced tests that occupational therapists have experienced as test-takers include driving tests, course exams, and the National Board for Certification in

Occupational Therapy examination. Some criterion-referenced tests that an oc-cupational therapist might use with a client are the School Function Assessment (SFA; Coster, Deeney, Haltiwanger, & Haley, 1998), the Klein–Bell Activities of Daily Living Scale (Klein & Bell, 1979), the Kohlman Evaluation of Living Skills (KELS; Kohlman Thompson, 1992), and the Árnadóttir OT–ADL Neu-robehavioral Evaluation (A–ONE; Árnadóttir, 1990).

Just as with normative tests, a therapist must examine the psychometric integrity of criterion-referenced tests and other limitations identified in the test manual. Again, the therapist must determine for each assessment if it is the most appropriate one to use.

Ipsative Assessments

An *ipsative assessment* is a test that has standardized procedures and is indi-vidualized so that the person compares himself or herself in the same domain across time. Frequently, the person contrasts present performance against the prior performance in a specific domain. Two common forms—*interview*- and *observation-based* assessments—do not have specific expected outcomes. A standardized method of collecting data is used in an ipsative assessment so that a therapist can obtain information from different clients under consistent conditions.

The test procedures for an ipsative assessment are standardized. The assess-ment developer outlines the specific procedures, the order in which they are to be followed, and sometimes the conditions that are most appropriate for admin-istering the specific test. A common ipsative assessment that has standardized (although not published) procedures is an *activity configuration* (Mosey, 1986), which consists of a series of questions that the therapist asks a client during the initial interview. The activity configuration begins with the therapist asking the client to describe a typical weekday in detail. During the interview, the therapist asks follow-up questions about specific activities and the amount of time spent in each activity. After outlining a weekday, the therapist asks the client to describe a typical weekend day. Again, the therapist asks follow-up questions about the specific amount of time spent in each activity. On the basis of the client's descrip-tions, the therapist forms a rough understanding of the client's activities. At this point, the therapist asks the client to indicate which activities he or she enjoys, dislikes, or finds dissatisfying. The therapist may also ask about difficult activi-ties and responsibilities. A standardized order of questions provides a clear and detailed understanding of the client's daily life. A change in the procedures (e.g., a change in the order of the questions) would result in less-thorough information about the client's life. Other ipsative assessments used by occupational therapists are the Canadian Occupational Performance Measure (COPM; Law, Baptiste, Carswell, McColl, Polatajko, & Pollock, 2005), the Pediatric Volitional Ques-tionnaire (PVQ; Geist, Kielhofner, Basu, & Kafkes, 2002), the Pediatric Interest Profiles (Henry, 2000), and the Occupational Performance History Interview (OPHI–II; Kielhofner et al., 1998).

Assessment Techniques

One method of grouping assessments tools is by the techniques used for gathering information. These categories can be labeled *watching* (observation), *measuring* (observation using instruments), *listening* (interviewing), and *asking* (written questionnaire). The most basic techniques are observation and interviewing. Observation involves a therapist directly perceiving the actions of a client and then recording what he or she sees. Observation can be aided (by the use of a tool) or unaided. Many assessments of activities of daily living (ADLs) and instrumental activities of daily living (IADLs) originated with unaided observation of activities and behaviors that led to the development of standardized observational tools. The Functional Independence Measure (FIM™; Uniform Data System for Medical Rehabilitation [UDSMR], 1997), one of the most widely used rehabilitation assessment tools, was developed from a standardized method of directly observing and rating ADLs.

Observation has advantages over interviews and questionnaires. First, observation allows the therapist to directly witness how a person performs in a given situation, without the rationalization or explanation a therapist might interject during an interview and without the bias inherent in a self-report or proxy-report questionnaire. Another advantage of an observational assessment is that it does not rely on the client's interpretation of questions or memory of events or activities. For an observational assessment to be accurate and consistent, however, the therapist must be unbiased and trained. Some observational tools require certification, which means the evaluator must receive advanced training. Another disadvantage of observational assessment is the extensive time required to gather the information. An assessment using the FIM can take a therapist an hour or more to perform and interpret, whereas a therapist can complete the self-report FIM in less than 30 minutes (Cohen & Marino, 2000).

An occupational therapist often selects performance tests to measure functional limitations. For example, the therapist can assess reaching, lifting, and standing balance with the Berg Balance Scale (Berg, Wood-Dauphinee, Williams, & Gayton, 1989) and walking speed with the Timed Get-Up-and-Go Test (Wall, Bell, Stewart, & Davis, 2000). Unlike ADL observations, performance tests often focus on a specific bodily function and its associated impairment. Performance tests are standardized as compared to observation assessments and often rely on calibrated instruments for measurement. Therefore, they are independent of individual judgment and not as susceptible to influence from the client or rater bias as observations, interviews, and questionnaires. However, because they focus on the function of a particular body part, performance assessments usually ignore the environment and the person as a whole. A study comparing performance tests to self-reported ADL ability noted cultural differences that could be due to sociocultural and environmental factors not accounted for in performance tests (van den Brink et al., 2003). Performance tests also assess cognitive functioning. These tests require the client to perform a cognitive task, such as telling time from an analog clock face or spelling or reading given words. Many of these cognitive tests are not standardized; therefore, it is difficult to interpret the results of such assessments.

Interviews are another common means of gathering information. The interview technique involves a conversation between the therapist and the client or a proxy. Although the observation assessment requires direct interaction with the client, a therapist can conduct an interview with the client or with someone who has sufficient knowledge of the client's situation to act on his or her behalf (e.g., caregiver, spouse, parent). A therapist can interview someone in person or via telephone or computer. Interviews range from formal (structured) to informal (open-ended). Structured interviews contain specific questions that the therapist asks in a specific order. When an interview is highly structured, the information obtained is more likely to be consistent across interviewees. Interview information can be recorded using written notes, audiotaping, or videotaping for later review. Taping the interview allows the data to be scored by independent raters, which can ensure reliability.

In general, interviews are less time-consuming than observations, and the training process is less rigorous than that required for a reliable observation. Therefore, the interview process is less expensive than the observation method but is still more expensive than administering a questionnaire. Another advantage to an interview is that it provides the therapist with an opportunity to probe for more or clarifying information. Probing is more likely to be used in open-ended, less-structured interviews. When a therapist asks clarifying questions, the client can explain answers to difficult-to-comprehend questions. One disadvantage of an interview is that rapport between the therapist and client or proxy is crucial to ensure that the client is answering truthfully. Moreover, the interview method (*face-to-face* vs. *remote*, *structured* vs. *open-ended*) can affect the reliability of the information obtained. Face-to-face and structured interviews provide information that is more consistent and require less training for the therapist. A therapist conducting an open-ended interview needs advanced training on how to effectively solicit information from the client. Less-structured interviews also require more effort to organize and analyze the information obtained. One of the most widely used health status assessments, the SF–36 (Ware & Sherbourne, 1992), was initially developed as an interview tool and is now extensively used as a self-report questionnaire.

The two major advantages of a questionnaire are the ease of administration and low cost. The client or proxy can complete questionnaires, like interviews. Questionnaires are likely to result in a less-biased interpretation of the information provided, particularly if the format is highly structured. A highly structured questionnaire in which the client answers multiple-choice or true–false answers (called *forced-choice responses*) provides highly reliable information. A client can complete a self-report questionnaire at his or her convenience and can be interrupted or stopped easily. Although questionnaires are easy for a therapist to administer, there are many disadvantages associated with them. Highly structured and clearly worded questions provide valid and reliable information; vague or difficult-to-interpret questions, however, provide questionable information. Moreover, the information obtained using questionnaires may be less accurate than information obtained from direct observations or interviews. For example, when completing a questionnaire, a client can easily misinterpret a question. Should a client misunderstand a question asked during an interview, a therapist has a chance to probe for clarification or additional information. A client can be less accurate when reporting his or her own behavior than when a therapist is directly observing it. Also, a client may be unable to judge his or her own abilities accurately or may answer a question with personal bias. Again, unlike during an interview or observation, the therapist does not have an opportunity to seek clarification or probe for more in-depth understanding. A well-designed questionnaire, however, provides the therapist with ways to detect untruths and biases via questions designed to test the veracity of the client's answers.

Considerations in the Administration of Assessments

An occupational therapist must consider a variety of issues when determining which assessment is best to use under which conditions. The use of a specific assessment depends on the purpose of the evaluation, the therapist's skills, the amount of time available to administer the test, and the tool's requirements (e.g., equipment, space, expertise). Typically, a therapist conducts an initial screening in an informal manner, using general information provided about the client. Screening often includes a review of referral information; general observations; or other information that the client, significant others (e.g., family, caregivers), or other professionals provide. At times, screening involves the administration of a standardized screening assessment.

If the therapist decides to proceed with a full evaluation, he or she must decide which assessments to administer and develop a plan to conduct the evaluation. The implementation plan must be realistic and created in such a manner that the therapist can appropriately carry it out under real circumstances. Sometimes space, equipment, resources, or expertise limit the choice of available tools. Because some assessments are used by professionals in many disciplines, an occupational therapist may revise the evaluation plan on the basis of which assessments are being used by others in the practice setting. If the assessment administered by another professional provides information needed to complete the occupational therapy evaluation, the therapist should use that information and reference the other professional's report in the final evaluation summary.

Once the therapist has developed an evaluation plan, he or she must inform the client about the process and the reasons for selecting each assessment. It is important to tell the client how long the evaluation will take and what exactly it will involve. Clients have the right to be informed about the purpose of each assessment and how the results will be used. Further, each client has the absolute right to refuse an evaluation or a specific assessment. It is the therapist's responsibility to explain the evaluation process in a manner that is appropriate to the client. When the client is a child, the family should be involved during the explanation process. If the client is an adult, but not capable of understanding the rationale for an assessment, the therapist should inform the designated health proxy about the focus and purpose of the selected assessments. In the past, it was customary to discuss such issues with family members and significant others. However, since passage of the Health Insurance Portability and Accountability Act of 1996 (Pub. L. 104–191), only those persons who have been formally designated by the client or hold a health proxy for the client can be involved in this process.

Developing Skill in the Use of Assessments

Standardized assessments are generally complex tools; often, they are not easy to master. Some require extensive training and certification prior to use. When a therapist is using a new or unfamiliar tool, he or she should study before administering that assessment to a client. First, the therapist should carefully read the test manual. This thorough reading provides an understanding of the scope and purpose of the assessment. Most manuals discuss the administration procedures, identify limitations of the assessment, and present facts about the psychometric integrity of the tool. The manual also explains what the therapist will learn about the client from the assessment. For example, the manual might explain that a therapist will learn about a client's strengths, limitations, performance skills, personal characteristics, roles, and values.

After reading the manual, the therapist must decide whether the assessment meets the expected needs of the client in his or her situation. The therapist makes this decision after considering the psychometric integrity and appropriateness of the data the assessment will provide. If the assessment seems to meet the expected needs, the therapist should examine published literature about the assessment. Research and clinical narratives provide important information about an assessment and its efficacy in a practice situation. Journal reports using research done with the specific assessment and reference books can provide valuable information about the assessment and its usefulness. Additionally, the Mental Measurement Yearbook Web site (www.unl.edu/buros), the Educational Testing Service Web site (http://ets.org/tests/), and the Health and Psychosocial Instruments (HAPI) database provide up-to-date and relevant information. These sources can give the therapist a broader understanding of an assessment and its appropriate use.

Once a therapist decides that an assessment is appropriate and will provide useful data, he or she must develop competence in administering the assessment efficiently. The therapist should practice administering the assessment until he or she is competent in the mechanics of giving directions and manipulating materials. The therapist should practice administering the assessment to several age-appropriate persons without disabilities. The therapist must also develop competence in interpreting the data appropriately by practicing scoring and interpreting the data. Administering and interpreting the assessment data for people without disabilities provides insight into the range and variety of responses for any test item. Optimally, once a therapist has obtained basic competence in administering an assessment, he or she should have someone with experience observe him or her administering the assessment and provide feedback to help the therapist refine skills and confirm that the data collected are reliable and accurate.

In most cases, a therapist uses a combination of standardized and non-standardized assessments (e.g., observation, checklist, interviewing, screening) to identify a client's overall strengths and limitations. Reports from nonstandardized instruments and clinical observations should include comprehensive descriptions of specific behaviors or performance. Data from nonstandardized instruments can establish the baseline occupational performance of a client. As with standardized assessments, the therapist must establish competence in the administration and interpretation of nonstandardized assessments. Therapists can practice administering nonstandardized assessments by observing and interviewing people without disabilities and then interpreting the data to enhance skill development and competence.

A therapist is competent in using a specific assessment when he or she can administer it and interpret the results in a clear, concise summary. In this summary, the therapist presents evidence and provides clear baseline data to either support the need for occupational therapy or illustrate that the client does not need occupational therapy because he or she is able to engage in daily life occupations independently. A therapist needs to be careful to be accurate and portray data honestly. When writing a report, the therapist should interpret data to provide a clear picture of the client's overall functional level, and when interpreting assessment scores, the therapist should report actual scores and interpret these scores accurately. A therapist should not overinterpret scores or make conclusions not supported by the data.

Setting Up the Assessment Environment

The therapist needs to consider the physical environment, as well as the psychological environment, when administering an assessment. The therapist is part of the environment, and he or she plays an important role in ensuring that the environment is optimal for obtaining the appropriate data. The assessment environment should be conducive to eliciting real skills and abilities from the client. The environments needed for standardized and nonstandardized assessments, as discussed in the following sections, are often distinctly different. The type of assessment and the performance the therapist is trying to elicit will determine the appropriate environmental setting for the assessment. The realities of the setting and the reimbursement system in which the therapist works may also influence the assessment environment.

Testing Environment for Nonstandardized Assessments

Most nonstandardized assessments do not specify the characteristics of the testing environment. Although a therapist may take many different approaches, he or she can gain the most trustworthy information when he or she conducts the assessment in a natural environment. A therapist can tell more about a child's attention skills in the classroom if he or she observes the child's performance in the classroom rather than in a clinical environment. Similarly, a therapist can gather more information about the home maintenance skills of a woman recovering from a cerebrovascular accident by observing her as she navigates her kitchen at home than by observing her performance in the adapted kitchen in the hospital. A therapist obtains more realistic information about the client's true performance skills when he or she uses the natural environment for a nonstandardized assessment. In addition, the client is often most comfortable in the natural environment; this comfort may be helpful in obtaining trustworthy data.

A therapist may use a simulated environment when it is not possible to perform an assessment in the natural environment. Simulated environments must be as close to the natural environment as possible to elicit realistic data about the client's skills and abilities. In addition, simulated environments may be helpful in increasing the client's comfort with the assessment process.

Sometimes a controlled assessment environment can yield a more valid performance. When assessing clinical observations of neuromotor performance, for example, the therapist might find that a child may not want to perform such specific tasks in the natural environment of the playground. The therapist might be more likely to elicit better results and more cooperation from the child in a quiet, controlled environment. Similarly, the therapist might get data on a client's range of motion and manual muscle testing that are more accurate in a private, controlled environment rather than in a large gym with many distractions. When assessing specific skills, the therapist should create an environment that will facilitate obtaining the most realistic results. Again, the therapist should try to ensure that the client is comfortable and in the best position to provide the most realistic results.

In a simulated environment, it is important that the equipment is ergonomically correct for both the therapist and the client to increase the comfort of both. The therapist should provide the client and himself or herself with a proper setting, appropriate table height, and a footrest for the client's feet and adhere to safety precautions. Proper ergonomics will increase the potential for optimal performance and comfort during the assessment.

Testing Environment for Standardized Assessments

Standardized assessments compare the performance of a person against normative or criterion-referenced data. Some standardized assessments prescribe the type of testing environment. If such a prescription exists, the therapist must follow it to achieve valid results. If the manual provides no description of the assessment environment, the therapist should create an environment that fosters the optimal performance of the client. In most situations, the natural environment may not be the best setting for standardized assessments because it tends to contain distractions that may impede optimal performance. Optimal assessment environments should be comfortable, private, well lit, distraction free, and quiet. When choosing the environment, the therapist must take into consideration the requirements of the assessment. Some assessments require specific equipment; others require a large amount of space. The therapist should make sure that the environment and equipment for a particular assessment are available before administering the assessment so that the results are not compromised.

Psychological Environment for Assessment

From a psychological perspective, the therapist should try to help the client become an active participant in the assessment process. Establishing rapport with the client increases the client's level of comfort, which can be critical because people tend to perform better when they are comfortable than when they are anxious. The therapist starts the process by introducing himself or herself to the client. It is important to find out what the client prefers to be called. Many older clients prefer to be called by their surnames and are offended when called by their first names, especially by someone who is younger. It is essential to build a rapport and not offend the client before the start of the evaluation. The therapist should explain the assessment to the client and answer any questions that the client may have. This communication will relieve anxiety and create a more client-centered atmosphere. In addition, when the client knows the rationale for the assessment and the therapist's expectations of the assessment process, he or she can be a more active participant in the process. Moreover, the therapist should consider the client's personality and timetable when scheduling the assessment. Whenever possible, the therapist should administer the assessment when the client is most alert and responsive. A therapist should not administer an assessment when a client is tired and upset. A client's mood and frame of mind will affect the quality of information obtained from the assessment.

The Therapeutic Relationship

The therapeutic relationship often begins with the therapist evaluating the client. In most situations, building rapport with the client assists the evaluation process. In the developing relationship between the therapist and the client, the client is in a vulnerable position. The client depends on the therapist to explain the nature of the evaluation and the intervention process. In most cases, the client relates to this information not from a position of knowledge but from one of trust. The client needs to trust the therapist and to believe that the information the therapist provides is accurate and honest. Moreover, the client needs to trust that the therapist has the required expertise to carry out the evaluation and intervention. Typically, people are more comfortable with those whom they feel they know. Rapport between therapist and client can help the client develop that trust. Once a relationship of trust has been established, the therapist must fulfill his or her ethical responsibility to not abuse this trust and to provide expert care to the best of his or her capabilities.

It is important to explore how building rapport can help the client. Once the client develops trust in the therapist, he or she may feel more able to reveal important aspects of his or her life, fears, and concerns. As the client reveals information that is more personal, he or she becomes more aware of his or her own thoughts and feelings, enabling him or her to come to terms with personal reactions to illness, injury, or disability. Strong rapport between client and therapist also can empower the client to feel comfortable enough to ask awkward or difficult questions that he or she might not have otherwise asked. The information gained from this relationship helps the therapist choose assessments that will meet the client's true needs. Ultimately, this information helps the therapist construct a client-centered evaluation and then a client-centered intervention. Throughout this process, the best interests of the client must be the primary concern of the therapist. Thus, the therapist must be careful that the nature of the evaluation does not impede the establishment of rapport.

Evaluator and Situational Issues

Each therapist has specific strengths and limitations that influence his or her selection and use of assessments. A therapist's knowledge, manipulative motor skills, and analytic reasoning all influence how he or she selects and uses assessments. When interpreting data, a therapist must consider other factors about himself or herself as an evaluator. Most commonly, a therapist gravitates toward assessments that he or she knows better and is more comfortable with, or that are readily available, rather than researching the best assessment to use. Thus, an awareness of the factors that influence his or her choice of assessments can be useful for the therapist as a reflective professional. Reflection on assessment practices may lead to a willingness to explore new or alternative assessments rather than repeatedly using one assessment tool. It is important to keep in mind that the therapist should choose an assessment that is most appropriate for the client and his or her needs rather than one that the therapist likes and feels comfortable administering.

A therapist's mindset or attitude at the time of the assessment may influence the administration of an assessment. For example, a therapist who is not feeling well or who is having a bad day may have difficulty attending to the tasks at hand. Therapists must maintain heightened awareness to prevent personal situations from influencing the evaluation. Thus, when interpreting evaluation data, a therapist must consider himself or herself as a possible intervening variable.

The environment of the assessment also may influence the data collected. Physical space, time of day, and distractions influence both the evaluator's and the client's performance and behaviors. When a therapist administers an assessment in an environment that is less than ideal (e.g., that has distractions or inadequate space), he or she should consider how this environment might influence the data and should reflect that in the evaluation summary.

The therapist must consider the whole evaluation experience. During an evaluation, a therapist and the client form an exclusive relationship within a shared experience. Although the primary focus is on the client, the therapist has the responsibility of analyzing the data to develop an appropriate intervention plan for the client. The knowledge that the therapist gains about the client during the evaluation; the rapport that is established; and the feelings, both emotional and intuitive, of the therapist toward the client make the evaluation experience richer. Any recommendations for the intervention plan must reflect both what has been learned from the total evaluation and this shared experience.

The evaluation summary can have an effect on the client's life. For example, when evaluating a child in a school system, the results of the data may result in a classification (e.g., class placement) that may follow that child for many years. In older adults, assessment data and the subsequent evaluation summary may determine whether the client is capable of living alone or must be in a supervised placement. Therapists must be certain of the integrity of the assessments and the accuracy of their data when writing evaluation summaries that may result in high-stakes decision making (Plake, 2002).

Types of Error in Assessment

A therapist makes important decisions, such as treatment protocols and disposition, on the basis of assessments. Therefore, it is critical that evaluators try to minimize error in the assessment process. Errors occur from the test itself in the form of item bias, or are made by the rater who scores the test or the client. A therapist should control for error in assessing a client to ensure that the assessment is an accurate reflection of the client's abilities. Choosing the best tool available for the purpose, ensuring that the therapist is competent in the administration of the assessment, and adequately preparing the client for the tasks he or she needs to perform can keep errors to a minimum.

Item Bias

Item bias occurs when people of similar abilities perform differently on a given test or test item because of age, gender, ethnicity, cultural, socioeconomic, or other group differences. Items can be biased when they contain content or language that is unfamiliar to, or interpreted differently by, different groups (Hambleton & Rodgers, 1995). When choosing an assessment or instrument, it is important to know the group of individuals for whom the instrument was originally designed and whether it was validated against other groups of interest. For example, the SF–36 (Ware & Sherbourne, 1992), one of the most widely used measures of health status, was originally designed as a generic health status measure and validated against large groups of people with various health problems. However, because none of these groups contained people whose primary means of mobility was a wheelchair, the developers wrote questions about mobility for people who could walk. To make this instrument un-biased for people who use wheelchairs, the word "walk" was replaced with the word "go." Item bias introduces errors into an assessment; people with equal abilities should be able to attain the same score. The therapist can apply measurement or test theory to assessments to determine their psychometric properties.

Classical test theory relies on the psychometric concepts of reliability, va-lidity, and responsiveness. This theory divides total scores into two components: the true score and a margin for error. This approach cannot separate individual ability from item difficulty. Recently, rehabilitation science has borrowed an approach long used in evaluating educational and psychological assessments: *item response theory.* This theory, developed in the 1960s as a means of sepa-rating item difficulty from underlying individual abilities *(respondent traits),* involves a series of statistical procedures. Item response theory is also called *latent* (or *underlying) trait theory* in the literature. This approach can also be used to evaluate whether items have equivalent meanings for different groups of respondents and whether items within a scale have the same response for-mat (difficulty). A variant of item response theory, *Rasch analysis,* was used extensively in evaluating the underlying response format of the FIM (UDSMR, 1997). These analyses have shown that the FIM has three underlying scales, including self-care, motor, and cognitive functions (Cohen & Marino, 2000). Although further discussion of psychometrics is beyond the scope of this chap-ter, the differences between classical test theory and item response theory and their implications for health care are discussed in detail in three publications (Chang & Reeve, 2005; Hays, Morales, & Reise, 2000; Schwartz & Rapkin, 2004). Item response theory analyses can also be used to determine whether raters are using the same standards of measurement and can assess whether physical functioning, as assessed by a particular measure, is based on the per-son's response, the properties of the questions asked, or the severity of a rater's observation.

Evaluator Variables

Rater or *observer bias,* another source of error in assessments, occurs when different evaluators disagree in their assessment of the same person *(interra-ter reliability)* or when the same evaluator scores the same person differently on repeated testing *(intrarater reliability).* If different therapists assessing the same person use different standards of measurement (i.e., if some are more lenient than others are), results are not comparable across therapists. Thera-pists need special training and testing against a standard to eliminate this possibility.

A more subtle rater bias takes the form of coaching a client (Victor & Abeles, 2004). A therapist may coach, or "push," a person to perform beyond his or her normal capacity so that the therapist or facility will appear in a better light. A therapist may notice what appears to be a loss of documented function when a client is transferred from one facility to another. The documented loss may be an actual loss, or it may reflect the effect of coaching on the part of the first facility (Segal, Ditunno, & Staas, 1993).

Other therapist factors also contribute to the validity of the assessment results. The therapeutic relationship, for example, contributes to the quality of a client's performance. A therapist facilitates the client's best performance when the client trusts the therapist and feels that the therapist is concerned about him or her. The amount of experience that a therapist has in administering and interpreting a specific assessment can influence the results. As a therapist gains more experience administering an assessment, he or she becomes more comfortable and skilled. When a therapist is new at giving an assessment, he or she usually focuses on the mechanics of administering the test, giving less attention to the client's performance. Practice and experience allow a therapist to become skilled in the mechanics involved in administering a tool. Likewise, multiple experiences provide the therapist with pragmatic knowledge about when to give a break; he or she is sensitive to the client's mood and manipulates the environment to ensure best performance within the standardized procedures. A skilled therapist uses the evaluation process to establish a solid therapeutic relationship with the client and his or her significant others.

Test-Taker Variables

Test-taker variables that can affect an assessment take many forms. Coaching, tolerance for pain or discomfort, and fatigue can influence a client's score on an assessment. In addition, the process of being evaluated may stress a client. A client realizes that the therapist will make decisions about him or her using the data collected and is conscious of the fact that information gathered using an assessment may determine the services he or she receives or the level of independence with which he or she will live. Even a very young child seems to realize that during an evaluation he or she is being observed and judged.

Anxiety and stress are always an important concern. A moderate amount of anxiety can enhance performance in a testing situation; however, too little or too much anxiety can result in poor performance. Therefore, the therapist should try to make the client at ease in the testing situation. The therapist should inform the client about what he or she expects from the client. Moreover, the therapist should outline to the client the procedures the evaluation will entail. This knowledge of the process can reduce anxiety. Questioning a client about prior experiences with testing and his or her views on testing can provide information that will help build rapport.

Likewise, depression and paranoia may be concerns. The therapist must continually reaffirm the purpose and goal of the occupational therapy evaluation. Should anxiety, stress, depression, or paranoia appear to interfere with the client's ability to complete the assessment, the therapist may have to adjust the evaluation plan.

Sometimes a client's beliefs and views about testing influence his or her performance. A person may not be motivated to perform well on an assessment when he or she believes that assessment scores do not reflect real abilities. A person who does not care about the results or who does not understand the purpose of the assessment may put little effort into the process of evaluation. When a client's beliefs or views about testing appear to be interfering with the collection of valid assessment data, the therapist needs to adjust the evaluation plan. The therapist may decide to report the limited data collected or may decide to explore other options with the client.

A client's physical status can interfere with his or her ability to complete an assessment. During the administration of an assessment, the therapist might observe that the client has limited energy, activity tolerance, or physical stamina. The therapist should modify the evaluation plan to match the client's physical capacity to complete the test. Sometimes a therapist needs to curtail the evaluation until the client has sufficient physical capacity.

Influence of Previous Testing Activities

A comprehensive evaluation usually involves several assessments, and the order in which they are administered needs to be planned. The activities involved in one test may influence performance on another test. Some testing demands may lead to fatigue or inability to attend to a task. Some assessments involve tasks that may excite a specific client, and other assessments contain questions that may upset a client, so it is critical that a therapist consider the order in which he or she administers specific tests. The therapist must consider what he or she has learned about the client from the screening and the demands of each assessment. The evaluation plan takes into account the demands that will be put on the client and any possible effects the assessment may have on the client. At times, facility policies and third-party payers determine how evaluations are administered, and the therapist may have to adhere to these policies. However, the therapist should make the experience as comfortable as possible for the client and should indicate any demands that the evaluation is placing on the client in the ensuing report. The therapist has a dual responsibility, to both the client and the facility.

Performance Versus Capacity

Performance is what a person can and does do in the real world, whereas *capacity* is what a person can do in a hypothetical or optimal situation (Spilker, 1990; Weingarden & Martin, 1989). Performance—what a person actually does in a given situation—provides a true picture of the person's functional status. Performance better reflects the assistance a person may need to function in the home environment, whereas capacity may be a better measure for determining the course and type of therapeutic intervention. Personal factors such as motivation and personality can influence performance. Coaching may influence capacity.

Implications for Intervention

The evaluation process requires therapists to obtain trustworthy data through the accurate administration of assessments and valid observations of the client's performance. The therapist derives a complete picture of the client through data from reliable and valid assessments, including observations and interviews with the client. These data are tempered by the therapist's judgment and clinical reasoning skills, often gained through experience. A thorough evaluation, combined with consultation with the client whenever possible, is a complex process, providing the foundation for the development of a sound intervention plan. A plan developed from inadequate data or data that were not gathered in an organized and standardized manner is like a house built on an inadequate foundation. Just as a house may not stand without the proper infrastructure, the intervention plan may not be adequate or successful without a basis in strong evaluative data.

The administration of a comprehensive and sound evaluation also may serve as the basis for identifying clear outcomes. If clear baseline data do not exist, it is difficult to determine the extent of the client's progress. Therapists often are able to identify tasks that clients are able to do after a course of intervention, but without clear baseline data, it is often hard to determine exactly what has changed to account for the improved performance. From a research perspective, it is impossible to analyze outcome data from interventions without reliable and valid evaluation data to serve as a baseline.

Conclusion

Administering an evaluation is a complex task. The role of an evaluator is one of the more daunting roles that an occupational therapist undertakes. Evaluation serves as the basis for understanding the client, determining his or her needs, and developing a plan for intervention. Performing an evaluation requires skill and competence. A therapist must become familiar and competent in administering a variety of assessments. He or she needs to understand the psychometric data and protocols used in standardized tests and the nature of the various assessments. Further, a therapist must consider the complexities of the assessments, the environment, and the potential variables that might affect the outcome of the assessments. Organizing and understanding all the necessary information for performing a comprehensive evaluation is like managing a three-ring circus: One must be aware of many factors at the same time to ensure a comprehensive and accurate evaluation.

Questions

1. Describe the process that an occupational therapist would use to develop skills in administering a standardized test. Why is such an extensive process necessary?

2. Select a criterion-referenced assessment. Review the manual and identify the elements used to determine mastery.
3. Select a norm-referenced assessment. Review the manual and identify the specific components used for the normative data.
4. Select an ipsative assessment. Review the manual and identify the specific components used to develop the test.
5. How would the environment influence the administration of a developmental assessment for a young child?
6. Consider your own life and self-observations. Can you identify any factors that would influence your ability to administer a standardized assessment? How?
7. Do you think it would be easier for you to administer a standardized assessment to a child or an adult? Why?

References

Árnadóttir, G. (1990). *The brain and behavior: Assessing cortical dysfunction through tasks of daily living.* St. Louis, MO: Mosby.

Ayres, A. J. (1989). *Sensory Integration and Praxis Tests.* Los Angeles: Western Psychological Services.

Berg, K., Wood-Dauphinee, S., Williams, J. I., & Gayton, D. (1989). Measuring balance in the elderly: Preliminary development of an instrument. *Physiotherapy Canada, 41,* 304–311.

Chang, C.-H., & Reeve, B. B. (2005). Item response theory and its applications to patient-reported outcomes measurement. *Evaluation and the Health Professions, 28*(3), 264–282.

Cohen, M. E., & Marino, R. J. (2000). The tools of disability outcomes research: Functional status measures. *Archives of Physical Medicine and Rehabilitation, 8*(12, Suppl. 2), 21–29.

Coster, W., Deeney, T., Haltiwanger, J., & Haley, S. (1998). *School Function Assessment.* San Antonio, TX: Psychological Corporation.

Fisher, A. G. (2003). *Assessment of Motor and Process Skills* (5th ed.). Fort Collins, CO: Three Star Press.

Fleiss, J. L. (1981). *Statistical methods for rates and proportions.* New York: Wiley.

Folstein, M. F., Folstein, S. E., McHugh, P. R, & Fanjiang, G. (2001). *Mini-Mental State Exam.* Odessa, FL: Psychological Assessment Resources.

Geist, R., Kielhofner, G., Basu, S., & Kafkes, A. (2002). *The Pediatric Volitional Questionnaire* (PVQ; Version 2.0). Chicago: Model of Human Occupation Clearinghouse, Department of Occupational Therapy, College of Applied Health Sciences, University of Illinois.

Hambleton, R., Rodgers, J. (1995). Item bias review. *Practical Assessment, Research, and Evaluation, 4*(6). Retrieved December 18, 2004, from http://pareonline.net/getvn.asp?v=4&n=6

Hays, R. D., Morales, L. S., & Reise, S. (2000). Item response theory and health outcomes measurement in the 21st century. *Medical Care, 38*(Suppl. 2), 28–42.

Health Insurance Portability and Accountability Act of 1996, Pub. L. 104–191, 45 C.F.R. §§160, 164. Retrieved October 27, 2004, from http://www.hhs.gov/ocr/hipaa/

Henry, A. D. (2000). *The Pediatric Interest Profiles: Surveys of play for children and adolescents.* San Antonio, TX: Therapy Skill Builders.

Itzkovich, M., Elazar, B., Averbuch, S., Katz, N., & Rahmani, L. (1990). *Lowenstein Occupational Therapy Cognitive Assessment.* Pequannock, NJ: Maddak.

Kielhofner, G., Mallinson, T., Crawford, C., Nowak, M., Rigby, M., Henry, A., et al. (1998). *A user's guide to the Occupational Performance History Interview–II* (OPHI–II; Version

2.0). Chicago: Model of Human Occupation Clearinghouse, Department of Occupational Therapy, College of Applied Health Sciences, University of Illinois.

Klein, R. M., & Bell, B. (1979). *The Klein–Bell ADL Scale manual*. Seattle: Educational Resources, University of Washington.

Kohlman Thompson, L. (1992). *Kohlman Evaluation of Living Skills* (3rd ed.). Rockville, MD: American Occupational Therapy Association.

Law, M., Baptiste, S., Carswell, A., McColl, M. A., Polatajko, H., & Pollock, N. (2005). *The Canadian Occupational Performance Measure* (4th ed.). Toronto, Ontario, Canada: CAOT Publications.

Mosey, A. C. (1986). *Psychosocial components of occupational therapy*. New York: Raven Press.

Nunnally, J. C. (1967). *Psychometric theory*. New York: McGraw-Hill.

Plake, B. S. (2002). Evaluating the technical quality of educational tests used for high-stakes decisions. *Measurement and Evaluation in Counseling and Development, 35*, 144–152.

Schwartz, C. E., & Rapkin, B. B. (2004). Reconsidering the psychometrics of quality of life assessment in light of response shift and appraisal. *Health and Quality of Life Outcomes, 2*, 16–26.

Segal, M. E., Ditunno, J. F., & Staas, W. E. (1993). Interinstitutional agreement of individual Functional Independence Measure (FIM) items measured at two sites on one sample of SCI patients. *Paraplegia, 31*, 622–631.

Spilker, B. (Ed.). (1990). *Quality of life assessments in clinical trials*. New York: Raven Press.

Uniform Data System for Medical Rehabilitation. (1997). *Guide for the uniform data set for medical rehabilitation* (Adult FIM™; Version 5.1). Buffalo: State University of New York.

van den Brink, C. L., Tijhuis, M., Kalmijn, S., Klazinga, N. S., Nissinen, A., Giampaoli, S., et al. (2003). Self-reported disability and its association with performance-based limitation in elderly men: A comparison of three European countries. *Journal of the American Geriatrics Society, 51*, 782–788.

Victor, T. L., & Abeles, N. (2004). Coaching clients to take psychological and neuropsychological tests: A clash of ethical obligations. *Professional Psychology: Research and Practice, 35*(4), 373–379.

Wall, J. C., Bell, C., Stewart, C., & Davis, J. (2000). The Timed Get-Up-and-Go Test revisited: Measurement of the component tasks. *Journal of Rehabilitation and Development, 37*(1), 109–114.

Ware, J. E., & Sherbourne, C. D. (1992). The MOS–36 Short-Form Health Survey (SF–36): I. Conceptual framework and item selection. *Medical Care, 30*, 478–483.

Weingarden, S. I., & Martin C. (1989). Independent dressing after spinal cord injury: A functional time evaluation. *Archives of Physical Medicine and Rehabilitation, 70*, 518–519.

7

Contextual Evaluation To Support Participation

Jane Case-Smith, EdD, OTR/L, FAOTA

Overview

Occupational therapists use assessments that enable understanding of people as occupational beings and focus on participation in life roles. In the evaluation process, the occupational therapist first asks the client to identify the occupations that are meaningful and important to him or her and then focuses on evaluating performance of and satisfaction with those occupations. Occupational performance is determined by a person's physical and psychological abilities and by the social, cultural, and physical contexts that support or constrain performance. In accord with the person–environment–occupation model (Law, Cooper, Strong, Stewart, Rigby, & Letts, 1996), assessment of the environment as it relates to the client's performance becomes an essential element of comprehensive evaluation. This chapter describes and illustrates

- Client-centered evaluation,
- Evaluation of client participation within natural contexts, and
- Evaluation of environments as they influence client participation.

Client-Centered Evaluation

Client-centeredness is a defining principle of occupational therapy practice. It guides how an occupational therapist evaluates performance strengths and concerns, selects goals, plans interventions, and evaluates the effects of an intervention program. This principle has been a defining construct of occupational therapy over time (Yerxa, 1967), across international borders (American Occupational Therapy Association [AOTA], 2008; Canadian Association of Occupational Therapists [CAOT], 1997; Wilcox, 1998), and across areas of practice (Law & Mills, 1998). Elements of a client-centered approach include demonstrating respect for clients, involving clients in decision making, advocating with and for clients in meeting their needs, and recognizing clients' experience and knowledge (CAOT, 1997).

In a client-centered evaluation, the occupational therapist assesses the client's ability to engage in meaningful occupations and the interplay among performance, activity demands, and context (Rogers & Holm, 2009). A primary goal of evaluation is to understand the person as an occupational being. Through evaluation of a client's participation in work, school, leisure, and play in natural physical, social, and cultural contexts, the therapist develops an occupational profile. The occupational therapist then can use this occupational profile to establish goals and to frame and interpret further analysis of performance. On the basis of data from the occupational profile and other assessments, the occupational therapist develops intervention goals and strategies that enhance the client's participation in the occupations most important to him or her (Law, 2002). Occupation-based intervention is a highly individualized process because it incorporates the unique perspective of the client, the client's occupational performance problems, and the performance context (Rogers & Holm, 2009). These principles—that the occupational therapist uses a client-centered approach, understands people as occupational beings, and focuses on client participation in life roles—have important implications for the evaluation process, the types of assessments selected, the methods used to evaluate clients, and the interpretation of evaluation results.

A client-centered approach recognizes that the client's perspective is the most important perspective in the intervention process. Almost always, the client, along with his or her caregivers, has the most accurate understanding of his or her strengths, limitations, and priorities. Client-centered evaluation includes the client's perceptions about performance, concerns about performance and roles, interests, goals, and priorities. A client-centered approach counters the traditional medical model, in which an expert determines a diagnosis and prescribes a treatment based on that diagnosis. In a traditional medical model, the client is the recipient of the treatment but is not actively involved in making treatment decisions. On the basis of the client's diagnosis and performance deficits, professionals determine the treatment approach. In such an approach, it becomes unlikely that treatment goals meet the client's interests and concerns. Because the traditional medical approach promotes passivity and dependency, it contradicts the goal of the occupational therapist—that clients actively engage and fully participate in work, daily living, and leisure roles.

In a client-centered evaluation, the occupational therapist helps the client identify and prioritize the occupations and activities that become the focus of intervention. By determining what occupations are most relevant to the client, the therapist can design meaningful interventions. When the therapist facilitates the client's self-direction and values the importance of the client's self-identified goals, the client becomes invested in the intervention program and is motivated to achieve the outcomes. As a result, outcomes are likely to be more satisfying and important to the client. In addition, the probability that outcomes are successfully achieved increases (Law, 1998).

A client-centered approach supports the client's perception that he or she can make decisions about intervention and can problem solve how to adapt activities to enhance participation. This approach encourages the client's sense of self-determinism and promotes his or her confidence in making decisions and directing therapy services toward his or her own goals. Many clients who receive occupational therapy have disabilities that endure throughout their lifetimes; therefore, promoting and respecting clients' self-determinism encourages them to independently manage services and direct the personal assistance they need.

In client-centered evaluation, the aim of the occupational therapist is to understand the client's perceptions of his or her occupational problems and identify desired outcomes. With these aims in mind, a primary method of assessment is self-report (McColl & Pollock, 2005). The occupational therapist asks what occupational concerns and goals are important to the client and family. This information is used to design individualized interventions that focus directly on the client's occupational priorities. Case Example 7.1 illustrates the importance of beginning the evaluation by assessing the client's concerns and priorities.

● ● ● ● ● ●

Case Example 7.1. Client-Centered Assessment: Matt, Who Has a C7 Spinal Cord Injury

Chris, an occupational therapist in a large rehabilitation center, used the Functional Independence Measure (FIM™; Uniform Data System for Medical Rehabilitation, 2009) to assess activities of daily living (ADLs) function in **Matt,** who was recently admitted to the center and was 2 months' post-C7 complete spinal cord injury. The FIM results showed that Matt was independent in feeding and verbal communication, was independent in mobility with his power chair, and required minimal assistance with transfers. He required moderate assistance in dressing and bathing. On the basis of these results, Chris selected the following goals for Matt: (1) improved technique and safety in chair-to-bed transfers, (2) increased independence in bathing, and (3) increased independence in dressing. However, when Chris asked Matt about his occupational priorities, Matt reported that learning to drive an adapted van was of greatest importance to him. Matt requested that intervention focus on identifying optimal adaptations that he could use to drive independently and practicing driving using this equipment with adapted techniques. Matt decided that a personal care assistant could assist him with dressing and bathing.

● ● ● ● ● ●

Despite the rehabilitation center's standard protocol that intervention sessions focus on self-care skills in the first weeks of therapy, Chris devoted the initial intervention sessions to adapted driving and providing Matt with information about the hand-controlled driving technology. She also discussed with Matt information about hiring and training a personal assistant. These sessions not only fully engaged Matt but also helped him develop confidence in making decisions and skill in managing his disability.

Client-Centered Assessments

In a client-centered evaluation, the testing paradigm shifts away from the notion that a standard set of items requiring a specific response and generating a standard score is required for valid testing. Some assumptions about client-centered assessments are

- Client-centered assessments measure the client's perception of health, performance, satisfaction, interests, or values;
- Client-centered, open-ended interviews elicit the unique concerns and priorities of the client;
- Client-centered assessments are occupation-based (focused on activities meaningful to the client);
- Client-centered assessments include measures of quality of life;
- Data from client-centered assessments may be qualitative or quantitative; and
- Client-centered assessments consider the client's natural context and, if possible, take place in the client's natural context.

Child-Centered Measures

Client-centered assessments for children become age-appropriate when the child can express a realistic perception about his or her occupations and can judge his or her own performance. It is somewhat difficult to determine when a child has sufficient sense of self to participate in a performance assessment. A child as young as 5 years may have a sense of what he or she does well and does not do well; however, the child may lack the ability to prioritize and plan. The Perceived Efficacy and Goal Setting System (Missiuna & Pollock, 2000) was designed to be used with a child as young as 5 years of age; the Child Occupational Self Assessment (Keller, Kafkes, Basu, Federico, & Kielhofner, 2004) is most appropriate for children 8 to 13 years of age. These two examples of client-centered assessments for children are described below.

Perceived Efficacy and Goal Setting System

The Perceived Efficacy and Goal Setting System (PEGS; Missiuna & Pollock, 2000) can be used to establish goals with a young child. It provides pictures of daily activities that can generate discussion with a young child to help that child identify his or her own goals. The child views pictures and rates his or her efficacy in performing the activities. Based on these ratings, the child selects goals for therapy.

The PEGS consists of 24 items, depicting 12 fine motor and 12 gross motor tasks that a child encounters on a daily basis. The 24 items are presented in pairs, with one picture showing a child performing a task competently and the other showing a child demonstrating less competence. The occupational therapist asks the child which picture is most like him or her. Next, the therapist asks the child whether the picture is "a lot" or "a little" like him or her. After reviewing all of the cards with the child, the therapist asks if there are additional tasks that the child would like to improve at or work on in therapy. The therapist uses the cards that the child has prioritized to further discuss the child's concerns, and the child determines which tasks he or she wishes to work on in a therapy program.

Missiuna and Pollock (2000) found that parents and their child had a moderate to high level of agreement about the child's competence on certain items (86.5% for bicycle riding and 75.7% for shoe tying); however, overall the correlation of competency scores between parents and child was low ($r = .29$). Although parents and their child agreed on certain goals, only 5 of 37 pairs agreed on the top four goals. Overall, the agreement between parents and child on what therapy should address was low, indicating that when parents and their child are compared, the child has different priorities than his or her parents. Studies using the PEGS (e.g., Missiuna & Pollock, 2000) recommend its use so that therapy programs match the child's interests and concerns. Attending to the child's priorities may facilitate the child's motivation and engagement in the therapy program.

Child Occupational Self Assessment

The Child Occupational Self-Assessment (COSA; Keller et al., 2004) is a client-centered assessment that measures a child's or youth's perceptions about his or her own sense of occupational competence and the importance of everyday activities. The COSA consists of a series of statements pertaining to everyday occupational participation and includes two versions, a card sort and a checklist (Keller et al., 2004). The scale measures a child's occupations and participation, including personal and contextual aspects of participation. Responses are from the child's perceptive (e.g., "I have a big problem doing this," "I am really good at doing this"). These statements give insight into the child's feelings of personal causation and indicate the level of support available in the environment.

The COSA is most useful for a client who is between the ages of 8 and 13 years, has adequate cognitive abilities for self-reflection and planning, and has a desire to collaborate in the development of therapy goals. It is not appropriate for a child with severe cognitive limitations or who lacks insight into his or her strengths and weaknesses.

A child can select the card sort version or the checklist. The child rates his or her own competency for different occupations and skills and then rates how much he or she values each activity or skill (i.e., its importance). The child's responses can be discussed as areas for goal development and should lead to an intervention plan. Keller and colleagues (2004) found discrepancy on the COSA between the child's self-perception and the therapist's observations (e.g., the child felt that he was competent in areas that the occupational therapist observed to be limited and incompetent in areas that the therapist judged to be a strength). Using the results of the COSA, the therapist and child can discuss differing perceptions about performance and establish priorities for change in an intervention program (Keller et al., 2004).

Client-Centered Measures for Adults

A number of client-centered measures have been developed for use with adults. These assessments work well at the initiation of an intervention program to establish the client's concerns and priorities. They align with the person–environment–occupation model (Law et al., 1996) and the Model of Human Occupation (Kielhofner, 2008).

Canadian Occupational Performance Measure

A prominent example of a measure of occupational performance and satisfaction, the Canadian Occupational Performance Measure (COPM; Law et al., 1998/2004; Law, Dunn, & Baum, 2005), is based on the concept of client-centered care. Law and colleagues (1991) originally developed the tool to improve objective measurement of client priorities when providing client-centered intervention. It measures a client's self-perception of occupational performance over time and is designed to be used as an outcomes measure. The COPM uses a semistructured interview format and structured scoring system to assess client outcomes in self-care, productivity, and leisure. It assists the therapist and client in identifying problem areas in occupational performance, setting goals, and measuring progress in occupational performance.

To administer the COPM, the occupational therapist asks the client to identify something he or she needs, wants, or is expected to do but cannot or does not do in the areas of self-care, productivity, and leisure. The client also identifies activities that he or she performs but with which he or she is not satisfied. Once the occupational performance problems have been identified, their importance is rated from "not important at all" to "extremely important." The five problems that are most important to the client are then scored for level of performance and satisfaction. Performance is rated from 1 *(not able to do at all)* to 10 *(able to do extremely well)*; satisfaction is rated from 1 *(not satisfied at all)* to 10 *(extremely satisfied)*. A total score can be computed by adding the scores for each problem and dividing by the number of problems.

The COPM is usually completed as an initial assessment and becomes the basis for establishing goals. Because the COPM scaled responses are unique to each client, scores for individuals should not be compared to each other; however, an individual's scores before and after intervention can be compared to evaluate progress. The COPM is responsive to client change in performance. In a series of pilot studies, Law and colleagues (1998/2004) showed that a typical change following occupational therapy intervention in performance and satis-faction on the COPM is 3 points, representing a significant change ($p < .001$; $n = 139$). A change score of 2 or more is considered clinically significant (Law et al., 1991, 1998/2004).

Carswell, McColl, Baptiste, Law, Polatajko, and Pollock (2004) com-pleted a systematic review of the research that has investigated the COPM psy-chometric properties or used the scale to measure outcomes. The goal of this review was to determine whether the COPM is a psychometrically robust and clinically useful outcomes measure for an occupational therapist (Carswell et al., 2004). These researchers found 88 articles that had used the COPM. Of these, 19 were research papers that examined the psychometric properties of the COPM. Three studies examined the test–retest reliability and found that reliability was high for both the performance and satisfaction scores (.76–.89). Eleven studies examined the validity of the COPM and generally supported its validity. In particular, it correlated with other measures of quality of life and functional performance. A particular asset of the COPM is that it is highly responsive to change in client outcomes over time. When compared to other measures (e.g., Short Form–36, the FIM™), the COPM is highly sensitive to client improvements in perceived performance level and satisfaction (Carswell et al., 2004).

The COPM appears effective in engaging the client in the therapeutic pro-cess. It provides a client-centered method for determining concerns and per-formance issues. One of the limitations of the COPM is that it cannot be used with all clients, particularly those who lack insight into their problems or who may not understand the rating scale. It also is limited as a precise measure of physical or psychosocial performance. Carswell and colleagues (2004) con-cluded that despite these limitations, the COPM is a useful tool for identifying clients' occupational needs, has demonstrated its ability to quantify change in performance, facilitates discussion and negotiation between clients and family caregivers, and gives the therapist important information for developing mean-ingful interventions.

Occupational Performance History Interview

Another client-centered measure is the Occupational Performance History In-terview (OPHI–II; Kielhofner, Mallinson, Forsyth, & Lai, 2001). This instru-ment focuses on occupational function and the client's routines and habits. The OPHI–II recognizes that a person is a dynamic system who is influenced by physical and social environments. It consists of a semistructured interview, scales for rating the information obtained in the interview, and a format for recording qualitative or narrative data. The three subscales measure

1. *Occupational competence:* The degree to which a person is able to sustain a pattern of occupational behavior that is productive and satisfying,
2. *Occupational identity:* The degree to which a person has internalized a positive occupational identity, and

3. *Occupational behavioral setting:* The impact of the environment on the person's occupational life.

The interview is organized into five categories: (1) activity or occupational choices, (2) critical life events, (3) daily routines, (4) occupational roles, and (5) occupational behavior settings. The occupational therapist asks about past and present roles. These categories appear to be helpful when a therapist interviews clients with newly acquired disabilities. The scale examines the client's ability to sustain behavioral patterns that are satisfying and productive and to understand the environment's influence on the person. The scale demonstrates high internal validity, as evidenced by all of the items fitting in the Rasch analysis results (Kielhofner et al., 2001). A sample of clients with psychiatric disorders and another sample with physical disabilities were used to evaluate the validity of the OPHI–II. The identity scale was lower for clients with psychiatric disorders, competence was affected for both groups, and environmental support was lower for clients with physical disabilities.

Occupational Self-Assessment

Similar to the COPM, the Occupational Self-Assessment (OSA; Baron, Kielhofner, Iyenger, Goldhammer, & Wolenski, 2003) is a self-report measure that an occupational therapist can use to establish the priorities and goals for intervention. The client rates himself or herself on occupational competence and the impact of environments on occupational adaptation. The OSA has two parts: *occupational performance* and *the environment.* Part one includes statements about the client's occupational behavior, how well it is done, its importance as a measure of competence, and values concerning competence. Part two measures environmental support for the client's occupations and the client's values concerning environmental support. The client is also asked about what he or she would like to change. This assessment seems most relevant for initiating intervention and establishing priorities for services. The authors indicate that it requires only 10 to 20 minutes to complete, and with its simplicity, clients can complete the scale independently. Kielhofner and Forsyth (2001) demonstrated that the scales were one-dimensional and that fit using Rasch analysis was excellent.

Client-Centered Assessments Summary

Client-centered occupational therapy assessments that use self-report have been developed for both children and adults. These assessments identify a client's perception of performance and ability, limitations, and disability. They also gather information about a client's interests, values, and concerns. Beginning an intervention program with the client's perspectives on performance establishes the client's priorities and contributes to establishing a rapport between the occupational therapist and client. In addition, these assessments allow the occupational therapist to explore the client's cultural values and contextual supports. Although client-centered assessments are key to developing the intervention plan, they do not stand alone, and the occupational therapist should administer additional observational and standardized assessments to further analyze performance problems and gain insight into the types of intervention strategies that will help improve performance.

Evaluation of Client Participation Within Natural Contexts

Participation means sharing with others, taking part in an activity, or involvement in a life situation. Participation in life's activities is an important aspect of health and quality of life. Law (2002) describes its importance: "Through participation, we acquire skills and competencies, connect with others and our communities, and find purpose and meaning in life" (p. 640). Participation in occupations is a central concept to occupational therapists and defines an essential goal of intervention.

The World Health Organization (WHO) defines *participation* as involvemental in a life situation and equates it to be a key indicator of health. The WHO (2001) recognizes the complexity of participation by stressing the interrelationships between body function and structure, activity, personal factors, and environmental characteristics. A person's participation does not occur in isolation and must be considered in relationship to his or her abilities and the environment in which he or she lives. Participation can be assessed only by considering the environments in which people live, work, and play. It implies engagement in a life situation or life activity but does not always mean performing the activity. For example, a person can meaningfully participate in an activity by observing that activity, partially performing it, performing it in an adapted way, or directing others to perform it. All of these types of performing imply "engaged involvement," which is the essence of participation. Key aspects of participation that relate to health are that the person can make decisions about participating, finds the activity to be meaningful, and participates in opportunities that are consistent with his or her life goals.

A majority of occupational therapy measures assess the client's performance (i.e., how a person completes an activity or task). Measures of participation are challenging to conceptualize, given the dynamic and evolving nature of participation. Scholars (e.g., Law, 2002; Law et al., 2005) have discussed the difficulty of measuring participation. It is not only a broad concept, but it is multidimensional and complex. Participation measures consider not only the person, environment, and occupation but also the interactions of these variables. Rather than defining specific attributes of the person, his or her occupations, and relevant environments, participation assessments evaluate the transaction of these variables.

It can be argued that measures of participation have certain characteristics. Scholars have attempted to define the characteristics of this broad, multidimensional concept and have made assumptions about how to measure it. The field has yet to reach consensus on how to measure participation (Coster & Khetani, 2008; Law, 2002; Law et al., 2005); however, in recent years, a number of participation measures have been published. Defining characteristics of existing participation measures include that they

- Use self-report or caregiver report,
- Focus on a person's everyday occupations or common occupations,
- Consider a person's natural environment or multiple environments,
- Focus on activities that are goal-directed, and
- Assess the perceived importance of participation and associated feelings of well-being or satisfaction.

The following sections discuss these characteristics.

Self-Report or Caregiver Report

Measures of participation are most often self-reported scales that define participation across environments and time. Coster and Khetani (2008) discussed the temporal/spatial aspects of participation that are inherent in the meaning of participation. Through self-report or caregiver report, participation is assessed as a personal and individualized experience. By using self-report, the evaluator gains a perspective on the opportunities and environmental supports available to the client and how he or she participates in those opportunities. A variety of methods have been developed to elicit self-report. Many instruments, such as the Life Habits Assessment (LIFE–H; Fougeyrollas, Noreau, Bergeron, Cloutier, Dion, & St-Michel, 1998) or the Late Life Function and Disability Instrument (LLFDI; Haley et al., 2002; Jette et al., 2002), use a questionnaire that can be administered as an interview or in paper-and-pencil format. Other measures (e.g., the Activity Card Sort [ACS]; Baum & Edwards, 2001, 2008) use a card sort activity in which the person identifies the amount and level of involvement in activities as depicted on the cards. Measures tend to be organized by activities, occupations, or roles and rate the frequency of participation, the supports necessary to participate, how well a person performs in that role or occupation, satisfaction with participation, and restrictions or limitations.

Everyday Occupations and Roles

Occupational therapy has traditionally categorized occupations as activities of daily living, instrumental activities of daily living, rest and sleep, education, work, play, leisure, and social participation (AOTA, 2008). As noted by Coster and Khetani (2008), measures of child participation are often organized by role or life situations. Examples of life situations defined in the *International Classification of Functioning, Disability and Health* (ICF; WHO, 2001) include recreation and leisure, engagement in play, education, self-care, and work. However, occupational therapy also recognizes the importance of assessing the subjective experience embedded in these occupations and roles. The meaning that a person gives to an occupation is essential to determining how it matches his or her life roles. For example, cooking may be leisure to one person, work to another, and an instrumental activity of daily living (IADL) to a third. In evaluating participation, perception of the experience can be as important as actual performance.

For example, a family may rate a child's performance as independent when it is actually supported by equipment, adapted methods, and physical assistance. When these adapted methods are integrated into a family's everyday life, family members often consider them as natural and routine and would not consider the child's dependence on supports to be a lack of independence.

Natural Environments and Multiple Environments

The environment is of particular interest when evaluating participation because it supports, enhances, or restricts participation. Assessments, including the Home Observation for Measurement of the Environment (HOME; Caldwell & Bradley, 1984) and the School Function Assessment (SFA; Coster, Deeney, Haltiwanger, & Haley, 1998), often specify the environment. When an assessment does not specify the environment, the occupational therapist should consider multiple environments to rate assessment items. Social, physical, temporal, and cultural contexts influence the extent, amount, and quality of a person's participation (AOTA, 2008). By observing or asking about participation in a person's everyday environments, the assessment obtains a valid measure, and the therapist can gain a realistic understanding about competence and participation of the client. The way in which environments are assessed as they contribute to a person's participation is discussed later in this chapter.

Goal-Directed Activities

Because participation in life activities is goal-directed and purposeful, participation measures consider the purpose of activity to the person. A person's goal in a specific activity (e.g., swimming, work) determines the meaning of participation and an intervention plan. For example, if the goal of going to the movies is to be with friends, then independent mobility in the theater or understanding the movie's plot may not be important aspects of participating in this activity. Activities such as housekeeping are perceived to be work to some people but leisure to those who derive great pleasure from maintaining a clean home. A child's learning in school can be work and lead to a career, but it is also social activity that enables learning about society and culture unrelated to work as an adult. The meaning a person assigns to an activity may determine whether that activity is a desired or appropriate focus for a rehabilitation program. For example, when a mother with multiple sclerosis finds that baking cookies with her 10-year-old daughter has become difficult, it is important to know whether baking is a valued leisure pursuit or a valued time for mother–daughter relationship. If baking is an important and desired activity, the therapist can adapt the techniques to bake; if mother–daughter interaction is most important, the therapist can recommend a substitute joint activity. The occupational therapist inquires about, rather than assumes, a client's goals or purposes in desired activities to fully interpret their meaning and value to the client.

Well-being and Satisfaction

Participation in meaningful occupations has a direct and substantial effect on health and quality of life (Coster & Khetani, 2008; Law, 2002; Wilcox, 1998). Most measures of participation include personal satisfaction, similar to measures of quality of life. The key difference between measures of quality of life and participation is that most scales that rate quality of life do not specify certain occupations or human functions (e.g., per the *ICF*). In contrast to measures of quality of life, participation measures link satisfaction and well-being to a client's involvement in specific activities.

By gaining appreciation of the client's satisfaction with performance and participation, the occupational therapist can establish intervention priorities. Measures of satisfaction are also essential outcomes for intervention programs.

Participation Assessments

As noted by Law and colleagues (2005) and Coster and Khetani (2008), measurement of participation only recently has emerged as a priority in rehabilitation and health care. Most occupational therapy assessments of participation focus on activities or occupations within specific environments or multiple environments. This section describes assessments that meet all or most of the characteristics defined above. Each assesses the interactions among person, environment, and occupation.

Child Participation Scales

Although a few measures of participation have been recently published, the number of available scales remains limited. This section describes three examples of participation measures for children: the Children's Assessment of Participation and Enjoyment/Preferences for Activities of Children (King et al., 2004), the School Function Assessment (Coster et al., 1998), and the Pediatric Evaluation of Disability Inventory (Haley, Coster, Ludlow, Haltiwanger, & Andrellos, 1992).

CHILDREN'S ASSESSMENT OF PARTICIPATION AND ENJOYMENT/PREFERENCES FOR ACTIVITIES OF CHILDREN

The Children's Assessment of Participation and Enjoyment/Preferences for Activities of Children (CAPE/PAC; King et al., 2004) was designed to measure how a child or youth (with or without disabilities) participates in everyday activities outside schoolwork or home chores. King and colleagues (2004) developed the CAPE to document what a child does in the context of his natural environment. It purposely does not rate adapted equipment, assistance, or environmental supports that may be necessary for the child to participate. It also does not rate the child's competence or gather information about how the family and environment influence the child's activity choices (Law et al., 2006). This 55-item questionnaire examines how a child or youth participates, including diversity (number of activities done), intensity (frequency of participation), and enjoyment of activities. The CAPE provides three levels of scores: (1) the child's overall participation in activities; (2) domain scores that reflect participation in formal and informal activities; and (3) scores that reflect participation in five types of activity: recreation, active physical, social, skill-based, and self-improvement. The scale also provides information about the context in which a child or youth participates in these activities. The PAC is a companion tool that assesses the child's preference for involvement in each of the 55 activities.

The CAPE has been used in a number of studies that describe participation in children with disabilities. Law and colleagues (2006) assessed participation of 427 children with health and developmental problems, approximately half of whom had cerebral palsy. This large survey showed that children with physical disabilities participated extensively in informal activities, particularly recreational, social, and self-improvement activities. Their participation in formal activities, such as sport teams or choir, was lower and less intense. They also participated less in active physical activities. Although this may be expected among children with physical disabilities, it is worrisome because physical activity is particularly important for maintaining physical function.

SCHOOL FUNCTION ASSESSMENT

The School Function Assessment (SFA; Coster et al., 1998) is a standardized, criterion-referenced assessment that measures a child's participation in academic and social school-related activities. Coster and her colleagues developed the SFA using the *ICF* model to conceptualize the scale's format. Therefore, the SFA measures participation in the school environment; task supports, including both equipment and personal supports; and activity performance. Coster and colleagues (1998) defined participation as the students' being involved in doing real-life activities. The items rate the extent to which the student can access, can make use of, or has the same opportunities in the environment as his or her peers without disabilities. The participation section measures the child's level of participation in six school activity settings: general or special education classroom, playground, transportation to and from school, bathroom, transition to and from class, and mealtimes. The task support section measures assistance and adaptations required to accomplish tasks. The activity performance section measures performance in school-related functional activities in two categories: physical tasks and cognitive/behavioral tasks. Each section comprises nine scales that measure specific tasks or areas of activity performance.

Given the comprehensive nature of the SFA, often multiple school-based professionals on the student's team (e.g., teacher, occupational therapist, speech–language pathologist) work together to complete one comprehensive assessment. It should be rated after the student has been observed for several weeks across all or most school environments, which is why multiple team members should complete the scales. The SFA is helpful when using a top-down assessment model in which the occupational therapist evaluates function and participation before analyzing performance of specific activities. The SFA accurately identifies areas where further analysis of performance or behaviors is needed (Coster et al., 1998).

In the SFA manual, Coster and colleagues (1998) stated that standard activity scale scores can be derived without administering the entire assessment. However, all items within the activity scale must be administered to obtain a standard or criterion-referenced score for that scale. Researchers have examined the reliability and validity of the SFA in a number of studies. Interrater reliability (using intraclass correlation coefficients [ICCs]) comparing 16 teacher and occupational therapist pairs was .70 for participation, .68 for task supports, and .73 for activity performance. Studies of interrater reliability (e.g., Davies et al., 2004) suggest that consistent results are obtained when the SFA is used by different professionals. Hwang, Davies, Taylor, and Gavin (2002) compared SFA scores for three different groups of children (general education students, students with learning disabilities, and students with cerebral palsy). These groups differed on all SFA subscales. In a more recent study (Davies et al., 2004), known groups' validity was studied by comparing students with three other types of disabilities (autism, learning disabilities, and traumatic brain injury). Using analysis of variance by ranks (Kruskal-Wallis one-way analysis) and discriminant analysis, scores on the SFA differed for students with autism and learning disabilities. Students with autism scored significantly lower on the cognitive–behavioral tasks than students with learning disabilities or traumatic brain injury, and the cognitive–behavioral scale was the most accurate predictor of disability across the different groups of students.

PEDIATRIC EVALUATION OF DISABILITY INVENTORY

The *Pediatric Evaluation of Disability Inventory* (PEDI; Haley et al., 1992) measures function and occupation in younger children (ages 6 months to 7 years). In contrast to most scales of young children that are based on a developmental framework, the PEDI, like the SFA, is based on the *ICF* (WHO, 2001). Its items measure the function–disability continuum from the perspective of the child's ability to participate in functional activities. The first section measures the child's functional capacity in self-care, mobility, and social function. The items are specific and list a number of developmental skills for each self-care area (e.g., eating, dressing). Caregivers must indicate that the child can or cannot perform each skill; therefore, partial performance is not rated for each specific skill. The second section rates caregiver assistance (i.e., how much assistance is needed for the child to perform the activity). The scale identifies the levels of assistance and task modification needed for the child to perform functional activities. The child's natural social and physical contexts are considered because these contribute to the child's ability to perform in functional activities.

A number of reliability and validity studies of the PEDI have been completed. Haley and his colleagues (1992) reported that internal consistency, based on the normative sample, ranged from Cronbach alphas of .95 to .99. These researchers measured interrater reliability by correlating the responses of primary caregivers with those of rehabilitation team members (ICCs ranged from .74 to .96). Nichols and Case-Smith (1996) also correlated parent ratings to those of occupational and physical therapists. They found more variation in scores (.20 to .93), probably because the therapists did not know the children as well as the rehabilitation team members did in the Haley et al. study. Wright and Boschen (1993) studied the test–retest reliability of the PEDI using a sample of children with cerebral palsy, ages 3 to 7 years. When children were measured 3 weeks apart, the ICCs were greater than .95 for total scores and above .80 for the functional subscales.

The validity of the PEDI has been well studied and found to be strong. The scale appears to be responsive to changes in performance and has been used to measure progress in children with spastic diplegia after selective dorsal rhizotomy (Nordmark, Jarnio, & Hagglund, 2000) and children who completed inpatient rehabilitation (Iyer, Haley, Watkins, & Dumas, 2003).

Adult Participation Scales

Measures of participation in adults have focused on specific occupations or roles or specific diagnostic groups. As defined in the previous section, adult participation tools assess a person's function in his or her natural environment, with emphasis on essential daily living activities, including ADLs, social participation, and mobility. Certain scales that were originally developed for specific populations (e.g., the Activity Card Sort for older adults with dementia, the Craig Handicap Assessment and Reporting Technique for spinal cord injury) have been revised and developed to apply to a broad range of disabilities. These tools are particularly useful in developing an initial occupational profile and in analyzing the effects of disabilities on life participation.

ACTIVITY CARD SORT

The Activity Card Sort (ACS; Baum & Edwards, 2001, 2008) is a standardized assessment that evaluates an adult's frequency and level of involvement in various activities. It measures human occupation and level of activity in four categories of human occupation: instrumental activities, low-demand leisure activities, high-demand leisure activities, and social activities (Baum & Edwards, 2001, 2008). The ACS uses pictures of people doing real-life activities so that the evaluator can discuss specific occupations and activities with a client in an easy and explicit way. The cards bring clarity to the conversation and create examples of activities that can be discussed. As a measure of occupation and participation, the ACS supports the common definition of occupation as a "complex dynamic involving individuals and their purposive behavior within environment contexts that have meaning and that change over time" (Sachs & Josman, 2003, p. 166).

The assessment uses a q-sort methodology, requiring the client being evaluated to sort cards depicting people engaged in real-life activities into categories. The sorting procedure allows the client to describe how and at what level he or she participates in various activities. The original version of the ACS was designed to capture activity level of people with Alzheimer's disease. A number of versions of the ACS are available, including a healthy older adult version, an institutional version, a recovering version, and an Israeli version. These versions have between 80 and 88 pictures and the assessment questions vary depending on which version is used.

A primary use of the ACS is to develop intervention goals. By identifying levels of occupation and activity participation, the occupational therapist can identify the client's concerns and the client's priorities emerge. The assessment allows the therapist to identify changes in activity patterns as a result of an intervention program. The ACS initiates client-centered intervention and provides a backdrop for discussing activity problems in a nonthreatening way.

In a factor analysis study of the ACS, Sachs and Josman (2003) confirmed the original factors with slight variation for older adults and young adults (students). The ACS items for the older adults clustered into four categories: IADLs, leisure, demanding leisure, and maintenance activities. For the young adults, the items clustered into five categories: IADLs, leisure, demanding leisure, maintenance, and social recreational activities. This analysis of construct validity suggests that the ACS measures slightly different constructs based on personal characteristics of the individual. This reinforces that participation measures are based on a person's perception of an activity's meaning and level of involvement in that activity.

In another validity study of healthy adults, healthy older adults, spouses or caregivers of people with Alzheimer's disease, people with multiple sclerosis, and stroke survivors who lived in Israel, Katz, Karpin, Lak, Furman, and Hartman-Maeir (2003) found that the ACS differentiated these groups. They differed significantly for activity level and individual activity areas. In healthy adults, participation changed with aging in social–cultural and high physical leisure areas. For caregivers of people with Alzheimer's disease, participation became restricted in leisure areas. For people with multiple sclerosis, the changes were manifested in IADLs and high physical leisure activities; for people with stroke, all activity areas were affected.

CRAIG HANDICAP ASSESSMENT AND REPORTING TECHNIQUE

The Craig Handicap Assessment and Reporting Technique (CHART; Whiteneck, Charlifue, Gerhart, Overholser, & Richardson, 1992) was developed to assess community participation in people with spinal cord injury. Originally, the scale included five domains or roles: physical independence, mobility, occupation, social integration, and economic self-sufficiency. It has items that relate to personal care and IADLs (e.g., shopping, meal preparation, laundering). The questionnaire asks the client to indicate time spent performing each task. The CHART was revised in 1999, and a cognitive functioning scale was added (Walker, Mellick, Brooks, & Whiteneck, 2003). The items are simple, objective, and observable. The subscale expands the use of the assessment to people with cognitive impairments, including those with traumatic brain injury, stroke, and multiple sclerosis. Currently there is a short form (17 items) and a long form (34 items). By design, the items correspond to different levels of the *ICF* (WHO, 2001), with the goal of quantifying participation in social roles. A client can complete the assessment independently, but ideally it is administered using interview so that the assessment administrator can ask follow-up questions.

A number of studies (e.g., Whiteneck et al., 1992; Whiteneck, Tate, & Charlifue, 1999) have examined the reliability and validity of the CHART, finding high correlations between family and client ratings and good scalability using Rasch analysis. Test–retest reliability was good (.83) for the total scores and .60 to .95 for subscales. Total CHART scores discriminated people with higher levels of handicap compared to those with low level as judged by rehabilitation professionals (Hall, Kijkers, Whiteneck, Brooks, & Krause, 1998; Salter, Foley, Jutai, Bayley, & Teasell, 2008). In a study of 1,110 individuals with spinal cord injury, traumatic brain injury, and other acquired disabilities, the CHART–Revised demonstrated a high correlation with level of disability as measured by the FIM (Walker et al., 2003). It has been demonstrated that CHART scores are affected by age, race or ethnicity, education, and occupation at the time of evaluation (Hall et al., 1998). Approximately one-third to one-half of the variance in CHART subscale scores is accounted for by age. Scores decrease with increasing age on all subscales except for the economic self-sufficiency subscale. Although the CHART's scores are based on normative data and it measures only objective aspects of participation, the CHART is a well-established measure of community integration in people with disabilities.

PERSONAL CARE PARTICIPATION ASSESSMENT AND RESOURCE TOOL

The Personal Care Participation Assessment and Resource Tool (PC–PART; originally the HART [Vertesi, Darzins, Lowe, McEvoy, & Edwards, 2000]) identifies individuals' functional abilities and the support provided by caregivers. It assesses what a person can do independently and what he or she can accomplish with the help of others. The assessment includes personal care and home management in the client's usual environments with the usual available assistance.

The PC–PART is appropriate for adults, including older adults and those with significant cognitive impairment or an inability to speak. The form of the tool is unique; the occupational therapist completes a chart on the basis of an interview with the client and then separately with a caregiver or key informant. A key informant can be an informal caregiver, a close friend, or a formal caregiver such as a nurse, who further describes concerns and adaptations for each activity. The assessment domains are clothing, hygiene, nutrition, mobility, safety, residence, and supports (Vertesi et al., 2000). The person indicates that he or she can complete each activity independently, with help, or cannot complete. Therefore, the PC–PART incorporates an understanding of the interaction between people and their environments (Barbara & Whiteford, 2005). The PC–PART gives multidimensional information about each performance area; however, it does not give a meaningful summary score. In a qualitative study using the PC–PART (HART) with older clients, occupational therapists indicated that the tool had clinical utility and furthered their clinical reasoning (Barbara & Whiteford, 2005).

LIFE HABITS ASSESSMENT

The Life Habits Assessment (LIFE–H; Fougeyrollas et al., 1998) is a measure of social participation in people with disabilities. The authors define social participation and life habits as the "daily activities and social roles that ensure the survival and development of a person in society throughout his or her life" (Fougeyrollas et al., 1998, p. 128). The LIFE–H assesses the degree of accomplishment of life habits in terms of the difficulty and assistance required in 12 areas (see Table 7.1). The individual appraises the quality of social participation by judging the difficulty of carrying out life habits in these areas.

Several studies have examined the validity and reliability of the LIFE–H. Fougeyrollas and colleagues (1998) estimated test–retest reliability using a sample of people with spinal cord injuries. They found good reliability for the overall score (ICC = .67 to .83) and moderate to high reliability for individual scales (ICC = .47 to .91). The LIFE–H has demonstrated significant differences in social participation in people with cerebral palsy and after a stroke (Noreau et al., 2004). In a recent study of test–retest and interrater reliability, Noreau and colleagues found excellent reliability for personal care and nutrition, with lower reliability for interpersonal relationships and social roles.

LATE-LIFE FUNCTION AND DISABILITY INSTRUMENT

The Late-Life Function and Disability Instrument (LLFDI; Haley et al., 2002; Jette et al., 2002) is a comprehensive assessment of physical function and disability in community-dwelling older adults. The LLFDI consists of items that measure *functional limitations* (inability to perform activities encountered in daily routines) and *disability* (inability to participate in major life tasks and social roles). The components (LLFDI Function Scale and Disability Scale) relate

Table 7.1. Domains for the Assessment of Life Habits (LIFE–H)

Daily Activities	Social Roles
Nutrition	Responsibility
Fitness	Interpersonal relationships
Personal care	Community life
Communication	Education
Housing	Employment
Mobility	Recreation

Source. Noreau, K., et al. (2004). Measuring social participation: Reliability of the LIFE–H in older adults with disabilities. *Disability and Rehabilitation, 26,* 345–352.

to the *ICF*; that is, the Function Scale measures performance of tasks or activities, and the Disability Scale measures participation or involvement in life situations. The Function Scale evaluates self-reported difficulty in performing 32 physical activities in three dimensions: upper extremity, basic lower extremity, and advanced lower extremity. Clients report how much difficulty they have doing a particular activity without the help of someone else and without the use of assistive technology (Haley et al., 2002). The Disability Scale evaluates self-reported limitations in and frequency of performing 16 major life tasks. The client reports how limited he or she feels in doing a particular task and how often he or she does that task.

Dubuc, Haley, Ni, Kooyoomjian, and Jette (2004) examined the concurrent validity of the LLFDI by comparing it to the Physical Function scale (PF–10) of the Short Form–36 (SF–36) and the London Handicap Scale (LHS; see below). In addition to calculating the correlations between the LLFDI and the SF–36 (PF–10) and the LHS, Dubuc and colleagues conducted a series of Rasch analyses to evaluate ceiling and floor effects and the precision of the measures. The correlation between the function component of LLFDI and the PF–10 was high for lower-extremity sections ($r = .85$) and moderate for upper-extremity sections ($r = .51$). The correlation between the disability component of the LLFDI and the LHS was moderate ($r = .47–.66$). The LLFDI measures a broader range of function than the other tools and is more precise than the PF–10. The disability component also is more precise than the LHS for the more challenging items and less precise than the LHS for the easier items. The authors concluded that a primary advantage of the LLFDI is that it has minimal ceiling and floor effects, making it suitable for a broad range of disabilities and sensitive to change over time when people may reach a high level of function.

LONDON HANDICAP SCALE

The London Handicap Scale (LHS; Jenkinson, Mant, Carter, Wade, & Winner, 2000) is a six-item instrument designed to measure global function and disability in adults with chronic, multiple, or progressive diseases. The LHS is based on the descriptive framework of handicap developed by the WHO in the *ICF*. Although the concept of handicap is now conceptualized as degrees of life participation, the dimensions of the LHS remain relevant (Jenkinson et al., 2000). The scale provides a profile on disability across the six dimensions and a severity score for degree of disability. The LHS rates a person's perceived level of physical independence, social integration, and economic self-sufficiency as these relate to health. Each dimension has a six-point rating scale, ranging from *no disadvantage* to *extreme disadvantage*. The scale can be self-administered or used by a therapist to interview the client or a caregiver. A weighted scoring system was developed for the original scale; however, Jenkinson and colleagues (2000) found that clients' overall rating was similar when using unweighted versus weighted scores.

In a study of concurrent validity for the LLFDI, Dubuc and colleagues (2004) found moderate correlations between the LHS and the LLFDI. The LHS is more comprehensive in coverage of basic requirements of living (e.g., orientation, socialization) than the LLFDI and therefore may be more sensitive for people with low functional levels. The LHS also demonstrated moderate correlations with the Barthel Index and the Frenchay Activities Index (Jenkinson et al., 2000).

COMMUNITY INTEGRATION QUESTIONNAIRE

The Community Integration Questionnaire (CIQ; Willer, Ottenbacher, & Coad, 1994) was developed as an outcomes measure for individuals with brain injury. The CIQ's 15 items are divided into sections of home integration (active participation in the operation of the home or household), social integration (participation in social activities outside the home), and productivity (regular performance of work, school, or volunteer activities). The items examine the frequency with which the individual performs activities and whether or not these activities are done jointly. Responses to the items can be collected through face-to-face interviews or phone interviews. The CIQ rates home, work, and community activities that require both physical and cognitive performance; therefore, it may be more appropriate for people with brain injury than the CHART. Using the CIQ, some interesting relationships among client factors, context, occupations, and community integration have been found in clients with head injury. Following rehabilitation, women tend to have greater home integration and men tend to have higher productivity. Young clients with head injury tend to be more integrated in terms of social and productivity dimensions, whereas older clients have more limited community integration (Dijkers, 1997).

The reliability of the CIQ is good, with test–retest reliability coefficients ranging between .63 and .91 for individual scales and .81 and .91 for total scores. Concurrent validity was demonstrated between CIQ and CHART scores (Zhang et al., 2002). CIQ scores correlate with scores that measure life satisfaction, community access, level of functioning, cognitive ability, and ADL ratings (Salter et al., 2008). Zhang and colleagues (2002) concluded that the CIQ appears to be the most appropriate instrument in quantifying rehabilitation outcomes for people with traumatic brain injury at the participation level.

Measures of Participation Summary

Measures of participation use self-report to obtain the client's perspectives on participation in specific life occupations and roles. Most measures of participation use the *ICF* as a framework, include broad categories of life activities, and make direct connections to the client's health (e.g., ask how health limits participation). Most participation scales include assessment of satisfaction with levels of participation, importance of participating in the activity, and supports required to participate. Some scales (e.g., PEDI, LIFE–H, LLFDI, PART–PC) measure functional levels, disability, and amount of caregiver assistance as distinct constructs; however, other scales (e.g., CAPE/PAC, LHS, CHART, CIQ) conceptualize participation holistically as the transaction between the person and his or her environment, including supports within the environment. Occupational therapists' use of participation measures appears to be increasing because these assessments provide a standardized method for developing the occupational profile. By focusing on life roles and satisfaction within those roles, participation assessments are important outcomes measures.

Assessments of the Environment

By definition, assessments of participation consider the contexts of a person's activities, recognizing that the physical, social, temporal, and cultural context can support or constrain participation. When measuring participation, the concept of environment is dynamic, that is, it varies across time and space, recognizing that contexts change with activities and roles. The environment has an essential role in determining the quality, frequency, and level of a person's participation in life activities. Because the environment can contribute to disability, comprehensive evaluation to understand the basis for disability and to plan intervention includes assessment of the environment. In the *ICF, environment* is broadly defined to include physical, social, cultural, economic, and organizational components. *Contexts and environments* also are broadly and comprehensively defined in the *Occupational Therapy Practice Framework: Domain and Process, 2nd Edition (Framework-II;* AOTA, 2008) as cultural, personal, temporal, virtual, physical, and social.

Assessments of the environment that are relevant to occupational therapists examine the interaction between person and environment that enables accomplishment of occupations. The goal of most environmental measures is to determine whether the environment constrains or supports a person's performance and what can be adapted or changed to enhance that person's performance. These assessments help the occupational therapist understand what contextual elements enable or interfere with a person's participation in life activities. By modifying or adapting the environment, an occupational therapist can improve a client's participation and decrease levels of caregiver assistance. In the following sections, measures of physical and social environments related to a person's occupations and participation are identified and explained. They are grouped by purpose: Child assessments emphasize the role of the physical and social environments in promoting skill development; adult assessments emphasize the safety and accessibility of the physical environment, workplace supports, or social supports within a community context.

Measures of Children's Environments

The goal of most assessments of children's environments is evaluation of the transactions between context and child. These assessments emphasize the elements of the environment known to promote development (e.g., parent support and responsiveness, availability of toys and learning materials). Assessments of a child's environment are often predictive of the child's future performance (Bradley et al., 2001).

Home Observation for the Measurement of the Environment

The Home Observation for the Measurement of the Environment (HOME; Bradley & Caldwell, 1994; Caldwell & Bradley, 1984) assesses the home context of young children and has widely been used in research and practice. The HOME was designed to describe and discriminate the quality and quantity of stimulation and support for cognitive, social, and emotional development available to a child in the home (Bradley, Corwyn, & Whiteside-Mansell, 1996). It is administered in the home by observing specific characteristics of the home and interviewing the parent about types of stimulation provided to the child. The items rate social behavior and socialization of the family, social support, communication, and family organization. Interpersonal relationships are assessed, including family, relatives/friends, community life, and use of services. The physical environment is also assessed, including lighting, safety, and equipment/toys. Although the HOME was originally developed to examine the home environment of infants and young children, the age range has been expanded and currently four forms are available for the following: infants, young children, school-age children, and adolescents.

The HOME appears to have a strong relationship to the family's socioeconomic context and family configuration (e.g., single mother, family with multiple children; Bradley et al., 2001). The HOME predicts children's cognitive and behavioral development (Bradley et al., 1989, 2001). In a study of families in Indonesia, Zevalkink, Riksen-Walraven, and Bradley (2008) found that HOME scores were significantly related to the quality of the mother–child relationship. Specifically, these researchers found that children with secure relationships lived in more organized home environments, where care was provided by regular substitutes when the mother was away and the child's play environment was safe. Children who lived in disorganized play environments with more play materials had less-secure relationships. In this study, a less-stimulating and more-organized environment related to a child who demonstrated higher social maturity. Studies using the HOME have clearly demonstrated the environment's influence on a child's development of occupations.

Test of Environmental Supportiveness

The Test of Environmental Supportiveness (TOES; Bundy, 1999; Skard & Bundy, 2008) assesses the supportiveness of the environment for play. This scale was developed as a companion tool to the Test of Playfulness (ToP; Bundy, 1997; Skard & Bundy, 2008) to explore how the environment affects a child's playfulness. Table 7.2 provides examples of the TOES items. A therapist can administer the TOES at home, at a preschool, or in other early childhood settings. It is designed for use with young children but can apply to school-age children (age range is 18 months to 15 years). The TOES consists of 17 items that are scored on a 5-point scale. The items rate caregivers, playmates, play objects, space, and quality of the sensory environment. The TOES can be scored in 15 to 20 minutes by observing the natural environment as the child

Table 7.2. Example Items From the Test of Environmental Supportiveness (TOES)

Item's Negative Anchor	Item's Positive Anchor
Caregivers interfere with player's activities and opportunities	Caregivers promote player's activities and opportunities
Caregivers enforce unreasonably strict boundaries or fail to set boundaries	Caregivers adhere to reasonable boundaries/rules
Peer (older and younger) playmates are dominated by player or dominate player	Peer (older and younger) playmates participate as equals with player
Peer (older and younger) playmates' response to player's cues interferes with transaction	Peer (older and younger) playmates' response to player's cues supports transaction
Peer (older and younger) playmates fail to give clear cues or give cues that interfere with transaction	Peer (older and younger) playmates give clear cues that support transaction
Space is not physically safe	Space is physically safe
Natural and fabricated objects do not support activity of player	Natural and fabricated objects support activity of player
Amount and configuration of space do not support type of play	Amount and configuration of space support activity of player
Space is not accessible	Space is accessible

Note. Adapted from "Test of Playfulness," by G. Skard and A. C. Bundy, *Play in Occupational Therapy for Children,* 2nd ed., edited by L. D. Parham & L. S. Fazio, 2008, St. Louis, MO: Mosby/Elsevier, pp. 71–94. Copyright © 2008, by Mosby/Elsevier. Adapted with permission.

plays. The assessment was developed using Rasch analysis; all items have good to acceptable fit and conform to the expectation of the measurement model. The TOES results can become the basis for discussing a child's play environment with caregivers and making recommendations to improve support of the child's play.

Bronson and Bundy (2001) examined the reliability and validity of the TOES and correlated results from the TOES with the ToP. Using a sample of 160 children, both playfulness (ToP) and the environment's support of playfulness (TOES) were measured. A positive significant correlation was found between playfulness and environmental supportiveness. This relationship was stronger for children who were developing typically than for children with disabilities. All TOES items had good fit with the scale except physical safety, which seems unrelated to the playfulness of the environment (i.e., a playful environment may contain certain features that are unsafe). The TOES complements the ToP in understanding a child's play and in intervention planning to enhance a child's play.

Measures of the Adult Environments

In much of occupational therapy practice, environments are informally evaluated, with a focus on understanding the supports and constraints available within the environment. Few assessments of the environment have been developed, perhaps because environments are dynamic and complex and change rapidly over time and space. It often is difficult to determine how a person will move through environments over time and how environments will change over time. The environmental assessments that have been developed tend to focus on one environment (i.e., home *or* work) and tend to focus on a single problem (e.g., physical access, fall prevention, social participation). Assessments of the home environment have focused on barriers to function, particularly for people in wheelchairs or mobility devices, and safety for older adults who are at risk for falling or other injuries. These assessments often identify barriers and problems that need to be modified to promote optimal function and safety.

Measures of a person's work environment have been developed to identify potential environmental modifications that can increase safety, access, and optimal function. They assess the worker's perception of the social environment, including peer and supervisor support. Research has shown that a supportive work environment is predictive of employee productivity and well-being (Billings & Moos, 1982; Dorman, 2009).

The Housing Enabler

The Housing Enabler (Iwarsson & Slaug, 2001) was developed in Sweden to measure physical or architectural barriers as they relate to a person's specific functional limitations. A primary focus for the assessment is home accessibility of older people. In the first step of administration, the therapist identifies a profile of the person's functional limitation (three scales). In the second step, the therapist completes a detailed observation of the environment (four scales). The therapist then calculates an accessibility score. For each environmental barrier, a severity score can be derived; therefore, the severity of the problem can be predicted.

The Housing Enabler has strong content and construct validity and has been used internationally (Iwarsson & Isacsson, 1997; Iwarsson & Slaug, 2001). The assessment has undergone revisions and development for the past 15 years. Recently, Carlsson and colleagues (2009) revised The Housing Enabler so that it requires less time to administer. Using previously established databases, they eliminated redundant items or ones that did not contribute to the variance. They also used a panel of experts to judge which factors were most important to safety and accessibility. Through this process, key housing barriers that constitute the revised version of The Housing Enabler (reduced from 188 items to 61) were identified. Table 7.3 shows examples of items on The Housing Enabler.

The Housing Enabler appears to be useful in identifying barriers to accessibility, particularly for older adults. By identifying hazards and safety issues in the home, this assessment can help distinguish the safety issues that need to be modified to allow an older adult to successfully stay in his or her home.

Table 7.3. Examples of Barrier Items on The Housing Enabler

Outdoors	Indoors
Narrow paths	Stairs/different levels
Irregular walking surfaces	Narrow passages
Steep gradients	Narrow doors
High curbs	No handrails in stairs
No handrails	Handrails too short
Poor lighting	Shelves extremely high
Narrow door openings	Sitting heights inappropriate
High thresholds	Shelves too deep
Heavy doors	No place to sit in shower
Complicated opening procedures for doors	Missing grab bars in shower
No level area in front of entrance	Shower knobs too high
Mailbox difficult to reach	Different levels in bathroom

Note. Adapted from "Toward a Screening Tool for Housing Accessibility Problems," by G. Carlsson et al., 2009, *Journal of Applied Gerontology, 28*, 59–79. Copyright © 2009, by Southern Gerontological Society. Adapted with permission.

Safety Assessment of Function and the Environment for Rehabilitation

The Safety Assessment of Function and the Environment for Rehabilitation (SAFER; Chiu, Oliver, Marshall, & Letts, 2001) is a comprehensive assessment of a person's ability to function safely in the home. It identifies and describes safety concerns of individuals in their homes, assisting occupational therapists in planning interventions that will improve the safety of the home (Chiu et al., 2001). The SAFER has 97 assessment items divided into 14 safety domains: living situation, mobility, kitchen, fire hazards, eating, household, dressing, grooming, bathroom, medication, communication, wandering, memory aids, and general issues.

The SAFER is completed in about an hour by examining all rooms of the home; specific observations are made in specific areas of the home (e.g., bathroom, kitchen). When the tool is completed, the occupational therapist examines specific items for safety concerns, summarizing those concerns and suggesting interventions. The SAFER manual suggests interventions for various safety problems (Oliver, Chiu, Marshall, & Goldsilver, 2003) with the goal of enabling clients to stay in their homes by increasing their safety. The tool can also be used to interpret ways to improve a client's independence and increase quality of life (Oliver et al., 2003).

The Safety Assessment of Function and the Environment for Rehabilitation–Health Outcome Measurement and Evaluation (SAFER–HOME) was developed by Chiu and Oliver (2006) to increase the SAFER's sensitivity to change. By adding a 4-point scale *(no problem, mild problem, moderate problem, severe problem)* for rating each item, the SAFER–HOME can be used as an outcomes measure useful in measuring environmental changes due to intervention. Examples of the SAFER–HOME domains include client's impairment, homemaking support, emergency communication, functional communication, personal care, family assistance, and medication. Chui and Oliver (2006) examined the factor structure, internal consistency, and construct validity of the SAFER–HOME. They found good internal consistency of the total score with lower internal consistencies for the subscale scores. Because the subscores have low reliability, the authors recommended that they only be used to describe safety concerns.

Westmead Home Safety Assessment

The Westmead Home Safety Assessment (Clemson, 1997) allows the therapist to identify physical environmental factors that appear to be a fall hazard. Its goal is to identify fall hazards in the home environment of older adults. The assessment is completed by observation of the home environment, focusing on potential fall hazards. The Westmead Home Safety Assessment can be used in home-based services with older adults where fall risk is great. The assessment provides a comprehensive list of recommended modifications that can be made to improve the home's safety and to increase the likelihood that the client can continue to stay in his or her own home. Clemson, Fitzgerald, Heard, and Cumming (1999) examined the interrater reliability of the Westmead Home Safety Assessment and found that the kappa values for 21 pairs of raters was fair to excellent, with most items excellent.

Work Environment Impact Scale

The Work Environment Impact Scale (WEIS; Corner, Kielhofner, & Lin, 1997) assesses the experience of people with disabilities in their workplace. Both physical and social factors are considered, including transportation, safety, lighting, time, equipment, tools, sound, and architecture. In addition, social environment is assessed, including attitudes, social climate, social support, communication, and expectations. The WEIS is a semistructured interview that gathers information about how the worker experiences and perceives his or her workspace, objects, and social supports as these affect his or her work performance, satisfaction, and well-being. This 17-item assessment includes the impact of environmental features such as the accessibility, arrangement, design, comfort, and sensory qualities of workspaces on the worker. The social environment includes time and productivity demands, work schedules, coworker interactions, supervisor communication, and client and customer interactions. The items do not measure positive or negative aspects of the environment but instead measure the fit between the client and aspects of the environment.

In a study of construct validity and internal consistency using 20 persons with acute psychiatric disability who had held jobs within the past 6 months, Corner and colleagues (1997) found that the WEIS items measure one construct, although a few items appeared to overlap or to measure redundant information. The workers with higher satisfaction, performance, and health rated their environments higher. Revisions were made to the WEIS items and manual to improve the redundant items so that they measured distinct characteristics of the environment.

Work Environment Scale

The Work Environment Scale (WES; Moos, 1994) measures worker's perceptions of a workplace's social environment. This scale measures the influence of the work environment on employee morale and well-being. It includes 90 true–false statements about the work environment. Three work environment dimensions have been found useful in assessing a work setting: relationship, personal

Table 7.4. Domains and Subscales for the Work Environment Scale

Domain	Subscales	Description	Example Items
Personal growth	Autonomy Task orientation Work pressure	Extent to which the employee can structure the day, make independent decisions; degree that employees are focused on getting the job done; extent to which the pressures of work and time demands dominate the job	"Employees are encouraged to make their own decisions" "There's a lot of time wasted because of inefficiencies" "There is no time pressure"
Relationship	Involvement Peer cohesion Supervisor	Degree of employee commitment, attachment to the organization, challenging work, degree to which employees are supportive of one another, overall ambiance of the work environment, degree to which management is supportive and caring of the employee	"The work is really challenging" "People go out of their way to help a new employee feel comfortable" "Supervisors often criticize employees over minor things"
System maintenance and system change	Physical comfort Control Innovation Clarity	Environment factors such as lighting, decor, and workspace; extent to which management uses rules and pressure to keep employees under control; level of variety, change, and new approaches; extent to which employees know what to expect in their daily routines and how clearly rules and policies are communicated	"Activities are well planned" "People are expected to follow set rules in doing their work" "Doing things in a different way is valued" "Workspace is awfully crowded"

Note. Adapted from *Work Environment Scale Manual,* 3rd ed., by R. Moos, 1994, Palo Alto, CA: Consulting Psychologists Press. Copyright © 1994, by Consulting Pyschologists Press. Adapted with permission.

growth, and system maintenance and change. The relationship dimension measures the degree of interpersonal interaction in a work environment, such as the social communication exchanges and cohesion among workers, and the friendship and support provided by coworkers and management. Social support by peers and supervisors has been shown to influence individuals' personal functioning at work (Billings & Moos, 1982). The personal growth section assesses the degree to which an environment encourages or stifles growth through providing for participation in decision making and autonomy, maintaining a task orientation, and providing job challenge and expectations for success and accomplishment. The system maintenance section assesses whether the work setting is orderly and organized, establishes clear expectations, and maintains control. See Table 7.4 for a description of the WES scales and items.

The WES has been used in a number of work environment studies that have focused on staff burnout, employee satisfaction, and employee emotional health. It has studied job satisfaction and well-being among physicians (Woodside, Miller, Floyd, McGowen, & Pfortmiller, 2008), nurses (Day, Minichiello, & Madison, 2007; Kotzer, Koepping, & LeDuc, 2006), and teachers (Dorman, 2009). The WES has shown validity in predicting outcomes with employees in health care, military, and correctional facility environments (Moos, 1994). Reliability of the scale is good; Cronbach alphas for each of the 10 subscales varied from .69 to .86 and test–retest reliability from .69 to .83 (Moos, 1994).

Assessments of Environments Summary

Occupational therapists generally measure the person–environment fit informally by assessing daily occupations within the client's natural environment. Standardized measures of the environment can assist in identifying specific aspects of the environment that create barriers to function, present as safety hazards, or interfere with well-being and satisfaction. The measures of environment described in this section emphasize the transaction among the client's capabilities, occupations, and the environment and specifically assess qualities of the environment that enable or enhance occupations, health, and well-being. These assessments help occupational therapists plan intervention by identifying the environmental modifications that will promote safety, well-being, and occupational performance. As we learn more about how the environment directly influences occupations and health, measures of the environment will continue to be developed and refined. Clearly, occupational therapy researchers need to continue development and testing of environmental assessments.

Conclusion

By evaluating the client's participation in life roles, the occupational therapist can construct an occupational profile for that person that considers his or her natural contexts. This occupational profile provides the basis for the occupational therapist and client to identify priority goals and essential outcomes that become the focus of intervention. Participation assessments often use self-report or interview with the client, consider the client's everyday occupations and natural environments, and evaluate goal-directed activities. These assessments also may assess the client's satisfaction with participation and his or her perception of barriers.

Assessment of the client's environment is included in holistic evaluation of his or her occupations and participation. Assessments of a child's environments often focus on contextual factors that promote development of specific skills, such as play. Assessments of an adult's environments tend to measure safety, accessibility, comfort, and social supports. The measures described in this chapter are part of the occupational therapist's evaluation toolbox and enable a comprehensive understanding of a client's occupations, the constraints and supports in the environment, and the ability of the client to participate across environments.

Questions

1. Why is client-centered evaluation important to an occupational therapist's evaluation process? How does it complement observational assessments of performance?
2. What is the purpose of the PEGS? Do parents and children often agree on the goals they select for the child's program?
3. The COPM measures a person's perception and satisfaction with performance. Discuss the research on the COPM's reliability and validity.
4. Discuss using the COPM to compare progress among different clients. Discuss using the COPM to measure progress across time for an individual client.
5. Explain what the CAPE/PAC measures. How would you use the CAPE and PAC results to identify intervention goals?
6. Compare the SFA with the PEDI. What is the contextual focus of each? What occupations are included in each? Both assessments consider task or activity supports; how does each scale rate activity supports?
7. Describe the Function and Disability subscales of the LLFDI. Compare the LLFDI with the London Handicap Scale.

References

American Occupational Therapy Association. (2008). Occupational therapy practice framework: Domain and process (2nd ed.). *American Journal of Occupational Therapy, 62,* 625–683.

Barbara, A., & Whiteford, G. (2005). The clinical utility of the Handicap Assessment and Resource Tool: An investigation of the use with the aged in hospital. *Australian Occupational Therapy Journal, 52,* 17–25.

Baron, K., Kielhofner, G., Iyenger, A., Goldhammer, V., & Wolenski, J. (2003). *The user's manual of the OSA* (Version 2.1). Chicago: Model of Human Occupation Clearinghouse, Department of Occupational Therapy, College of Applied Health Sciences, University of Illinois.

Baum, C. M., & Edwards, D. (2001). *Activity Card Sort.* St. Louis, MO: Washington University.

Baum, C. M., & Edwards, D. (2008). *Activity Card Sort* (2nd ed.). Bethesda, MD: AOTA Press.

Billings, A. G., & Moos, R. H. (1982). Social support and functioning among community and clinical groups: A panel model. *Journal of Behavioral Medicine, 5,* 295–311.

Bradley R. H., & Caldwell, B. M. (1994). The HOME inventory and family demographics. *Developmental Psychology, 20,* 315–320.

Bradley, R. H., Caldwell, B. M., Rock, S. L., Barnard, K. E., Gray, C., Hammond, M. A., et al. (1989). Home environment and cognitive development in the first 3 years of life: A collaborative study involving six sites and three ethnic groups in North America. *Developmental Psychology, 25,* 217–235.

Bradley, R. H., Corwyn, R. F., McAdoo, H. P., & Garcia Coll, C. (2001). The home environments of children in the United States: Part I. Variations by age, ethnicity, and poverty status. *Child Development, 72,* 1844–1867.

Bradley, R. H., Corwyn, R. F., & Whiteside-Mansell, L. (1996). Life at home: Same time, different places—An examination of the HOME Inventory in different cultures. *Early Development and Parenting, 5,* 251–269.

Bronson, M. R., & Bundy, A. C. (2001). A correlation study of a Test of Playfulness and a Test of Environmental Supportiveness for play. *Occupational Therapy Journal of Research, 21,* 241–259.

Bundy, A. (1997). Play and playfulness: What to look for. In L. D. Parham & L. S. Fazio (Eds.), *Play in occupational therapy for children* (pp. 36–62). St. Louis, MO: Mosby.

Bundy, A. (1999). *Test of Environmental Supportiveness.* Ft. Collins: Colorado State University.

Caldwell, B., & Bradley, R. (1984). *Home Observation for Measurement of the Environment.* Little Rock: University of Arkansas.

Canadian Association of Occupational Therapists. (1997). *Enabling occupation: An occupational therapy perspective.* Ottawa, Ontario, Canada: CAOT Publications.

Carlsson, G., Schilling, O., Slaug, R., Fange, A., Stahl, A., Nygren, C., et al. (2009). Toward a screening tool for housing accessibility problems. *Journal of Applied Gerontology, 28,* 59–79.

Carswell, A., McColl, M. A., Baptiste, S., Law, M., Polatajko, H., & Pollock, N. (2004). The COPM: A research and clinical review. *Canadian Journal of Occupational Therapy, 71,* 210–222.

Chiu, T., & Oliver, R. (2006). Factor analysis and construct validity of the SAFER–HOME. *OTJR: Occupation, Participation, and Health, 26,* 132–141.

Chiu, T., Oliver, R., Marshall, L., & Letts, L. (2001). *Safety Assessment of Function and the Environment for Rehabilitation (SAFER) tool manual.* Toronto, Ontario, Canada: COTA Comprehensive Rehabilitation and Mental Health Services.

Clemson, L. (1997). *Home fall hazards: A guide to identifying fall hazards in the homes of elderly people and an accompaniment to the assessment tool, the Westmead Home Safety Assessment (WeHSA).* West Brunswick, Victoria, Australia: Co-ordinates Publications.

Clemson, L., Fitzgerald, M. H., Heard, R., & Cumming, R. G. (1999). Inter-rater reliability of a home fall hazards assessment tool. *Occupational Therapy Journal of Research, 19,* 83–100.

Corner, R. A., Kielhofner, G., & Lin, F-L. (1997). Construct validity of a work environment impact scale. *Work, 9,* 21–24.

Coster, W., Deeney, T., Haltiwanger, I., & Haley, S. (1998). *School Function Assessment.* San Antonio, TX: Psychological Corporation.

Coster, W., & Khetani, M. A. (2008). Measuring participation of children with disabilities: Issues and challenges. *Disability and Rehabilitation, 30,* 639–648.

Davies, P. L., Soon, P. L., Young, M., Clausen-Yamaki, A., Davies, P. L., Soon, P. L., et al. (2004). Validity and reliability of the School Function Assessment in elementary school students with disabilities. *Physical and Occupational Therapy in Pediatrics, 24*(3), 23–43.

Day, G., Minichiello, V., & Madison, J. (2007). Self-reported perceptions of registered nurses working Australian hospitals. *Journal of Nursing Management, 15,* 403–413.

Dijkers, M. (1997). Quality of life after spinal cord injury: A meta analysis of the effects of disablement components. *Spinal Cord, 35,* 829–840.

Dorman, J. P. (2009). Statistical tests conducted with school environment data: The effect of teachers being clustered in schools. *Learning Environments Research, 12,* 85–99.

Dubuc, N., Haley, S., Ni, P., Kooyoomjian, J., & Jette, A. M. (2004). Function and disability in late life: Comparison of the Late-Life Function and Disability Instrument to the Short-Form–36 and the London Handicap Scale. *Disability and Rehabilitation, 28,* 362–370.

Fougeyrollas, P., Noreau, L., Bergeron, H., Cloutier, R., Dion, S. A., & St-Michel, G. (1998). Social consequences of long-term impairments and disabilities: Conceptual approach and assessment of handicap. *International Journal of Rehabilitation Research, 21,* 127–141.

Haley, S. M., Coster, W. J., Ludlow, L. H., Haltiwanger, J. T., & Andrellos, P. F. (1992). *Pediatric Evaluation of Disability Inventory (PEDI).* San Antonio, TX: Psychological Corporation.

Haley, S. M., Jette, A. M., Coster, W. J., Kooyoomjian, J. T., Levenson, S., Heeren, T., et al. (2002). Late Life Function and Disability Instrument–II: Development and evaluation of the function component. *Journals of Gerontology Series A—Biological Sciences and Medical Sciences, 57*(4), M217–M222.

Hall, K., Kijkers, M., Whiteneck, G., Brooks, C. A., & Krause, J. S. (1998). The Craig Handicap Assessment and Reporting Technique (CHART): Metric properties and scoring. *Top Spinal Cord Injury and Rehabilitation, 4,* 16–30.

Hwang, J., Davies, P. L., Taylor, M. P., & Gavin, W. J. (2002). Validation of School Function Assessment with elementary school children. *Occupational Therapy Journal of Research, 22*(2), 1–11.

Iwarsson, S., & Isacsson, A. (1997). Quality of life in the elderly population: An example exploring interrelationships among subjective well-being, ADL dependence, and housing accessibility. *Archives of Gerontology and Geriatrics, 26,* 71–83.

Iwarsson, S., & Slaug, B. (2001). *The Housing Enabler. An instrument for assessing and analysing accessibility problems in housing.* Nävlinge and Staffanstorp, Sweden: Veten & Skapen HB & Slaug Data Management.

Iyer, I. V., Haley, S. M., Watkins, M. P., & Dumas, H. M. (2003). Establishing minimal clinically important differences for scores on the Pediatric Evaluation of Disability Inventory for inpatient rehabilitation. *Physical Therapy, 83,* 888–898.

Jenkinson, C., Mant, J., Carter, J., Wade, D., & Winner, S. (2000). The London Handicap Scale: A re-evaluation of its validity using standard scoring and simple summation. *Journal of Neurology, Neurosurgery, and Psychiatry, 68*(3), 365–367.

Jette, A. M., Haley, S. M., Coster, W. J., Kooyoomjian, J. T., Levenson, S., Heeren, T., et al. (2002). Late life function and disability instrument: I. Development and evaluation of the disability component. *Journals of Gerontology Series A—Biological Sciences and Medical Sciences, 57*(4), M209–M216.

Katz, N., Karpin, H., Lak, A., Furman, T., & Hartman-Maeir, A. (2003). Participation in occupational performance: Reliability and validity of the Activity Card Sort. *OTJR: Occupation, Participation, and Health, 23,* 10–17.

Keller, J., Kafkes, A., Basu, S., Federico, J., & Kielhofner, G. (2004). *The Child Occupational Self-Assessment* (COSA; Version 2.0). Chicago: Model of Human Occupation Clearinghouse, Department of Occupational Therapy, College of Applied Health Sciences, University of Illinois.

Kielhofner, G. (2008). *Model of Human Occupation: Theory and application* (4th ed.). Baltimore: Lippincott Williams & Wilkins.

Kielhofner, G., & Forsyth, K. (2001). Measurement properties of a client self-report for treatment planning and documenting occupational therapy outcomes. *Scandinavian Journal of Occupational Therapy, 8,* 131–139.

Kielhofner, G., Mallinson, T., Forsyth, K., & Lai, J-S. (2001). Psychometric properties of the second version of the Occupational Performance History Interview (OPHI–II). *American Journal of Occupational Therapy, 53,* 260–267.

King, G., Law, M., King, S., Hurley, P., Hanna, S., Kertoy, M., et al. (2004). *Children's Assessment of Participation and Enjoyment (CAPE) and Preferences for Activities of Children (PAC).* San Antonio, TX: Harcourt Assessment.

Kotzer, A. M., Koepping, D. M., & LeDuc, K. (2006). Perceived nursing work environment of acute care pediatric nurses. *Pediatric Nursing, 32,* 327–332.

Law, M. (1998). Does client-centered practice make a difference? In M. Law (Ed.), *Client-centered occupational therapy* (pp. 19–29). Thorofare, NJ: Slack.

Law, M. (2002). Distinguished scholar lecture. Participation in the occupations of everyday life. *American Journal of Occupational Therapy, 56,* 640–649.

Law, M. C., Baptiste, S., Carswell-Opzoomer, A., McColl, M. A., Polatajko, H., & Pollock, N. (1991). *The Canadian Occupational Performance Measure.* Toronto, Ontario, Canada: CAOT Publications.

Law, M. C., Baptiste, S., Carswell, A., McColl, M. A., Polatajko, H., & Pollock, N. (1998/2004). *The Canadian Occupational Performance Measure* (4th ed.). Toronto: CAOT Publications.

Law, M., Cooper, B., Strong, S., Stewart, D., Rigby, P., & Letts, L. (1996). Person–environment–occupation model: A transactive approach to occupational performance. *Canadian Journal of Occupational Therapy, 63,* 9–23.

Law, M., Dunn, W., & Baum, C. (2005). Measuring participation. In M. Law, C. Baum, & W. Dunn (Eds.), *Measuring occupational performance: Supporting best practice in occupational therapy* (2nd ed., pp. 107–128). Thorofare, NJ: Slack.

Law, M., King, G., King, S., Kertoy, M., Hurley, P., Rosenbaum, P., et al. (2006). Patterns of participation in recreational and leisure activities among children with complex physical disabilities. *Developmental Medicine and Child Neurology, 48,* 337–342.

Law, M., & Mills, J. (1998). Client-centered occupational therapy. In M. Law (Ed.), *Client-centered occupational therapy* (pp. 1–18). Thorofare, NJ: Slack.

McColl, M.A., & Pollock, N. (2005). Measuring occupational performance using a client-centered perspective. In M. Law, C. Baum, & W. Dunn (Eds.), *Measuring occupational performance: Supporting best practice in occupational therapy* (2nd ed., pp. 81–92). Thorofare, NJ: Slack.

Missiuna, C., & Pollock, N. (2000). Perceived efficacy and goal setting in young children. *Canadian Journal of Occupational Therapy, 67*(2), 101–109.

Moos, R. (1994). *Work Environment Scale manual* (3rd ed.). Palo Alto, CA: Consulting Psychologists Press.

Nichols, D., & Case-Smith, J. (1996). Reliability and validity of the Pediatric Evaluation of Disability Inventory. *Pediatric Physical Therapy, 8,* 15–24.

Nordmark, E., Jarnio, G., & Hagglund, G. (2000). Comparison of the Gross Motor Function Measure and Pediatric Evaluation of Disability Inventory in assessing motor function in children undergoing selective dorsal rhizotomy. *Developmental Medicine and Child Neurology, 42,* 245–252.

Noreau, K., Desrosiers, J., Robichaud, L., Fougeyrollas, P., Rochette, A., & Viscogliosi, C. (2004). Measuring social participation: Reliability of the LIFE–H in older adults with disabilities. *Disability and Rehabilitation, 26,* 345–352.

Oliver, R., Chiu, T., Marshall, L., & Goldsilver, P. (2003). Home safety assessment and intervention practice. *International Journal of Therapy and Rehabilitation, 10,* 144–150.

Rogers, J., & Holm, M. (2009). The occupational therapy process. In E. B. Crepeau, E. S. Cohn, & B. A. B. Schell (Eds.), *Willard and Spackman's occupational therapy* (11th ed., pp. 428–434). Philadelphia: Lippincott Williams & Wilkins.

Sachs, D., & Josman, N. (2003). The Activity Card Sort: A factor analysis. *OTJR: Occupation, Participation, and Health, 23,* 165–176.

Salter, K., Foley, N., Jutai, J., Bayley, M., & Teasell, R. (2008). Assessment of community integration following traumatic brain injury. *Brain Injury, 22,* 820–835.

Skard, G., & Bundy, A. C. (2008). Test of Playfulness. In L. D. Parham & L. S. Fazio (Eds.), *Play in occupational therapy for children* (2nd ed., pp. 71–94). St. Louis, MO: Mosby/Elsevier.

Uniform Data System for Medical Rehabilitation. (2009). *Functional Independence Measure.* Buffalo: State University of New York.

Vertesi, A., Darzins, P., Lowe, S., McEvoy, E., & Edwards, M. (2000). Development of the Handicap Assessment and Resource Tool (HART). *Canadian Journal of Occupational Therapy, 67,* 120–127.

Walker, N., Mellick, D., Brooks, C. A., & Whiteneck, G. G. (2003). Measuring participation across impairment groups using the Craig Handicap Assessment and Reporting Technique. *American Journal of Physical Medicine and Rehabilitation, 82,* 936–941.

Whiteneck, G., Charlifue, S., Gerhart, K., Overholser, D., & Richardson, G. (1992). Quantifying handicap: A new measure of long-term rehabilitation outcomes. *Archives of Physical Medicine and Rehabilitation, 73*, 519–526.

Whiteneck, G., Tate, D., & Charlifue, S. (1999). Predicting community reintegration after spinal cord injury from demographic and injury characteristics. *Archives of Physical Medicine and Rehabilitation, 80*, 1485–1491.

Wilcox, A. A. (1998). Reflections on doing, being, and becoming. *Canadian Journal of Occupational Therapy, 65*, 148–157.

Willer, B., Ottenbacher, K. J., & Coad, M. L. (1994). Community Integration Questionnaire. *American Journal of Physical Medicine and Rehabilitation, 73*, 103–111.

Woodside, J. R., Miller, M. N., Floyd, M. R., McGowen, K. R., & Pfortmiller, D. T. (2008). Observations on burnout in family medicine and psychiatry residents. *Academic Psychiatry, 32*, 13–19.

World Health Organization. (2001). *International classification of functioning, disability and health*. Geneva: Author.

Wright, F. V., & Boschen, K. A. (1993). The Pediatric Evaluation of Disability Inventory (PEDI): Validation of a new functional assessment outcome instrument. *Canadian Journal of Rehabilitation, 7*, 41–42.

Yerxa, E. J. (1967). Authentic occupational therapy. *American Journal of Occupational Therapy, 21*, 1–9.

Zevalkink, J., Riksen-Walraven, J. M., & Bradley, R. H. (2008). The quality of children's home environment and attachment security in Indonesia. *Journal of Genetic Psychology, 169*, 72–91.

Zhang, L., Abreu, B., Gonzales, V., Seale, G., Masel, B., & Ottenbacher, K. (2002). Comparison of the Community Integration Questionnaire, the Craig Handicap Assessment and Reporting Technique and the Disability Rating Scale in Traumatic Brain Injury. *Journal of Head Trauma Rehabilitation, 17*, 497–509.

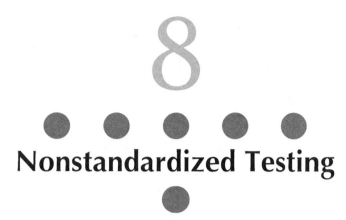

Nonstandardized Testing

Aimee J. Luebben, EdD, OTR, FAOTA
Charlotte Brasic Royeen, PhD, OTR, FAOTA

Overview

This chapter begins with an introduction to nonstandardized testing as a method of information gathering, including a comparison of nonstandardized to standardized assessment instruments. It then discusses why, when, and how occupational therapists use nonstandardized testing. The remainder of the chapter reviews nonstandardized testing methods in four major testing categories: observation, interview, questionnaire, and performance test.

Standardized Versus Nonstandardized Testing

What makes an assessment tool standardized? According to Anastasi and Urbina (1997), "Standardization implies uniformity of procedure in administering and scoring the test" (p. 6). *Standardization* means that each time an occupational therapist administers a standardized assessment, the tool is given in the same manner and is scored in the same manner. Standardization also means that the environmental conditions under which the assessment tool is administered are prescribed. Standardized assessments have psychometric data regarding their reliability and validity. In addition, most standardized assessments can be categorized as either criterion-referenced or norm-referenced. A *criterion-referenced* instrument allows comparison of the results for an individual to a criterion, also called a *standard*. A *norm-referenced* tool allows comparison of the results for an individual to a group of people, often people with similar characteristics and/or conditions. A standardized assessment instrument used in a manner not prescribed in the manual may no longer be considered standardized. To compare characteristics of nonstandardized and standardized assessment instruments, see Table 8.1.

Table 8.1. Comparison of Nonstandardized and Standardized Assessment Characteristics

Characteristic	Nonstandardized Assessment	Standardized Assessment
Focus	Ipsative-referenced	Norm-referenced
		Criterion-referenced
	Individual, system	Standard, groups
	Individualized, self	Others
Personal	Intrapersonal	Interpersonal
Setting	Naturalistic	Laboratory controlled, prescribed
Type of evidence	Individuated	Class
Examples	• DNA	• Blood type
	• Fingerprints	• Percentile rank
	• Performance observation	• Standard score
	• Ethnographic observation	• Derived score
Data generated	Qualitative and quantitative	Primarily quantitative
Procedures	Less formal	Formal
Structure	Less structured	More structured
Clinical reasoning	Requires strong clinical reasoning for assessment and interpretation	Less dependent on clinical reasoning for administration and interpretation
Validity	Strong internal validity	Strong external validity

Nonstandardized assessment tools may not be uniform in administration or scoring. In addition, full and complete psychometric data about the assessment tool may not exist. Because nonstandardized testing is not built on prescribed processes of administration and scoring, it allows for flexibility and individualization. Just as standardized tools are norm-referenced or criterion-referenced, nonstandardized tests are individualized. Individualized can also be called ipsative-referenced; the word *ipsative* (ipsitive is an alternate spelling) is Latin for herself, himself, or itself. Anastasi and Urbina (1997) stated,

> While the ipsative frame of reference may be the most suitable for intra-individual comparisons, such as those needed in the assessment of interests and other preferences, normative reference data are necessary for the sort of interindividual comparisons used, for example, in the assessment of ab-normality. (p. 370)

Nonstandardized assessments using an ipsative reference provide unique opportunities for occupational therapists to delve deeply into the individual or a group within the natural environment. Just as research methods evolve to meet a particular field's need, methods of assessment develop in response to a discipline's need. For occupational therapy evaluation, ipsative-referenced nonstandardized assessment tools are becoming more recognized and useful as individualized assessment instruments. In fact, Donnelly and Carswell (2002) reviewed the literature to report on individualized outcomes measures that are client-centered.

Why Use Nonstandardized Testing?

Nonstandardized testing results in the collection of individuated information that can be traced to a single entity. Individuated evidence (e.g., fingerprints; DNA; a well-written, detailed performance observation) provides strong internal validity: The information collected is indicative of a person's uniqueness, an intrapersonal comparison. If interpersonal comparisons are the goal, then occupational therapists need to use standardized assessment tools that have strong external validity. A standardized assessment allows comparison of a person's ability, behavior, performance, and so on to a standard (criterion-referenced) or a group (norm-referenced). The resulting information from many standardized assessments, however, is considered class evidence: classification within a category (e.g., blood type, perceptual–motor percentile). Class evidence does not offer the corresponding intrapersonal uniqueness that individuated evidence provides.

Evidence-Based Practice and Nonstandardized Testing

Evidence is at the center of evidence-based practice, a movement driving many health care disciplines. Although occupational therapy is currently focused on empirical research as the primary and sometimes only approach to evidence-based practice, Ilott (2004) differentiated three distinctive evidence-based practice approaches: empirical research, experiential evidence, and theoretical knowledge. She observed that "It is important to . . . remember that all sources of evidence—whether from theory, experience, or research—are equally valid" (Ilott, 2004, p. 348). Using empirical research alone to drive evidence-based practice would be a disservice to the people who occupational therapy serves and be potentially harmful to the profession of occupational therapy. Occupational therapists who generalize their strong theoretical foundation to synthesize experiential evidence gained through evaluation—including nonstandardized testing—are using two of the three approaches to evidence-based practice.

Controlling Bias and Nonstandardized Testing

The goal of any type of testing—standardized or nonstandardized—is to ascertain some aspect of the individual being evaluated. To achieve this goal, the evaluator is obligated to control for as much testing variance or bias as possible. The acronym PIE can help occupational therapists remember three aspects of testing bias—*person*, *item*, and *environment*. There are two types of *person-related* (the *p* in PIE) testing bias: evaluator or rater bias and test-taker bias. To determine actual occupational performance, an evaluator must control for his or her expectations and rating tendencies that could result in error: severity/leniency, central tendency, and halo effect. For the evaluator to gather critical information, the person being tested must demonstrate genuineness in any performance and be a good *historian* (a person who provides the truth about a situation) when responding to questions. The middle letter (*i*) of PIE signifies *item bias*, which involves the degree to which the specific element being tested fits the actual occupation the test-taker performs in real life. *Environment* (the *e* of PIE) relates to the degree to which the testing context matches the natural environment. In addition to the three aspects of bias, there is a certain unnaturalness in the observation event itself, which can lead to testing variance and possible error.

To apply PIE to a testing situation, consider the example of Mr. O'Neill, an 83-year-old widower who usually brushes his teeth alone in the bathroom of his home. Marty, an occupational therapist testing this task in a hospital setting, needed to control for all three aspects of PIE testing bias. To reduce testing error, both types of person bias would need extra attention: Marty would need to control for her expectations and rating tendencies and determine Mr. O'Neill's genuineness and historian abilities in his response to her questions about the toothpaste container (manual squeeze or pump) and toothbrush (manual or battery-operated). Marty's presence in observing Mr. O'Neill may result in him performing this seemingly mundane task differently than usual. Just by changing context—by observing Mr. O'Neill in his home—she could eliminate environment bias, and most of the bias related to item and to the person, especially related to the person being tested. The variance corresponding to observer presence, however, would remain.

The outcomes (e.g., behaviors) of nonstandardized assessment must be double-checked to make certain the findings are considered usual, typical, average, and representative (Brentnall & Bundy, 2009). Making nonstandardized testing as systematic as possible and controlling for bias can result in objective information that has great relevance to the client receiving occupational therapy services.

Organizing Structures and Nonstandardized Testing

Nonstandardized testing can be used with various naming systems (taxonomies) and theoretical approaches that provide an organizing structure for evaluation. The American Occupational Therapy Association (AOTA) provides a system of naming the various aspects of the occupational therapy profession's domain of concern in the *Occupational Therapy Practice Framework, 2nd Edition* (*Framework–II;* AOTA, 2008). Nonstandardized testing can be used to assess the *Framework–II* aspects that include areas of occupation, client factors, performance skills, performance patterns, contexts and environment, and activity demands. Nonstandardized assessment can be used on a global scale by using the World Health Organization's (WHO's) system: the *International Classification of Functioning, Disability and Health* (*ICF;* WHO, 2001). In the ICF, areas for nonstandardized testing include assessment of a person's participation or involvement in a life situation, activity limitations or challenges an individual may have in executing activities, participation restrictions or challenges an individual may experience when engaged in life situations, and external and internal influences related to a person's functioning. Nonstandardized testing also can be used with theoretical approaches that have an organizing structure. For example, the Canadian Model of Occupational Performance (CMOP; Canadian Association of Occupational Therapists [CAOT], 1997) provides structure to allow assessment of person, environment, and occupation (P–E–O). For the CMOP (CAOT, 1997), *Framework–II* (AOTA, 2008), and *ICF* (WHO, 2001), Figure 8.1 provides a comparison of three aspects: life areas (occupation), foundational components (body-level), and contextual factors.

Nonstandardized Testing Components

When thinking about using a nonstandardized assessment, the occupational therapist should consider three important components: elements of nonstan-

	CMOP (CAOT, 1997)	Framework–II (AOTA, 2008)	ICF (WHO, 2001)
Life Areas (Occupations)	**Occupation**: Self-care, Productivity, Leisure	**Areas of Occupation**: Activities of daily living, Instrumental activities of daily living, Rest and sleep, Education, Work, Play, Leisure, Social participation	**Activities and Participation (Daily Life Area Domains)**: Learning and applying knowledge, General tasks and demands, Communication, Mobility, Self-care, Domestic life, Interpersonal interactions and relationships, Major life areas, Community, social, and civic life
Foundational (Body-Level) Components	**Person**: Spirituality; Physical, Cognitive, Affective	Client factors, Performance skills, Performance patterns, Activity demands	**Body Functions and Structures**: Mental, Sensory, Voice and speech, Cardiovascular, hematological, immunological, and respiratory, Digestive, metabolic, and endocrine, Genitourinary and reproductive, Neuromusculoskeletal and movement-related, Skin and related structures
Contextual Factors	**Environment**: Physical, Institutional, Cultural, Social	**Context and Environment**: Cultural, Personal, Physical, Social, Temporal, Virtual	**Contextual Factors** — **Environmental Factors**: Products and technology, Natural environment and human-made changes to the environment, Support and relationships, Attitudes, Services, systems, and policies; **Personal Factors**

Figure 8.1. Comparison of the CMOP (CAOT, 1997), *Framework–II* (AOTA, 2008), and *ICF* (WHO, 2001).

dardized testing, operations of nonstandardized testing, and outcomes of non-standardized testing. Each component will be discussed in turn.

Elements of nonstandardized testing refers to the characteristics of tools, including centeredness, equipment and supplies, training, invasiveness, responsivity, needs, and expenses. Nonstandardized testing

- Is client-centered. *Client* is defined as "a person, group, program, organization, or community for whom the occupational therapy practitioner is providing services" (AOTA, 1995, p. 1029).
- Involves equipment that is often highly portable and usually does not involve the purchase of additional supplies and equipment. Some standardized tools require that buyers purchase additional equipment (e.g., a tricycle) not included in test kits.
- Does not typically require extensive training or certification for use. For some standardized assessments, costs are incurred not only with the instrument, but also for training in the use of the instrument.
- Is typically noninvasive and involves little risk.
- Permits responsivity to change. In many cases, standardized instruments do not have enough sensitivity to detect small changes observed by the occupational therapist. In cases when standardized testing results might indicate that a client has reached a plateau, nonstandardized testing may be responsive enough to ascertain small outcome changes in the performance of a client.
- Fulfills unmet need. It is appropriate when a standardized assessment related to a specific occupational performance aspect does not exist.
- Is inexpensive. Many standardized assessment instruments are costly; after buying the initial tool, individual test or scoring forms must be purchased on an ongoing basis.

Operations of nonstandardized assessments refers to the manner of administering the tool, including ease of administration, time, environment, ease of analysis, and clinical reasoning. Nonstandardized testing

- Is relatively easy to administer. The procedural steps in administering nonstandardized tests are usually straightforward, compared to the complex procedures of some standardized tests.
- Takes less time to administer in comparison with many standardized assessment instruments, but may take more time to document. Taking care to select unique language to describe testing and test results is the reason why documentation time of nonstandardized testing may be longer.
- Is typically conducted in the client's natural environments. Using natural environments helps control for the environmental aspect of PIE testing bias. For example, observing a child in the classroom provides assessment information about a student in an environment that is natural to the child.
- Is relatively easy to analyze. Unlike standardized assessment instruments, which often have complex scoring procedures that frequently take a great deal of time, nonstandardized testing often allows for simple analysis.

- Involves clinical reasoning for interpretation. Interpreting nonstandardized testing may require considerable clinical expertise to provide an understanding of multiple data points. Some standardized assessment tools, however, substitute computer scoring and interpretation for professional clinical reasoning.

Outcomes of nonstandardized assessments refers to the manner of administering tools, including validity of findings for an individual, control of PIE bias, and validity of findings from natural environments. Nonstandardized testing

- Provides valid results for an individual client. Nonstandardized testing taps into the uniqueness of an individual, offering assessment results with strong internal validity.
- Offers opportunities to control for the person aspect of PIE testing bias, particularly evaluator or rater variance, by establishing rater reliability. A single occupational therapist can start with intrarater reliability by making sure he or she performs nonstandardized assessment methods the same way each time. Interrater reliability can be established across all therapists within a practice setting. Within clinical settings, all occupational therapists can formalize establishment of interrater reliability for commonly used nonstandardized testing methods. In fact, formalizing a system to assure and document interrater reliability competence across therapists in a practice setting can serve to fulfill some requirements mandated by national agencies that accredit hospitals and clinics.
- Provides information related to naturally occurring behaviors. Instead of testing performance based on sterile conditions or contexts (sometimes associated with standardized assessment instruments), assessing behaviors that occur naturally can help control for the item aspect of PIE testing bias.

When To Use Nonstandardized Testing

Nonstandardized testing is used throughout the occupational therapy process, both at the information-gathering stages of screening and evaluation and after the initial information-gathering stages: during intervention planning, intervention, and reevaluation. During the screening and evaluating process, nonstandardized assessment tools can be used to collect information for both parts of the *Framework–II*'s evaluation process: the occupational profile and the analysis of occupational performance (AOTA, 2008).

Using nonstandardized testing is common during screening, a time when occupational therapists collect information related to a potential client to determine the need for further evaluation and the possibility of intervention. Not intended as a comprehensive evaluation, screening provides preliminary information to determine whether further occupational therapy services are needed. Screening typically involves observation and interview, two nonstandardized assessment tool categories. Nonstandardized screening in a school setting may consist of observing a student on the playground or interviewing the teacher to gather information related to the background and basis for the occupational therapy referral. In an adult day care setting, an occupational therapist might perform a screening during a group craft activity to identify individuals who are interested and have the functional capacity to participate in a gardening group.

During evaluation, the other initial information-gathering stage, occupational therapists use nonstandardized testing alone or in an integrated approach by using nonstandardized assessment methods to supplement standardized assessment instruments. Although the recommendations and examples of nonstandardized testing provided later in this chapter can be used for either screening or evaluation, the level of detail of certain methods is more relevant for evaluation.

Nonstandardized testing is also used after the initial information gathering stages: during intervention planning, intervention, and reevaluation. Occupational therapists interpret nonstandardized testing results to plan intervention and use nonstandardized methods—primarily observation, interview, and performance testing—to monitor progress during intervention. At the time of reevaluation, occupational therapists compare the client's performance with initial results to gauge improvement. Nonstandardized testing can play a significant role in the area of reevaluation to determine the effectiveness of occupational therapy.

How To Use Nonstandardized Testing

The appropriate and effective use of nonstandardized testing requires the occupational therapist to have a solid theoretical knowledge base and sound clinical reasoning, two of the three evidence-based practice approaches. Using nonstandardized assessment instruments appropriately and effectively is dependent upon selection and use of tools in four major categories: observation, interview, questionnaire, and performance test. For effective use of nonstandardized testing, Table 8.2 provides questions and directions.

Nonstandardized Testing Categories

The two most common forms of nonstandardized testing are observation and interview. The two remaining categories—performance test and questionnaire—have less coverage in this chapter because observation is often used as a method of collecting performance testing information and interviews often include a questionnaire component. Box 8.1 provides a process that expert occupational therapists use before, during, and after evaluation to improve validity.

Observation

Observation, which comes from the Latin *observo* (meaning to watch, pay attention to, and take careful note of) has come to signify a systematic examination of some type of phenomenon. In occupational therapy, observation is

Table 8.2. Effective Use of Nonstandardized Testing

Question	Directions
1. What is the theory base?	Base all information gathering on theory. Because theory and practice must be linked consistently, theory needs to provide the foundation for evaluation and intervention. Theoretical knowledge is one of three approaches to providing evidence-based practice.
2. How does nonstandardized testing relate to evidence-based practice?	Use an ipsative, client-centered approach to underpin nonstandardized information gathering. According to Ilott (2004), "The perspective of the patient and their caregivers is a critical component of experiential evidence, especially their views about what constitutes desirable or successful outcomes" (p. 348). Experiential evidence (the product of occupational therapy clinical reasoning) is one of the three approaches to providing evidence-based practice.
3. What organizing structure (e.g., taxonomy) is being used, and how is the nonstandardized testing relevant?	Select the nonstandardized testing method based on relevance to what is being measured and the organizing structure being used. For example, an occupational therapist using the *ICF* (WHO, 2001) would choose a method to assess (a) the two components of functioning and disability (activities and participation, body functions and structures) or (b) the two components of contextual factors (environmental factors, personal factors). Another example is a therapist who uses the *Framework–II* (AOTA, 2008) to assess areas of occupation, client factors, performance skills, performance patterns, context and environment, and activity demands.
4. What are the sources of nonstandardized testing, and how are assessment data triangulated?	Use multiple assessment tools in testing a client. Although a therapist-designed checklist can offer some information about a person, documenting observations adds to the richness of data collection. Using more than one testing tool allows occupational therapists to triangulate the data collection process, fulfilling the nonstandardized testing goal: determining the actual occupational performance of the person being tested.
5. How will the client be monitored during nonstandardized testing?	Use assessment tools as means to an end, never as an end in themselves. Occupational therapists should be sensitive to client cues and careful not to stress, fatigue, or invade the personal and cultural space of a client. Therapists can reschedule the session, stop and take a break, or switch to a different information-gathering approach if client cues indicate need for change.
6. How does nonstandardized testing accommodate diversity?	Respect the diverse nature of humans who vary in gender, class, cultural background, and many other ways. Sensitivity to diversity can be addressed by selecting nonstandardized assessment tools that allow for variation in client response. Nonstandardized assessments provide individuated evidence, not class evidence. Therefore, when working with individuals of diverse backgrounds, nonstandardized assessment tools may be the preferred method of testing to accommodate cultural differences and offer cultural sensitivity.

(Continued)

Table 8.2. Effective Use of Nonstandardized Testing (*cont.*)

Question	Directions
7. What is the secret of getting true nonstandardized testing results?	Establish rapport with the client. When gathering information about people, especially through nonstandardized testing, rapport is crucial. For a variety of reasons, an occupational therapist who is highly skilled in the interpersonal aspect of clinical reasoning may not be able to establish rapport that is optimal to the assessment session. Regardless of the level of rapport established, the nonstandardized testing documentation must include information about the status of rapport to help readers interpret adequacy and accuracy of testing information.

Box 8.1. Validity Format

Before the assessment, ask
- Am I biasing this assessment in any way?

During the assessment, monitor autonomic nervous system functioning of the person:
- Is the person unduly stressed (sweating, repetitive behavior, self-stimulating, fast breathing, blanching)?
- Are the responses consistent? Does the message from body language match message from verbal statements?
- Are there signs of fatigue?

After the assessment, ask
- Was this a novel experience for the person?
- Did an event occur that could change the findings of the nonstandardized assessment?
- Were the responses average and typical of how the person usually functions?
- How can the outcomes of this assessment be corroborated?

---

probably the most common procedure for collecting knowledge for evaluation purposes. In fact, occupational therapists at all competence levels—novice to expert—include observation as an integral part of their assessment information-gathering repertoire.

The following are examples of ways to observe phenomena (e.g., behaviors, activities, functions, participation, environments):

- Look at the posture, symmetry, and fluidity of motion while someone engages in gait;
- Look at the posture, symmetry, and fluidity of motion while someone engages in an activity;
- Inspect a classroom for flow patterns, noise levels, and visual demands;
- Watch a person who has had a stroke getting dressed in the morning at home; and
- Diagram the manner in which an individual who has had a head injury moves from one end of the occupational therapy clinic to the other while navigating around tables, people, and chairs.

Although the process of observation involves visually sampling phenomena, the other senses (i.e., hearing, smelling, touching, tasting) often provide additional information. For example, using vision alone to sample an environment such as a kitchen might involve a description of the physical layout, level of lighting, and efficiency of workstations. Additional sensory information about a kitchen—a lingering natural gas smell, sticky counters that hinder gravity-eliminated horizontal movements of pots to the stove, or a floor that is gritty with sand—may raise safety issues. For the purposes of this chapter, *observation* is used synonymously with *visual sampling* and includes obtaining information through all senses.

Because of the nature of observation, occupational therapists must control for all three aspects of PIE testing bias. Both types of the person aspect of PIE testing bias must be controlled, particularly the type related to the evaluator. To control for the item aspect of PIE testing bias, an occupational therapist must ensure that the specific testing element corresponds to the actual occupation the client being tested performs in real life. Performance testing conducted in a natural environment (e.g., the client's home, church, public library, social club) has built-in controls for the environmental aspect of PIE testing bias. Although not optimal, performance testing also occurs in simulated contexts (e.g., a clinic) when natural environments are not readily available. The validity of performance testing and its generalization to the natural environment are based on the match or fit of the simulated context to the natural environment. Test validity improves when a simulated context more closely resembles the natural environment, increasing the probability that the client will be able to generalize skills practiced in the clinic to a natural setting such as home. In addition, therapists must account for the unnaturalness of the observation itself, which may lead to some testing variance and potential error in information gathering.

Occupational therapists use varying degrees of formality and structure to systemize the procedure of collecting evaluation information through observation. Information collected through observation can include nonnumeric descriptions of characteristics that provide qualitative, measurable information that results in numeric data that are quantitative or a combination of qualitative and quantitative aspects. The systematic, procedural component of observation affects the degree of formality, level of structure, and balance of the qualitative and quantitative information. Observations related to standardized testing are frequently formal and structured because therapists must follow specific protocols that were refined during instrument development. Results of information obtained through standardized testing often start as qualitative but are transformed into quantitative information: Observations are usually classified or ranked into categories, then assigned numeric values. The numeric values, based on observation of performance levels, factor into the scoring of the standardized assessment. For example, an occupational therapist watches Mark, an 8-year-old boy in second grade, string eight blocks within a 15-second time period, which correlates with a point score of 7 on the Manual Dexterity subtest of the Bruininks–Oseretsky Test of Motor Proficiency (2nd edition, BOT–2; Bruininks & Bruininks, 2005).

Without a routine systematic procedure, an observation is likely to be classified as informal and unstructured. For instance, an occupational therapist used an informal, unstructured approach to observation when he entered the home of Mrs. Jameson, an 83-year-old widow who lived alone prior to hospitalization. The therapist watched her move from the foyer through the rooms and took notes for a home accessibility visit prior to her discharge. His observations probably included both qualitative and quantitative information (e.g., Mrs. Jameson's motor and praxis skill performance as she reached for drinking glasses on a top shelf, the size and number of throw rugs on the floor, the time she required to move from the couch to the bathroom).

As procedures become more systematic and routine, observations become semiformal and semistructured. An occupational therapist who systematically works sequentially through a self-designed checklist as a guide to collecting observations is using a semiformal, semistructured approach. The expert therapist who has an established routine for evaluating people demonstrating similar occupational patterns is also using a semiformal, semistructured approach, although less official-looking (there are no written guidelines).

Observations that are semiformal or informal and semistructured or unstructured are not necessarily inferior to formal, structured observations. Formal, structured observation (which is part of standardized testing) is frequently a sterile procedure with resulting outcomes that can be different from what happens under customary conditions in a natural environment. In other words, standardized conditions in a prescribed setting may yield reliable information but may not be valid for the person. For example, a person may be able to transfer in a simulated clinic bathroom but may have difficulty transferring in the home bathtub if the shower nozzle is in the opposite direction from the nozzle in the clinic shower. The clinic evaluation would provide documentation that the patient was successful in tub transferring.

Visual sampling that is less systematized often results in an increased richness of information. Interestingly, formal, structured observation that is part of the information-gathering process for a standardized instrument is frequently augmented with less formal, less structured observation. In the earlier example of Mark, the occupational therapist made additional observations as follows: Mark, a right-handed boy, used his left thumb and finger pads to hold the string (1 inch from the end) in a vertical direction 6 inches in front of his chest. With his right hand, he picked up three blocks at once, placing one block at a time on the tip of the string while retaining the other blocks fisted in his middle, ring, and little fingers. As Mark dropped one block on the string, he grasped the string tip (above the block) in his right thumb and index finger pads, allowing gravity to move the block down the string held vertically. He then transferred the string back to his left thumb and finger pads to begin sliding another block onto the string.

The procedures developed during the standardization of the BOT–2 resulted in observations about Mark that were formal, structured, and quantitative: Mark's raw score of eight (blocks) equated to a point score of 7 for that subtest item. The supplemental nonstandardized testing information, however, provided valuable unstructured and informal information that was qualitative in nature. On the basis of the additional observations, the occupational therapist improved the richness of information related to Mark's ability to organize a task, sequence steps, and use strategies (in this case, a gravity-assist method).

Collection Methods

To collect observation information, particularly in quantitative format, occupational therapists use four common methods: event recording, duration recording, rate recording, and time sampling. In occupational therapy, the two most common methods of collecting information are event recording and duration recording. *Event recording,* the simplest of the four methods, provides a count of each occurrence of a specific type of phenomenon within a testing period. For event recording, an occupational therapist keeps a tally of occurrences, resulting in an understanding of the frequency of a phenomenon. Using Mrs. Jameson's home accessibility evaluation as an example, the occupational therapist could keep track of the number of times Mrs. Jameson slipped on throw rugs, used the towel bars in the kitchen and bathroom for stability in transitions, or steadied herself with both hands on the counter in preparation for reaching for a glass. An occupational therapist assisting in the decision of whether Mrs. Jameson can return home to live alone could keep a tally of unsafe acts. When therapists use timing devices such as stopwatches or kitchen timers, they are performing *duration recording.* For a particular phenomenon (e.g., behavior, activity engagement), duration recording determines the length of time of an occurrence, the amount of time needed for completion, the length of time spent, or latency (the length of time a phenomenon is not observed). Using duration recording in Mrs. Jameson's case, the occupational therapist could measure how much time she required to move from driveway into the house; how long she spent moving from her foyer to the kitchen; the length of time she needed to complete the task of getting a glass of tap water; or *latency,* the time interval between unsafe acts.

To use duration recording, the therapist must determine which "end" of time is considered optimal by determining whether the focus is either speed (a shorter time) or endurance (a longer time). For example, if the focus is speed, then the optimal end of the timescale is a low number: the fewest number of time units. In terms of speed, a person who assembled a five-piece work task in 10 seconds is 3 times faster than someone who took 30 seconds to assemble the same five-piece work task. If the focus of duration recording is endurance, then the optimal end of the timescale is a high number of time units. For instance, when working on increasing attention to task (a type of endurance), a student who attended to task for 12 minutes without becoming distracted performed four times better than another student who was able to pay attention without distraction for 3 minutes.

Rate recording, a combination of event and duration recording, is calculated by dividing frequency (event recording) by length of time (duration recording). Mrs. Jameson's occupational therapist, who is interested primarily in determining whether she can return to live alone, used event recording to keep a simple tally of the number of times she performed unsafe acts. A tally of one unsafe act provides little meaning unless duration of the home accessibility evaluation is known. For the case of an evaluation lasting 15 minutes, the rate recording is calculated by dividing the event recording of unsafe acts (one act) by the duration recording of the evaluation (15 minutes). In this instance, Mrs. Jameson performed one unsafe act every 15 minutes. Extrapolating that information to a 16-hour day, allowing 8 hours for sleep, Mrs. Jameson had the potential for 64 unsafe acts per day and 448 unsafe acts per week. On this basis, the occupational therapist may recommend that it is not safe for Mrs. Jameson to return home to live alone. One unsafe act during a 4-hour evaluation (240 minutes), however, results in an extrapolation of 4 possible unsafe acts per day and 28 potential unsafe acts per week. Although 4 unsafe acts per day is better than 64, Mrs. Jameson's occupational therapist still would need to determine whether it is safe for her to return home alone. In this case, the quantitative information generated by rate recording may not be enough to make a final recommendation. If her occupational therapist supplemented the rate recording with qualitative information that indicates all 4 unsafe acts during the visit occurred when Mrs. Jameson tripped on throw rugs, a simple recommendation of removing the throw rugs would eliminate all 64 potentially unsafe acts per day predicted in the shorter evaluation, as well as the 4 possible daily unsafe acts observed during the longer evaluation.

According to Ottenbacher (1986), *time sampling* (also called *scan sampling, instantaneous time sampling, discontinuous probe time sampling,* and *interval sampling*) "involves recording the state of a behavior at specific moments or intervals in time" (p. 71). This most sophisticated method of collecting observation data requires signaling specified intervals by a timer, recorded cues, or other means. The observation times are interspersed with intervals of no observation, which are usually used for recording results of preceding observation intervals. Time sampling can be used in combination with event recording, duration recording, or rate recording. To apply time sampling to Mrs. Jameson's case, her occupational therapist could use an audio recording indicating 5-minute observation times followed by 10-minute intervals of no observation to record the frequency (event recording) of unsafe acts within that observation interval. If the one unsafe act seen in the earlier rate recording example did not occur during the observation interval, then the occupational therapist would record that he observed no unsafe acts. As this example shows, time sampling (although a potent research strategy) can be time-consuming and burdensome and has the potential to produce inaccurate information in practice settings.

Format for Observation

We have developed the following format, which provides fundamental steps of observation-based nonstandardized testing:

- *Step 1:* Describe the setting. Note whether the assessment is occurring indoors or outdoors; note whether the environment appears cluttered or uncluttered; note the number of people, animals, and objects in the setting; note the lighting, temperature, sounds/noise, and smells.
- *Step 2:* Judge the emotional/social tone of the setting and provide a label that connotes the feeling evoked. For example, is the setting safe? Is the setting peaceful? Is the setting chaotic?
- *Step 3:* Conduct an activity analysis by making note of activities and actions.
- *Step 4:* Judge how society would label the ongoing activities (i.e., is there occupational engagement and participation?).
- *Step 5:* Make note of how long the observation occurred and during what time of day.
- *Step 6:* Summarize findings.
- *Step 7:* Make an interpretation including actions to be taken if necessary.

Interview

Interview refers to the process of inquiry during which an individual asks another person one or more questions. Virtually all occupational therapists use interviewing—and more often than not, nonstandardized interview methods—to collect information about almost every client from the very first moment of meeting. Beginning prompts (e.g., "Describe how you are doing," "Tell me how it has been going") often lead to follow-up probes or additional questions (e.g., "Tell me more about that," "And what did you do then?"). Using prompts, probes, and questions such as these reveals a great deal to the occupational therapist about the clients' activities and participation in life and their challenges while engaging in life situations and occupational therapy aspects, including areas of occupation, client factors, performance skills, performance patterns, contexts and environment, and activity demands (AOTA, 2008). The previous questions are considered open-ended questions, which are designed to elicit responses to direct the content of the interview by what the person reveals. Closed-ended questions have forced-choice options. An example of a forced-choice response format is selection of one item from an exclusive number of possible responses. Closed-ended questions are often found on questionnaires, a nonstandardized assessment category that will be discussed later in this chapter.

Like observations, nonstandardized interviews vary in degree of formality (formal, semiformal, or informal), structure (structured, semistructured, or unstructured), and information type (qualitative vs. quantitative). Generally, as a format becomes increasingly systematic, the interview tool is correspondingly considered more formal and structured. Some interview tools, considered semiformal and semistructured, offer an integrated approach to the collection of qualitative and quantitative information.

Interviews factor heavily into an occupational therapist's clinical reasoning process. For most occupational therapists, interviewing provides the foundation for three forms of clinical reasoning: narrative reasoning, interactive reasoning, and conditional reasoning. Occupational therapists use *interactive reasoning* (client-centered interchange) to piece together the fragments of a client's life story and the unique perspective of the client (*narrative reasoning*) into a holistic pattern that guides interpretation and intervention planning. The therapist's *conditional reasoning* allows for selection of the instruments and questions needed for the interview. Obtaining useful information during the data collection stage of an interview is contingent upon controlling for item and person aspects of PIE testing bias. Because interviews involve the interaction of two persons—the evaluator and the individual being tested—both types of person-related testing bias require close attention.

Format for Interview

We view the following as the fundamental steps of interview-based nonstandardized testing:

- *Step 1:* Tell me about yourself? Who are you?
- *Step 2:* What is the issue or problem?
- *Step 3:* Why is it an issue or problem?
- *Step 4:* When is it an issue or problem?
- *Step 5:* How have you addressed the issue or problem in the past? How can I, as a therapist, solve or modify the problem?

The series of questions provided in these steps may be easily adapted to switch the emphasis of the interview from a problem-based nonstandardized assessment tool to a different focus as needed.

Individualized Interview Instruments

Occupational therapy has several individualized interview instruments, including the Occupational Performance History Interview (Kielhofner et al., 2004) and the Canadian Occupational Performance Measure (Law et al., 1998). Both interview instruments are occupation-centered, and each is based on a different frame of reference.

The Occupational Performance History Interview (OPHI–II; Version 2.1; Kielhofner et al., 2004) is an ipsative-referenced tool based on the Model of Human Occupation (MOHO; Kielhofner, 2008). The OPHI–II is an individualized, client-centered, semistructured interview that systemizes the collection of occupational history information that can be used in developing a person's occupational profile. Using the structure of the occupation-based OPHI–II to obtain client narratives, therapists help clients "integrate their past, present, and future into a coherent whole" (Kielhofner et al., 2004, p. 9). The OPHI–II, which is designed to allow flexibility while exploring a client's occupational life history, includes three scales: Occupational Identity, Occupational Competence, and Occupational Settings (Environment). Version 2.1 of the OPHI–II includes scale keyforms (Kramer, Kielhofner, & Forsyth, 2008), designed using Rasch measurement, that convert Likert-responses into interval measures.

The OPHI–II manual (Kielhofner et al., 2004) has other reproducible forms, including the OPHI–II Clinical Summary Report Form and Life History Narrative Form.

The Canadian Occupational Performance Measure (COPM; Law et al., 1998) is an ipsative-referenced tool that is based on the Canadian Model of Occupational Performance (CAOT, 1997). The individualized COPM was designed to examine interactions among the person, environment, and occupation (P–E–O). A client-centered, occupation-based interview tool, the COPM identifies problem areas in occupational performance, provides a rating of the client's priorities in occupational performance, evaluates performance and satisfaction relative to those problem areas, and measures changes in a client's perception of his or her occupational performance over the course of occupational therapy intervention (Law et al., 1998, p. 1).

The COPM allows flexibility in interviewing clients. According to the COPM manual, "it is essential that therapists use their skills in interviewing, probing for full responses, validating assumptions and motivating respondents to obtain the most thorough and comprehensive assessment" (Law et al., 1998, p. 34). The test form provides additional directions as follows:

> To identify occupational performance problems, concerns, and issues, interview the client, asking about daily activities in self-care, productivity, and leisure. Ask clients to identify daily activities which they want to do, need to do or expected to do by encouraging them to think about a typical day. Then ask the client to identify which of these activities are difficult for them to do now to their satisfaction. (Law et al., 1998, p. 2)

Deceptively simple in appearance, the COPM is a powerful, time-saving assessment tool that gathers salient client-centered information. Box 8.2 provides a SOAP note (subjective, objective, assessment, and plan) for Sandy, a typical college student considered a member of the well population. Sandy is right-handed, 21 years old, female, and a junior at a midwestern university and lives in a campus apartment with three roommates. A business major, Sandy became engaged to an engineer in Alaska on Valentine's Day and plans to be married the week after graduation. The SOAP note for Sandy shows application of the COPM and uses the P–E–O language of the Candian Model of Occupational Performance.

Questionnaires

Questionnaires used in information collection during the evaluation process include client self-report measures that a client or caregiver completes by paper and pencil or by instruments administered via electronic devices such as computers. Because this type of assessment tool can be completed with or without an occupational therapist present, selection of completion method may help control for person-related PIE testing bias that involves the evaluator. Questionnaires have the potential to control for the person-related testing bias involving the test-taker if the individual is a good historian, can read and compre-

Box 8.2. Occupational Therapy Initial Evaluation: The SOAP Note

S: Sandy indicated that she was relieved to be working on her occupational performance (OP), saying her "life was such a mess." She said that she can't seem to get anything done, is failing her business law course, and forgets simple things.

O: On the Canadian Occupational Performance Measure (COPM), a client-centered, interview-based assessment instrument that detects self-perceived change in OP over time, Sandy identified nine OP problems. Of these OP problems, two (22%) were in self-care (taking too long in morning routine and forgetting to brush teeth), four (56%) were in productivity (decreased time management skills because of high levels of electronic social networking, misplacing homework, getting unorganized easily, running out of gas, and falling asleep in business law class), and two (22%) were in leisure (paying high communication bills and having no fun at all). Using the importance scale (COPM–I), Sandy prioritized her most critical five OP problems and then rated her performance (COPM–P) and satisfaction (COPM–S) for each. The table below lists Sandy's COPM scores, which indicate overall decreased performance and satisfaction levels associated with two underlying person components related to cognition: time management and organizational skill difficulties.

OP Problem	COPM–I Score	COPM–P Score	COPM–S Score
1. Time management	10	2	1
2. Homework	10	3	2
3. Brushing teeth	9	4	3
4. Organizational skills	9	3	3
5. Paying bills	8	2	2
COPM Total Score (average)		2.8	2.2

Note. COPM–I, COPM–P, and COPM–S scales consist of a 1–10 rating, with 10 indicating *the optimal level of each.*

A: Rapport was established, and testing indicated that Sandy is a good historian, so the results of this evaluation reflect a reliable and valid estimate of Sandy's OP at the current time. Use of the COPM showed functional deficits in Sandy's OP related to self-care, productivity, and leisure performance and satisfaction, secondary to inadequate time management and organizational skills. Sandy's problem list consists of the five OP problems listed in the previous table. Sandy, who has an excellent potential for improvement, would benefit from skilled occupational therapy to improve her OP through compensatory strategies.

P: Sandy is to be seen for 45-minute sessions semiweekly for 2 weeks for skilled occupational therapy instruction in compensatory time management and organizational strategies. By discharge, Sandy will exhibit independent utilization of these strategies, demonstrating improved self-care, productivity, and leisure performance and satisfaction as evidenced by improvements in COPM–P and COPM–S reevaluation scores compared with initial COPM–P and COPM–S scores. The following table lists Sandy's long- and short-term goals.

Box 8.2. Occupational Therapy Initial Evaluation: The SOAP Note *(cont.)*

OP Problem	Short-Term Goal (1 week)	Long-Term Goal (by discharge)
Time management	Decrease electronic social networking to a scheduled 5 times per day.	Decrease electronic social networking to a scheduled 3 times per day.
Homework	Place finished homework for one course in an expandable folder.	Place finished homework for all courses into color-coordinated, expandable folders.
Brushing teeth	Brush teeth 1 time per day.	Brush teeth 2 times per day.
Organizational skills	Organize work related to school.	Organize work related to school and personal life.
Paying bills	Decrease monthly communication bill by $20.	Decrease monthly communication bill by $50.

Ashley Dodson, MS, OTR

Date: _____

---

hend the information requested, has the requisite motor skills (using a writing instrument or a computer), and makes appropriate decisions among choices. Medical histories that patients complete in a medical setting are an example of questionnaires that document an individual's past.

In occupational therapy, the Occupational Self-Assessment (OSA; Baron, Kielhofner, Iyenger, Goldhammer, & Wolenski, 2006), which is based on the MOHO (Kielhofner, 2008), is one example of an ipsative-referenced questionnaire. The OSA was "developed to assess the MOHO concepts of occupational competence and value for occupation through self report" (Kramer et al., 2008, p. 173). The individualized, client-centered questionnaire consists of two primary self-assessment forms: OSA Myself and OSA My Environment. The OSA helps clients establish priorities for change, which translate into intervention goals. Included in the assessment are reproducible forms for planning and implementing goals and showing progress and outcomes.

Performance Tests

Performance tests are different from questionnaires. Rather than rely on self-report, occupational therapists use their strong activity analysis skills to use performance testing as a means of collecting information about how a client carries out a task in context. Because observation is a primary tool in the collection of data related to performance tests, occupational therapists who use this method of collecting information must control for the three aspects of PIE testing bias. Additionally, occupational therapists must take into account the unnaturalness of the observation itself, which can lead to testing variance.

Examples of nonstandardized performance tests include activities such as cooking lunch in a kitchen, buttering a piece of toast while seated at a dining table, changing the sheets on a king-sized bed, or creating a pinch pot out of clay. Performance testing can be based on the client's real-time performance of predetermined criteria such as making a sandwich, operating the stove efficiently and safely, moving from one room to another and within rooms, or preparing a space for completion of a specified craft project. In performance testing, the client demonstrates an aspect of occupational performance that is rated qualitatively and quantitatively by the occupational therapist.

Conclusion

In occupational therapy, nonstandardized testing and standardized assessment instruments are important tools. Standardized assessments are limited in number and must be used within the restricted and prescribed conditions, which often impose sterile or artificial conditions on the client. Moreover, standardized assessment instruments sometimes provide little usable information related to the complexity of the occupational therapy domain of concern. Nonstandardized testing, however, produces ipsative-referenced results that may offer stronger internal validity and more sensitivity for an individual than information produced by standardized instruments.

Occupational therapists are called upon to consider nonstandardized testing as a sound method of gathering rich information about clients and are challenged to improve the reliability and validity of nonstandardized assessment tool use. Any assessment tool—standardized or nonstandardized—should be used in systematic or standard ways to provide consistency and control for all three aspects of PIE testing bias. Making the nonstandardized testing process as systematic as possible should provide equally valid results, regardless of the person conducting the assessment.

Nonstandardized testing can be used alone effectively to gather information during evaluation. For various reasons, nonstandardized testing may be the only way an occupational therapist can perform a particular evaluation.

An optimal method of data collection uses nonstandardized testing and standardized assessment devices in an integrated approach. Integration of nonstandardized testing offers ipsative-referenced information about individual clients to supplement standardized assessment information that compares client performance with criterion-referenced standards or norm-referenced peer groups.

To use nonstandardized testing appropriately and effectively, an occupational therapist must have a solid theoretical knowledge base and sound clinical reasoning, two of the three evidence-based practice approaches. Therapists who wish to implement evidence-based practice should consider Ilott's (2004) reminder that all sources of evidence—empirical research, experiential evidence, and theoretical knowledge—are equally valid.

Questions

1. Discuss the role of theory in nonstandardized assessment.
2. Discuss the role of clinical reasoning in nonstandardized assessment.
3. Describe three actions the occupational therapist can take during nonstandardized assessment that incorporate PIE to assure validity of the testing situation.
4. Describe and discuss three clinical situations in which nonstandardized assessment would be appropriate.
5. When does a standardized test become nonstandardized?
6. What are the benefits and drawbacks of evaluating a client in his or her natural environment (e.g., home, work, school)? What are the benefits and drawbacks of evaluating a client in a specialized intervention environment (e.g., hospital clinic, outpatient rehabilitation center)?
7. Relate Ilott's (2004) perspective of evidence-based practice approaches to nonstandardized assessment.

References

American Occupational Therapy Association. (1995). Concept Paper—Service delivery in occupational therapy. *American Journal of Occupational Therapy, 49*, 1029–1031.

American Occupational Therapy Association. (2008). Occupational therapy practice framework: Domain and process (2nd ed.). *American Journal of Occupational Therapy, 62*, 625–683.

Anastasi, A., & Urbina, S. (1997). *Psychological testing* (7th ed.). Upper Saddle River, NJ: Prentice Hall.

Baron, K., Kielhofner, G., Iyenger, A., Goldhammer, V., & Wolenski, V. (2006). *A user's manual for the Occupational Self Assessment* (OSA; Version 2.2). Chicago: Model of Human Occupation Clearinghouse, Department of Occupational Therapy, College of Applied Health Sciences, Unversity of Illinois.

Brentnall, J., & Bundy, A. C. (2009). The concept of reliability in the context of observational assessments. *OTJR: Occupation, Participation, and Health, 29*(2), 63–71.

Bruininks, R. H., & Bruininks, B. D. (2005). *Bruininks–Oseretsky Test of Motor Proficiency* (2nd ed.). Circle Pines, MN: AGS Publishing.

Canadian Association of Occupational Therapists. (1997). *Enabling occupation: An occupational therapy perspective.* Ottawa, Ontario, Canada: CAOT Publications.

Donnelly, C., & Carswell, A. (2002). Individualized outcome measures: A review of the literature. *Canadian Journal of Occupational Therapy, 69*, 84–93.

Ilott, I. (2004). Evidence-Based Practice Forum—Challenges and strategic solutions for a research emergent profession. *American Journal of Occupational Therapy, 58*, 347–352.

Kielhofner, G. (2008). *Model of Human Occupation: Theory and application* (4th ed.). Baltimore: Lippincott Williams & Wilkins.

Kielhofner, G., Mallinson, T., Crawford, C., Nowak, M., Rigby, M., Henry, A., et al. (2004). *A user's manual for the Occupational Performance History Interview* (OPHI–II; Version 2.1). Chicago: Model of Human Occupation Clearinghouse, Department of Occupational Therapy, College of Applied Health Sciences, Unversity of Illinois.

Kramer, J., Kielhofner, G., & Forsyth, K. (2008). Assessments used with the Model of Human Occupation. In B. J. Hemphill-Pearson (Ed.), *Assessments in occupational therapy mental health: An integrative approach* (2nd ed., pp. 159–184). Thorofare, NJ: Slack.

Law, M., Baptiste, S., Carswell, A., McColl, M. A., Polatajko, H., & Pollack, N. (1998). *Canadian Occupational Performance Measure* (3rd ed.). Ottawa, Ontario, Canada: CAOT Publications.

Ottenbacher, K. J. (1986). *Evaluating clinical change: Strategies for occupational and physical therapists*. Baltimore: Williams & Wilkins.

World Health Organization. (2001). *International classification of functioning, disability and health*. Geneva: Author.

9

Reliability and Validity: The Psychometrics of Standardized Assessments

Patricia Crist, PhD, OTR, FAOTA

Overview

No one wants a car mechanic to work on his or her car without a good diagnostic procedure. No one wants a physician to perform surgery without first carrying out diagnostic tests. No parent wants his or her child screened for developmental problems without using an accurate test. Likewise, no one would want to receive occupational therapy without first undergoing an evaluation process. In each scenario, confidence in the outcomes of the evaluation process is dependent on both the skill set of the evaluator and the quality of evaluation assessments used.

Evaluation should result in the accurate definition of the occupational problem or deficit to support professional decision making in the following areas:

- *Diagnostic:* Determine the presence and severity of a problem.
- *Descriptive:* Give details regarding the current state of the problem.
- *Predictive:* Provide a prognosis based on current conditions or performance problems.
- *Conclusive:* Determine the effectiveness of or outcomes from intervention for individuals or programs.

An occupational therapist is responsible for choosing the best assessments available for his or her practice and accurately scoring and interpreting the results. Confidence in test results is critical in identifying problems in people needing attention, planning intervention, monitoring changes as a result of occupational therapy intervention, and determining accumulated outcomes at the termination of services. Better standardized assessments provide reliable and valid information related to the purpose and intended use of the tool. Methodological research establishes the reliability and validity of assessments.

The purpose of this chapter is to provide an overview of critical measurement, or *psychometric characteristics,* of standardized tests, which is essential to having confidence in evaluation results. Validity is more critical than reliability for the assessments used in occupational therapy. However, both reliability and validity support the quality, accuracy, and generalizability of assessment outcomes for intervention planning, program evaluation, and applied research to support evidence-based practice. Assessment manuals report reliability, validity, and related statistics about the development and use of the assessment. Often, additional information is reported in journal articles, research summaries, and reviews. This chapter provides a foundation for clinical reasoning and professional confidence in assessment selection, application, and interpretation of the evaluation across the intervention process. An occupational therapist must be familiar with measurement, or psychometric, concepts to evaluate and defend the "goodness" of the assessments he or she uses daily.

Although much of the evaluation process is based on the "art" of administration, this and the following chapter focus on the "science" underlying assessment use. *Psychometrics* is the science of testing (Anastasi & Urbina, 1997). The science of assessment selection and use is based on the "theory of test and measurements," which determines the goodness of a standardized test. The goodness of a test is a reflection of a test's reliability, validity, and accuracy. These three issues form the guiding questions each therapist needs to ask about the assessment(s) he or she is using or planning to use:

1. *Validity:* Does the test measure what it is supposed to measure?
2. *Reliability:* Does the test consistently yield the same or similar scores?
3. *Accuracy:* Does the test fairly and closely approximate an individual's true level of ability, skill, or aptitude? (Kubiszyn & Borich, 2003, p. 299)

The occupational therapist should seriously consider using only tests that yield sufficient evidence supporting these three dimensions. The occupational therapist is responsible for knowing the technical adequacy of a test (the psychometric qualities), the purpose of the test, and the population for which the test is intended, and competently using the assessment.

Standardized Tests

From a clinical perspective, the goodness of an assessment is a combination of its quality (science) and the skills (art) of the evaluator. The psychometrics supporting the intended use of the assessment determines the assessment's quality. A standardized assessment has reported norms from a specific population, relevant reliability and validity studies to support the assessment's intended clinical use, and, most importantly, interpretation of test scores to report individual assessment outcomes, called *test results.*

Standardization of Administration Versus Standardized Tests

Uniformity, consistency, and competency in administering tests are essential during the evaluation process. *Uniformity* in assessment procedures means that the evaluator consistently administers the assessment the same way each time, called *intrarater reliability,* which will be discussed later. To maintain uniformity, an assessment must have (at the very least) comprehensive published instructions for administration and scoring. The evaluator also must be well versed, trained, and consistent in administering the assessment according to these specified instructions. Some assessments require that an occupational therapist be certified in the administration to ensure that the test is administered and used accurately.

An occupational therapist must realize that a screening tool or assessment with published administration and scoring procedures may have standardized procedures but may not necessarily be a standardized test. A standardized assessment has published procedures for administering and scoring, along with reliability and validity studies to support the intended use of the tool during service delivery. A standardized assessment provides

- *Objectivity* (a measure that is not dependent on the personal opinion of the examiners);
- *Quantification* (numeric precision enabling finer discrimination in performance or characteristics and interpretation);
- *Communication* (enhancement of interprofessional use); and
- *Scientific generalizations,* including program evaluation, outcomes studies, and reimbursement documentation (Nunnally & Bernstein, 1994).

A *standardized assessment* is an instrument that has undergone rigorous psychometric procedures to support its intended purpose and use. All standardized assessments publish their standardized administration and scoring procedures, sometimes including normative data and suggested interpretations of results, in the form of a test manual. A standardized assessment also will have information about its reliability and validity studies as evidence that a therapist using this assessment is measuring the same way every time (reliability) and measuring what he or she intended to measure (validity). Studying the reliability and validity of an assessment contributes to evidence-based practice. An instrument is fully standardized when two different evaluators observe the same assessment of a person and independently arrive at the same score.

The foundation for having confidence in a standardized assessment is reliability and validity as a result of measurement and methodological research. A therapist interprets an assessment's reported reliability and validity using the correlation statistical test and examining the resulting correlation coefficient.

Overview of Basic Test and Measurement Concepts

Some important concepts in basic test and measurements are psychometric properties of an assessment, measurement, test scores, reliability, validity, and correlation coefficient. Understanding these concepts is critical to being a competent evaluator.

Psychometric Properties of an Assessment

Understanding the psychometric qualities of a standardized test requires a foundational knowledge of statistics, especially correlation, and the basic approaches used to demonstrate the goodness or various qualities of an assessment. Table 9.1 lists key statistical terms used in reporting the reliability and validity of tests.

Measurement

The basis of all assessment is the meticulous and precise observation of what is being evaluated. Objective measures give predictable meaning and accuracy

Table 9.1. Basic Statistical Terms Used in Tests and Measurement

Term	Description
Correlation	The degree of relationship between two sets of scores. It implies the degree of relationship or association, but does not imply causality.
Correlation coefficient	A statistical indicator that quantifies the degree of relationship between two sets of scores. The coefficient varies from –1.0 to +1.0. The *strength* of the relationship is represented by how close the correlation is to a perfect +1 or –1. The *direction* of the relationship indicates if the variables are related to each other positively (+) or negatively (–). • *Positive correlation (+1):* A high score on one assessment is related to a high score on another, or two low scores are related. • *Negative correlation (–1):* A high score on one assessment is related to a low score on another.
Measurement research	The rules for assigning numbers to behavior, characteristics, or performance to quantify the results of an assessment.
Methodological research	Approach used to study and report norms, reliability, and validity to establish evidence of the quality of an assessment's outcomes for practice-related planning and decisions.
Psychometric	Test and measurement statistics provided to support the technical or scientific quality of an assessment.
Reliability	The degree of precision consistency between two scores; reliability indicates that a tester comes up with the same results each time he or she conducts an assessment, given that there are no intervening variables.
Test statistic	The reported statistical/numeric result from a study to describe a type of reliability or validity.
Test score	An individual's current obtained score *(Os)* on a test is the sum of his or her true score *(Ts)* and the negative influence of error *(Te)* from sources that prevent the current score from fully reflecting the individual's true abilities: $Os = Ts + Te$
Validity	The degree to which a test accurately measures the specific construct, trait, behavior, or performance it was designed to measure.

to these observations. Measurement contributes to the reliability of scoring processes through methodically defining and thoroughly labeling what is being measured. Explicit rules for assigning numbers to assessment observations are an inherent component of the standardization process. The therapist is responsible for following these standardized rules during the scoring. Using standardized measures enhances the therapist's ability to communicate his or her findings accurately, and the assignment of numbers allows for more specific reporting of outcomes. Thus, measurement is a systematic way to report assessment findings and reflects the therapist's adherence to professional traditions regarding measurement.

Test Scores

Ideally, assessment scores reflect what is being measured by the assessment, frequently a person's ability. In reality, however, a person's score on a test is not always accurate; it is a combination of the person's "true score" plus the negative influence of testing error that influences test outcomes:

$$\text{Obtained score } (OS) = \text{True score } (TS) + \text{Testing error } (TE)$$

Errors in measurement are the disagreement between a person's true score and the obtained score. Measurement errors are generally viewed as a random, unpredictable influence on test scores. However, using standardized procedures for performing assessments increases the chance that a person's real abilities have been identified because consistent assessment delivery decreases outside distractions or influences on performance. The goal for the occupational therapist during assessment is to decrease the influence of error on testing results.

A person's experience as a student illustrates this point. As a student, one may experience the concepts of true score and error when taking a test. Does the score on an exam accurately reflect the student's degree of knowledge or ability? This can be answered affirmatively only when outside influences are not present to introduce inaccuracies (testing error) that might negatively influence or mask the student's actual capabilities (true score). Testing errors might include insufficient sleep before a test, having the flu on the day of a test, test items based on content not covered in class, the test room being too noisy or too cold, a major stressful life event occurring before or during the test, and so on. Thus, the obtained score is only an estimate of the student's real (or true) capability. A true score (by definition) contains no error; this evaluation goal is never truly obtained because error can be reduced but not eliminated.

The occupational therapist's goal is precision in measurement. Precision in measurement is reduced and replaced by error when there is variability due to inconsistencies in the observer's ratings or scores, including skilled delivery; measurement tool calibration and accuracy; environmental conditions; and subject's physiological, emotional (mood and motivation), and current health condition. A therapist can have precision in measurement and reduce errors by

- Using standardizing measurement methods;
- Having appropriate and sufficient training in assessment procedures (including certifying and rechecking periodically);
- Having experience in administering and scoring the instrument (learning standardized procedures, reliability, validity); and
- Repeating the measurement to verify evaluator, subject, and instrument consistency (Hulley, Cummings, Browner, Grady, & Newman, 2007).

If the score obtained is closer to a true score, the better the test's overall reliability and validity. Because true scores are constant or never change between one test administration and another as long as the condition of the individual has not changed, reliability reflects (1) the degree of true score differences contributing to the observed score and (2) the portion of performance or function that will remain constant over time if conditions remain the same.

Likewise, the more sources of error influencing test results, the less the true score will make up a person's obtained score. As a result of the degree of error influencing testing outcomes, intervention decisions might be based on incorrect or misleading information.

Reliability and Validity

The two most important concepts arising from psychometric or measurement theory are reliability and validity. *Reliability* refers to consistency betweens two scores. Typically, an assessment's reliability is established by correlating the scores from an individual on the same test given at two different times using equivalent sets of items or testing conditions (Anastasi & Urbina, 1997). Reliability contributes to predictability and reproducibility of results if the evaluator administers the assessment without changes in the individual or conditions for testing. *Validity* is ensuring that what is measured is what is intended to be measured, or the degree to which the test measures what it purports to be measuring. An assessment's validity is established by comparing scores on a given assessment of a specific construct, trait, behavior, or performance with another measure of the same construct. Specific types of reliability and validity will be discussed later in this chapter.

The author or publisher of an assessment, or an interested professional, performs the studies of reliability and validity that the occupational therapist uses in selecting quality tests or interpreting results. Often, an author of an assessment establishes the types of reliability and validity that support the purpose and application of his or her assessment. The occupational therapist in practice does not establish test reliability or validity but depends on studies conducted by third parties and published manuals and articles to learn about the reliability and validity of a particular assessment. A therapist gains confidence in the use of a particular assessment for evaluating a client by referring to the published reliability and validity. Moreover, a therapist can determine whether the assessment is appropriate for assessing outcomes or identifying deficits or dysfunction.

Correlations and the Correlation Coefficient

Correlation statistics establish many of the types of reliability and validity. *Correlation* is defined as what is common between two measures. A brief introduction to the concept of correlation is provided to assist with understanding the remaining content of this chapter. Readers should refer to statistical texts for more extensive explanations.

Correlation does not imply causality, only that a relationship exists between two measures or variables; a third external factor may be the cause. For instance, the number of sexual overtures markedly increases when college women sunbathe in bikinis. Although these two factors positively correlate, a third factor—seasonal weather changes (hot vs. cold temperatures)—might be the causal factor in these two occurrences increasing or decreasing in frequency at the same time.

The correlation coefficient (indicating the degree of agreement between two measures) is another important statistic in tests and measurements. Most assessments use a specific statistical test to arrive at a correlation coefficient called the *Pearson product-moment correlation coefficient,* reported as *r.* However, there are many other correlation coefficients, and each uses a symbol other than *r.* Test manual correlation reports can be overwhelming. Just remember that a statistician selects a particular correlation approach on the basis of how the assessment converts an observation to a number and scores responses and that the correlation approach adopted is not as important as the final coefficient value, which is what actually appraises test quality. Correlation coefficients can range from –1.00 to +1.00. A correlation of 0.00—the midpoint of the continuum between the two extremes—indicates that the two sets of test scores are unrelated. As the scores move to the ends of the continuum, the magnitude or strength of correlation increases. In other words, the *relationship* between the two variables of measure—how much they have in common or share with each other—increases.

A second important correlation concept is the *direction* of the relationship, indicated by a positive or negative coefficient. A positive correlation is an association between two variables going in the same direction. As one variable becomes large, the other also becomes large, and vice versa. Positive correlation is represented by correlation coefficients greater than 0 (0 to +1.0). A negative correlation is an inverse association between two variables. As one variable becomes larger, the other becomes smaller. Negative correlation is represented by correlation coefficients less than 0 (–1.0 to 0).

The labels + and – have nothing to do with the quality of the correlation. For example, a therapist would expect a positive correlation coefficient between the degree of deformity and the reported pain for arthritis. The hypothesis is that as hand deformity increases, reported pain increases and as hand deformity lessens, less pain will be reported. A therapist would expect a negative correlation between the amount of pain and increases in pain medication in arthritis. In this case, a therapist hypothesizes that as pain medication is increased, reported pain decreases. Likewise, a therapist would want a negative correlation between calorie consumption and weight loss and a positive correlation between food calorie intake and weight gain. Always analyze whether the coefficient is in the direction desired by thinking through the expected direction of the relationship when the two variables are compared. A therapist will not see a perfect prediction from correlation (+1.00 or −1.00), because this means the scores are error-free, which can never happen when evaluating human performance. For instance, only correlations that are unavoidable can be without error. The correlation between eating pickles and dying is +1.0, because 100% of people who eat pickles die. The same relationship can be found with drinking bottled water and growing older!

The *strength* of the correlation found between two measures is also central to determining the quality of the reliability or validity of an assessment. The higher the correlation coefficient (ignoring the + or − sign), the greater its strength. As a general guideline, industry standards use the following coefficient ranges to judge reliability and validity studies reported by test developers and publishers:

- .90 – .99   High and preferred, but not frequently observed
- .80 – .89   Satisfactory or adequate
- .70 – .79   Weak or minimally acceptable
- Below .70   Caution—inadequate or unacceptable.

A publisher also may publish specific correlation standards for certain types of reliability and validity.

The correlation statistic measures the amount of agreement between two assessment methods. Therefore, if the reported correlation coefficient between two versions of the same test is .90, and one squares the coefficient to determine the percentage of agreement, or *explanation in common,* between the two tests, the result is 81% [(correlation coefficient)^2 = $(r)^2$ = $(.90)^2$ = 81%]. In other words, performance on the second test will be 81% in common with the first, but 19% of the performance variance remains unexplained by the two measures.

Some people do not consider r^2, but it is another way to understand results. For instance, an occupational therapist and a physical therapist each administer different but widely used self-reporting pain scales. The supervisor asks the two therapists to use a single measure to increase efficiency. The literature comparing the two scales states that the correlation between them is .25. Using r^2, this means that approximately only 6% of the information gained from both assessments is in common, leaving 94% that is explained differently by each assessment. This means that a loss of information may occur if only one assessment is selected. On the other hand, if the coefficient is .90, r^2 is equal to 81%, and there is great overlap in information across the two assessments. In this case, the therapists could afford to drop one, choosing whichever has other features most relevant to their practice needs.

Reliability

Reliability is the extent to which a test captures an individual's true score in spite of limiting error possibilities. Reliability has two important properties:

1. Reliability is that portion of a subject's performance that will remain constant over time (*score reliability*).
2. Reliability is that portion of observed score variance pooled across all subjects that is the result of true score differences (*test reliability*). (Thorndike, 2001, p. 33)

The next sections discuss score reliability—the standard error of measurement—and the various forms of test reliability in greater detail.

Score Reliability: Standard Error of Measurement

The *standard error of measurement (SEM)* is a measure of the reliability of the obtained score. The SEM is the standard deviation of the distribution of error in measurement (Bolton & Parker, 2008). SEM reflects the degree of true score versus error in an obtained score from an individual. It supports the notion of accuracy in assessment and answers the question, How closely does the assessment score approximate the true score of an individual? (Kubiszyn & Borich, 2003). The SEM estimates the possible deviation of an individual's obtained score from his or her true score. If a test is repeatedly given to the same person under similar conditions, his or her obtained score will vary within a certain range of total scores. The statistical average of all these obtained scores is a good indicator of one's true score. As a result of the variance between true and obtained scores, the occupational therapist needs to treat the final test score as an estimate, not as a definitive true score. To increase the accuracy and interpretation of an individual score obtained during an assessment, a therapist can use the published SEM for the assessment.

The SEM is an estimate of the reliability of the obtained score—in other words, a measure of the inconsistencies (attributed to various sources of error or pure chance) calculated from the standardization sample. The SEM is the measurement error for a particular assessment and is likely to be the gap between the obtained score and one's true score. A smaller SEM indicates that the obtained score better reflects the true score. In practice, this means that if an assessment has a small SEM, a therapist can be confident that the client's obtained score is close to the true score as long as the therapist used standardized procedures for administration and scoring. If the obtained score does not reflect a person's true score, the SEM will likely be larger than published and will not be an accurate estimate, because more error may be contributing to the obtained score than what was found in the standardization sample.

The SEM is established during the standardization of the assessment by accumulating repeated scores from the standardization sample to see how much scores in performance or function stay constant over time, when nothing has occurred that could cause change. The SEM is reported in test manuals or other measurement publications. In practice, one uses the reported SEM to describe the degree of consistency or preciseness related to obtaining a true score. Other resources to calculate the SEM statistically are beyond the scope of this chapter.

Interpreting Scores Using the SEM

Although the SEM reports reliability, its importance (from an intervention perspective) is that it indicates the degree of confidence that a client's obtained score is a reflection of his or her real performance ability rather than some random influence or error.

The SEM is typically reported in the test manual accompanying the assessment. Adding the SEM to the obtained score and then subtracting the SEM from the obtained score gives the boundary of confidence (the *score band of uncertainty*) within which the individual's true score is likely to lie. For instance, if the obtained score is 50 and the reported SEM for the test is 3, the estimate of a client's true score is somewhere between 47 and 53. A therapist would have less confidence in this estimate of true score if the SEM was large, meaning that more error contributes to the obtained score. In the previous example, imagine the implications if the SEM was 12, giving a much larger range of uncertainty regarding the individual's true score.

Although the SEM is important for interpreting an individual score, it has additional utility in occupational therapy. An assessment often is used to determine a person's eligibility for criteria-based services or programs; the obtained score can determine whether a person qualifies for occupational therapy or other related services. For instance, many developmental programs require that a child have an intelligence quotient (IQ) score below 70 to participate. A child may not qualify for this program if a recent IQ test reported that he or she had a 72 IQ. However, if the IQ test manual reports an SEM of 6, then the child's score could range from 66 (72 − 6) to 78 (72 + 6). This lower score would mean that the child would be eligible for services. If a therapist felt that the child might benefit from the program, the therapist could use the assessment's SEM as evidence to support program admission.

A therapist sometimes administers a retest to see whether the person receives the same or a different result. Of course, if the same therapist administers the retest, he or she could be biased, so it is best if the same therapist does not conduct the repeat test. In such a case, having another therapist administer the retest would mean that the new score is more defensible and fairer.

Test Reliability

There are several types of assessment reliability. Authors or psychometrician groups emphasize only certain reliability types that support the purpose and use of a given assessment. Because the purpose of this chapter is to provide an overview of common approaches only, the major or most common types of reliability will be discussed here. Readers are reminded that

- *Reliability* is the consistency with which an assessment performs.
- All reliability is established by test developers or others to improve the quality of the assessment. Occupational therapists use this information to select tests and help interpret individual scores; typically, they never do their own local (mini) reliability studies to support intervention decision making.
- The only types of reliability that must be reported for an assessment are ones that support the intended purpose and use of the assessment by an evaluator. For instance, if the purpose of a test is to measure intervention changes, then test–retest reliability must be reported.
- All reliability is reported using some type of correlation coefficient.

Table 9.2 summarizes the forms of reliability typically reported for assessments used in occupational therapy. Each type of test reliability is listed according to the various names seen in the literature. A brief description and

Table 9.2. Types of Reliability

Type	Description	Coefficient Standard
Standard error of measurement	The inconsistency or unreliability of the obtained score for an individual. (Also noted as SEM or Sem.)	.90 or higher
Test–retest reliability or stability	A measure of test score stability on the same version of the assessment over two occasions.	.90 or higher
Alternate, parallel forms of reliability or equivalence	The correlation in scores using two different forms of the same assessment.	.85 or higher
Internal consistency	*Split-half reliability:* The extent to which the score from one half of an assessment correlates with the other half.	.70–.95
	Kuder-Richardson (KR): The extent to which any one item on an assessment correlates with other items on the same assessment.	
	Coefficient alpha: Similar to KR, but used when an assessment has items with multiple response options.	
Scorer reliability	*Interrater reliability:* The degree of agreement between two raters following observation of the same subject during an assessment.	.90 or higher
	Intrarater reliability: Administering and scoring an assessment consistently the same way each time it is administered.	

the preferred reliability coefficient required for satisfactory reliability also are included. Each section below discusses two different aspects of the form of reliability: First, the reliability is discussed along with the procedures used to establish the test reliability, and second, the clinical relevance for this reliability is described.

Test–Retest Reliability or Stability

Test stability is established by giving the same test to the same individual in the same context at two different times. This procedure is repeated until data from a large group of similar individuals have been collected. A sufficient amount of time must pass between the administration of the test and retest in order for the individual to forget his or her responses to test items, as well as to prevent other intervening factors from influencing the second set of scores. Typically, the average time between tests is 1 to 2 weeks. The first set of scores is compared with the second set of scores to derive a correlation. Poor test–retest reliability for tests used in occupational therapy can reflect changes in disability or illness, new learning, or practicing of the target performance.

The occupational therapist looks for *test–retest reliability* on tests he or she will use to measure change over time as a result of intervention. The therapist wants the test to be a stable measure of what is expected to change and not be easily influenced by other outside events. With good test–retest reliability, the therapist has increased confidence that any changes in the score reflect true changes in the area measured, not unreliability entering from external sources.

Alternate or Parallel Forms of Reliability or Equivalence

The assessment developer obtains an estimate of the reliability of an assessment by using two equivalent forms of the assessment. To establish equivalence between two forms of the assessment, the developer gives two groups of individuals both assessments at the same time and correlates their scores. This approach eliminates the influence of practice and memory present in the test–retest situation. However, developing two equivalent tests with different items testing the same information or skill is not easy. Most often, alternate forms of reliability are used when test security is an issue, such as with large-scale tests like the SAT or the GRE.

An occupational therapist should look for alternate forms of a test when responses to items are easily remembered, stimulate learning, or possibly even practice specific skills. For instance, during a test of motor abilities with a child, the therapist might ask the child to model skipping as a test item. Afterward, the therapist observes the child practicing this skill regularly during recess. Asking the child to skip during the reassessment would result in measuring the effects of practice in addition to the effectiveness of the intervention provided. In this case, having two forms of a test of motor ability would be beneficial. If the therapist administers the assessment to determine whether a change has oc-curred because of intervention, the therapist needs to know whether the assess-ment will teach or whether the person will remember the items. If the assess-ment uses scenarios that trigger specific memories, then having two equivalent forms of a test to determine intervention effectiveness is beneficial.

Internal Consistency

Internal consistency determines the degree of agreement or commonality be-tween items in an assessment that measures a single concept or skill. It is logical that if a person gets one item correct on an assessment, he or she should get others correct also, if the assessment truly measures a single concept. Test items are then internally consistent with each other. The goal in designing a reliable instrument is for scores on similar items to be related (internally consistent), but for each also to contribute some unique information. A commonly accepted rule is that an r of .60–.70 indicates acceptable reliability, and .80 or higher indicates good reliability. High reliabilities (.95 or higher) are not necessarily desirable because this indicates that the items may be redundant.

Split-Half Reliability for Assessment

Split-half reliability involves splitting a single form of an assessment into two equivalent, shorter forms. One method for doing this is to create one form of the test using the first half of the items and a second form using the items from the second half of the assessment. Another approach is to put all even-numbered items into one test and all odd-numbered ones into another. An assessment developer uses this approach when varying item difficulty is not evenly spread throughout the assessment, for example, in assessments in which items get in-creasingly difficult. Reliability of this form of an assessment is called *odd–even reliability*. An assessment developer should examine the internal consistency to find alternate form reliability or shorten an assessment by 50%.

An occupational therapist seeks split-half reliability information in three situations. First, a therapist may find that this method was used to create a new shorter form of the assessment and as a result may want to know how this was done and to what degree the new shorter test correlates with the longer version that is no longer available. Second, the short form and the long form of the test both may be available, and an occupational therapist might want to have options in choosing the short versus long form of a test when individuals fatigue easily or when a lesser amount of time can be allocated to a specific assessment than at other times. Third, this method may result in two equivalent forms of the same test that can be used, like forms developed through alternate reliability.

Inter-Item Internal Consistency

An occupational therapist is interested in *internal consistency reliability* to ensure that the same skill, ability, or knowledge is measured with each item on the assessment. Items that do not contribute to the overall score because they are measuring something else lower a test's reliability and, as a result, the ability to identify problems warranting intervention or measuring change.

The following are measures of internal consistency:

- The *Kuder-Richardson (KR) method* refers to the "item-total correlation," called the *KR20* and *KR21*. The KR20 handles only responses that can be scored correct or incorrect (i.e., objective answers). The KR21 can be used to report internal consistency for a wider array of response types.
- *Cronbach alpha statistic,* or *coefficient alpha,* is used when multiple responses to the same item can be made. This method is used on assessments where responses are acquired using response scales like *never, some of the time, most of the time,* and *all of the time.*

Scorer Reliability

Scorer reliability is important because the therapist does not want to be responsible for introducing error into an assessment process. A therapist's scorer reliability improves through training in the assessment's standardized procedures and rechecking skill maintenance over time.

As an assessment is used over and over, unintentional deviations in delivery and skill creep in, modifying the standardized approach. As a result, it is important that a therapist periodically recalibrate his or her skills on a specific assessment as well as compare outcomes from other raters.

Intrarater Reliability

Intrarater reliability is not a formal type of reliability used in tests and measurements. Rather, it is supported through a therapist's professional values and ethical commitment to providing a quality occupational therapy evaluation. Its presence is reflected in behaviors that ensure continuous competence in the assessments used in an occupational therapy evaluation program. Training in an assessment according to published standardized procedures and habitual recalibration activities must be present to ensure intrarater reliability. A therapist also needs regular recalibration for all assessments—used frequently and infrequently—because consistency in the therapist's skills deteriorates over time. Recalibration includes, but is not limited to, restudying standardized procedures and fine-tuning skills, having another trained evaluator review and critique current administration skills, and attending a workshop on the administration of the assessment. Only regular recalibration gives a therapist the competence to use assessments consistently as they were designed and intended to be used. Scorer reliability is the fundamental requirement underlying intrarater reliability.

Interrater Reliability

Test manuals report *interrater reliability* to demonstrate that with adequate training (as described in the test manual), practice, and recalibration, two different raters will consistently arrive at essentially the same score. The key idea here is training and adherence to published standardized procedures for both raters.

An occupational therapist should look for interrater reliability information when more than one therapist in a setting or across settings might assess or reassess the same individual over time. Interrater reliability also may be important when multiple therapists evaluate different individuals but come together to assign individuals for intervention purposes to like groups based on similar test scores. Knowing that an assessment has good interrater reliability is important, but not sufficient for a therapist; a therapist must learn and adhere to published administration and scoring procedures at minimum. Preferably, a therapist also should periodically determine his or her own interrater reliability by conducting assessments simultaneously with another trained colleague to compare their independent scoring results. In assessment training and recalibration, the two raters compare scores and discuss those that are different to arrive at the one expected by the test publisher. Later, a therapist might want to administer co-evaluations without discussion; the percentage of agreement between the two raters' scores can be hand-calculated. When this informal way of establishing interrater reliability approaches the published numeric value, a therapist can be confident that he or she is trained or recalibrated sufficiently in the standardized procedures for administration and scoring. Further, the therapist can rest assured that regardless of who sees a client for evaluation, he or she would arrive at the same scores.

Sometimes in a setting it is necessary, and even valuable, to establish interrater reliability between two therapists who work in two different areas between which patients or clients are readily transferred. With interrater reliability established between two therapists, the necessity to reevaluate assessment scores when a patient is transferred may be eliminated, or the current therapist's scores may be directly compared with previous scores from another therapist to determine changes in ability or to modify the intervention plan.

Validity of Assessments

Assessment validity provides support that the assessment measures the correct target construct, trait, behavior, or ability. Table 9.3 outlines the major types of validity found in assessments used by occupational therapists. The validity of an assessment is supported when the assessment demonstrates that it actually measures what it claims to measure. Typically, the correlation between two assessments of the same trait, behavior, or ability provides evidence that supports the validity of an assessment. A validity coefficient of an assessment enables a therapist to assess how well the individual assessment results compare with an external criterion measure. An occupational therapist wants to know that he or she is measuring validly what he or she wants, not some undesirable aspect contributing to performance. Assessment reliability is important, but only once test validity is known.

Table 9.3. Types of Validity

Type	Description
Standard error of estimate	The inaccuracy or invalidity in determining an individual's true score. (Noted as SEE or Seest.)
Face validity	Established through the appearance of the items as related to the purpose of the assessment. It is not based on statistical proof.
Content validity	The extent to which the items on the assessment represent a sufficient, representative sample of the domain or construct being examined.
Criterion-related validity	*Concurrent or congruent criterion-related validity:* The extent of agreement between two simultaneous measures of the same behavior or trait. *Predictive or criterion-related validity:* The extent to which scores on an assessment forecast future behavior, abilities, or performance.
Construct validity	*Convergent validity:* The degree to which two tests being conducted measure the same ability or behavior; the amount of agreement between the two. *Discriminant validity:* The degree to which each of two assessments being conducted measure a different ability or behavior; the amount of disagreement between the two.
Ecological validity	The degree to which the test mimics and measures similar activities or events that can be observed in a typical, daily living context.
Factorial validity	The identification of interrelated behaviors, abilities, or functions that contribute to collective abilities or functions. Sometimes referred to as *multi-trait–multi-method validity.*

Score Reliability: Standard Error of Estimate

Just as the standard of error of measurement indicates the margin of error as a measure of unreliability across the standardization sample, the *standard error of estimate (SEE or SEest)* is the result of the margin of error that gives imperfect reliability in determining a person's score as correct. The SEE is not a major measure used in score reporting and is seldom mentioned for the assessments that an occupational therapist might use.

Face Validity

Face validity is not testable because it rests in the eye of the beholder. In assessment manuals, *face validity* usually presents the subjective and logical judgment used by the author or experts to declare this type of validity. Face validity is initiated by showing measurement items to potential individuals with conditions or behaviors to be assessed and/or a group of experts on the condition or behavior. The goal is to seek their confirmation that the test contained relevant items or behaviors to be measured. Face validity of an assessment also is important for the client or patient. As long as the assessment appears to address the client's health concerns meaningfully, the client will be motivated to do it well. Face validity can be considered a primitive form of content validity.

Content Validity

Content validity examines how well an assessment represents all aspects of the phenomenon being evaluated or studied (Hulley et al., 2007). The assessment developer establishes an assessment's content validity by examining the degree to which items on the assessment are an accurate representation of content; the test developer examines test questions to see how well they cover the content. Content validity is simple to establish as long as what is being assessed is not complex. In order to analyze content validity, the test developer must use specific objectives for the test or a test blueprint. A *test blueprint* is an outline of the major content areas covered in an assessment. Many times, the test blueprint also includes the percentage of items from each subcategory to be included in the final draft of the test. This percentage can be supported by the literature, analysis of experiences, or some desired goal. For instance, the national certification examination in occupational therapy is derived from a test blueprint that allocates the number of items to be included based on the percentage of time in activities, such as evaluation and intervention, as reported by the participants in a national study of entry-level practice. Thus, the content validity of the national certification examination is established by confirming whether the number of items on the exam reflects current practice percentages.

Content validity is based on logical judgment using assessment objectives, a blueprint, literature-supported criteria, or some other systematic resource on which to evaluate the presence and degree of content validity. In fact, inter-judge agreement is becoming an increasingly popular method of supporting content validity claims. The published assessment manual or other scientific publications should provide sufficient descriptive information about the process used to arrive at content validity assertions.

Criterion-Related Validity

Criterion-related validity is the extent to which one measure is systematically related to similar measures. To establish criterion-related validity, the scores from one assessment are correlated with an external criterion, typically one that is better known and already used, usually a well-established or widely accepted measure or assessment of the same criterion. This often is referred to as comparing to the "gold standard." Assessment developers also use a correlation statistic, called a *validity coefficient,* to verify criterion-related validity. Two types of criterion-related validity are concurrent and predictive.

Concurrent or Congruent Criterion-Related Validity

Concurrent validity compares a new assessment with one that is considered a measurement standard, sometimes referred to as the "gold standard" in measurement tools. Determining the concurrent criterion-related validity across tests is useful in occupational therapy to validate our specific professional assessments with others outside the field. The assessment developer compares the scores of a new test to an established test of the criterion by conducting both assessments at the same time. When one assessment has good concurrent validity with the other, one of them can be eliminated. Reasons to select an assessment are the following:

- It is more cost-effective,
- It takes a shorter amount of time to administer,
- It has better face validity to encourage participation,
- It can be given in groups, or
- Its results reflect greater congruence with program goals or purpose.

Predictive Criterion-Related Validity

The ability of an assessment to predict future abilities or outcomes, the test's *predictive validity,* is very important to a therapist. Typically, this kind of validity relates a current characteristic to anticipated future abilities or setting(s). Predictive validity is established by taking a measurement at one point in time and correlating it with later findings. A therapist can develop these findings by assessing the status of a person with respect to an important skill and then conducting another test of the skill at a future point to see what portion of the earlier test predicted the current abilities of the person studied.

If the purpose of an assessment is to forecast future abilities, problems, or outcomes based on the assessment results, then the predictive validity of a test is important. In early intervention, a therapist wants to know the relationship between current developmental abilities and future academic and social competence issues that may arise without intervention. An occupational therapist might use a coma scale in acute care to predict future rehabilitation potential and aptitude tests to predict future work options. A therapist would want to know the predictive ability of a coma assessment or aptitude test because the results might give or limit access to services or limit the individual to certain types of care systems. Sometimes, predictive validity can even guide the selection of therapy as therapists study intervening variables or activities between the two test administrations. Sometimes, test manuals compare interventions through their discussion of the outcomes from their predictive validity sample. However, predictive validity is a challenge to establish. When predictive validity is not possible, a therapist would find construct validity valuable.

Construct Validity

Construct validity is how well a measurement conforms to theoretical constructs. This validity is established by providing evidence supporting the relationship of a given assessment and a given theory. A theory provides a set of predictions and is used to establish construct validity. For instance, if a theory states that certain improvements in handwriting will occur after certain interventions, then a construct validity assessment using a pre- and post-intervention study can determine whether the theoretically expected changes actually occurred. If the assessment results demonstrate that the theoretically predicted changes did occur, then the assessment will have good construct validity. In other words, scores on the first assessment correlate with the second. Convergent validity and discriminant validity are two specific forms of construct validity.

Convergent Validity

A therapist looks for high positive correlations between two assessments, or *convergent validity*. When a new assessment becomes available, a therapist may compare it to an established assessment to determine the amount of agreement between the two assessments. If a high validity coefficient is achieved, then both tests measure the same construct and consequently the therapist can choose the assessment that best meets his or her needs. However, if the two assessments for the same construct have poor convergent validity, each measures something different. In this situation, the therapist should try to uncover the reason for the difference. This information will support the therapist's decision to conduct both assessments because each assessment provides different kinds of information.

Discriminant Validity

Discriminant validity is the opposite of convergent validity. With *discriminant validity,* high negative correlations between the two assessments are desirable when measuring the same general content or construct in very different areas. An assessment that has good discriminant validity will detect only individuals with similar conditions or abilities and rule out all others. The more consistently the assessment rules out others, the better the discriminant validity. Meaningful comparisons are essential. For instance, in occupational therapy a therapist would expect a test of cognition to better identify cognitive deficits in people with Alzheimer's disease than in those without it. Or, if the assessment is designed to isolate cognitive dysfunction in the presence of Alzheimer's, a meaningful discriminant validity test should be able to detect a worsening of cognitive abilities at each stage of the illness. Another approach could be to compare the performance of individuals suffering from various illnesses, such as multiple sclerosis, with different cognitive issues to see whether test results accurately separate the two groups on cognitive performance.

Ecological Validity

Ecological validity is a form of validity discussed in research design and psychometrics regarding the issue of generalizability. Ecological validity relates to the generalizability of study findings to other similar events or activities; in tests and measurements, it has to do with an assessment's ability to measure, collect, and record behaviors or observations that would be observed in a typical, daily living context. For practice, ecological validity is important when considering current or predicted level of independence, discharge criteria, and even community functioning. The potential utility of an observation or behavior gathered during an evaluation or by an assessment tool is framed within the cues associated with natural contexts or habitats, called ecological validity.

In an occupational therapy assessment, this concept is important because we want to know how much our scores and observations from a test reflect the individual's current or predicted performance abilities in natural contexts. For instance, if we measure cognition in the clinic, knowing the ecological validity of the test to predict cognitive capacities or deficits at home or work would be useful. With the heavy reliance on assessments that measure body functions, body structures, and performance skills, ecological validity is important to our evaluation processes and outcomes for intervention planning and documentation.

Ecological validity of an assessment tool can be established two ways: (1) Performing the assessment of function in a controlled clinical setting and then repeating it as soon as possible in the individual's home to see whether scores vary because of the natural cues in the home versus the controlled, distraction-free environment during clinical assessment or (2) correlating the assessment with accepted assessment tools of functional performance in natural contexts. Practitioners can use the reported ecological validity of an assessment to provide reference between clinical observations and potential for community or independent living. In other words, ecological validity is the relevance of the tool to daily living.

Factorial Validity

Factorial validity is a preferred approach to establish the validity of measures for complex behaviors. This type of validity is seldom necessary in most assessments because typical assessments look at isolated, single-performance abilities or problems. However, an occupational therapist is interested in occupations and daily living activities, which are complex and require multiple performance abilities. To establish the factorial validity of an assessment, the assessment should be correlated with a variety of other assessments that measure common traits, typically one factor or variable at a time. Sometimes, only the portion of the complex assessment that is similar to a single factor or construct is correlated with another, not the entire assessment.

Assessment Responsiveness

The bottom line on reliability and validity is the quality of the assessment to consistently and accurately measure a behavior or ability. This leads to the next most critical issue, responsiveness to measure change as a result of intervention, called sensitivity and specificity. *Sensitivity* is the ability to accurately detect those with a condition; *specificity* is the ability of an assessment to identify or to detect those who do not have the condition. Responsiveness is related to both reliability and validity of an assessment regarding the extent to which the assessment can practically or theoretically measure the current state of an individual to diagnose current status, but most importantly, to determine whether and how much change has occurred. The degree of fit between the construct and what is actually measured is important. For instance, applying an assessment tool with a similar construct, but one that is not reflective of the individual's demographics compared to those in the standardization sample (a question of specificity), may alter the sensitivity of an assessment.

In addition, responsiveness to change may be related to avoiding ceiling and floor effects and having scales in assessment tools that are unable to detect changes in performance. *Ceiling and floor effects* are when the assessment is not able to detect additional changes at the bottom (floor) or top (ceiling) of the scale. Assessments with good reliability and validity, used as intended in terms of standardization sample and procedures, have a wide enough scale to detect changes without a ceiling or floor effect and will enhance the chance of detecting change due to intervention (Domholdt, 2005).

Final Thoughts About Reliability and Validity

Before closing this chapter, which has primarily focused on reliability and validity from conceptual (definition and description), methodological (research), and applied (practice) perspectives, some additional considerations related to determining the quality of different measurement approaches need to be raised. Two timeless questions must be asked and the therapeutic value of the answers understood clearly:

1. Can a test have good reliability but poor validity?
2. Can a test have poor reliability but good validity?

The answers demonstrate one's understanding of these critical test and measurement concepts. Establishing the validity of tests is more important than reliability. Validity is a check against some established external criterion, demonstrating that the test measures what it is designed to measure (Anastasi & Urbina, 1997).

Conclusion

Quality assessments are critical to an occupational therapist's decision-making process. As occupational therapists, we must seek all possible avenues to explore the quality of the assessments we use. Ensuring the quality of a test is no easy task. Much of the time and financial responsibility rests on the test developer until a test publisher becomes invested in marketing the tool. Both test developers and publishers are bound by ethics, but as occupational therapists we must always be slightly skeptical when a test is being marketed, because an unethical publisher may choose to withhold certain reliability and validity studies that do not support their particular assessment tool. Occupational therapists should not rely solely on a test manual or even the knowledge that the test is frequently used in occupational therapy circles and should always conduct their own investigations. Also, prior to selecting a new assessment or reusing an existing test, occupational therapists should look at external reviews of these instruments reported in the profession's literature, as well as critical reviews from outside the profession.

Questions

1. How can error in testing results be controlled or dampened to ensure accurate measurement of an individual's condition or change due to intervention? Compare reliability and validity. Can an assessment be reliable but not valid? Can an assessment be valid but not reliable? What is the clinical relevance of using a reliable assessment? Using a valid assessment?
2. What strategies or approaches can an occupational therapist use to make sure the final score of an assessment is a more true score than error?
3. What guides an occupational therapist in looking for the right or best type(s) of established reliability or validity during the selection of an assessment?
4. How can test specificity and sensitivity be enhanced or supported during assessment in practice?
5. Describe the differences in measurement among standard deviation, standard error of measurement, and standard error of estimate. What do they mean and how are they applied in interpreting an individual's performance following assessment?
6. For each type of reliability and validity, summarize the following: how and why an assessment developer would want to establish this type of validity, why knowing that the assessment had this characteristic would be important to an occupational therapist, and why this type of reliability or validity is important to know when interpreting the scores obtained from an individual for diagnostic or intervention planning purposes.

References

Anastasi, A., & Urbina, S. (1997). *Psychological testing* (7th ed.). Upper Saddle River, NJ: Prentice Hall.

Bolton, B. F., & Parker, R. M. (2008). *Handbook of measurement and evaluation in rehabilitation* (2nd ed.). Gaithersburg, MD: Aspen.

Domholdt, E. (2005). *Rehabilitation research: Principles and applications*. St. Louis, MO: Elsevier/Saunders.

Hulley, S. B., Cummings, S. R., Browner, W. S., Grady, D. G., & Newman, T. B. (2007). *Designing clinical research*. Philadelphia: Lippincott Williams & Wilkins.

Kubiszyn, T., & Borich, G. (2003). *Educational testing and measurement: Classroom applications and practice* (7th ed.). New York: Wiley.

Nunnally, J. C., & Bernstein, I. H. (1994). *Psychometric theory* (3rd ed.). New York: McGraw-Hill.

Thorndike, R. (2001). Reliability. In B. F. Bolton (Ed.), *Handbook of measurement and evaluation in rehabilitation* (3rd ed., pp. 29–48). Gaithersburg, MD: Aspen.

10

Scoring and Interpretation of Results

Patricia Crist, PhD, OTR, FAOTA

Overview

The primary goal of evaluation is to determine intervention needs or changes after assessment-based intervention. A critical aspect of the evaluation process for a therapist is the ability to accurately interpret assessment results. Comprehension of scoring processes and interpretation of results leads to effective evaluation documentation and facilitates best practices in intervention planning. Such understanding has as its foundation a therapist who knows both the psychometrics that underpin the scores and the influence of error on obtained assessment results. This chapter provides the knowledge required to score and interpret assessment scores.

Scoring

Cronbach (1990) defined a *test* as a "systematic procedure for observing behavior and describing it with the aid of numerical scales or fixed categories" (p. 32). *Measurement* is the scientific process of quantifying characteristics to develop an integrated picture of a person based on information (Bolton & Brookings, 2001). A *test score* is a numeric representation of a response to an assessment or, more specifically, an item or collection of items on an assessment. *Measurement research* is the science of scoring and interpreting findings using universal principles from measurement science.

The goal of scoring an assessment is to transform an observed or acquired performance on a test item to an accurate, defensible, and meaningful interpretation that can contribute to clinical reasoning and provide understandable assessment results for problem solving, intervention planning, and communication purposes. Converting an observed performance during an assessment to a usable result follows a systemic process:

raw score → derived or obtained score → (standard score) → test interpretation

The evaluator's first step in scoring a test behavior is marking a *raw score* for the observed performance or response using a *response scale* or *marking system* provided in the assessment manual. The second step is using a scale useful for understanding assessment results to convert the raw score. This score is called a *derived* or *obtained score*. One of the few times raw scores are used, other than the initial step of scoring an assessment, is during research data collection, because a raw score is a pure score without other transformation. In some instances, assessment manuals (or the therapist as an evaluator) convert the derived score to a *standard score,* which sometimes makes scores even more meaningful to stakeholders. Standard scores also allow comparisons between assessments. The parentheses around this step in the diagram reflect that the conversion to standard scores is optional because a therapist can accurately interpret from either obtained or standard scores. Certainly, the ability to complete all these steps in scoring is dependent on the development and standardization of procedures published for the assessment. Some procedures will be developed more thoroughly than others.

A score or *test result* is only a snapshot of current abilities or conditions. In intervention planning and clinical decision-making processes, a therapist should consider other important information, such as observations, records, reports from other disciplines, patient and program resources, predictions regarding recovery or skill development, and, most importantly, the client's goals and needs, along with the evaluation results.

The compelling goal of any assessment is definitively and accurately identifying what is being measured. This is called *test validity.* The validity of a test is an indication of how well it measures what it says it does. Validity is a primary determinant in our final decisions. According to Anastasi and Urbina (1997), there are essentially four decisions from assessment that are the outcome of a test's validity; two are correct decisions and two are incorrect decisions:

- *Two correct decisions:*
    1. Assessment correctly detects the presence of something when it truly does exist.
    2. Assessment correctly does not find anything when there is nothing.
- *Two incorrect decisions:*
    1. Assessment finds something when really it is not present (false acceptance).
    2. Assessment does not find anything when the condition truly does exist (false rejection).

With the first incorrect decision (false acceptance), an assessment result would support providing unneeded interventions that could be harmful, such as a drug (which causes uncomfortable side effects) for an illness a client does not have. With false rejections, the client does not receive treatment from which he or she could have benefited. False acceptances are a waste of valuable resources and add unnecessary health care costs. False rejections are a more serious testing failure. Thus, along with the reliability and validity of an assessment, scoring interpretation becomes very important in maximizing the frequency of correct findings and minimizing the frequency of incorrect decisions that are very costly to individuals and the health care system. This is the essence of scoring validity.

Response Methods for Test Items

When selecting an assessment with the best quality for a given program need, the occupational therapist has a number of choices for assessment tools. Ultimately, the quality of test scores begins with the type of response method or rating scales included in the assessment. *Response methods* or *rating scales* provide a mechanism for gathering the strength of a response, feeling, or performance. In addition, the quality of the method or scale influences the value of the information obtained for future intervention or program evaluation purposes. Although covering all rating scales or response methods is impossible, the typical ones seen in occupational therapy are

- *Observation of performance* using a standardized protocol that directs attention to preidentified issues.
- *Likert scales,* a highly used response type in which specific rank-ordered responses are presented in the scale. Likert scales are response rating scales with three to seven linearly related test response options differentiating the degree of response. The response anchors vary and include *strongly disagree to strongly agree, very much like me to not at all like me,* and *0% of the time to 100% of the time.* Likert scales with midpoints, especially those that read *don't know* or something similar, are test-taker friendly but give no real response for the basis of diagnosing or interrupting problems. A midpoint for *no response, not sure,* or *no opinion* increases test-taker comfort, but repeated use as a selected response significantly limits a therapist's understanding of the client's problems or needs. When the assessment does not provide a midpoint item (especially of the type that allows "fence sitting"), the test-taker is forced to choose a side. This ultimately will give the therapist better information about the client's true needs or interests. However, this approach to testing may lower test-taker motivation to complete the test.
- *Checklist scales* are a scale of responses in which all the possible adjectives or characteristics relating to the purpose of the assessment are included using a "present" or "absent" response format. Checklists can give wide coverage of characteristics but cannot give information regarding the strength of contribution of the characteristics that are marked.
- *Forced-choice scales* attempt to reduce bias in responses by forcing the test-taker to choose one of the assessment items. There is no midpoint for no decision and no "no response or not observed/present" category. Forced-

choice scales provide an evaluation of strength of response. An example would be "Indicate the degree to which the following statement describes your interest."

- *Semantic differential* is a subjective evaluation of concepts along a continuum with end anchor words such as goodness descriptors *(good–bad, fair–unfair)*, potency or strength responses *(heavy–light, hard–soft)*, or activity dimensions *(active–passive, fast–slow)*. Semantic differential is most effective when a multipoint scale is provided for marking answers, remembering the concern about including a *don't know/not sure* midpoint.
- Q *sort* asks the responder to sort a series of items such as pictures or words into specific stacks according to stated criterion categories such as "which activities you currently engage in" or "do now; used to do; would like to do in the future; not interested in doing."

These are the major types of response and rating scales seen in occupational therapy; there are many more. The best scales most clearly approximate what the therapist wants to assess and use a method that thoroughly elicits potential responses. Regardless, the most important rule for increasing response rate, ensuring a true score, and providing validity is to ask only about what one wants to know.

Norm-Referenced and Criterion-Referenced Tests

Before discussing scoring, it is important to understand the two major types of assessments: norm-referenced and criterion-referenced. *Norm-referenced testing* compares the results of the person being tested against the population or representative sample. Norm-referenced testing allows a therapist to place or rank the individual's performance in relation to others who have taken the test. *Criterion-referenced testing* uses a criterion or a standard of performance or skill attainment to measure mastery. Criterion-referenced testing provides a therapist with knowledge regarding the test-taker's level of proficiency or mastery of the skill or ability that the assessment measures.

All of us are familiar with both types of testing. The college entrance boards compare each person to the standardization group to score performance. Most classes use norm-referenced testing, assuming that a student who gets an A knows about 20% more information than a student who earns a C. Criterion-referenced approaches are used in high school physical education classes (where a student has to demonstrate a certain level of physical condition before passing) and in some schools in which a student needs to achieve a certain minimum test score to graduate. In occupational therapy, the national evaluation for Level II fieldwork is based on mastery learning concepts. The occupational therapy national certification examination is criterion-referenced, because the test-taker must accumulate enough correct answers out of the total number of valid test items to demonstrate that he or she is at least minimally competent to be an entry-level occupational therapist.

Norm-referenced assessments provide comparative information from a *standardization sample* of individuals with defined demographic characteristics. The outcomes from the standardization sample are called *norms*. Norms are the comparative basis for interpreting the results of the person the therapist assesses. To make a valid comparison, the test-taker's characteristics must be similar to the demographic characteristics of the norm sample. In creating a norm-referenced assessment, the developer selects test items that promote variance and spread performance results along a continuum of complexity. Norms provide a comparison of the possible range of scores rather than simply show the presence or absence of a characteristic, ability, or skill as criterion-referenced approaches do. Norm-referenced assessments permit a broader testing of behaviors or abilities, whereas criterion-referenced testing measures a narrow, frequently very specific, area of mastery.

When creating a criterion-referenced assessment, the developer chooses items that reflect different levels of mastery. Thus, content validity is very important. Criterion-referenced or mastery tests are important in occupational therapy when deciding whether to discharge a client or place him or her in certain learning or therapeutic groups based on similar capabilities or deficits. Criterion-referenced assessments are very useful in measuring skill or performance attainment of activities of daily living because a therapist simply wants to know what a person can and cannot do. Although findings from this type of assessment can be used to request more intervention time from third-party payers, norm-referenced information usually is more effective in supporting the need for intervention.

Both types of tests can be standardized in terms of test items, administration, and scoring. To ensure the quality of the assessment processes and have confidence in scores, a therapist must always

- Read the test manual before administering the assessment,
- Practice delivering the assessment before using it to assess a client,
- Adhere exactly to the published administration and scoring instructions in the assessment manual without deviating or adapting the assessment to a specific situation, and
- Convey the importance of the assessment to the client so that he or she will be encouraged to do his or her best.

If a therapist deviates from the published procedures for any reason, he or she must use caution when reporting the results. When a therapist does not follow the standardized procedures, he or she has no way to determine the effect of this choice on the obtained scores. The results received are not necessarily accurate because of the deviation from the standardized procedure. When writing a report after deviating from the standardized procedures, the therapist must describe the deviation from prescribed procedure and describe what occurred, indicating that this might affect the results and caution against using the data.

Essential Statistical Concepts for Scoring and Interpretation

A test score is typically the sum of responses to test items or tasks. The goal in scoring is to convert an observation to a numeric quantity so that the therapist can record, analyze, and meaningfully interpret the results. Interpreting scores requires that the therapist understand this process and apply related statistics, called *psychometrics* or *measurement science*. With increased accountability expected in practice, an occupational therapist must understand the statistics used in tests and measurements.

This textbook provides only a conceptual understanding of certain test statistics applied to the evaluation process. The next section is a review of the psychometrics that are essential to a competent evaluator. Readers are advised to use other resources for a more thorough discussion on statistics and a deeper understanding of what is discussed here. The concepts discussed in the following section are defined or described in Table 10.1

Measurement Scales

Tests and measurements use four different measurement scales. These levels or scales are important to know in testing because the required response or answer method dictates the boundaries for quantifying and reporting test results. The scales are presented from the simplest to the most sophisticated.

Table 10.1. Basis Statistical Concepts for Scoring and Interpretation

Concept	Description
Score	*Raw score:* an individual's response to a specific test item before it is converted to some other number via test manual instructions; what is marked by the test-taker or evaluator during the process of the evaluation. *Obtained/derived score:* a conversion of the raw score to some other form using a method published for the test. *Standard score:* a conversion of the derived score to a form that permits comparison of the test results with others.
Levels of measurement	*Nominal:* a score that identifies an individual as having or not having the characteristic. *Ordinal:* a score that rank orders a given characteristic across all individuals. *Interval*:* a score that reflects the magnitude of difference between responses; contains a standard unit of measurement, making it possible to quantifiably measure differences between individuals. *Ratio*:* a score that is like an interval scale but is ratio-based using a scale with a zero point (complete absence of characteristic). *Can be combined to create a "metric scale."
Normal distribution	A mathematically determined curve representing the theoretical distribution of scores or some other characteristic across the population that clusters around a central point called a mean or average.

Nominal Scale

Nominal scale scores identify individuals as having or not having a particular characteristic. Test items with responses resulting in mutually exclusive categories are nominal, such as yes or no, male or female, marital status (single, married, widowed, divorced), pain or no pain, having a symptom or not, being able to run or not, and being able to fix breakfast or not. The condition, characteristic, ability, or whatever the test item is measuring is marked either as present or not present. Checklists and *Q*-sort response scales result in nominal data. Examples include the assigned number for a Special Olympics competitor or indicating that the loss of sensation is or is not present with carpal tunnel syndrome.

Ordinal Scale

An *ordinal scale* ranks the characteristic being measured along a continuum. Ordinal scales provide information only about position, not magnitude or degree of a condition or an ability. Some examples of test items whose responses result in ranking or ordering of an ordinal nature include tallest to smallest, most to least pain, total number of medications, and high to low stress. The condition, characteristic, ability, or attribute that the test item is measuring must vary in a linear progression and along a continuum in which the anchors at each end are polar opposites. The use of Likert and semantic differential response scales results in ordinal data. Examples are winning a gold, silver, or bronze medal and reporting sensation loss in one, two, or three fingers with carpal tunnel syndrome.

Interval Scale

An *interval scale* has a standard unit of measure related in response sets that allow a person to estimate the magnitude of difference between responses. It is an ordinal scale with equal units along its length. For instance, when measuring the number of minutes it takes workers to sort hardware into three different canisters, a person who finishes the test item in 5 minutes is twice as fast as a person who does the same task in 10 minutes. Examples are time to run the 50-meter race in the Special Olympics and temperature.

Ratio Scale

A *ratio scale* is like the interval scale with an underlying measurement, but a major difference is that this scale has a true zero point (ratio-based). Some examples are miles per hour and feet per second. For an occupational therapist, ratio scales are often physical measures, such as top running speed in the 50-meter race in the Special Olympics or rate of nerve conductance with carpal tunnel syndrome.

Most measurement scales use either ordinal or interval scales to gather their responses to test items. Some experts argue that there is no real difference in response data tabulated using an interval or ratio scale, so they collapse the two and call it a *metric scale*.

Understanding the item response method and the related scale of measurement used to gather scores is important because it influences how a therapist interprets scores. For instance, a checklist collects nominal data on characteristics. All a therapist knows when scoring this test is which characteristics the individual reports or identifies to describe himself or herself or some other activity. A therapist does not know the strength of the response that likely varies from one checklist item to another.

Central Tendency

With a normal curve, all three measures of *central tendency*—the mean, median, and mode—are equivalent (at the peak of the normal curve). Figure 10.1 depicts a normal curve, which will be discussed extensively later. Each of the three measures is a different approach to describing the most common or average characteristic in a group or set of scores. Table 10.2 describes the different types of central tendency.

Mean

The *mean* is the average of the group of scores. The formula is

$$\overline{X} = \frac{\Sigma X}{N} \qquad\qquad \text{average score} = \frac{\text{sum of all scores}}{\text{total number of scores}}$$

Some texts use M rather than $\overline{X}$ as the symbol for the mean or mathematical average. $\overline{X}$ is referred to as "bar x."

- Σ The sigma symbol, used to indicate the sum of the scores obtained
- X The scores obtained
- N The total number of scores gathered.

The mean has several features that make it the preferred measure of central tendency. It is the most stable because each score contributes to the calculation, but it is greatly affected by extreme scores. The implications of this characteristic of the mean are discussed later in this chapter.

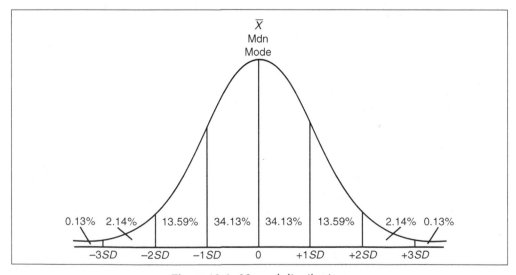

Figure 10.1. Normal distribution.

Table 10.2. Central Tendency and Variability in Scoring

Concept	Description
Central tendency	*Mean:* the average of a group of scores; noted as $\overline{X}$ or *M*.
	Median: the score that splits the distribution in half; 50% of the scores are above and 50% below the median; called the *midpoint score;* noted as *Mdn.*
	Mode: the score that occurs most frequently in the distribution of scores.
Variability	*Standard deviation:* the estimate of variability that normally accompanies the mean due to accumulated error; noted as *SD, S,* or *σ*.
	Variance: also called the *mean square deviation,* is a variation on the *SD*; noted as *MSD.*
	Semi-interquartile deviation or range: based on the range of the middle 50% of the scores around the median instead of the entire range of scores; noted as *SIQR.*
	Range: usually the high and low score are given as the range; another method is to subtract low score from high score, and this gives one number for the range; noted as *R.*

Median

The *median* is the second most frequently encountered measure of central tendency. It evenly divides the population in half, with 50% above the median and 50% below. The median is favored over the mean when extreme scores are present, discussed later in this chapter. Also, it may be favored with ordinal response items on a test. The measurement abbreviation for the median is *Mdn.*

To calculate a median, a therapist orders scores from low to high and then selects the score that divides the group equally in half. If there are an even number of items, then the median is the average of the two center-most numbers. Following are examples of the calculation, with arrows indicating the score(s) that divide the total number in the group into 50% on each side:

$$\frac{(56 + 62)}{2} = 59$$

	45		45		45
	52		52		52
→	56	→	56	→	56
	62	→	56	→	62
	<u>109</u>		62		65
			<u>109</u>		<u>109</u>
	Mdn = 56		*Mdn* = 56		*Mdn* = 59

Mode

The *mode* is the least reported score unless it permits the author to make a significant point regarding the interpretation of the results. This is because the mode provides very little information beyond which scores occur most frequently. If two scores occur most frequently, this is a bimodal distribution. If each score appears an equal number of times, then there is no mode.

Variability

Variability is the spread of scores around a measure of central tendency. Variation provides information regarding how condensed or widely spread the scores are in the distribution. Variation is important because a smaller variation around the measure of central tendency indicates that the score is accurate (a true score) and not due to random variation (error).

Standard Deviation

The *standard deviation (SD)* is the estimate of variance that accompanies the mean. Standard deviation is powerful because it considers every score obtained. The notation for the standard deviation is *SD*. Standard deviation as a measure of test variability is related to the standard deviation concept discussed under the section on Normal Distribution. The *SD* provides the basis to compare results from different tests taken by an individual. Here, essentially, the variance is similar to the *SD*. If item responses were collected using ordinal scales of measurement, extreme caution must be taken in reporting the mean and related standard deviation because the initial data were not sophisticated enough to warrant this application.

The calculation for a standard deviation is more complex. Most assessment manuals report the *SD*, and calculators make it easy to determine. Here is one approach a therapist can use to calculate *SD*:

$$SD = \sqrt{\frac{\Sigma x^2}{N}}$$

Semi-Interquartile Deviation or Range

The *semi-interquartile deviation* or *range* is based on the range of the middle 50% of the scores around the median instead of the entire range of scores. It is noted as the *SIQR*. Like the median, this variance measure compensates for extreme scores and is preferred when test items were gathered using ordinal response scales. Calculation of the SIQR is a bit more challenging, and because a table will be provided in most test manuals with which to match the obtained score, only the formula is presented here:

$$SIQR = \frac{Q_3 - Q_1}{2}$$

where 75% of the scores are below Q3 and 25% of the scores are below Q1.

One disadvantage of the SIQR is that it uses only half of the acquired scores, so it is more stable than the range but not as good as the standard deviation, which considers all scores.

Range

Range is the easiest estimate of variance but also the least sophisticated. The notation for range is *R*. The range is calculated by subtracting the lowest score from the highest score. Sometimes, the range is called an *inclusive range*. The inclusive range is calculated by subtracting the lowest score from the highest score and adding 1.

Scores: 33   45   47   51   62   79   88   93

Various ways to calculate and report *R* for the above set of scores:

$$R = 93 - 33 = 60$$

$$\text{Inclusive } R = (93 - 33) + 1 = 61$$

Most often seen in reports:

"The scores range from 33 to 93."

$$R: (33 < x < 93)$$

$$R = 33 \text{ to } 93$$

A therapist seldom sees the calculated range reported to describe variance in scores because it provides little valuable information. What a therapist sees are the lowest and highest scores reported, so that he or she knows the general spread and, if the therapist has an individual score, he or she would know where it would generally fit in the norm sample results. The reported range might be interesting in terms of showing whether individuals passed all items. If so, this would mean there is a *ceiling,* which is difficult with norm-referenced testing because the therapist is not seeing any differences between individuals detected in the "ceiling score area." Likewise, in norm-referenced testing, a therapist wants a range as wide as possible with no extreme score outliers, giving the best possible variation to detect differences between scores.

Normal Distribution

The *normal distribution* is a standard developed in 1733 by Abraham deMoivre from theory and mathematical calculations (cited in Pearson, 1924; definition included in Table 10.1). For test and measurement purposes, the underlying premise is that if a person gathered responses to any variable from a very large number of individuals, the numbers of people achieving each score most likely would distribute themselves in a *normal curve,* the model used to make comparisons among scores or statistical decisions. Normal distribution is shown in Figure 10.1.

In the normal distribution, the mean ($\overline{X}$), median (*Mdn*), and mode are all equal because the distribution is symmetrical on both sides. The previous section included a description of the measures of central tendency (see Table 10.2). In addition, the percentages of scores represented under each area that equate to each SD are a standard derived from the normal curve. Each SD is set at a place where the direction of the curve changes mathematically.

Remember that standard deviation refers to an error in measurement. If there is no error (which does not occur in testing), a therapist could dismiss the concept of SD altogether, but since error is present in any assessment administered, a therapist always will introduce some measurement of variance into the interpretation of results.

This simple curve should be committed to memory because recalling this information with ease will help immensely in listening to or giving reports in team meetings or in reading client records regarding assessment outcomes. Some helpful information from the normal curve includes the following:

- The percentage of scores between 0 and +1 SD or 0 and –1 SD is 34.13% (commonly referred to as 34%)
- The percentage of scores between +1 SD and +2 SD or –1 SD and –2 SD is 13.59% (commonly referred to as 14%)
- The percentage of scores between +2 SD and +3 SD or –2 SD and –3 SD is 2.14% (commonly referred to as 2%)
- 99% of the scores fall between –3 SD and +3 SD

Typically, all scores on an assessment will be between –3 SD and +3 SD.

Further, a therapist can add the areas under the curve to gain reference information:

68% of the scores are between –1 SD and +1 SD (34% + 34% = 68%)

Or, a therapist can calculate the percentage of scores above or below a standard deviation: What percentage of individuals scored less than +2 SD? Add the areas to the left of this mark: 2% + 14% + 34% + 34% = 84%. These numbers always correlate with percentile scores (cumulative percentages). If a therapist understands the standard deviation in relation to the normal distribution, he or she can easily convert scores to *percentile scores* because they are equivalent to the areas under the curve. So in the last example, the individual score was in the 84th *percentile*.

The therapist should never automatically interpret a score on the left of the center of the normal distribution as being bad or negative. Sometimes a therapist would prefer scores to be on that side of the mean, with a negative SD reported, for example, if the normal distribution reflects the degree of disability present, the current cholesterol, or bone density score. Always interpret assessment data or norms with reference to the direction of the measure used.

Relationships Between Central Tendency and Variation in Testing

The mean and standard deviation are the most sophisticated and sensitive measures for evaluating data because they are based on the assumption that the obtained scores were based on interval or ratio levels of measurement and all

Table 10.3. Measures of Central Tendency and Variance Commonly Reported, by Type of Measurement Scale

Measurement Scale	Central Tendency	Variance
Ratio and interval	Mean	Standard deviation
Ordinal	Median	Semi-interquartile deviation or range
Nominal	Not applicable	Not applicable

scores in the distribution were used. The least sophisticated measure is the mode because it gives little information; thus, modes are seldom reported. More often, the upper and lower limits of the range are reported to indicate the variation of the scores. The level of sophistication is related to the way in which responses were gathered (i.e., the level of measurement; see Table 10.3).

When a response to a test item results in interval or ratio data, sometimes combined and called *metric data,* it is legitimate to calculate a mean and standard deviation. However, with ordinal data, a therapist can use only those test statistics listed. An interval or ratio measure can be converted to the less-sophisticated forms related to ordinal and nominal items; an ordinal response can be converted to a nominal one. However, a category cannot be converted to a more-sophisticated one because there is not sufficient information to make a valid conversion.

Skewing in Score Curves

In the real world of testing, many tests result in skewed curves, which affects the use of the normal distribution and related measures of central tendency. Figure 10.2 shows examples of a positively and negatively skewed distribution.

As illustrated and discussed previously, the mean is the most sensitive to clustering at one end of the curve and to extreme scores. The median is not as unstable. Thus, using the mean is problematic when extreme scores skew a curve. One arena where skewed distributions get much attention is in the classroom. Grade-conscious students realize two things:

1. Everyone prefers a negatively skewed test over a positive one, especially if the instructor sticks to the published grading scale in the syllabus, because scores cluster toward the high end of the scale.
2. When a test is positively skewed, everyone in the class is shocked by their low grades and hopes that the instructor does not use the earned grade without somehow adjusting the scores (i.e., through bonus points or curving).

More-sophisticated instructors use test and measurement principles and statistics to aid in fair, accountable decision making regarding test scores and logical communication to others using standards accepted in testing practices. When the instructor uses test statistics with skewed test results, decision making should center on the median, not the mean. Sometimes an instructor

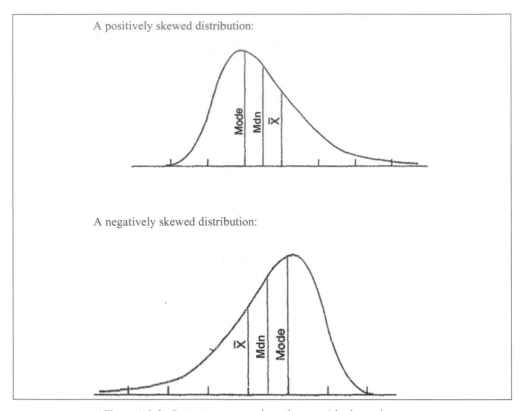

Figure 10.2. Impact on central tendency with skewed curves.

is lenient and curves the test using the mode, instead of the median or mean, and applies the test's standard deviation to determine the cutoff score needed for each percentage or letter grade.

When an assessment has skewed results, the author of the assessment usually will address this issue in the manual and provide a guide for interpreting the assessment outcomes.

Sensitivity

Sensitivity relates to the degree of stability or the pull on a variable away from the mode of the curve. In skewed curves, the mean is pulled faster than the median, and the median is always between the mean and mode, so the mean is more sensitive.

What is the clinical importance of this concept? If a therapist has a group of scores and there are a few very high or low outliers, reporting the mean will misrepresent the scores. Thus, the median is more suitable to use with outlying scores. Another administrative example applying the concept of skewed distributions shows the effect of outliers on the measure of central tendency. An administrator challenged an occupational therapy department to prove that average department salaries were below market value. He included the salary of the department head (an outlier; it was much higher than those of frontline staff) with all other occupational therapy salaries to arrive at a department average. According to the administrator's monthly expense printout, the average occupational therapist salary in the department was $50,100, which was $8,000 above the average reported by area hospitals. When the salary of the department head was removed from the average, however, the average occupational therapist salary was only $37,000. The staff explained their rationale using statistical information about outliers and were each rewarded a permanent $5,000 salary increase!

Item Analysis

The reliability and validity of an assessment are important, but another quantitative feature to consider is item analysis. The effectiveness of any item on a test can be studied by analyzing responses to it. Item analysis reflects two different features: *item difficulty* and *item discrimination*. Item analysis is used to perfect a test, or in other words, to improve its reliability and validity. It can shorten the test by eliminating test items that do not contribute significantly. The *significance* of an item measures what the assessment purports to measure (validity) and whether it does so accurately (more true than error score). Some assessment developers try to use random selection for this process, which is better than serendipity but is not the best approach to adding or removing test items. For instance, a test item may be very difficult and the majority of test-takers might not be able to answer it, but if the high scorers on the test always get the item correct, then it is a good item to retain because it discriminates this high-scoring group from the rest. According to Miller, Linn, and Gronlund (2009, p. 362), item analysis is designed to answer questions such as the following:

1. Did the items function as intended?
2. Were the test items of appropriate difficulty?
3. Were the test items free of irrelevant clues and other defects?
4. Was each of the distracters effective (in multiple-choice items)?

The assessment developers ask these questions when constructing their test, but these also are good questions for a therapist to consider when choosing an assessment for practice. It is important for the therapist to look for this information in the assessment's standardization manual and reflect on subjective feelings or experiences with the assessment in the context in which it will be used.

In practice, it is useful to review items that the client did not answer correctly. This may give the therapist clues as to what the client does not understand or what skills are not yet acquired. This reflective review of missed or wrong responses to items can include

- Discussion with the client to discover what he or she does not know,
- Looking for groupings of similar problems to focus intervention around skills that are least acquired across a given time,

- Uncovering how a therapist might improve the intervention approach to prevent recurrence in future clients, or
- Looking for another assessment that better relates to the goals of the intervention program.

Item Difficulty

The *difficulty* of an item is defined as the percentage of individuals who pass it. An item that 75% of test-takers pass is easier than one that only 15% pass. In the process of test construction, a spread on item difficulty is usually desirable. Easier items are frequently placed at the beginning of the assessment to build the test-taker's confidence and motivate the person to continue with the assessment when items get more difficult.

A common rule is to choose a set of items with a spread in difficulty but with the average of the spread around 50%, or .50, if the goal is to maximize differentiation between individuals. On the other hand, screening tests might cluster around .20 to .30 to ensure that individuals are not missed initially (false rejections) by this quick method. In mastery testing, the item difficulty should be around .80 to .90 to ensure that the individual has adequately mastered the desired skill consistently. Item difficulty can be calculated as

$$P = 100 \ (R/T)$$

where the statistical notation for item difficulty is P, R is the number of people who got the item right, and T is the total number who responded to the item.

Item Discrimination

Item discrimination is the degree to which an item differentiates correctly among test-takers for the behavior or skill that the assessment is designed to measure (Anastasi & Urbina, 1997). On a criterion-referenced assessment, items may be selected only because of their ability to discriminate between having mastered or not mastered the desired level of competency. Item discrimination can be established in two ways: (1) The assessment can be given to individuals who have known varying levels of mastery in a criterion, or (2) each item can be studied in reference to the rank orders of how each person performed on the assessment overall.

For instance, professors who use computerized scoring on a test get item discrimination statistics that reflect each item's ability to predict who was most likely to get the answer right. If an equal number of low scorers and high scorers on the test answered the item correctly, then the item is a poor discriminator. On the other hand, if only the high scorers got the item right, the item discrimination index would be very high. If a professor is examining a test from a norm-referenced perspective, he or she would not necessarily throw out a question if a large number of students did not answer it correctly; he or she would first consider the item's discrimination statistics. Also, the professor can get response discrimination statistics that would tell him or her which responses were good distracters and which were not. The higher the distraction value of all non-right answers, the better the item will differentiate the scorers. Creating a good test is hard work, and it takes multiple efforts to refine good questions. Each improvement to a test improves test-takers' chances of receiving a final score that reflects a true score rather than random error.

There are many specific statistical approaches to testing item difficulty and discrimination. One easy formula for calculating item discrimination is

$$D = (RU \times 2 \times RL) / (.5T)$$

where D is the item, RU is the number of students in the upper group who answered the item correctly, RL is the number of the students in the lower group who answered correctly, and $.5T$ is half of the total group who took the test item. This is not a measure of true item validity because it compares the item against an internal criterion based on how the current test-takers performed, not an external criterion. Items with low discrimination power should be studied for misleading clues, vagueness, or other technical problems. Typically, this information is presented in an assessment manual. Therapists need to understand conceptually how item difficulty is determined to appropriately use the assessments when discussing this issue in practice.

Two other methods to provide support regarding the value of the scores obtained from a group of test-takers are *extreme groups validation* and *cross-validation*. *Extreme groups validation* is when the responses of the lower 27% to 33% of test-taker scores on a test are correlated with the responses of the top 27% to 33% of test-taker scores. *Cross-validation* is when a different sample of individual responses is used to determine test validity than the sample used to study item difficulty. Conceptually, items with the highest negative correlation are retained. With the advent of computers, this difficult process is made easier, and test precision is improving with new computer-assisted approaches.

Rasch Analysis

Rasch analysis is not really an item analysis procedure but is included because it is a method to arrive at standard results on assessments that are highly reliant on evaluator observation, in which all items have a variance in individual task difficulty, such as complex daily living tasks, or items require analysis of multi-skilled activities (not single-focus test items). Rasch is a method to stabilize your reliability and validity as a scorer.

Rasch analysis or *scoring* is valuable in occupational therapy because therapists must subjectively observe complex task performance, which creates a greater chance for bias to introduce errors into scores. (If Rasch analysis were used by judges of ice skating, gymnastics, or diving competitions, the raters would have fewer crises related to scoring discrepancies and final decisions.) Each task, especially daily living tasks, has its own level of difficulty. In occupational therapy, Rasch analysis of scores sees wiping a spill on a kitchen counter as less difficult than cleaning a spill on a carpet. The Rasch approach to item analysis reflects

- The performance ability of the person observed or tested,
- The item or task difficulty in comparison to other test items,
- The severity or leniency of the rater in scoring the task performance, and
- The degree of difficulty in declaring a rating for the task.

Each item on an inventory has a Rasch score calculated from repeated studies of the consistency of ratings for a test item. Each evaluator is standardized in becoming a reliable, valid scorer through training on standardized administration procedures that also includes interrater reliability checks with test experts. This is followed by an independent rating of observed performance in which the average error of severity or leniency in scoring on the test is calculated for every time the scorer administers the test in the future. Anyone who goes through training to use the Assessment of Motor and Process Skills (AMPS; Fisher, 2003) understands this approach once they have been calibrated on the test. The AMPS is computer scored using the raw data the administrator provides, mixed in with the item difficulty pretested for each daily living task item and the administrator's calibration as an evaluator (accounting for scorer error) using this specific test. Thus, a client's score on the test reflects his or her true score because the score has been adjusted for typical common scorer errors attributed to task difficulty and evaluator misjudgments.

Norms

In norm-referenced assessments, the comparison of scores to a well-defined group is expected. This group is referred to as the test's *norm group* or *norms*. To establish norms, the standardized test is given to a large group of people for whom the assessment was developed, or groups or individuals likely to use the test because of its stated purpose. These norms are published in the assessment manual, allowing future evaluators to compare the results of their individual scores to those of a larger norm group. Ideally, the more the norm group data parallel the assumptions of the normal curve, the better.

Norms frequently use one or more standard ways to report findings from an assessment. These are discussed under the next section on Reporting Scores. Norms are helpful in defining a person's strengths or weaknesses or describing the amount of skill or ability (progress) within a given intervention sequence or across time. To use norms accurately, a test-taker should have characteristics similar to those of the norm group; otherwise, the evaluator introduces a new source of error into data interpretations.

The evaluation report should specify the type of norm group, each of which has implications for interpreting the client's test score:

- *Multiple norm group comparisons* enable comparison of one person's score on a test to more than just a single norm group. An evaluator might compare a test-taker's results on a vocational readiness inventory to the norms of several different occupational groups.

- *Local norm groups* provide information for norms using only local test-takers. These groups are used frequently in schools where curricula are unique, either within a school or within a school district or region. Sometimes, rehabilitation agencies find that a certain assessment is very useful but that no norms are specific enough to their group; they may establish local norms for comparisons of individual scores with those from their group. This is not a simple process, but it can be done validly, especially if agencies consult a psychometrician. Over time, local norm groups can provide new evidence for practice.
- *National norms* represent individuals from across the country. Test developers may conduct a national norm standardization study. Because a thorough national norm study is nearly impossible to conduct (it would be too complicated and expensive), the evaluator must consult the manual to identify the rationale and process used to establish the national norms and to judge the quality of the approach. Although it is difficult and costly to establish true national norms, most tests are perceived to be of higher quality if their norms are at the national, rather than local, level.
- *Special group norms* are norms for a test that may be used with more than one population of like individuals whose performance may vary because of their special problem or condition. Some call this *fixed reference group norms*. This type of norm often is used in occupational therapy evaluation. For instance, a test measuring social adjustment may be valid for people with social adjustment problems who also fit one or more disability groups or social conditions. Separate norms should be presented for each special group or use.

Other terms you might hear are *developmental norms, mental age norms,* and *national anchor group norms.* Reading the test manual closely should give the rationale for the norm group selection and process. For interpretation purposes using norms, a client's characteristics should be similar to those reported in the norm group.

Reporting Scores

An *obtained score* reflects a known distribution of test scores, including central tendency and variance estimates. Such scores can be found in most, if not all, assessments. Obtained scores only have meaning when considering the assessment itself, but when a therapist reports tests to clients, their families, other practitioners, and third-party payers, he or she needs to give scores that are easily communicative and possibly permit comparison with other assessment results. The scores offered by standardized tests and standard scores are two ways to report score results. Standard scores provide an easy way to report how a person performs in relation to others on the assessment as well as a simple way to compare the outcomes of different tests.

As a review, the number assigned to a test-taker's performance on a test item is the *raw score.* The assessment manual will instruct the therapist on which, if any, method should be used to convert the raw score to an *obtained* or *derived score,* which is usually incorporated into the evaluation report. Sometimes raw and obtained scores are the same; other times, they are not. Then a third, optional step is translating the derived score to a *standard score.* Sometimes, the assessment manual publishes a table explaining how to convert the obtained score into a derived or standard score. Other times, if needed, a therapist can convert the test score into a standard score as long as he or she knows the score's standard deviation. This may make it easier to communicate assessment results of similar problems.

Scores From Standardized Tests

Standardized tests frequently convert their results into some type of externally accepted standard, such as percentages or grade or age equivalence. Table 10.4 provides brief definitions of the types of standardized scores, and Figure 10.3 presents many of the standard score reporting methods in relation to the normal distribution, showing how the scoring methods relate to the distribution and to each other.

Percentile Scores

A *percentile score,* sometimes called a *cumulative percentage score,* correlates exactly with the percentage areas under the normal distribution (see Table 10.4). A percentile score relates the obtained score in terms of the percentage below the score and the percentage above it. It explains one's relative standing within a larger group who also took the assessment. For instance, in a test of motor ability given to a child, the number of items passed out of the total number of items and a score of the child's ability are compared to the number of tasks the norm group of children of the same age are able to pass. This percentile score for completed motor ability tests allows for interpretation of how the child performed in relation to peers in the norm group.

Stanine Scores

Stanine scores were developed by the military, the first group to promote testing for aptitude. The objective was to get the best match between the skills of applicants and the skills the military needed. Education was the next group to actively pursue testing as valuable in describing human performance and decision making. The distribution of stanine scores is divided into 9 segments, with 5 as the midpoint and 5 ± 2 as nearly equivalent with –1 and +1 SD. Note in Figure 10.3 how the percentage within each of the stanines changes in relation to its location within the normal curve. Another similar linear scale is *sten,* where the bottom line is divided into 10, not 9, segments.

Percentile Equivalent or Rank

Percentile equivalent or *rank measures* are considered to be better than age or grade equivalents or norms because the characteristic being measured may vary

Table 10.4. Types of Score Reporting

Concept	Definition
Percentile	Scores are assigned that indicate what percentage of the sample scored above and below the individual.
Stanine	Scores are assigned on the basis of an underlying scale broken into 9 standard sections. The basis for this scale is 5 ± 2.
Reporting Equivalencies in Some Standardized Tests	
Grade equivalent	Scores are assigned on the basis of data gathered from children in several different grades to identify what level of grade performance a student is currently exemplifying.
Developmental age	Scores are assigned on the basis of data gathered from children in several different grades to identify what level of developmental performance a student is currently exemplifying.
Percentile ranks	Scores are assigned on the basis of a comparison of expected performance from children with the individual's same grade.
Standard Scores	
z scores	Scores relate to the standard deviation of the normal distribution; midpoint is 0, and 1 SD = z of 1.0; the basis is 0 ± 1.0.
T scores	Scores relate to the standard deviation of the normal distribution; midpoint is 50, and 1 SD = T of 10; the basis is 50 ± 10.

widely but unevenly across the standardization sample. Percentile equivalents and ranks avoid problems with unequal growth and differential learning experiences that are common to children. As an evaluator, if a therapist uses percentile equivalent or rank measures, he or she cannot simply explain that this is a percentage of correct items. It is different and reflects the variance within the normal distribution.

Reporting Equivalencies in Some Standardized Tests

Norm-referenced standardized tests frequently compare their findings to external scales to give meaning to their scores.

Grade Equivalent

Grade equivalents are established by issuing a test to students in a specific grade. These norms then can be used to compare an individual's score with

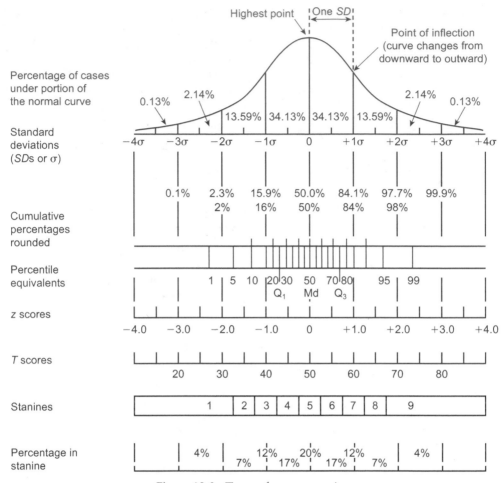

Figure 10.3. Types of score reporting.

the expected patterns for the norm group. The performance of an individual is matched with the norms for a grade equivalence test to describe the individual's current academic abilities common to a specific grade.

Much dissatisfaction is created by grade equivalencies, which are norms and not standards. Equal differences in scores do not necessarily mean equal differences in performance abilities, and grade equivalents are not comparable across schools. A detailed discussion is beyond the scope of this chapter, but the issue of grade equivalence is currently undergoing great debate in this country because of the high-stakes educational testing now widespread following passage of the No Child Left Behind Act of 2001 (Pub. L. 107–110). Although the intentions of the policy sound positive, the reality is that a local or state group might not be able to design the correct tools to administer a test that fully meets the program criteria.

Developmental Age Equivalent

Age-equivalent scores are determined similarly to grade-equivalent scores. In this case, the goal is to determine how close the individual's performance is to patterns of people from a certain developmental age. Frequently these tests measure one developmental issue at a time, such as physical, cognitive, or social growth and development. This scoring procedure has weaknesses similar to those of age equivalence.

As can be seen in Figure 10.3, all the major types of scores relate to the normal distribution including standard deviation. Studying this chart shows the relationship between the reported scores that can use this distribution.

Standard Scores

Standard scores provide an easy way to report how a person performed in relation to others on the assessment, as well as a simple way to compare the outcomes of different administrations of a test. The therapist can convert the derived score into a standard score if he or she obtained the score's standard deviation from the test manual.

z scores

When a therapist has information about the standard deviation of an individual's score, he or she can easily calculate a z score and T score (see Figure 10.3).

The basis for the z score is 0 ± the equivalent number associated with the identified standard deviation for the individual from the test. The formula for transforming an obtained score into a z score to tell how far above or below the mean the *SD* units lie is

$$z = \frac{x - \overline{X}}{SD}$$

where z is the z score, x is the obtained or raw score, $\overline{X}$ is the mean score, and *SD* is the standard deviation. For example, occupational therapists measure for improvements in activities of daily living and physical therapists measure for improvements in mobility after 1 week of intervention:

Occupational therapy	Physical therapy
$x = 85$	$x = 90$
$\overline{X} = 75$	$\overline{X} = 140$
$SD = 10$	$SD = 25$
$z = \dfrac{85 - 75}{10} = +1.0$	$z = \dfrac{90 - 140}{25} = -2.0$

This does not mean that one therapy is better than the other; what it does mean is that the individual showed more positive improvement in activities of daily living than they did in mobility after 1 week of therapy.

T scores

At times, the *z* score can be confusing if it is a negative value. *T* scores avoid this problem because the midpoint of the *T* score is 50 ± 10 from each *SD*. Using the example from the previous page:

<table>
<tr><td>Occupational therapy</td><td>Physical therapy</td></tr>
<tr><td>*T* = 10(*SD* or *z*) + 50</td><td>*T* = 10(*SD* or *z*) + 50</td></tr>
<tr><td>= 10(1.0) + 50</td><td>= 10(–2.0) + 50</td></tr>
<tr><td>= 10 + 50</td><td>= –20 + 50</td></tr>
<tr><td>= 60</td><td>= 30</td></tr>
</table>

One can report either a *z* score or *T* score, depending on preference. If one test reports a *z* score and the other a *T* score, the therapist can convert one so that the results can be compared, giving meaning to the obtained scores between two assessments.

Controlling Error in Test Scores for Better Interpretation

So far in this chapter, we have reviewed issues in scoring, generic interpretation concerns, and effective reporting of results. This section provides a brief review of error and explains how to control its intrusion into testing administration and interpretation. The goal is to ensure that test scores consist of true score, with limited error. (Chapter 9 discusses the makeup of any given test score.) Sources of error include the test-takers themselves, the testing instrument, the procedures used in administering the test, and the scoring of results. Just as one must fast before a blood test to achieve a more accurate reading of one's blood glucose level, evaluators must consider how to reduce error before and during testing related to occupational therapy assessment.

Error Attributed to Test-Takers

Error attributed to test-takers is called *intra-individual error* and includes factors that an individual brings to a test, or experiences as a result of completing the test, that negatively alter the obtained score. For instance, fatigue, illness, or a distracting stressful event, such as a personal or medical crisis or an intense rehabilitation session, just before the evaluation are some of the test-taker factors that can introduce error. In occupational therapy, there may be regional, ethnic, or language barriers and differences that contribute to errors.

Entry-level occupational therapists, and even some more experienced ones, fail to ensure that our test-takers can hear them, can clearly see test items, and are familiar with test objects and requests. Therapists must make sure that clients have their eyeglasses, hearing aids, mobility aids and splints, false teeth (if they are undergoing an eating evaluation), and so on, before beginning an assessment. It is surprising how many individuals will attempt to complete tests without these devices and announce afterward that they believe that this negatively influenced their test results. Time is too precious to readminister assessments; this also may be problematic because test-takers have already been exposed to the test items.

Error Introduced by the Test

Although error introduced by the assessment should be removed through good test standardization procedures, some always will exist because total perfection is not achievable, even if it is a worthy goal. Error is introduced through poorly written items that may be too difficult and through unclear standardization procedures, such as using oral instructions with the test-taker when reading level is not adequate.

Even though a test has been standardized rigorously for client populations similar to the one a therapist is going to use it with, the test still may not work for some reason. Always consider unexpected errors that arise from the test itself.

Error in Test Administration

Errors may be introduced during test administration simply by not following the published standardized instructions or because the administrator has not trained himself or herself adequately in the assessment's standardized procedures. In addition, physical discomfort for either the test-taker or examiner, the therapist's attitude toward the test, or problematic instructions or explanations also can negatively influence the score an individual obtains on a test.

Error in Scoring

Errors in scoring can result from not recording the correct responses to test items and also from not closely following the published scoring instructions in the test manual. The errors—sometimes referred to as *personal bias errors* (Miller et al., 2009)—are classified as the following types:

- *Generosity* or *leniency error* occurs when there is a tendency to rate performance favorably or use only the high end of the scale.
- *Severity error* is the opposite of generosity error, when there is a tendency to unfavorably rate performance or use lower scores more frequently than warranted.
- *Central tendency errors* occur when a rater tends to give midpoint ratings, or ratings in the middle of the distribution of responses that effectively mean no rating, ultimately preventing a true score.
- *Halo effect* occurs when the evaluator's general impression of the test-taker affects the accuracy of the performance rating.
- *Logical error* occurs when performance or behaviors are rated as more alike or dissimilar than they actually are because of evaluator information bias from other sources (e.g., insufficient opportunity to observe test behavior, prior knowledge that is inaccurate, test performance that does not relate to the current situation).

- *Proximity error* occurs when an unexpected event immediately preceding an assessment or something highly unusual triggers a reaction to the next test item and, as a result, uniquely contributes error to test results. Proximity error is already accounted for by using standardized administration procedures, so the expected influence of previous test items has been calculated into the norms via the standardized administration to a sample.
- *Ambiguity error* occurs when, for some unknown reason, the rater's interpretation of a response to a test varies from the typical interpretation made by others.
- *Contrast error* occurs when the evaluator's subjective response to certain characteristics of the test-taker influences scoring or results. This may start with the evaluator feeling negatively about a particular characteristic of the test-taker.

These sources of error can be very perplexing. However, by following standardized procedures and reflecting on how and when you see these errors creeping into your scoring, you can at least limit, if not prevent, their negative influence, ensuring the maximum contribution of true score to the obtained score.

Controlling Error in Scores

The influence of various errors can be controlled by the occupational therapist, maximizing the percentage of true score in an obtained score. This begins with constant awareness of error sources and vigilance to prevent their intrusion. Also, you can ensure you

- Are properly trained and qualified to perform a specific assessment,
- Regularly recalibrate your skills on both frequently and infrequently used tests,
- Follow standardized procedures and adapt tasks as infrequently as possible, and
- Avoid test-taker pretesting and testing conditions, including environmental concerns, that might negatively affect performance.

These conditions are refined by both artful skill and applied science during testing procedures.

Steps in Scoring and Interpreting Performance on a Standardized Test

Interpreting individual outcomes from an assessment requires translating published standardization into meaningful interpretation of assessment results for treatment planning and outcomes. This process engages both the art and science of evaluation. In the evaluator role, the occupational therapist uses a standard set of steps to translate scores. These six steps are

1. Verify that the assessment is an appropriate choice to use by checking
   - That the purpose of the test matches the desired need to describe client performance;

- That the individual being tested has demographic characteristics similar to the standardization sample reported in the test manual (e.g., age, diagnosis, condition, norms);
- That the evaluator has the proper administration preparation/calibration/training and adequate resources to deliver the assessment in a standardized manner; and
- That the best order is chosen, if doing more than one assessment, and that fatigue and other factors that may affect the client are controlled for.

2. Assess the client.
   - Note any exceptions related to modifying standardized assessment delivery procedures or unexpected responses to assessment activities.
3. Debrief the client at the end of the assessment session and after the final report regarding assessment outcomes (oral and written).
4. Go over the manual to
   - Follow scoring instructions, including transforming raw data into derived scores and standard scores.
   - Compare scored results to the appropriate standardization sample in the published manual. Sometimes more than one set of norms is available. Choose the one that most closely approximates the individual being evaluated, noting any exceptions.
   - Use the interpretation guidelines that apply to your obtained scores to describe the evaluation results and related interpretations.
5. Document outcomes in client records:
   - The results from the test.
   - Meaningful interpretation related to occupational therapy intervention planning or documentation of outcomes (state which norm sample was used; use clinical reasoning and critical thinking).
   - Any deviation from standardized procedures, including using a norm-referenced group that does not approximate the individual being evaluated. When this occurs, state cautionary use of results along with how this change may have affected outcomes or influenced intervention planning.
   - Any further action recommended, including additional testing, reevaluation, or referral.
6. If you are going to an intervention planning or goal-setting meeting, be prepared to comment on the scores obtained in reference to standard scores and standard deviation and include assessment recommendations so that you can contribute to discussions and prioritization of team planning.

Conclusion

The purpose of assessment is to quantify the skills or abilities observed in an individual. The information presented in this chapter provides the science for administering, scoring, and interpreting assessments in occupational therapy.

Much of the art of being an evaluator is woven throughout this text. Both art and science are fundamental requirements to qualify as a competent evaluator in occupational therapy.

Ethical, professional, legal, and political concerns will always influence our use of assessments. Therapists cannot acquiesce to these pressures without considerable negative impact on themselves as professionals and occupational therapists. Through a scientific or psychometric-based approach to assessment, therapists ensure professional-level competence and uphold the valuable contribution our evaluation process provides to our clients, as well as serve as accountable partners in the health care system.

Questions

1. Select one behavior, characteristic, or function that occupational therapists evaluate. Try writing an assessment item using the following response methods:
   - Observation scale
   - Likert scale
   - Forced-choice scale
   - Checklist scale
   - Semantic differential scale
   - Q sort
   - Rasch analysis.

   What challenges did you face in writing good items using each of these methods?
2. Apply the four measurement concepts (nominal, ordinal, interval, and ratio) to something that you could measure in each of the following situations:
   - Running a marathon race
   - Determining upper-extremity edema
   - Coping with stress
   - Describing a child's ability to cut a shape out of paper with scissors
   - Reporting experience with pain
   - Making a peanut butter and jelly sandwich.

   What did you find in trying to apply these concepts to the variables to be measured?
3. Calculate the mean, median, and mode for the following set of test scores: 8, 1, 3, 14, 35, 5, 4, 8, 9, 10, 11, 2, 10, 9, 8, 7, and 6. Plot these scores on a graph, and label the mean, median, and mode. Remove the score of 35, and redo the exercise. What happened to the measures of central tendency? What is the clinical relevance of this exercise?
4. Referring to the types of score reporting in Table 10.4, determine the following standard scores for an individual's score that result in the following standard deviations reported on two different tests: $SD = +5$ and $SD = -2$.

- z score
- T score
- stanine
- cumulative percentage
- percentile.

What percentage of individuals scored above and below each of these scores?

5. Why control for error in scoring tests? Choose a situation in which you score a test. Give an example of how the errors in scoring might influence the scores you assigned to an individual's performance or might influence the individual's response on a questionnaire. What are five ways to control error in scoring?

References

Anastasi, A., & Urbina, S. (1997). *Psychological testing* (7th ed.). Upper Saddle River, NJ: Prentice Hall.

Bolton, B. F., & Brookings, J. B. (2001). Scores and norms. In B. F. Bolton (Ed.), *Handbook of measurement and evaluation in rehabilitation* (3rd ed., pp. 3–28). Gaithersburg, MD: Aspen.

Cronbach, I. J. (1990). *Essentials of psychological testing* (5th ed.). New York: Harper-Collins.

Fisher, A. G. (2003). *Assessment of Motor and Process Skills* (5th ed.). Fort Collins, CO: Three Star Press.

Miller, M. D., Linn, R. L., & Gronlund, N. E. (2009). *Measurement and assessment in teaching* (10th ed.). Upper Saddle River, NJ: Merrill/Pearson.

No Child Left Behind Act of 2001, Pub. L. 107–110, 20 U.S.C. 6301.

Pearson, K. (1924). Historical note on the origins of the normal curve of errors. *Biometrika, 16*, 402–404.

11

● ● ● ● ●

Interpretation and Documentation

●

Aimee J. Luebben, EdD, OTR, FAOTA

Overview

This chapter focuses on the interpretation and documentation aspects of the evaluation process. The section on interpretation includes information on factors that contribute to the transition from interpretation to intervention planning, including applying a theoretical foundation, accounting for testing bias, synthesizing multiple data points, and defending evaluation results. The section on documentation discusses purposes and classification, information confidentiality and privacy, and general recommendations. The chapter features a documentation mystery woven throughout the sections, highlighting key points.

Introduction

When mystery surrounds why a person was not recommended for direct occupational therapy services, occupational therapists need to figure out why by the use of documentation, the only permanent record remaining after services are rendered. Using documentation to refute not one, but two direct service ineligibility decisions is exactly what happened in the mystery of Morgan (a pseudonym). The mystery began when Al, a veteran pediatric occupational therapist, received an impassioned plea from Morgan's parents, who wished to have their 19-month-old son evaluated. Certain he would benefit from direct early intervention services, the parents disclosed that evaluations performed within the previous 4 months by two facilities in different states indicated Morgan was not eligible for direct occupational therapy services.

The mystery of Morgan's ineligibility for services deepened when Al learned that Morgan was born at 36 weeks' gestation and was a twin. Hesitant about evaluating the same child a third time within 4 months, Al requested from the parents all documentation related to the previous evaluations. The documentation evidence, which included team reports from more than one profession, provided clues that helped solve the mystery of Morgan's ineligibility. This evidence showed that the testing had been adequate, but the quantitative evidence from the standardized assessment tool used did not substantiate the eligibility decision of either facility. The mystery was solved when Al determined that neither facility had provided satisfactory interpretation of the assessment findings. Morgan did not require a reevaluation. The reports of both facilities, however, needed reevaluation in the form of reinterpretation of results.

Solving mysteries is an appropriate metaphor for occupational therapy practice. Occupational therapists are lifestyle detectives who search for clues, test hypotheses, interpret findings, determine conclusions, and disseminate discoveries. They solve mysteries by profiling clients, examining clues within contexts, and synthesizing multiple data points to give order to the complexities of life. Adept at interpreting and applying information, occupational therapists are also masters of generalization. Lessons learned from solving the mystery of Morgan's evaluations are interwoven throughout this chapter, providing a focus on two occupational therapist–as–detective aims: interpretation of assessment findings and dissemination of discoveries through documentation.

Interpretation

Interpretation is a primary part of the occupational therapist's job. Even though many standardized assessment instruments have computer applications that score a client's performance and are advertised as capable of interpreting scores, interpretation is a principal realm of the occupational therapist. Interpretation of assessment information is an art that requires reflection, theoretical knowledge, clinical reasoning, and practice.

During the evaluation process, interpretation is the key to making meaning of information collected through various assessment methods, including standardized assessment instruments, nonstandardized testing, and an integrated approach that uses nonstandardized assessment techniques to supplement standardized assessment tools. Making informed service delivery decisions requires accurate interpretation. Moreover, precise assessment interpretation is fundamental to intervention planning.

Multiple factors contribute to interpretation, which is then translated into intervention planning. Factors that contribute to the transition from interpretation to intervention planning include applying a theoretical foundation, accounting for testing bias, synthesizing multiple data points, and defending evaluation results. Because the mystery of Morgan began for Al with the same decision about intervention planning—both facilities determined that Morgan was ineligible for direct service intervention—Al decided to test each of these factors to solve the mystery of Morgan.

Applying a Theoretical Foundation

To link theory and practice consistently, intervention planning must rely on a theoretical foundation. Occupational therapists use theory to organize thinking and begin the clinical reasoning process.

In the case of Morgan, Al quickly determined that the theoretical foundation was a developmental approach, which was appropriate and understandable considering that both facilities performing the evaluations were pediatric facilities. Because Morgan's evaluating therapists used a reasonable theoretical foundation, the mystery of his direct service ineligibility continued.

Accounting for Testing Bias

If the goal of testing is to determine the actual performance of the person being evaluated, then testing conditions can influence an evaluation. Although ideal conditions are optimal in collecting testing information, optimal conditions are not always possible. Optimizing testing conditions involves controlling for as much testing variance or bias as possible. Designed to be used during the testing process, the PIE acronym that is designed to help therapists identify sources of bias during the testing process (see Chapter 8) can be used to confirm whether the evaluators accounted for the three testing bias aspects—*p*erson, *i*tem, and *e*nvironment—in written documentation.

Applying PIE to Morgan's reports, Al found little supporting evidence of difficulties related to the two types of the person-related testing bias (the *P* of PIE). Al presumed the prior evaluators controlled for their expectations and rating tendencies that could result in error. After meeting the family, Al believed that Morgan demonstrated genuineness in his performance and that his parents were good historians. As for item bias (the *I* of PIE), both facilities used a typical pediatric standardized criterion-referenced and norm-referenced assessment instrument that tests children as they play with toys, a natural occupation for Morgan. The only extraordinary testing bias aspect was the environment (the *E* of PIE). For Morgan, arriving at each facility for testing was the first time he visited either place. Morgan was not only out of his natural environment, he was observed by teams of people who were unfamiliar to him. The fact that Morgan was expected to perform typically in an unfamiliar environment was the first loose end Al found, but this aspect of testing bias was not enough to unravel the full mystery of his ineligibility.

Synthesizing Multiple Data Points

To interpret assessment findings, summarizing multiple data points is not enough. Occupational therapists must *synthesize* multiple data points, making certain that the qualitative information and quantitative information collected during evaluation provide similar pictures of performance.

The mystery of Morgan demonstrates how easily interpretation can go awry. Although therapists in both facilities used an integrated approach, using nonstandardized testing (observation, in particular) to supplement the standardized tool information, therapists at each facility based the direct service ineligibility decision on the standardized instrument's age equivalents that were available for each scale, but not for individual subtests. Using age-equivalent scores to determine service provision presents a significant potential for misinterpretation and should be handled with caution. In fact, Anastasi and Urbina (1997) stated that "scores based on developmental norms tend to be psychometrically crude and do not lend themselves well to precise statistical treatment" (p. 55).

For individual subtests, each facility also reported percentile ranks (one facility used the term *percentile* and the other clinic used the symbol %, but both were incorrect), which is a normalized derived scale with unequal intervals, but neither facility provided any interpretation of these norms. Beyond style variations, the differences were many: One facility provided raw scores, adjusted for preterm birth, and the other supplied a normalized standard score with equal intervals, but neither did both.

For the facility reporting normalized standard scores but no corresponding interpretations or raw scores, Al was able to reconstruct subtests and scale scores. (In the narrative part of the report, what initially looked like detailed clinical observations of Morgan was actually the language of individual test items from the assessment instrument.) The reconstructed raw scores showed that normalized standard scores for the total scale and one subtest were incorrect—the facility staff had not performed hand calculations required by the standardized instrument manual for raw scores lower than the upper limit of the smallest percentile rank in the table.

Al gave Morgan's parents a document that included reconstructed raw scores, hand-calculated standard scores, and interpretations of all derived scaled scores. Al told the family that the reports should have included, at minimum, raw scores and normalized standard scores with equal intervals. To compare Morgan's performance with children in his age group, the interpretation of his performance and the eligibility decision should have been based on the standard scores with equal intervals.

The mystery of Morgan was solved. He was eligible for direct services because he had serious developmental delays that were evident in the evaluation documents from two facilities. Solving the mystery showed that Morgan's other therapists summarized but did not *synthesize* his testing findings into an accurate interpretation. In the case of both facilities, Morgan did not qualify for direct service provision because of therapist error in interpreting testing information collected through a standardized instrument.

Defending Evaluation Results

Once occupational therapists have finalized and disseminated evaluation reports, their jobs are not done. The reports, which live forever in records, must be defensible. Dissection of Morgan's reports led to a third report to the parents that defended the validity of his testing, but not the accuracy of the findings. Although Morgan had been denied direct services, his evaluation results were not defensible.

Solving the mystery of Morgan's previous evaluations revealed the power— both positive and negative—of interpretation and launched Al's crusade against the common use of norms based on age to determine developmental delay and eligibility for occupational therapy services. After analyzing Morgan's two evaluation reports, Al realized that using chronological age and age equivalents (or

Table 11.1. Effects of Being 5 Months Behind on Delay Percentage at Various Chronological Ages

Child	Chronological Age (Months)	Age Equivalent (Months)	Delay %
Lily	6	1	83
Mei	12	7	42
Hannah	18	13	28
Callie	26	21	19
Michaela	45	40	11

perceptual age, motor age, or whatever other form or terminology age-based scores take) is not a good choice given that older children who are delayed are penalized because both chronological age and age equivalents start at zero and keep getting larger. An older child would have to be many more months behind age level compared with a younger child, although the percentage of delay could be the same. To see this phenomenon in action, see Table 11.1, which summarizes the effects of being 5 months behind on delay percentages for 5 girls at various chronological ages.

The mystery of Morgan and the examples in Table 11.1 show that using chronological age and age-based norms can result in turning away individuals who really need occupational therapy. The ethical implications of using age equivalents to calculate developmental delay are therefore serious.

Documentation

The purpose of documentation, according to the *Guidelines for Documentation of Occupational Therapy* (American Occupational Therapy Association [AOTA], 2008, p. 684), is to

- Articulate the rationale for provision of occupational therapy services and the relationship of these services to the client's outcomes;
- Reflect the therapist's clinical reasoning and professional judgment;
- Communicate information about the client from the occupational therapy perspective; and
- Create a chronological record of client status, occupational therapy services provided to the client, and client outcomes.

Without a doubt, the primary purpose of documentation—evaluation reports, in particular—is communication. Documentation is also important for public relations, education, reimbursement, and research. With some care in writing reports and descriptions, documentation can serve as an advertisement for the value of occupational therapy services and teach people outside the profession more about occupational therapy. For third-party payers, documentation is the sole source of determining whether occupational therapy services will be reimbursed.

Documentation serves as the basis for research, including outcome studies, quality assurance, and other forms of program review. On a smaller scale, an outcome study at the case report level can be completed each time an occupational therapist delivers services. With many reimbursement sources mandating significant practical improvement in a person's function, occupational therapists are obligated to demonstrate significant improvement as an outcome if services are authorized. Although some occupational therapists believe a fine line divides research and evaluation, the line is more likely to represent an investigation continuum with research at one end and evaluation at the other. Documentation indicative of best practices is located in the middle of the research–evaluation continuum.

Documentation using single-case reporting with empirical data can provide evidence of significant clinical change resulting from occupational therapy services. Like single-subject research designs, single-case reports have inherently strong internal validity but correspondingly low external validity: Generalizing to others may be difficult. To improve external validity, single-case reports need to be replicated and accumulated. The technology of electronic health records offers an integrated way of accumulating information. If occupational therapists collect similar information and report findings in a consistent format, the data mining capabilities of electronic health records can provide opportunities to capture the outcomes of similar people, aggregate results, analyze outcomes, and demonstrate irrefutable evidence of the effectiveness of occupational therapy.

Classification

Documentation varies. Most documentation can be classified according to four aspects: process stages, timing types, setting styles, and design formats.

Process Stages

Because the occupational therapy information-gathering process consists of two stages, documentation often is classified according to the stages: screening or evaluation. *Screening,* which provides preliminary information to determine whether further occupational therapy services are needed, is not intended as a comprehensive evaluation. A formal document related to a screening should be labeled as such—*a screening report.* In practice, however, many occupational therapists begin with gathering information by screening; quickly determine whether or not a formal evaluation is warranted; and then, when potential performance problems are discovered, start gathering more definitive information through various assessment tools. An *evaluation report* summarizes and synthesizes the findings of multiple assessment tools.

Timing Types

Because evaluation reports provide snapshots of a client's occupational performance at a particular point in time, evaluation documentation often is classified according to the following types: initial, progress, or discharge (can be termed *discontinuation*). If treatment is recommended in the initial report, then the other types of report correspond with intervention timing. Often, at least one other reevaluation report before discharge or discontinuation is completed during treatment, and a discharge (or discontinuation) evaluation is performed, usually as part of the final intervention session. Initial and progress evaluation reports are considered *formative evaluation;* discontinuation documentation is considered *summative evaluation.* If the initial evaluation recommendation is "no services are needed," the first report also serves as a discharge or discontinuation document. An initial evaluation report that does not recommend occupational therapy services can be considered summative.

Setting Styles

Evaluation documentation can also be classified according to three general format styles: acronym, narrative, and template-based. Although originally designed to serve as progress notes, acronym-style documentation often is used in documenting evaluation findings for all points in time. In medical-model settings, there is a variety of acronym-style documentation. One example is the SOAP note, named for the section labels: Subjective, Objective, Assessment, and Plan. Another example is the DAP note: Description, Assessment, and Plan. The DAP combines the S and O of the SOAP note into D, the description section.

Some settings use narrative reports as documentation and provide site-specific guidelines for expected content and format. Narrative documentation usually consists of written information in paragraph form, often with headings that show key assessment areas. Narrative documentation is common in many community-based settings, such as schools.

Some facilities use template-based documentation, such as a checklist or other specially designed form. When a therapist completes the form, documentation is done. Each facility determines the appropriate documentation style to use. Because the intricacies of documentation style are beyond the purview of this chapter, readers should consult two application-based textbooks: Borcherding's (2005) *Documentation Manual for Writing SOAP Notes in Occupational Therapy* and Sames's (2010) *Documenting Occupational Therapy Practice.*

Regardless of the style used, a therapist is responsible for accurate and thorough reporting based on assessment outcomes, documented observations, and clinical reasoning. When a checklist does not permit sufficient description of individual evaluation outcomes, the therapist is responsible for ensuring complete documentation is recorded.

Design Formats

Evaluation documentation also can be classified according to design format: paper-based or electronic. In some facilities, some occupational therapists continue to document services using the traditional handwritten method. However, the electronic format has become the rule, so many facilities are working to scan older paper-based documentation into client records.

Community occupational therapists have known for decades the benefits of the electronic format. Many community therapists have developed electronic report systems that make documentation efficient. In medical-model facilities, electronic health records now have become common because of the Health Insurance Portability and Accountability Act of 1996 (HIPAA, Pub. L. 104–191). To comply with federal regulations, many facilities use digital template formats that provide an outline of the required documentation. Therapists provide documentation by completing checklists, selecting appropriate choices from drop-down menus, making connections to other parts of the electronic record, and inputting specific information. The electronic format has unique storage and retrieval opportunities as well as data-mining capabilities. Data mining allows comparison of a single person to *norm-referenced* information (a typical group) or *criterion-referenced* information (a standard) as well as *ipsative-referenced* data that allow comparison of a single person with his or her own information to track changes over time.

Electronic client records bring up other issues related to availability, access, and security. Availability of digital records can be a problem if the machine is down, the server is overloaded, the system has crashed, the router has difficulties, or the power has gone out. To provide continuity of care despite electronic glitches, some clients have started carrying printed versions of their basic electronic records. Access and security are addressed in the next section, and the section on general documentation recommendations, particularly the last five recommendations, provides further information about using an electronic format for documentation purposes and protecting privacy.

Information Confidentiality and Privacy

Information related to people receiving health care services has had confidentiality protections for centuries. From the times of Hippocrates, professional codes of ethics have emphasized confidentiality as a basic tenet. In the occupational therapy profession, confidentiality is addressed in the *Occupational Therapy Code of Ethics* (AOTA, 2005). Failure to comply with professional code of ethics tenets can result in sanctions, including suspension from practice for life.

When professional codes of ethics did not adequately protect confidentiality of individuals, governmental entities enacted privacy laws. Many states have had privacy statutes for years, protecting various aspects of an individual's life. The federal government also has enacted legislation related to privacy. Financial information was one of the first areas to receive federal privacy protections. Educational records are protected by the Family Educational Rights and Privacy Act of 1974 (FERPA, Pub. L. 93–380). HIPAA is an extension of earlier privacy legislation.

HIPAA's two main goals are reflected in its name: health insurance portability and accountability. The electronic health record is the key to complying with portability mandated by HIPAA. In theory, electronic records allow the capture and storage of all health-related information related to a person and permit a person to transfer to another insurance company. HIPAA also mandates accountability: explanation of costs in an effort to decrease waste and fraud. Electronic health records improve the efficiency of accountability.

HIPAA comprises four standards (also called *rules*): transactions, identifiers, security, and privacy. Although the HIPAA standards corresponding to transactions, identifiers, and security cover electronic information only, the privacy rule protects personal health information delivered in any fashion. Many facilities require that a therapist be trained and certified in the basic HIPAA regulations and processes.

The privacy rule was implemented first. Implementation of the three electronic information standards is having an interesting and stealthy effect, resulting in a documentation evolution similar to that of FERPA. In educational settings, FERPA served to open student records to parents upon written request. As a result, evaluation reports written for educational settings have evolved into documentation that is understood on multiple levels by people with diverse backgrounds and varied education. Once the bastion of professional eyes only, medical-model facility documentation is now being accessed by patients and clients exercising their HIPAA rights to access their personal health information.

Increased access affects information confidentiality and privacy. Access and security are indirectly related: As access increases, security decreases. The movement to wireless devices also decreases security and, by extension, privacy and confidentiality. Early electronic health systems were perhaps more secure than some newer Web-based systems accessed with wireless devices. Earlier systems often were interfaced with a wired network with machines for input. In these closed systems, security risks were primarily with people who accessed the input devices.

More recently, some facilities and organizations have moved to electronic health care systems that are designed for access via secure Web sites on the Internet. Secure Web sites offer some safety in these open systems, but many of these Internet-based systems allow wireless access from any device (often unsecured) from any wireless hotspot. This can be problematic because on the Internet, hosting devices (sometimes called *nodes*), not the network, are responsible for transmitting information. Devices connected to different internal systems and routers to outside networks send information until the relay machine indicates the information has been received. Information is then sent to the next node of the network (and the next and the next) until the information gets to the secure Web site.

On the network of networks—the Internet—if something happens to one node, the network still functions. Even though a secure Web site is accessed, many personal access devices (e.g., smart phones, Web book or netbook computers) may not be secure. Additionally, having a secure device does not guarantee a safe device. Malware (a contraction of the words *malicious software*) is a reality. Started as pranks, early malware included viruses and worms that disabled system functions or shut down computers. The current generation of malware is more hostile. Newer malware applications (e.g., spyware, bots, keystroke loggers) are designed to steal data for profitable use. At any one time, the

Internet functions with a number of hosting devices that are infected with one or more forms of malware. To improve security of personal access devices, users can employ various types of security applications (e.g., firewalls, encryption).

Using a secure access device and a secure Web site helps improve security, but the connection between the device and Web site is equally important. The safer hard-wired, closed system is not an option when accessing the Internet. Although a computer terminal may be hard-wired to a facility system, the facility system at some point will "open" when connected to an outside system to access the Internet. Additionally, the movement to wireless connectivity presents new perils. Theoretically, if a personal access device is open, any file saved internally or by connection (via memory device or linking Web site) can be accessed and stolen. A secure wireless connection offers some safety, but many wireless hotspots are essentially radio-based, which allows opportunities for stealthy electronic eavesdropping and robbery. Sometimes, personal access devices switch from one wireless connection to another without the user being aware that a change occurred. It is important to know how and where personal access devices are connected at all times. To protect Internet-based electronic health records from danger, occupational therapists need to ensure security at four points: personal access device, transmission, connection, and Web site. With wireless connections, new security concerns arise daily.

To summarize, occupational therapists must adhere to the confidentiality standards set in the profession's code of ethics and comply with privacy rules or standards mandated by state and federal legislation. Because the complexity of privacy legislation is beyond the scope of this chapter, readers are referred to the online tutorials of the University of Miami's Privacy/Data Protection Project (2002a, 2002b).

General Documentation Recommendations

Solving the mystery of Morgan—reinterpreting the evaluation evidence to prove he was well qualified for direct occupational therapy services—was tantamount to justifying the early intervention services this child and his family needed. For the other therapists involved, however, this mystery represented a worst-case scenario, demonstrating what might happen when documentation is read by another health professional.

Documenting occupational therapy services is of equal importance to providing services in the first place. Long after services have been provided, documentation remains as evidence of the occupational therapy services a client received. Occupational therapists display their public presence through their documentation. From documentation, another therapist can determine the clinical reasoning skills, therapeutic abilities, and general competence of the occupational therapist(s) who originally wrote the documents. Documentation can be well written or poorly developed and uninformative. Both writing styles have equal longevity. One poorly written note could be damaging to a professional's reputation. Professional reputations may be protected by adhering to the following general recommendations.

Realize That Recordable Equals Recoverable and Discoverable

Occupational therapists are well aware that documentation becomes a legal document, but many are not equally cautious about creating other records that become permanent. With technology readily available, just about any kind of record is recoverable and discoverable; information can be subpoenaed and used in court cases. Digital information, which can last forever, leaves traces even after being "erased."

Occupational therapists are trained to exercise caution when documenting for occupational therapy services. Some are unaware, however, that other documents are discoverable. Discoverable records include e-mail, personal notes, texts, voicemail, and answering machine messages. Occupational therapists should keep in mind the legal ramifications whenever they make a permanent record.

Time is likely to become a new issue related to service provision. In the future, there may be challenges to billing for occupational therapy services for duplication of time. For example, a client who sees a therapist on a personal communication device during a treatment session may dispute whether occupational therapy services were delivered. The third-party payer could request phone records to determine whether the communication was professional in nature and related to the person being billed for the time period.

Using time to look for discrepancies between professional and personal activities is becoming easier. Today's world includes automatic record keeping of time, date, and location. Many individuals can be traced throughout the day. For example, an occupational therapist might be tracked on the way to work through transactions such as credit card purchases for fuel or use of automatic toll booths. She may be traced from one traffic light to the next via cameras mounted at intersections. If she stops at a store, the camera in the parking lot and building may shadow her. There are credit cards (and some library books) equipped with radio devices that are recognized by equipment at multiple sites and time-stamped even without a transaction. Computer systems provide a record of all actions, including signing on, making records related to a client, using the Internet, and logging off. At home, the therapist leaves a record of phone, cable, satellite, and Internet access. This example provides an indication of why occupational therapists need to make certain there is an accurate record of service provision without time duplications.

Follow the Guidelines for Documentation of Occupational Therapy

The *Guidelines for Documentation of Occupational Therapy* (AOTA, 2008) is an official AOTA document that provides recommendations for report writing. This document offers suggested content with examples for various types of reports and a listing of fundamental elements present in all documents. An example of a fundamental element is including the "client's full name and case number (if applicable), on each page of documentation" (p. 689). For the most current version of this document, use the search feature in www.aota.org and key in the following search string: *"guidelines for documentation"* (including the quotation marks).

Request Examples of Best Practice in Documentation

Documentation varies from facility to facility. And certainly, as any occupational therapy student who is supervised by more than one fieldwork educator can attest, report writing within a single facility can vary from therapist to therapist. Although some variation is purely style, facilities often have specific requirements or regulations that documentation must meet. One of the best ways to become proficient in the documentation of a new facility (or for more than one supervisor) is to request and study examples of previously written documentation the facility (or supervisor) considers best practice. Report examples need to be *de-identified* (a HIPAA term), that is, stripped of all identifying personal health information.

Respect the Readers

If the primary purpose of documentation is communication, respecting the reader is necessary. The first step in respecting the readers is determining who will read the occupational therapy report. The second step is writing the documentation for the readers, who may include clients receiving occupational therapy services, their families, referral sources, third-party payers, and other professionals. Occupational therapy evaluation findings need to be consolidated into one document that communicates to all readers. Keeping report readers satisfied enough to finish an entire document is the third step of respecting the reader. Harris (1998) emphasized the effectiveness of brevity in documentation: "Long, wordy notes are not read, the most effective documentation reports are those that are short and to the point" (p. 179). If evaluation reports are lengthy, the occupational therapist can make reading easier by dividing information into short paragraphs, using various levels of headings, and designing tables to summarize data.

Do Not Make the Readers Work

Each evaluation report should stand alone and include all information readers need to come to the same conclusion as the report writer. Initial reports can provide information related to delay, decline, or dysfunction in terms of percentages for an individual, justifying the need for occupational therapy services. Progress and discharge reports should include all necessary preliminary information so report readers do not have to search for and read old documentation to make comparisons to determine clinical change.

Demonstrate Effectiveness by Showing Improvement

To show effectiveness of services, occupational therapists need to show clinical change in the direction that shows improvement. At minimum, the discharge report should include comparisons of current performance with performance documented in a previous report, with improvement percentage

$$\text{Improvement Percentage} = \frac{\text{New (Evaluation)} - \text{Old (Evaluation)}}{\text{Old (Evaluation)}} \times 100$$

Figure 11.1. Easy calculation for improvement percentage.

changes calculated. Figure 11.1 provides an easy way to calculate improvement percentage.

Determining direction of improvement is key. In many cases, the direction of improvement is a higher value. For example, Charlie, a 10-year-old boy with severe and profound disabilities, is working to improve head control. As intervention, his occupational therapist added a mercury switch to the headset of Charlie's personal listening device. The switch activates the device to play music when Charlie holds his head up; the switch stops the music when his head is down. During the initial evaluation, Charlie was able to control his head for an average of 61 seconds. For a progress note a week later, the occupational therapist found that Charlie controlled his head for an average of 113 seconds. Figure 11.2 shows the calculation for improvement percentage for Charlie. The occupational therapist was able to provide evidence of occupational therapy intervention effectiveness: Her documentation indicated that Charlie showed an 87% improvement in head control performance.

Electronic systems can be set up to provide automatic calculation of improvement and demonstrate effectiveness of service delivery. In fact, the sophistication of some electronic systems allows comparisons as part of the available data mining capability.

When in Doubt, Leave It Out

Documentation must include only information pertinent to the person receiving occupational therapy services. In some styles of documentation, the therapist can check whether a phrase or sentence is really necessary by removing it and seeing how the document reads. The phrase or sentence should be deleted if the document if the document is stronger without the segment. Careful proofreading, coupled with spelling and grammar checking, can find other unnecessary or inaccurate information. If the therapist trips over a sentence or component during proofreading, chances are the intended readers will also stumble. The passage should be rewritten or deleted to protect the reading rhythm.

$$\text{Improvement Percentage} = \frac{113 - 61}{61} \times 100 = 87\%$$

Note. The direction of improvement can be a lower value. If a client is working on improving speed, then the desired improvement is less time.

Figure 11.2. Easy calculation for improvement percentage: Charlie.

Explain Professional Jargon

Using frequent parenthetical phrases often allows the option of using "chart talk" familiar to health care professionals and words readers without the same educational background can understand. A combination of professional and explanatory styles helps readers at various educational levels understand the documentation. For example, rather than write "ATNR has already begun to integrate," the following description provides more information about this 6-month-old baby:

> Sam showed signs of the asymmetrical tonic neck reflex (ATNR), a primitive reflexive motor pattern, which is typical for infants of his age. He demonstrated the ATNR, primarily in supine (on his back), when he either (1) moved his head out of midline (the "invisible" middle of his body) toward his left or right side or (2) extended (straightened) an arm to the side. The stimulus of Sam turning his head sideways or extending his arm resulted in his exhibiting the typical ATNR pattern: his arm and leg on the "nose side" extended and his arm and leg on the side opposite the nose flexed (bent). Sam was able to move out of the ATNR pattern (especially in sitting positions), a sign that the influence of this primitive reflex is disappearing. As expected when the session progressed and he became more tired, Sam demonstrated increasingly more instances of the stimulus-response ATNR pattern.

If explaining professional jargon is difficult, consider generalizing information using the document *Plain Language Principles and Thesaurus for Making HIPAA Privacy Notices More Readable*, developed by the Health Resources and Services Administration (2009). Although this document was designed to assist facilities in developing appropriate privacy notices, the principles and thesaurus contain many useful ideas for simplifying terminology.

Use Descriptions as Educational Teaching Tools

By providing professional jargon and parenthetical explanations, written documentation can help teach people outside the profession more about occupational therapy. Every report should include an occupational therapy–to-English dictionary that educates readers to be advocates of occupational therapy. In the case of Sam's ATNR, readers learn the full name of the reflex, that the reflex is typical for him at his age, and the components of the reflex. Later, if another therapist mentions ATNR without explanation, the readers of Sam's report will already have the necessary background information.

Use Appropriate Terminology

Occupational therapy students often overuse the word *patient*, using this term (especially the abbreviation *pt.*) when referring to any person receiving occupational therapy services. In many settings, particularly medical-model facilities, the word *patient* is most appropriate. Other settings, however, may have specific terminology that must be used when referring to the individual receiving services. The term *client*, for instance, has been popular for a number of years. In school settings, the person receiving occupational therapy services is called a *student,* whereas in an industrial setting, the individual may be known as a *worker* or *employee* or as a *resident* in a skilled nursing facility. Before making any assumptions, the therapist should check with the facility to determine appropriate terms and use the terms consistently.

Use Past Tense

An experienced occupational therapist learned the hard way to use past tense for documentation verbs. After hard questioning from parents, who heartily maintained that their child did not have a specific skill included in the formal report, the therapist had to admit she had seen the behavior only once. By using present tense, the therapist implied that the behavior is always present, either ongoing or happening all of the time. Had the therapist used the past tense, however, she would have indicated that the action happened before the current time, either as a one-time occurrence or on an ongoing basis in the past. This underscores the importance of selecting the appropriate verb tense when writing documentation.

Present-tense observations that signify ongoing behavior should be in the past tense, indicating that something happened at least once. For instance, the past-tense version—"Lee sat with a straight back"—indicates that the behavior was observed one time or more. The present-tense versions—"Lee sits with a straight back" or "Lee is sitting with a straight back"—indicate a behavior Lee accomplished 100% of the times he was sitting during the session.

Can and *able* (as in "Lee can sit with a straight back" or "Lee is able to sit with a straight back") deserve special note. Although some occupational therapists make liberal use of *can* and *is able to* in their notes, use of these present-tense terms leaves doubt in readers' minds about whether these behaviors were seen during an evaluation or whether the therapist may simply have believed that the client had the potential to exhibit the behaviors. If the phenomenon was observed, using the past tense—*was able to*—is more appropriate; for example, "Lee was able to sit with a straight back."

Use Active Rather Than Passive Verbs

What is the difference between the following two observations: "Mandy moved from prone into sitting" and "Mandy was moved from prone into sitting"? In the first observation, which used an active verb (i.e., *moved*), Mandy was an active participant, accomplishing the action herself. In the second observation, with the passive verb (*was moved*), Mandy did not actively participate in the action; she was passively manipulated from one to another position.

Written descriptions of observations should reflect what happened during an evaluation session. In most cases, the person observed is an active participant, so the observation should include an active verb. Expanding the active-verb example provides additional information: "Mandy moved from prone (on her stomach) into side-sitting by pushing down with her left arm, leaning to her left side, and swinging her legs around to the right side." If passive action is observed, use passive-voice verbs, but include the identity of the active agent in the description. For instance, in the expanded passive verb, the identity of the active agent is the therapist: "Mandy was moved into sitting from prone (on her stomach) through four-point (hands and knees) by the therapist."

Use Seem *and* Appear *Judiciously*

Although some facilities may allow the use of *seem* and *appear,* administrators in other settings believe that professionals such as occupational therapists should have the expertise to make documentation-writing decisions that eliminate the words *seem* and *appear.* The observation "Mr. Oberfeldt demonstrated difficulty seeing objects within 6 to 12 inches of his eyes, such as a newspaper" provides much more definitive information about his skills than the observation "Mr. Oberfeldt appeared to have difficulty seeing nearby objects."

If the habit of using these two words is difficult to break when writing, the therapist can fix the results when proofreading. Using the find feature available in many applications can help the therapist search for *appear* and *seem.* If either word is present, the therapist should rewrite the section. Interestingly, Soccio (2006) agreed with judicious use of these two words, using the phrase "weasel claims" (i.e., "sneaky") for statements written with *seem* or *appear.*

Eliminate *Will, Would, Should, and* Could

The words *will, would, should,* and *could* mean that the client may show the behavior if given the chance—in other words, the behavior did not happen during the evaluation session. Therapists using these four words in documentation are predicting future behaviors on the basis of their observations. Occupational therapists should not document an observation that they did not specifically see; records of observation must be legally defensible.

In the example "Mollie would visually track an object," readers of the report have no idea whether Mollie showed visual tracking skills during the session; *would* may indicate only that this behavior was possible in the therapist's professional opinion. The observation is transformed by eliminating *would,* changing the verb to past tense, and expanding observation to provide additional information:

> As expected for her age, Mollie used whole-head movements (rather than moving her eyes only—as anticipated when she gets older) to track visual objects. At the starting point of Mollie looking straight forward, she tracked objects 4 inches to the left and right in the horizontal plane, 2 inches up and down in the vertical plane, and 1 inch in each direction in the diagonal planes.

Use Articles and Personal Pronouns

Writers of evaluation reports should individualize descriptions of the client by using articles *a, an,* and *the* and personal pronouns (e.g., *she, him, her, his, him*). Reports should match what the facility considers best practice in documentation, taking shortcuts (e.g., approved abbreviations) as allowed. In narrative reports, particularly those that are read by the client or families of people receiving occupational therapy services, write full sentences with all appropriate parts of speech (e.g., "The mother reported that her son did . . ." instead of "mom said son did. . . .").

Separate Judgments From Descriptions

The written description should describe exactly what the therapist observed during the session documented. By "painting a picture" that is clear, the therapist enables the reader to make a judgment or draw an appropriate conclusion. Judgmental language can be included in a separate interpretation section, a consecutive sentence, or a separate table column or clearly labeled as interpretation if included in the same location as the corresponding description. Instead of writing "Mrs. Martinez did a better job of walking today," the description and judgment are divided into separate sentences as follows:

> Mrs. Martinez walked 500 feet, from her room to the independent living kitchen, within 10 minutes without resting. Her functional mobility performance showed an improvement compared with a week ago, when she walked 100 feet toward the kitchen over a period of an hour and required four 5-minute rest breaks.

Justify Professional Opinions Using Behavioral Examples

When a therapist makes an observation on the basis of his or her knowledge of the underlying aspects of the client's situation, the report should cite a specific example to justify a professional opinion. The following two descriptions provide examples of using the phrases *as evidenced by* and *as indicated by*.

> Mr. Martin showed difficulty discriminating three-dimensional space, as evidenced by his tripping on the 4-inch step at the entrance of his house.

> In the classroom, Sarah continued disregarding her central vision (looking straight at a task or object), as indicated by her viewing tasks with her head turned at a 45-degree angle and using her peripheral vision to complete activities.

Use Spell Check, If Available

Typos happen. But errors in documentation can make the occupational therapist look careless and sloppy, and by extension, incompetent. If a spell check is available in the documentation system, the therapist should take advantage of it. Some spell-check programs permit adding practice-related, technical terms to the dictionary. Adding common ones used in documentation can save time and increase accuracy.

Use Readability Statistics, If Available

For some types of documentation, reading level may become an issue. With the rise in client-centered care and improved client access to their own records, documentation may need to be written at a level that matches the educational background of the person receiving services. Fortunately, many electronic applications have features that provide statistics related to readability. To find and activate the readability statistics feature, the therapist can click on the application help menu and search for the term *readability*. When activated, a dialog box appears after every standard spelling and grammar check. The box includes counts of words, characters, sentences, and paragraphs; averages of sentences per paragraph, words per sentence, and characters per word; and readability, which includes passive sentences percentage, a reading ease score, and grade level score. The Flesch Reading Ease score has a 100-point scale; a score higher than 60 is considered a good reading ease score, whereas lower scores indicate a document that is more difficult to read. The Flesch–Kincaid Grade Level corresponds to a grade in school; for example, a Flesch–Kincaid Grade Level of 13 corresponds to the reading level of first-year college students. If an occupational therapist knows she is working with a client with a seventh-grade reading level, she can adjust her writing to provide documentation that reaches that level. The Flesch Reading Ease and Flesch–Kincaid Grade Level are inversely related: As one increases, the other decreases. Strategies to improve reading ease and decrease grade level include decreasing the length of words, number of words, and number of words per sentence and increasing the number of sentences, paragraphs, and sentences per paragraph.

Use Autocorrect, If Available

Some electronic applications offer an autocorrect feature that can improve quality and speed of writing. Autocorrect can be found by accessing the help menu and searching for the term *autocorrect*. When the feature is accessed, an autocorrect dialog box appears with a blank area called *Replace* and another blank area named *With*. To improve efficiency of writing, an occupational therapist can develop codes for frequently used words or phrases. For example, a therapist who has grown weary of typing *occupational therapy* can save time by accessing the autocorrect feature, inputting *ot1* into the Replace area and *occupational therapy* into the With area, clicking on the Add button, and then on the OK button. From that time (until the option is removed from autocorrect), the application will replace *ot1* with *occupational therapy*.

Autocorrect also can be used to fix unique writing difficulties. For instance, a person intends to write the word *assess* but instead types *asses*. Both words are included in standard spell-check features. The person can use autocorrect to replace *asses* with *assess* and not have to worry about the problem. Other recommended additions to autocorrect include replacing *posses* with *possess* and replacing *defiantly* with *definitely*. Once added to autocorrect, the word cannot be used in writing. For instance, many people may not have a need to use the plural of the words *ass* and *posse*. Autocorrect comes with a listing of replacement items and has a removal feature. For example, autocorrect converts (c) to the symbol ©. To stop the conversion, a person needs to access the autocorrect dialog box, click on the Replace (c) with © line in the autocorrect listing, click on the Delete button, and then click on the OK button.

Collect Descriptions in a Database

Writing a description well (e.g., of a behavior or performance) sometimes takes more time than scoring a standardized assessment instrument. Rather than writing from scratch each time, therapists should think about gathering well-crafted descriptions into a central place for later use. The centralized descriptions, which serve as templates for customizing the information for individuals, can be stored in an electronic master file. All identifying information related to clients should be carefully removed from the descriptions.

An efficient therapist can develop two databases based on gender. The male version (with *he, his, him, himself*) can be developed first, then converted to a female version (with *she, her, herself*) by using the replace feature, available in most applications, to replace both *his* and *him* with *her* and *he* with *she*. These replacements will also convert *himself* to *herself*.

When writing a new report, the therapist can search the file for similar descriptions using key words in the find feature of most applications or add descriptions newly written for the current report. The descriptions also can be printed as a checklist, with a hard copy for use during the evaluation session. Over time, as the electronic master file grows, the descriptions can be re-arranged and categorized by content, age, setting, and so on.

Protect the Privacy of Electronic Information

Because personal health information is used and stored electronically, ensuring the security of electronic information is of utmost importance. Newspaper accounts contain horror stories of electronic health information inadvertently released to the general public through computers—with confidential reports still stored on hard drives—stolen or given to charitable organizations. Less spectacular violations of confidentiality occur frequently with information available to multiple people who use a single computer station. Personal access devices (e.g., phones, netbooks, PDAs) containing client information get lost, stolen, or cloned. Unsecured digital information can be replicated more than once. Privacy is becoming increasingly problematic.

If a computer is shared by other people, a simple way to secure electronic information is to make sure that confidential files are closed before leaving the computer station. Saving all work to a password-protected folder is a good option. Another method of protecting client records is to save electronic information to portable storage devices (e.g., USB memory drives) with appropriate password protection and encryption. The storage devices must be kept safe.

Interconnections and wireless capabilities increase security dangers exponentially. For Internet-based health records, occupational therapists need to ensure security of four points: Web site, personal access device, transmission, and connection. Any Web site used for client information must have security. Personal access devices also need security. Keeping current with the most recent versions of security applications such as encryption and firewalls may help. Working from a secured access point may offer additional security. The connection also must be secured. Occupational therapists need to be cautious of how and where an access device is connected at all times. If a therapist is documenting while in transit, the personal access device may change connection sites many times without the occupational therapist knowing it. One way to make certain of secured connections is to work offline with wireless capabilities turned off. Later, the occupational therapist can make the connection manually with full knowledge of the wireless access point. Occupational therapists working on client records need to exercise extreme caution if using unsecured wireless access sites.

To protect privacy of electronic information, occupational therapists need to be careful when documenting. For additional information related to privacy in general and electronic information in particular, please see *University of Miami's Privacy/Data Protection Project* for computer practices (2002a) and office practices (2002b), and University of Miami's Ethics Programs for protection recommendations related to e-mail (2003a), passwords (2003b), and portable computing and storage (2003c).

Conclusion

The mystery of Morgan, threaded throughout this chapter, serves as a reminder of the importance of interpretation in occupational therapy and the lasting power of documentation. To show effectiveness, occupational therapists must solve the mystery of each person by becoming lifestyle detectives who profile clients, examine clues within contexts, and synthesize multiple data points to give order to the complexities of life. Documenting occupational therapy is of equal importance to providing the original services. Because documentation remains as evidence of occupational therapy, occupational therapists must remain cognizant that their writing is part of their professional image. To ensure a legacy that shows the record of a competent therapist, this chapter offers general documentation recommendations.

Questions

1. Identify 10 words specific to occupational performance aspects that occupational therapists might assess and explain these terms as if you were using them in documentation targeted toward the specified audience:
   - Another rehabilitation team where the client will be transferred
   - A child's parent with a high school education
   - A referring physician
   - A child's parent with a sixth-grade education
   - A classroom teacher of a student with a disability
   - A third-party payer interested in function and functional outcomes
   - An older adult with mild cognitive difficulties
   - A Hispanic mother who speaks and understands minimal English.
2. Discuss how you can protect the confidentiality and privacy of your evaluation reports. If you use a computer or computer network for documentation, identify the personal and administrative steps you would take to

protect this information. If you are using a personal access device that is wireless, identify the personal and administrative steps you would take to protect this information.

3. Occupational therapists frequently perform audits on documentation for fieldwork students, junior staff occupational therapists, occupational therapy assistants, and other non–occupational therapist team members. Prepare a chart audit form that you could use to audit the quality of evaluation documentation by synthesizing the characteristics of best practices discussed in this chapter.

4. You are at your desk at work and see an individual who presents you with a written letter from a lawyer requesting immediate release of all your documentation on a specific client for a legal issue being investigated. You do not know whether the lawyer represents your facility or someone else. What do you do?

References

American Occupational Therapy Association. (2005). Occupational therapy code of ethics (2005). *American Journal of Occupational Therapy, 59,* 639–642.

American Occupational Therapy Association. (2008). Guidelines for documentation of occupational therapy. *American Journal of Occupational Therapy, 62,* 684–690.

Anastasi, A., & Urbina, S. (1997). *Psychological testing* (7th ed.). Upper Saddle River, NJ: Prentice Hall.

Borcherding, S. (2005). *Documentation manual for writing SOAP notes in occupational therapy* (2nd ed.). Thorofare, NJ: Slack.

Family Educational Rights and Privacy Act of 1974, Pub. L. 93–380, 20 U.S.C. § 1232g *et seq.*; 34 C.F.R. § 99.

Harris, C. H. (1998). Documentation. In J. Hinojosa & P. Kramer (Eds.), *Occupational therapy evaluation: Obtaining and interpreting data* (pp. 165–183). Bethesda, MD: American Occupational Therapy Association.

Health Insurance Portability and Accountability Act of 1996, Pub. L. 104–191, 45 C.F.R. §§160, 164.

Health Resources and Services Administration. (2009). *Plain language principles and thesaurus for making HIPAA privacy notices more readable.* Retrieved August 7, 2009, from http://www.hrsa.gov/servicedelivery/language.htm

Sames, K. M. (2010). *Documenting occupational therapy practice* (2nd ed.). Upper Saddle River, NJ: Prentice Hall.

Soccio, D. (2006). *How to get the most out of philosophy* (6th ed.). Belmont, CA: Wadsworth.

University of Miami's Privacy/Data Protection Project. (2002a). *Computer practices to preserve privacy.* Retrieved August 7, 2009, from http://privacy.med.miami.edu/tutorials/xtb_computer_practices.htm

University of Miami's Privacy/Data Protection Project. (2002b). *Office practices to preserve privacy.* Retrieved August 7, 2009, from http://privacy.med.miami.edu/tutorials/xtb_office_practices.htm

University of Miami's Ethics Programs. (2003a). *Kinder, gentler, safer emailing.* Retrieved August 7, 2009, from http://privacy.med.miami.edu/tutorials/email_etiquette.pdf

University of Miami's Ethics Programs. (2003b). *Picking and protecting passwords.* Retrieved August 7, 2009, from http://privacy.med.miami.edu/tutorials/password_pick_protect.pdf

University of Miami's Ethics Programs. (2003c). *Protecting portable computing and storage.* Retrieved August 7, 2009, from http://privacy.med.miami.edu/tutorials/portable_protect.pdf

12

Reassessment and Reevaluation

Fern Silverman, EdD, OTR/L

Overview

This chapter discusses reassessment and reevaluation as integral components of the evaluation process. Reassessment and reevaluation are defined in terms of their purpose and their client-centered and collaborative focus. Following a discussion of two approaches to reevaluation—continuous monitoring (ongoing reassessment) and systematic reevaluation at a discrete point in time—the chapter addresses some of the factors influencing the scope, nature, and type of reevaluation, looking at contextual factors and appropriate evaluative tools. It examines the reasoning processes supporting reevaluation, along with the competencies and skills required in conducting reevaluations. The chapter includes a brief examination of the relationships among reevaluation, treatment outcomes, and evidence-based practice and a section on the role of reevaluation in the termination of services. It concludes with a brief overview of the writing of the reassessment report.

Introduction

Reevaluation stands alongside initial evaluation as a critical part of occupational therapy practice. It helps an occupational therapist answer some of the essential questions that guide his or her treatment planning, such as, "Is this client making progress toward his goals?" and "Is the frequency/intensity/duration of treatment appropriate?" Reevaluation parallels initial evaluation as a conceptual process of collecting reliable and relevant information to support making informed clinical decisions (Krishnamurthy et al., 2004; Spruill, Rozensky, Stigall, Vasquez, Bingham, & Olvey, 2004). Both processes involve complex problem solving as the therapist generates, interprets, and translates client data into decisions and actions. In each process, the therapist strives to understand the client as an occupational being and to describe the "gap between capacity and performance" (World Health Organization [WHO], 2001, p. 20) that prevents full participation and engagement in the client's chosen occupations. In both situations, the therapist describes the client's current occupational performance status (either comprehensively or focused on a discrete aspect) and makes projections about future performance. The common purposes of initial evaluation and reevaluation center on the need to have accurate and complete information about the client as a basis for treatment planning. Hocking (2001) described this as a primary practice issue for a professional because both the initial evaluation and the reevaluation serve as the "basis from which occupational therapists define their clients' occupational performance challenges, determine clients' priorities, and negotiate the goals of interventions" (p. 468). Although initial evaluation and reevaluation share a basic procedure and overarching purpose, as well as many of the same skills and thought processes, they represent distinct components of the evaluation process with differing characteristics.

Inherent Complexity of Reevaluation

There are fundamental differences between evaluation and reevaluation. The initial evaluation establishes an occupational performance baseline; the reevaluation seeks to describe a new performance baseline and document change in the client's performance resulting from intervention. The therapist obtains an updated view of the client's performance that must be compared both retrospectively to the initial status to determine the degree and nature of change that has occurred and prospectively to the client's desired status to determine the performance issues still to be addressed. Simultaneously, the therapist reviews the intervention plan to understand how or why the change has occurred. That review requires self-reflection to consider how the therapist's skills have contributed to changes in the client's status. The therapist then integrates all of this information to determine if, how, and why occupational performance has improved, regressed, or stayed the same and to make the next set of decisions regarding the subsequent course of intervention (Moyers & Dale, 2007).

WHO Guidelines and an Environmental Perspective to Reevaluation

The complexity of the reevaluation process also relates to the changing context of a client's natural environment. Occupational therapists increasingly use a societal model to consider the needs of a client during reevaluation, in alignment with the philosophy of the WHO. Disability is viewed as a normal part of life that affects everyone at various times during the course of his or her life. The WHO recognizes that health and well-being can be affected by environmental barriers, as well as by body structure or body function problems (WHO, 2001). Using this as a guideline, occupational therapists must examine a client's limitation in participation as it relates to factors in the environment. An older client who moves to a first-floor, senior-friendly new apartment, for example, might have different treatment needs than one on the third floor of an old building. Reassessment must consider the barriers and supports in the environment to gauge the client's needs during any reevaluative process.

The increasing use of universal design principles in architecture, product manufacturing, and interior design can enable a client to participate fully in his or her environment, even when reassessment indicates continued limitation or a decline in skills. *Universal design,* "the design of products and environments to be useable by all people to the greatest extent possible without the need for adaptation or specialized design" (Center for Universal Design, 1997), promotes full access, embracing the philosophy of inclusion (Darragh, 2007). Typically, universal design results in a more functional environment or product for everyone (McGuire, Scott, & Shaw, 2006). The American Occupational Therapy Association (AOTA) aligns with the WHO perspective on health, social justice, and inclusion (AOTA, 2008c), and universal design plays an important role in promoting these values. The availability or lack of availability of universally designed products or environments should therefore be considered when a client's status is reassessed, reflecting the focus on society's role and responsibilities in enhancing participation for all citizens.

Reevaluation and the *Occupational Therapy Practice Framework–II*

AOTA's *Occupational Therapy Practice Framework: Domain and Process, 2nd Edition (Framework–II;* AOTA, 2008b) complements the WHO guidelines. Its language and spirit focus on function and participation ahead of client factors and disabilities. The *Framework–II* states that "despite their importance, the presence or absence of specific body functions and body structures do not necessarily ensure a client's success or difficulty with daily life occupations" (pp. 630–631). The overarching stated goal of the domain of occupational therapy is "to support health and participation in life through engagement in occupation" (p. 636). Participation and health therefore frame the reevaluation process. A reevaluation must consider a client's skills alongside factors in the physical and social environment to determine the need for further treatment.

The *Framework–II* uses language similar to that used in the *International Classification of Functioning, Disability and Health (ICF;* WHO, 2001) in an effort to create a meaningful picture of health and functioning. The *ICF* is applied at the individual level, the service/institutional level, and the population/community and social policy level for service provision. In occupational therapy, the *Framework–II* looks at performance patterns of the client across the same parameters. Using these categories, the occupational therapy reevaluation process should take into account the client's occupational performance and patterns of behavior on multiple levels and in multiple contexts.

The *Framework–II* addresses reevaluation specifically by including "Intervention Review" as a substep within the intervention phase of service delivery and also explicitly delineating outcomes assessment in the outcomes phase of service delivery. The intervention review, as described in the *Framework–II,* consists of three steps: reevaluating the plan and its implementation, modifying the plan as appropriate, and considering the need for further treatment. The

Framework–II describes the review phase of occupational therapy intervention as one that is continuous and collaborative in nature, to best address the current and future needs of the client.

Purposes of Reevaluation

Reevaluation serves the multiple purposes of evaluating client progress, exchanging feedback and information with the client or other professionals, establishing progressive goals, modifying intervention approaches and techniques, changing the intensity of service, and evaluating the efficacy of intervention (AOTA, 2005; Egan & Dubouloz, 2000; Moyers & Dale, 2007; Polgar, 2003). Reevaluation provides the therapist with information to support a range of potential decisions, including continuation of the intervention plan, changes in the intervention plan, discharge or discontinuation of services, or referral to another service or therapist (AOTA, 2008b). Reevaluation is a simultaneous review of the many client, therapist, and procedural factors that make up occupational therapy intervention and that provide valuable insight into the dynamic relationship among the client's occupational performance status, the therapist's repertoire of skills, and the integrity of the intervention plan.

Collaborative Nature of Reevaluation

The therapist is not the sole evaluator or decision maker in the reevaluation process. The importance of collaboration between client and therapist in reevaluation is clear (Egan & Dubouloz, 2000; Krishnamurthy et al., 2004; Tickle-Degnen, 2002; WHO, 2001). Although the therapist and client and family or caregiver collaborate during the initial evaluation, the relationship between the two parties strengthens and develops as intervention progresses and becomes even more intense during reevaluation. The client is the expert on how he or she has experienced changes in capacity and how those changes have altered performance in activity and participation across contexts. It is the client who feels the dynamic interactions between health conditions and contextual factors (WHO, 2001) and who can inform the reevaluation from that unique perspective. The therapist is the expert in understanding causal links and associations. Together, these co-experts make sense of the results of the reevaluation and construct a new plan. As Egan and Dubouloz (2000) described in the reevaluation stage of the Occupational Performance Process Model, a client-centered treatment planning model, "therapist and client determine whether or not the desired results have been obtained" (p. 99).

Reevaluation also can be considered a broader collaborative process by using a systems lens. The *Framework–II* (AOTA, 2008b) looks at the client from multiple angles and viewpoints that emphasize context and interrelationships. The word *client* is interpreted to mean any entity that receives occupational therapy services (AOTA, 2008b). Clients are thus categorized in the *Framework–II* as people, including families, caregivers, teachers, employers, and relevant others; organizations such as businesses, industries, or schools; and populations within a community, such as refugees or veterans. A reevaluation therefore may require that the therapist collaborate with multiple people involved in the well-being of the client. Spouses of patients with Alzheimer's disease or parents of students with autism are examples of those who may collaborate in the decision-making process that occurs during reevaluation. Communications among those who collaborate with the occupational therapist may occur during official contacts, such as individualized education plan meetings or discharge planning conferences, or informally, in hallway conversations or during an observation of treatment by a family member. Research suggests that both may influence the final therapy decision with regard to therapy duration and amount (Silverman, 2007), and therapists must be aware of the effect of all contacts and collaborations among those involved.

Differentiating Ongoing Reassessment and Discrete Reevaluation

Ongoing reassessment occurs during intervention where monitoring is a continuous part of treatment (AOTA, 2005; Clark & Miller, 1996; Krishnamurthy et al., 2004). In contrast, reevaluation is a distinct step along an evaluation–intervention–reevaluation continuum (AOTA, 2008a; Egan & Dubouloz, 2000; Fisher, 1998; Moyers & Dale, 2007). A therapist must acknowledge the need for both ongoing monitoring of the client's status within intervention (reassessment) and conducting discrete periodic reevaluations (Sames, 2004). Both approaches, either used exclusively or integrated, produce information used to modify the intervention approach. In each approach, evaluation, intervention, and reevaluation are interdependent processes. A therapist should approach reevaluation with an awareness of the interdependencies within each clinical situation and understand that in either approach, reevaluation itself can produce change (Krishnamurthy et al., 2004).

Ongoing Reassessment as Continuous Monitoring

Spruill and colleauges (2004) described continuous monitoring as an approach to reassessment used in psychology: "As treatment progresses, the clinician's initial assessment of the problem may change; as the assessment changes, so should the intervention" (p. 746). Within the occupational therapy literature, there is support for this approach to reassessment (Clark & Miller, 1996; Opacich, 1991). Ongoing reassessment is a necessary component of treatment between initial evaluation and discharge, where the therapist "modifies the intervention process to reflect changes in client status, desires, and response to intervention" (Prabst-Hunt, 2002, p. 162).

Opacich (1991) described the continuous nature of reassessment by saying,

> But as we have seen, information-gathering and decision making do not stop with the initial assessment and establishment of treatment goals. . . . Data and clinical observations regarding changes in human performance are continuously collected in the course of therapy. The information serves

to support, refute, or amend the treatment hypothesis and allows the clinician to make informed decisions. Furthermore, such evidence, systematically collected, can help determine the efficacy of treatment. If the therapy is not beneficial, the practitioner can decide to alter or terminate therapy. (p. 361)

Clark and Miller (1996) presented a systematic approach to continuous reassessment. The authors describe occupational therapy participation in the Heartland Problem-Solving Model, a four-level "problem-solving approach to special education service delivery" (p. 702). In the model, occupational therapy progress monitoring is a system of intertwined intervention and assessment of children with special needs, where comprehensive information about the student's functioning and instructional, curricular, and environmental accommodations is collected on an ongoing basis using multiple data collection methods and sources. As information is gathered, the therapist reflects on the information and makes immediate decisions to modify current intervention. Students are included in self-monitoring and contribute to the database as they are ready. Progress monitoring, as presented by Clark and Miller, is an example of a highly developed formal system of continuous reevaluation.

Another example of progress monitoring is the Response to Intervention (RtI) approach that is part of the Individuals With Disabilities Education Improvement Act of 2004 (Pub. L. 108–446). *RtI* is a tiered approach to intervention in schools that is designed to help all students who are in general education succeed, providing early intervening services through targeted interventions with progress monitoring (Fairbanks, Sugai, Guardino, & Lathrop, 2007). Occupational therapy delivered as part of RtI services makes use of ongoing progress monitoring to document and assess change.

Reevaluation as a Discrete Activity

Occupational therapy literature describes reevaluation as a discrete activity (AOTA, 2008a; Egan & Dubouloz, 2000; Fisher, 1998). *AOTA Documentation Guidelines* (AOTA, 2008a) names the reevaluation report as a specific type of documentation and provides guidelines for the content to be addressed in the reevaluation report. In her 1998 Eleanor Clarke Slagle Lecture, Fisher (1998) presented the Occupational Therapy Intervention Process model, a top-down approach to intervention planning. In this model, Fisher included reevaluation as a specific step in intervention planning. She labeled the step "Reevaluate for Enhanced Occupational Performance" and described it as a time when the therapist uses "performance analyses to verify whether the client has met his or her goals" (p. 518). The therapist identifies additional problems, redefines performance discrepancies, and cycles back through previous steps in the model to modify and implement new intervention strategies. Fisher also made the key point that focused reevaluation provides critical information about the effectiveness of occupational therapy services.

How Often Should Reassessment and Reevaluation Occur?

Progress monitoring, by its very nature, implies ongoing reassessment that yields data gathered on a regular basis with regard to client performance. The frequency of this reassessment process is straightforward because, by definition, it is ongoing and continuous. Progress notes, which a therapist can maintain in various ways, serve as a record of a client's change in occupational performance.

Given the complexity of reevaluation and the number of ways available to collect data, discrete reevaluation also takes place on a regular basis (Watson, Kanny, White, & Anson, 1995). Barnett (2004) addressed the issue of timing and sequence of reevaluation in the decision-making process. He questioned the use of a one-point-in-time assessment for related service providers, advocating multiple assessment points over a longitudinal timeline to acquire meaningful information and suggesting a data-driven model that measures outcomes when service intensity is increased or decreased.

Legal and administrative policies set by the educational or health facility involved determine the frequency of the discrete reevaluation process. Funding sources sometimes predetermine therapy duration periods on the bases of diagnoses or protocols established by institutional agencies. However, it is the responsibility of the occupational therapist to request a reevaluation at any time, independent of set policies and guidelines, if he or she ethically believes that the changed needs or status of a client warrant formal reexamination.

In clinical practice, reassessment and reevaluation result in a comprehensive database for the therapist's reflection and use in decision making. Although either process can stand alone, ideally both should be done together. The weaving together of the subjective and objective data provides a basis for the therapist to understand the client as an individual and evaluate both the client and the intervention plan. An example might be an occupational therapist working in an inclusive early intervention center. Reevaluation in his or her practice would have formal and informal aspects and be both continuous and discrete. This therapist would use a day-to-day comparison of current and past performance with initial goals as an informal means of reassessing children in order to be child-centered and make incremental modifications in daily treatment activities (i.e., reassessment as continuous monitoring). Formal reevaluation would occur on an annual basis when the interdisciplinary team, including the parents, sat down and reviewed the results of standardized tests and conducted a structured and systematic review of the child's goal attainment status (i.e., reevaluation as a distinct step). Like the clinician in this example, each therapist must develop an approach to reassessment and reevaluation in response to a number of factors affecting his or her practice and clinical setting.

Influencing Factors

Although the therapist and the client are the evaluators and decision makers, numerous contextual factors influence the therapist's approach to reevaluation within a particular clinical setting. Schell (2003) framed these influences as part of pragmatic reasoning and elaborated on the "everyday issues that have been identified over the years that affect the therapy process" (p. 136). She explained how factors such as available resources, organizational and professional culture, and reimbursement and regulation, along with the therapist's "clinical competencies, preferences, commitment to the profession, and life role demands outside of work" (p. 137), create practice and personal contexts that shape decision making around the scope and timing of services, including reevaluation. Practice context and the choice of reevaluative tools are two contextual factors particularly relevant to an understanding of the reevaluation process.

Practice Context

Characteristics of the practice context have a clearly identifiable effect on reevaluation. Krishnamurthy and colleagues (2004) made the case that within psychology, the volume and type of reevaluations vary within specialty areas of the profession. This same argument can be made for occupational therapy. Therapists in different practice areas respond to very different regulatory requirements for reevaluation, such as IDEA (AOTA, 2004; Clark & Miller, 1996) in school-based settings or Medicare in skilled nursing facilities (AOTA, 2008c). The short length of stay in acute care settings, for example, may force the rapid integration of evaluation, intervention, and reevaluation within one or two sessions, whereas the residential environment of a group home for individuals with developmental disabilities may allow monthly or even annual reevaluations.

Relevant legislation, reflected in new case law, continually alters the contextual parameters of reassessment and reevaluation. In school-based assessment in Pennsylvania, for example, the Gaskin settlement (*Gaskin v. Commonwealth of Pennsylvania*, 1995) heightened the need for therapists to consider a child's ability to participate in an inclusive classroom context as part of the reassessment and reevaluation process. The Gaskin settlement resulted from a class action suit by parents of children with disabilities who felt that their children's right to an education with their typical peers was being denied. Expanding to an international perspective, occupational therapists in different countries encounter different cultural and geopolitical factors that may influence the frequency and nature of reassessment and reevaluation procedures. In Australia, for example, funding for occupational therapy services in schools must be applied for annually from a set amount provided by the government for each child with a qualifying disability *(Disability Act 23/2006)*. The amount awarded each year is allocated by the principal and the Student Support Group (SSG), who determine which services (e.g., instructional aide, occupational therapy, speech, physical therapy) should be supported. Therefore, an extensive formal occupational therapy reevaluation must occur each year to put forth a strong case for continued funding.

Reevaluation Tools

A second factor influencing reevaluation is the availability of appropriate assessment tools. As Davies and Gavin (1999) put it, "The most common method used to demonstrate a change in clients' performance as a result of the treatment is to measure the client's abilities before and after treatment" (p. 363). Occupational therapists across specialty areas of practice have vastly different assessment tools available to them, contingent on the client's occupational performance problems, age, or diagnosis. Assessments used by occupational therapists also vary greatly in the psychometric qualities that influence their appropriate use in reevaluation. Experts in evaluation (Davies & Gavin, 1999; Polgar, 2003) caution occupational therapists on the psychometric issues relevant to selecting appropriate assessment tools that are particularly applicable to the selection of tools for reevaluation. Additionally, therapists must be cognizant of the fact that standardized instruments often focus on discrete underlying skills rather than performance of the activity and participation levels, and thus give limited information about the client's volitional aspects, integrated performance, or the environmental components of occupational performance (Fisher, 1992).

Fisher (1992) noted that the prevalent use of "home-grown evaluation tools" (p. 278) is problematic because validity and reliability are not adequately established, limiting the appropriateness of comparing pre- and posttreatment evaluation scores. Polgar (2003) explicitly addressed the need for an instrument to have strong test–retest reliability or stability over time, because "an estimate of the test's stability is necessary when the measurement is used as an outcome measure" (p. 304).

Polgar (2003) directed attention to another form of reliability relevant to reevaluation. Alternate form reliability is a concern when a therapist must repeatedly evaluate a specific area of client performance. As Polgar explained, client performance may artificially improve when given the same test at both evaluation and reevaluation because of a memory or practice effect. In this situation, rather than use the same test at reevaluation, the therapist identifies and uses a different test that measures the same performance area, computing the reliability coefficient to establish the equivalence of the two measures.

Often, a therapist will use the same evaluative tool for reevaluation that was used for the initial evaluation. The use of the same evaluation tool at targeted points across the duration of treatment yields data that facilitate comparison to a baseline level of skill performance. For example, a therapist could evaluate the range of motion of a client with a joint problem using a goniometer. By measuring the range of motion of a specific joint the same way using the same tool at the same time of day (i.e., under the same conditions), the therapist can quantitatively assess any changes made.

Although initial evaluation directs reevaluation and provides a clear baseline for assessing progress, the narrow focus that results from some initial evaluations also can constrain the reevaluation process. A therapist might use the initial evaluation to qualify the client for therapy and to describe performance. Therefore, at the point in time when the therapist selects the initial evaluation tools, the full impact of occupational therapy is not established. A reevaluation using the same tools might not capture the qualitative information gained through the collaborative relationship with the client, resulting in documentation of restricted outcomes and constricted views of treatment effectiveness. For this reason, the therapist may decide to alter the evaluative tool used for reassessment on the basis of the unique factors that frame the reassessment process. The following scenarios exemplify situations in which the therapist might choose to select a different evaluation tool than the one used during the initial evaluation or augment the reevaluation process by adding an additional evaluation tool to the reevaluation.

1. The client progresses across the developmental continuum from one age category to the next, and the initial evaluative tool is no longer appropriate. *Example:* An occupational therapist administers the Peabody Developmental Motor Scales (PDMS; Folio & Fewell, 2000) to a boy 5 years, 8 months of age with a delay of approximately 2 years in developmental skills who is enrolled in a preschool for children with special needs. A year later, the child has reached a chronological age of 6 years, 8 months, and his scores on some subtests might surpass the ceiling of the PDMS (5 years). The therapist decides to administer the Bruininks–Oseretsky Test of Motor Proficiency (Bruininks & Bruininks, 2005), which is normed for children ages 4 through 21.

2. The client transitions from one type of service delivery setting to another with a different focus and legal parameters, triggering a need for a different evaluation. *Example:* The DeGangi–Berk Test of Sensory Integration (Berk & DeGangi, 1983) is given to a girl who is 4 years, 1 month old as part of an assessment for occupational therapy services in a private clinic. A year later, she enters kindergarten in a typical classroom, where occupational therapy is now a related service. As part of the reassessment, the therapist may choose to administer the Sensory Profile School Companion (Dunn, 2006) instead of the previously given test to assess sensory processing issues that might be particularly relevant to school-based practice.

3. The client's condition (client factors) has changed since the last evaluation with regard to the extent of his disability or medical status. *Example:* An occupational therapist evaluates a 65-year-old diabetic patient with neuropathy for bilateral hand function. His medical condition worsens, and he undergoes an amputation 4 months later. At the point of his 6-month reassessment, the therapist must include evaluation tools that look at prosthesis use.

4. An additional performance area has gained importance to the client's overall well-being and sense of self and needs to be addressed in the reevaluative process. *Example:* A client 38 years of age who had a spinal cord injury and lower-extremity paralysis was initially evaluated in the acute care unit, with a focus on range of motion and activities of daily living. At the time of his 6-month reevaluation, he had improved to the extent that he was ready to resume his job as an accountant at a nearby accounting firm. The therapist added a work site assessment in the reas-

sessment process to assist the client in reentering his work environment with his disability, increasing the value of the reassessment by making it contextually appropriate (Law, Baum, & Dunn, 2001).

The therapist uses a holistic, flexible, and reflective therapeutic thought process when determining which assessments to use. The therapist must understand the limits of each individual test in reevaluation and avoid the expectation that a single evaluation can address all client performance issues with psychometric integrity. The therapist also must consider the changing dynamics of client factors and context that may necessitate an alteration of evaluation tools.

Reevaluation as an Iterative Process

The multiple purposes of reevaluation dictate an organized yet flexible integration of three steps: data collection, reflection, and decision making. Each step is distinct, involving specific thought processes and actions and producing requisite data to inform the next step. The steps flow from one to another, yet they are iterative, allowing the therapist to revisit steps in any order to produce a concurrent picture of the client, the intervention process, and the therapist's role in the process. The therapist gathers information about the client, the intervention, and his or her own reactions and responses to the client and the treatment. The therapist then considers all of this information to understand what has transpired in the intervention process and to gain an insight into why and how the intervention has had this effect. This process leads to well-informed decisions to modify, maintain, or discontinue discrete or comprehensive intervention strategies and actions.

Step 1: Data Collection

To initiate collection of data, the therapist makes the key decision about how extensive the data collection will be and identifies the sources and methods to collect information about the client, the intervention, and the therapist self-review. This begins with a retrospective review of what has occurred from the point of initial evaluation until the current point in time, including the evaluations performed initially, the client's initial status in all areas evaluated, and the client's current status on both short- and long-term goals. The collaborative review of the client's status includes not only recognition of his or her measured progress toward goals, but also recognition of his or her emotional and affective responses to treatment and his or her views on if and how treatment has addressed what is important to him or her (Kielhofner, Hammel, Finlayson, Helfrich, & Taylor, 2004). The therapist also reviews the course of treatment to confirm what was done and to clarify how it was done (i.e., the therapist's skills in providing the services).

Data collection itself is a multistep process in which the therapist collects all readily available information about the client and the treatment and quickly analyzes that information to decide where more focused or in-depth information is needed and how to acquire that information. The therapist and client decide which assessments to repeat, if any, and how to obtain additional information from other sources. Actual testing may be less extensive than that at the time of initial evaluation, because the reevaluation focuses on discrete problems or functional areas. The therapist seeks to answer two interconnected questions: (1) How has the client's occupational performance status changed since the initial evaluation? and (2) How has therapy been conducted?

Step 2: Reflection

The second step in reevaluation is reflection. In this step, the therapist seeks to answer two additional interconnected questions: (1) Why has change occurred? and (2) What does the change mean for the client's future? The therapist considers all of the information obtained during data collection, including reports from other health care providers, educators, or other documented providers to understand better the client's current occupational performance status. As Schell (2003) described, "More data are collected and the occupational therapy practitioner gains a sharper clinical image. The clinical image is the result of the interplay between what the occupational therapy practitioner expects to see (such as the usual course of the disease or disability) and the actual performance of the client" (p. 135). The therapist and client carefully compare current status to the client's desired future status to determine the nature and extent of the changes in the client's occupational performance and the continued potential for reaching the original goals and outcomes.

In this step, the therapist also seeks to understand why change has occurred. The therapist considers the overall effectiveness of the intervention plan. At this point, the therapist asks questions such as

- Did change occur as expected?
- Is there evidence to explain the change or to direct therapy from this point?
- Are the changes in the client's status meaningful to the individual or family?
- Are the changes important for functioning within the client's environment?
- Will the client and family or caregiver be able to maintain these changes after discharge from therapy?
- Are the changes occurring at an appropriate rate and amount relative to the frequency and duration of treatment?
- How much more change can be expected?
- How much time is needed for the client to achieve the changes?
- Do I have the knowledge and skills necessary to continue the treatment?
- Are there services in addition to occupational therapy that are needed?
- Is the client invested and engaged in treatment?

- Am I engaged, and do I believe in the client's ability to reach his or her outcomes?

The therapist asks and answers questions like these alone and together with the client in order to move to decision making, the final step of the reevaluation process.

Step 3: Decision Making

In this step of reevaluation, the therapist faces a choice of three decisions regarding the client and the intervention plan. As with the other steps, the therapist makes a decision in collaboration with the client and family or caregiver. This step appears straightforward, but it involves an analysis of the pros and cons and potential ramifications of each decision before a selection is made. The decision of what to do with the results of the reevaluation is an ethical decision as the therapist sorts through the options to determine what could be done, what should be done, and ultimately what is done (Schell, 2003). Questions generated during the reflection stage serve as the basis for evaluating the options in the decision-making step. The therapist arrives at the decision having considered all available information and can provide a rationale for the decision.

One decision is that the therapist can continue the intervention plan. The decision to continue the intervention without alteration indicates that the therapist and client agree that the client is progressing satisfactorily and that the plan can continue to provide just the right challenge to achieve further progress. The therapist can decide to modify the intervention plan. When the therapist decides to modify the intervention plan, he or she and the client also must make subsequent decisions regarding the nature, timing, and implementation of the changes. The therapist may elect to adjust discrete treatment activities or approaches within the plan or may substantially alter the frequency, duration, and intensity of the entire plan, including goals and outcomes. Or the therapist can decide to discontinue intervention and discharge the client from services. Typically, the therapist and client make this decision in one of several situations. The therapist and client choose discharge when the client has achieved all intervention objectives and can sustain that progress outside the treatment environment. The therapist may discontinue services when the client is not able to meet all of the objectives but has met maximum therapeutic benefit. A therapist also may discontinue services when the client's personal needs, goals, or context changes.

If the therapist continues or modifies an intervention plan, he or she then continues to cycle through the steps of reevaluation as needed. A decision to terminate services ends the process of reevaluation. Throughout the three steps of reevaluation, collaboration with the client and family or caregiver is fundamental to the success of the reevaluation. The therapist draws upon a mixture of thinking and reasoning processes during reevaluation to ensure that the client is an active collaborator and that all of the multiple factors are drawn together and considered.

Reasoning Processes Supporting Reevaluation

Occupational therapists use multiple reasoning styles during reevaluation to evaluate overall treatment effectiveness and make decisions while maintaining the client–therapist relationship and managing a large volume of diverse information. In their textbook on clinical reasoning, Mattingly and Fleming (1994) described the process of clinical reasoning in occupational therapy as "deliberation about what an appropriate action is in this particular case, with this particular patient, at this particular time" (p. 10). They went on to describe procedural, interactive, conditional, and narrative reasoning. Schell (2003) defined clinical reasoning as a complex and multifaceted "process used by practitioners to plan, direct, perform and reflect on patient care" (p. 131). (Readers are encouraged to read Schell's work for a discussion of scientific, narrative, and ethical reasoning.) Through the use and integration of all of these modes of reasoning, a therapist learns the particulars of each case as he or she implements the intervention plan and the relationship with the client unfolds. During reevaluation, the therapist shifts fluidly across all of the modes of reasoning.

In the data collection and reflection steps of reevaluation, the therapist uses scientific and procedural reasoning when comparing the client's current performance status to his or her initial level of performance to identify changes in the client's status and response to specific interventions. The therapist then shifts to interactive and conditional reasoning as he or she incorporates subjective information from the client about his or her response to treatment, personal goals, and situation. A final shift to narrative reasoning occurs as the therapist and client look ahead and compare the client's current status to the desired intervention outcome. If the therapist makes a decision at any point to readminister a formal assessment, the therapist again switches to procedural reasoning in parallel with the thinking process of the initial assessment.

During the decision-making step in reevaluation, the therapist again uses multiple modes of reasoning. In continuing an existing intervention plan or selecting new intervention strategies, the therapist once more uses scientific and procedural reasoning to match the plan and strategies to the problem or deficit. However, the therapist simultaneously moves to interactive reasoning as the intervention plan is modified for the client, who is involved in decisions of how and when to modify the plan. When the therapist makes the decision to terminate services, a final switch to conditional and narrative reasoning occurs. The therapist and client together must consider the client's life beyond the treatment setting and determine how able the client is to meet the demands and challenges of his or her life. Throughout the reevaluation process, the therapist uses pragmatic reasoning as he or she negotiates the service delivery system with the client. The therapist considers the ethical implications of each decision as he or she decides on the best option for the client.

Therapist Skills Needed for Reevaluation

The skills involved in reevaluation parallel the skills needed in the initial evaluation phase, with specific emphasis on unique application of specific competencies. One of the most obvious skills needed is that of selecting and interpreting formal assessments with specific consideration of the psychometric issues identified earlier in this chapter. Given the nature of reevaluation in occupational therapy, in which the challenge is to understand and integrate the multiple physical, social, cultural, and emotional features of a person and translate that information into occupational performance in various temporal and performance contexts, additional skill areas are equally vital to an efficient and effective reevaluation process (Coster, 1998). Spruill and colleagues (2004) described six foundational competencies of clinical psychologists that also apply to the skill set needed by an occupational therapist in the reevaluation phase: scientific foundations, relationship skills, communication skills, individual and cultural differences, ethical and legal guidelines, and critical thinking. The complexity of reevaluation, in which the client relationship has evolved and the amount of information available to be synthesized and used has multiplied, intensifies demands in all of these areas. Krishnamurthy and colleagues (2004) reinforced the notion of integrating technical assessment skills with the ability to synthesize information with inferences and communicating results and feedback in a way that is understandable and useful to the client. Both Spruill and colleagues and Krishnamurthy and colleagues stressed the importance of self-reflection and analysis as components of the skill set used in evaluation and reevaluation.

Reevaluation: Linked to Treatment Outcomes and Evidence-Based Practice

Reevaluation, through its reiterative nature, serves as a way to look at a client's needs in relation to his or her initial status when therapy commenced. The therapist collects information that informs clinical decision making through the reevaluative processes of ongoing reassessment and systematic reevaluation. The data also provide a way for the occupational therapist to demonstrate the measurable treatment outcomes resulting from occupational therapy. Reevaluation therefore aligns with evidence-based practice principles as a process that collects and uses data to guide therapy decisions and interventions.

Connection to Outcomes

Reevaluation can serve the dual purposes of determining a client's progress toward the therapy goals and contributing to the evaluation of the service program (Fisher, 1992; Krishnamurthy et al., 2004; Polgar, 2003). Due in part to fiscal issues, therapists may be under pressure to use reevaluations to document outcomes and demonstrate the efficacy of occupational therapy intervention (Unsworth, 2000). Yet the occupational therapist also must recognize that change is not always the sole object of intervention (Fawcett, 2007). And the therapist must recognize that outcomes measures need to be sensitive to protective and preventive effects, as well as to improvements (Heaton & Bamford, 2001, p. 347). Kielhofner and colleagues (2004) identified four interrelated components of outcomes research that demonstrate the overlap between reevaluation of the individual client and measurement of effectiveness at the programmatic level: "(1) identifying client needs, (2) creating the best possible services to address those needs, (3) generating evidence about the nature of specific services and their impact, and (4) accumulating and evaluating a body of evidence about specific occupational therapy services" (p. 16). Kielhofner and colleagues also included "understanding the process of therapy" as an important element of treatment effectiveness research. The client's perspective on how therapy has progressed and what the experience has meant can inform outcomes research in much the same way that the reevaluation process is enhanced by the inclusion of the client's subjective information.

Outcomes are also central in the *Framework–II*. The *Framework–II* addresses outcomes as "the end result of the occupational therapy process" (AOTA, 2008b, p. 660), and occupational therapists must therefore assess "observable outcomes" (p. 660) to determine the client's success in achieving the goals set at the beginning of the intervention process. The *Framework–II* also points out that the assessments and variables selected for measurement shape the definition of the outcome. Therefore, outcomes measurements must be holistic in nature, considering the client's occupational profile, contextual factors, and the needs and desires of the client himself or herself. The therapist may modify the measures chosen during the treatment process to reflect a change in priorities as needed.

Connection to Evidence-Based Practice

Reassessment and reevaluation provide concrete evidence to guide decision making. Such evidence can help answer prognostic questions (Bennett & Bennett, 2001) such as "Was the treatment effective?" or "Should treatment be altered?" Despite the importance of evidence, evidence and data alone cannot lead to appropriate decision making without clinical judgment and reflexivity. Lee and Miller (2003) proposed that decision making for the occupational therapist must be contextualized, not just evidence-based, to truly serve the needs of clients. A contextualized therapy decision takes into account the client's perspective and the values of occupational therapy. Lee and Miller suggested that therapy decisions emerge from a triad of data: formal assessment/reassessment, therapist clinical observations, and client self-report.

The number of sources of evidence determines the effectiveness of reevaluation. Some sources of evidence are the client as expert and the research literature. These sources allow the therapist to judge whether his or her interpretations are accurate and whether decisions about intervention modifications or discharge reflect best practice. Evidence-based practice requires an "approach that integrates the best external evidence with individual clinical expertise and patient's choice" (Sackett, Rosenberg, Muir Gray, Haynes, & Richardson, 1996)—the same factors that frame the reevaluation process. Reevaluation also can contribute to the development of evidence-based practice as a therapist examines in aggregate the results of individual client reevaluations.

Bennett and Bennett (2001) made this connection, commenting that "evaluating the effectiveness of the treatment of clinical practices implemented, in terms of improvement in relevant outcomes, makes it possible to determine if the evidence-based decision-making process has been successful. Evaluation leads to more questions and so the cycle continues" (p. 178). Although reevaluation at the client level is not synonymous with outcomes research or the generation of evidence-based practice, if the therapist conducts the reevaluation systematically and collects and analyzes the results in aggregate, the processes clearly can be mutually informative.

Reevaluation and the Termination of Services

Reevaluation, as a process, can be used to determine continued eligibility, program planning, or discharge. However, there are no uniform eligibility criteria for occupational therapy services (Muhlenhaupt, 2000), and similarly, there is no single criterion to establish when to terminate services. A therapist should terminate direct services "when the goal has been met or when the means of achieving the goals is no longer best accomplished through our legitimate tools" (Nesbit, 1993, p. 846). Although there have been multiple attempts to unify or standardize discharge decisions (Kaminker, Chiarello, O'Neil, & Dichter, 2004; Long, 2003; Lovell & Russell, 2005), success has been limited and setting-specific. Therefore, the skills and expertise of the occupational therapist are critical to the reevaluation process, which often guides the pace and timing of service termination.

Termination of services is subject to the rules and regulations of the institution, including relevant laws, policies, and practices. However, termination of services also can occur in a way that is client-centered. To ensure that the termination of services is client-centered, communication is vital. It is incumbent upon the therapist to be certain that he or she communicates effectively with all stakeholders involved about the purpose of the therapy at the beginning of the therapeutic relationship, when the initial evaluative process takes place. The client, significant family members, and administrators should understand the scope and domain of occupational therapy practice as it relates to the needs of the client. It is equally important to communicate the results of reevaluation and ongoing progress monitoring. By keeping the client and other stakeholders informed, a change in amounts of service delivery will be more understandable and less of a surprise to those involved. If multiple treatment notes for a client with a brain injury, for example, repeatedly show no further gains, and a thorough reevaluation verifies this trend, the client and his or her family members might be more likely to agree with a therapist's decision to terminate services. A clear delineation of therapy goals and progress toward these goals can preempt unrealistic expectations among stakeholders and facilitate a smoother transition when therapy is no longer warranted.

In many cases, therapists can reduce therapy services gradually, tracking the success of each reduction with progress monitoring. A therapist can terminate services slowly in several ways. For example, a therapist might shift the delivery model for therapy services from direct services to consultation, cutting back on the hands-on nature of the interaction between the therapist and the client. Second, a therapist can change a service from individual sessions to a group session, reducing the intensity of the client–therapist relationship. Finally, frequency can also be changed; for example, services can be decreased from once a week to once every other week, with further reductions in frequency occurring until service termination is complete.

There are a number of advantages to a step-down approach to service termination. First, the therapist can use progress monitoring to test the ability of the client to maintain his or her new performance level and goals reached as services are reduced. In this way, a gradual reduction in services acts as a vehicle for ongoing progress monitoring. Second, the client and family members can separate more easily from any dependence on the therapist, transitioning from relying on the supportive role of an occupational therapist to an increased state of independence. The client is able to apply new skills to meaningful, functional activities and transfer them to the natural setting while still receiving some occupational therapy support. Therefore, the client is more likely to generalize outcomes appropriately, enhancing his or her sense of empowerment and facilitating a smoother transition to life beyond occupational therapy.

A therapist must use a moral compass when using reassessment and reevaluation to terminate services. Ethical decision making relates directly to discharge planning, which is the end product of the reassessment and reevaluation processes (Atwal & Caldwell, 2003). Atwal and Caldwell identified the ethical breaches that occur when a therapist fails to heed the AOTA *Code of Ethics*. In their research, they identified unintentional gaps in an occupational therapist's adherence to the values of autonomy, beneficence, nonmaleficence, and justice in treatment and discharge decisions. Careful reevaluation is essential for making treatment decisions regarding frequency or service termination while maintaining high ethical standards.

Documentation and the Reevaluation Report

Once the process of reevaluation concludes, the therapist documents the results. The therapist can record reevaluation results, if brief, in the regular progress note by recording the changes in client status and resulting adjustments in the intervention plan. Lengthy, comprehensive reports may entail a separate format. A facility or source of reimbursement may determine the specific formats of reports.

AOTA documentation guidelines (2008a) include the reevaluation report as a specific form of clinical documentation. The guidelines suggest five content areas to be included in the report:

1. *Client information*
2. *Updated occupational profile*—Identification of performance areas that have been resolved or that continue to be problematic, as well as changes in the client's priorities or desired outcomes

3. *Reevaluation results*—Specification of assessments used, client performance, and response
4. *Summary and analysis*—Interpretation of data, including comparison with previous evaluation results
5. *Recommendations.*

According to this document, the reevaluation report provides documentation of periodic reassessments that are readministered at intervals established by the practice setting.

Conclusion

Reevaluation is a critical component of the occupational therapy process. Mattingly and Fleming (1994) repeatedly reinforced the notion that reevaluation is an essential component of occupational therapy intervention. They identified "a process of nearly continuous hypothesis generation, evaluation, and revision" (p. 336) in occupational therapy. This continuous process of revision is essential no matter how thorough the initial assessment. The therapist, through reevaluation, is able to adjust the intervention to adapt to client improvement, regression, or the evolution of the therapeutic relationship.

Reevaluation requires that the therapist collaborate with the client to work through the steps of data collection, reflection, and decision making to incorporate multiple pieces of information into a cohesive and responsive decision to continue or update the intervention plan or terminate treatment. The data collection step includes gathering information from a variety of sources about the client, the intervention process, and the therapist. The therapist and client reflect on the client's initial status and desired future status, and consider both the client's and the therapist's subjective responses in determining the effectiveness of the intervention plan. The evaluation of treatment effectiveness leads to decisions about continuing, modifying, or discontinuing treatment. Through the three reiterative steps of reevaluation, the therapist is continually drawing on a blend of reasoning modes and evidence to make intervention decisions that are clinically sound, holistic, and responsive to the unique situation of the client.

Questions

1. When performing a reevaluation, the therapist may choose to use the same tools used previously or different tools. Give some examples of why the therapist might use the same tools and why he or she might use different tools.
2. Reflection is a complex process. Discuss the various elements of the reflection process during reevaluation.
3. Describe the clinical reasoning modes that are often used in the reevaluation process.
4. This chapter mentions that the term *outcomes* may vary. What are different types of outcomes one may find from intervention?
5. Describe the relationship between reevaluation and evidence-based practice.

References

American Occupational Therapy Association. (2004). *Occupational therapy services in early intervention and school-based programs.* Retrieved June 16, 2004, from www.aota.org/practitioners/official/statements/40881.aspx

American Occupational Therapy Association. (2005). *Standards of practice for occupational therapy.* Retrieved September 24, 2009, from http://www.aota.org/Practitioners/Official/Standards/36194.aspx

American Occupational Therapy Association. (2008a). Guidelines for documentation for occupational therapy. *American Journal of Occupational Therapy, 62,* 684–690.

American Occupational Therapy Association. (2008b). Occupational therapy practice framework: Domain and process (2nd ed.). *American Journal of Occupational Therapy, 62,* 625–683.

American Occupational Therapy Association. (2008c). *Reimbursement and regulatory resources: Information you need to successfully advocate for your patients and your profession.* Retrieved November 30, 2009, from www.aota.org/Practitioners/Reimb/Resources/2008conf/2008C.aspx

Atwal, A., & Caldwell, K. (2003). Ethics, occupational therapy, and discharge planning: Four broken principles. *Australian Occupational Therapy Journal, 50*(4), 244–251.

Barnett, D. W. (2004). Response to intervention: Empirically based special service decisions from single-case designs of increasing and decreasing intensity. *Journal of Special Education, 38,* 66–79.

Bennett, S., & Bennett, J. W. (2001). The process of evidence-based practice in occupational therapy: Informing clinical decisions. *Australian Occupational Therapy Journal, 47,* 171–180.

Berk, R. A., & DeGangi, G. A. (1983). *DeGangi–Berk Test of Sensory Integration.* Los Angeles: Western Psychological Services.

Bruininks, R., & Bruininks, B. (2005). *Bruininks–Oseretsky Test of Motor Proficiency* (2nd ed.). Circle Pines, MN: AGS Publishing.

Center for Universal Design. (1997). *The principles of universal design, version 2.0.* Raleigh: North Carolina State University. Retrieved October 9, 2009, from http://www.design.ncsu.edu/cud/about_ud/udprinciplestext.htm

Clark, G. F., & Miller, L. E. (1996). Providing effective occupational therapy series: Data-based decision making in school-based practice. *American Journal of Occupational Therapy, 50,* 701–709.

Coster, W. (1998). Occupation-centered assessment of children. *American Journal of Occupational Therapy, 52,* 337–344.

Darragh, J. (2007). Universal design for early childhood education: Ensuring access and equity for all. *Early Childhood Education Journal, 35*(2), 167–175.

Davies, P. L., & Gavin, W. J. (1999). Measurement issues in treatment effectiveness studies. *American Journal of Occupational Therapy, 53,* 363–372.

Disability Act 23/2006. (2006). Victoria, British Columbia: Parliament of Victoria.

Dunn, W. (2006). *Sensory Profile School Companion.* San Antonio, TX: Psychological Corporation.

Egan, M., & Dubouloz, C. J. (2000). Evaluating client performance related to targeted outcomes. In V. G. Fearing & J. Clark (Eds.), *Individuals in context: A practical guide to client centered practice* (pp. 99–107). Thorofare, NJ: Slack.

Fairbanks, S., Sugai, G., Guardino, D., & Lathrop, M. (2007). Response to intervention: Examining classroom behavioral support in second grade. *Exceptional Children, 73*(3), 288–310.

Fawcett, A. (2007). *Principles of assessment and outcome measurement for occupational therapists and physiotherapists.* New York: John Wiley & Sons.

Fisher, A. G. (1992). Functional measures, part 2: Selecting the right test, minimizing the limitations. *American Journal of Occupational Therapy, 46,* 278–281.

Fisher, A. G. (1998). Uniting practice and theory in an occupational framework (Eleanor Clarke Slagle Lecture). *American Journal of Occupational Therapy, 52,* 509–521.

Folio, M. R., & Fewell, R. R. (2000). *Peabody Developmental Motor Scales* (PDMS–2–1; 2nd ed.). Austin, TX: Pro-Ed.

Gaskin v. Commonwealth of Pennsylvania, 23 IDELR 61 (Pa. 1995).

Heaton, J., & Bamford, C. (2001). Assessing the outcomes of equipment and adaptations: Issues and approaches. *British Journal of Occupational Therapy, 64*(7), 346–356.

Hocking, C. (2001). Implementing occupation-based assessment. *American Journal of Occupational Therapy, 55,* 463–469.

Individuals With Disabilities Education Improvement Act (IDEA) of 2004, Pub. L. 108–446, 20 U.S.C. § 400 *et seq.*

Kaminker, M., Chiarello, L., O'Neil, M., & Dichter, C. (2004). Decision making for physical therapy service delivery in schools: A nationwide survey of pediatric physical therapists. *Physical Therapy, 84*(10), 204–213.

Kielhofner, G., Hammel, J., Finlayson, M., Helfrich, C., & Taylor, R. R. (2004). Documenting outcomes of occupational therapy: The Center for Outcomes Research and Education. *American Journal of Occupational Therapy, 58,* 15–23.

Krishnamurthy, R., VandeCreek, L., Kaslow, N. J., Tazeau, Y. N., Miville, M. L., Kerns, R., et al. (2004). Achieving competency in psychological assessment: Directions for education and training. *Journal of Clinical Psychology, 60,* 725–739.

Law, M., Baum C., & Dunn, W. (2001). *Measuring occupational performance: Supporting best practice in occupational therapy.* Thorofare, NJ: Slack.

Lee, C., & Miller, L. (2003). The process of evidence-based clinical decision making in occupational therapy. *American Journal of Occupational Therapy, 57*(4), 473–477.

Long, D. (2003). Predicting length of service provision in school-based occupational therapy. *Physical and Occupational Therapy in Pediatrics, 23*(4), 79–93.

Lovell, K. R., & Russell, K. (2005). Developing referral and reassessment criteria for drivers with dementia. *Australian Occupational Therapy Journal, 52*(1), 26–33.

Mattingly, C., & Fleming, M. H. (1994). *Clinical reasoning.* Philadelphia: F. A. Davis.

McGuire, J., Scott, S., & Shaw, S. (2006). Universal design and its applications in educational environments. *Remedial and Special Education, 27*(3), 274–278.

Moyers, P., & Dale, L. (2007). *The guide to occupational therapy practice* (2nd ed.). Bethesda, MD: AOTA Press.

Muhlenhaupt, M. (2000). OT services under IDEA 97: Decision-making challenges. *OT Practice, 5*(24), 10–13.

Nesbit, S. (1993). Direct occupational therapy in the school system: When should we terminate? *American Journal of Occupational Therapy, 47,* 845–847.

Opacich, K. J. (1991). Assessment and informed decision making. In C. Christensen & C. Baum (Eds.), *Occupational therapy overcoming human performance deficits* (pp. 356–372). Thorofare, NJ: Slack.

Polgar, J. M. (2003). Critiquing assessments. In E. B. Crepeau, E. S. Cohn, & B.A.B. Schell (Eds.), *Willard and Spackman's occupational therapy* (10th ed., pp. 299–312). Philadelphia: Lippincott Williams and Wilkins.

Prabst-Hunt, W. (2002). *Occupational therapy administration manual.* Albany, NY: Delmar.

Sackett, D. L., Rosenberg, W., Muir Gray, J., Haynes, R., & Richardson, W. (1996). Editorial— Evidence-based medicine: What it is and what it isn't. *British Medical Journal, 312*(7023), 71–72.

Sames, K. M. (2004). *Documenting occupational therapy practice.* Upper Saddle River, NJ: Prentice Hall.

Schell, B.A.B. (2003). Clinical reasoning: The basis of practice. In E. B. Crepeau, E. S. Cohn, & B. A. B. Schell (Eds.), *Willard and Spackman's occupational therapy* (10th ed., pp. 131–138). Philadelphia: Lippincott Williams & Wilkins.

Silverman, F. (2007). *A study of occupational therapy service negotiations in educational settings* (Doctoral dissertation, Arcadia University, Philadelphia). Retrieved April 17, 2009, from ProQuest Digital Dissertations database (Publication No. AAT 3289777).

Spruill, J., Rozensky, R. H., Stigall, T. T., Vasquez, M., Bingham, R. P., & Olvey, C. D. V. (2004). Becoming a competent clinician: Basic competencies in intervention. *Journal of Clinical Psychology, 60,* 741–754.

Tickle-Degnen, L. (2002). Client-centered practice, therapeutic relationship, and the use of research evidence. *American Journal of Occupational Therapy, 56,* 470–474.

Unsworth, C. (2000). Measuring the outcome of occupational therapy: Tools and resources. *Australian Occupational Therapy Journal, 47*(4), 147–158.

Watson, A. H., Kanny, E. M., White, D. M., & Anson, D. K. (1995). Use of standardized activities of daily living rating scales in spinal cord injury and disease. *American Journal of Occupational Therapy, 49,* 229–234.

World Health Organization. (2001). *International classification of functioning, disability and health.* Geneva: Author.

13

● ● ● ● ●

Evaluating Special Populations

●

Jaime Phillip Muñoz, PhD, OTR/L, FAOTA

Overview

An occupational therapist must be able to screen and evaluate a wide variety of patient populations. On any given day, occupational therapists choose assessments to evaluate premature babies in an intensive care unit; children in school; and adults with conditions as varied as strokes, traumatic brain injuries, spinal cord injuries, and depression and dementia, to name only a few. Evaluation is one of the most fundamental yet most complex aspects of what therapists do in day-to-day practice. In its broadest sense, evaluation helps a therapist make reasoned and informed decisions about intervention. Best practice in evaluation requires that a therapist establish what the client wants and needs to do, consider critically the contexts in which the person performs, and determine barriers and supports to occupational performance (Dunn, 2000). Best practices also require that a therapist select valid, reliable measures that fit the client and his or her context. This includes selecting assessments that are *culture-fair*—assessments that do not discriminate against a person on the basis of age, race, ethnicity, gender, sexual orientation, or economic or disability status (Padilla & Borsato, 2008).

This chapter explores issues surrounding the implementation of culture-fair evaluation processes when assessing special populations. *Special populations* are defined here as people with disabilities, populations with limited English proficiency, and groups and communities that are marginalized and economically disadvantaged. Accommodations to the evaluation process that may be required because of a client's age or developmental level, functional capacity, or sociocultural context are discussed. Clinical reasoning processes to consider when evaluating special populations are examined in three broad areas: person-related issues, assessment-related issues, and evaluator-related issues. Although these categories are discussed separately, it is essential to recognize that in the context of the evaluation process, these components interact.

Purpose of Accommodations in the Evaluation Process

Chapter 10 discusses standardized testing, focusing on the scoring and interpretation of results. By definition, in standardized testing the evaluator administers and scores the assessment uniformly. This uniformity is a critical dimension of standardization. If instructions, time limits, the way items are presented, and the way test-takers respond are all the same, then the evaluator can be confident that any differences in performance are differences in ability, not differences in the conditions of the assessment process (Harnis, Amtmann, Cook, & Johnson, 2007). This uniformity helps a therapist, as an evaluator, maintain a high level of confidence in his or her findings regardless of the construct being measured.

Test accommodations are attempts to ensure that evaluation processes are fair and unbiased toward all. *Accommodations* are changes in the way an assessment is administered or the way a person responds to test items; these changes often are categorized as changes in setting, scheduling, timing, presentation, and method of responding (Goh, 2004). Accommodations often influence the uniformity of testing processes (Thurlow & Thompson, 2004).

Federal laws and regulations such as the American with Disabilities Act (ADA, 1990), the Individuals with Disabilities Education Act (IDEA, 1997), and the No Child Left Behind Act (NCLB, 2002) are intended to guarantee the right of all students to be evaluated fairly. Thus, in the context of these federal laws, testing accommodations are reasonable accommodations. A therapist has a responsibility to be familiar with local, state, and federal guidelines and legislation that might regulate the evaluation of people with disabilities (e.g., IDEA, ADA, NCLB). Clear understanding of these regulations is particularly significant when the results of an evaluation may determine the presence or nature of a disability or when the results will be used to determine service eligibility or placement.

Much of the literature on testing accommodation focuses on educational, not health, assessment (Pitoniak & Royer, 2001). The emphasis on evaluation in the educational testing literature is on the impact of accommodations on the psychometric properties of the assessments used to measure students' educational and psychological performance (Harnis et al., 2007). Nonetheless, the abundant educational assessment literature provides effective frameworks for examining the range of accommodations that a therapist can and should make to ensure fair testing. Categories of accommodations are changes in the setting, timing, or scheduling of a test; presentation of test items; or changes in the subject's method of responding to items (Bolt & Thurlow, 2004; Goh, 2004). Hollenbeck, Tindal, and Almond (1998) provided a clear and useful description of the purpose of accommodation that helps a therapist remember that the purpose of an accommodation is to elicit a culture-fair evaluation of performance:

Accommodations do not change the nature of the construct being tested, but differentially affect a student's or group's performance in comparison to a peer group. Also, accommodations provide unique and differential access (to performance) so certain students or groups of students may complete the test and tasks without other confounding influences of test format, administration, and responding. (p. 175)

Person-Related Issues

Evaluation is an interpersonal process. It is often the first contact that a client and his or her family have with occupational therapy. Thus, evaluation is often the first opportunity for a therapist to demonstrate an interpersonal stance that reflects intentional respect for the client, the client's family, and the client's lifestyle (Dunn, 2000). Attention to the interpersonal process in evaluation is of primary concern in any occupational therapy evaluation, but it becomes even more important when the client has a disability or differs culturally from the therapist in terms of ethnicity, race, religion, gender, sexual orientation, age, or socioeconomic status (Weinstock-Zlotnick & Hinojosa, 2004). A therapist must consider the person-related issues that can influence evaluation practices. Further, a therapist's clinical reasoning processes should include consideration of the person's disability, life stage, and culture.

Consider the following practice scenario. Mr. Ortega is a 77-year-old man referred to an outpatient rehabilitation center with a diagnosis of arthritis, which affects his lumbar spine and right hip. His chief complaint is back pain. Mr. Ortega speaks conversational English, but his native language is Spanish. He moved to the United States 2 years ago from El Salvador after his wife died. His eldest son, his son's family, and two friends from the small Salvadoran community he has settled in accompany him to the clinic. His son has brought copies of his father's health records from when he was hospitalized in El Salvador. These records are in Spanish, but it appears Mr. Ortega suffered a cerebrovascular accident (CVA) in the left temporal lobe 6 years ago.

In this case story, there are multiple issues that might influence the evaluation process. The occupational therapist might consider whether Mr. Ortega's CVA resulted in an expressive aphasia, which, combined with English being his second language, could result in poorer scores on tests requiring verbal responses. The therapist also needs to consider that Mr. Ortega's advanced age, with its related life stage factors, could influence testing. For example, does Mr. Ortega have any problems with visual acuity or hearing that could influence accurate evaluation of his performance? A therapist who intentionally considers how culture might influence the evaluation process would question whether Mr. Ortega and his family have had any experience with standardized testing or whether this type of testing will represent a novel situation for them. The therapist might consider whether the assessments chosen have valid and reliable

Spanish versions or whether the therapist has a level of Spanish fluency that will allow effective assessment of Mr. Ortega.

Disability

An occupational therapist who evaluates people with physical disabilities uses assessments designed to assess such populations. Some considerations for effective test administration for people with disability seem obvious. For example, a person with a hearing impairment may be significantly disadvantaged by an oral test even when oral content is provided visually. An oral test usually can be adapted easily for a person with visual impairments, but a test requiring motor performance is likely to present some challenge (Pitoniak & Royer, 2001). On the other hand, some considerations are less obvious. For example, the Nottingham Health Profile (McEwen & McKenna, 1996) is a well-known and frequently used measure of quality of life, yet it includes several questions concerning mobility that are ill suited for people in wheelchairs. When a therapist uses and scores this assessment in the standard way, the physical functioning scores for people who are wheelchair-bound are overstated (Post, Gerritsen, van Leusen, Paping, & Prevo, 2001).

A therapist cannot assume that a person with a physical limitation will automatically perform less well, or that a tool designed for a nondisabled population will elicit an accurate measure of performance for people with disabilities. Braden (1994) reviewed more than 200 studies of the intellectual performances of children who were deaf and found that those with parents who also were deaf performed better than nonimpaired children on psychological performance tests. A person with a disability may or may not require an accommodation, and people with similar disabilities may not require the same accommodation. The main point here is that the therapist must thoughtfully consider the person and the area of occupational performance he or she wants to measure to ensure a valid and reliable evaluation process.

Accommodations include any change in the conditions under which a standardized test is administered (Bolt & Thurlow, 2004). This includes any changes in the way the test is delivered (when, where, how long), changes in the way the test items are presented, and modifications in the manner in which the person responds to test items, including the use of special equipment (Fuchs, Fuchs, Eaton, Hamlett, & Karns, 2000). When choosing to make an accommodation because of a client's disability status, the therapist must judge whether the client needs an accommodation and, if so, what the nature and extent of such accommodations will entail. When choosing the most appropriate assessment tool, the therapist must consider the nature of the client's disability and the design of the assessment. For example, people with limitations in dexterity, vision, or perception may be allowed extra time to complete a test. It is the evaluator's responsibility to tailor the accommodation to the person's need. The therapist must be knowledgeable about testing accommodations and, when appropriate, encourage the client to be part of the decision-making process about accommodations.

Clinical reasoning related to test accommodation may include the therapist's reflection on whether to modify the test instructions or materials, allow for changes in the response format, decrease or eliminate expectations for speed of response, or modify the test setting (Anastasi & Urbina, 1997; Goh, 2004). When the therapist has completed the testing, he or she should reflect on any accommodations made to determine which were most effective. Documentation of these findings may support clinical reasoning in future testing situations where accommodations also may be required.

When testing a client with special needs, the accommodations a therapist institutes may represent deviations from standardized testing protocols. For example, a person with a visual limitation may need manual guidance in a fine motor task or adapted materials that help compensate for low vision, and a person with poor motor control may need assistance stabilizing his or her body or materials. Whenever an accommodation is made to a standardized assessment, issues of validity and reliability of the results become critical considerations in the interpretation of the results. A therapist must specify clearly in the evaluation report any changes made to standardized protocol. If accommodations are made, standard scores from the normative sample cannot be used to describe the client's performance, because reliability and validity of the tool would be affected (Richardson, 2001).

Evaluators must thoughtfully consider issues of test psychometrics when making accommodations. The American Psychological Association's (APA's) *Standards for Educational and Psychological Testing* emphasize that test scores obtained under different testing conditions must be assumed to have a different meaning unless the accommodations have been shown to not alter the meaning of the test (APA, 1999). The impact of accommodation on test reliability and validity or on test performance continues to be researched, and contradictory findings have spawned much debate and disagreement (Cox, Herner, Demcyzk, & Nieberding, 2006).

One widely discussed categorization of testing accommodations was created by CTB/McGraw-Hill, which publishes many educational and psychological tests (CTB/McGraw-Hill, 2005). CTB/McGraw-Hill's three-level categorization of accommodation states that Category 3 accommodations, such as reading items aloud, using a scribe on writing tests, or allowing the use of a dictionary or calculator, "change what is being measured and are likely to have an effect that alters the interpretation of individual criterion- and norm-referenced scores" (p. 9).

Although an occupational therapist is far more likely to complete health assessments that do not require these specific types of accommodations, the principle remains the same. Accommodations can influence test psychometrics, and therefore the use of accommodations when administering standardized tests should occur only after thoughtful consideration of the potential impact on test validity and interpretation of test results. A therapist must document in the evaluation summary a clear description of and rationales for the accommodations used.

Life Stage

A client's age and stage of life also can have implications that a therapist must consider when selecting and interpreting evaluation results, particularly if standardized tests are selected. Many therapists work in pediatric settings where public policies such as IDEA (IDEA, 1997), Individuals with Disabilities Education Improvement Act (IDEA, 2004), or No Child Left Behind (NCLB, 2002) and programs such as Head Start and Medicaid have helped to create and maintain a practice context that emphasizes standardized assessment procedures (Swinth, 2009). For example, norm-referenced measures that establish a child's performance often are used by the pediatric team to make a determination about a child's eligibility for services (Case-Smith, 2005; Swinth, 2009). In many cases, eligibility decisions are based on whether a child's score falls 1 to 2 standard deviations below the test norm in particular developmental areas or is in the bottom 25% of scores.

When interpreting the results of a pediatric assessment, it is essential that the therapist reflect on contextual factors that may influence the child's performance. For example, research suggests that poverty can be a powerful determinant of a child's cognitive development (Duncan & Brooks-Gunn, 2000). From an environmental perspective, low-income families frequently live in neighborhoods characterized by social disorganization, such as high rates of crime, joblessness, social isolation, and few resources for child development (Brooks-Gunn & Duncan, 1997; Zins, Weissberg, Wang, & Walberg, 2004). When selecting an assessment or interpreting the results, the therapist not only must consider whether the assessments used are standardized on a U.S. population norm that includes children with disabilities, children from cultural and ethnic groups, or children who have recently emigrated to the United States but also must consider and report alternative explanations for the client's test performance (Stewart, 2001).

A person's stage of life always should be a consideration in the evaluation process and is often a critical concern when evaluating elderly people. Growing older does not inevitably mean becoming disabled; however, compared to younger cohorts, older people have a much higher incidence of functional limitations (Ekstrom & Smith, 2002). Elderly people may present with mild to moderate sensory impairments, diminished memory, or a decreased attention span, and there will always be a subgroup of the older population that will experience a significant level of functional disability requiring the extended use of health services. With such people, the evaluation process is multidimensional and often complicated (Caplan & Shechter, 2008; Hills & Bernstein, 1997). When evaluating an older client, the therapist must recognize that functional impairments, as a result of pathology, often are superimposed on physical and psychological features that may be part of the normal process of aging. The evaluation process often is more challenging with older people, because the client's clinical presentation is frequently complicated by multiple diagnoses. A client's physical, mental, and social well-being are interrelated, necessitating an evaluation plan that considers how best to determine the client's occupational status from these multiple vantage points. If the client is confused or has trouble communicating, the evaluator may need to rely on a family member for assessment data.

Andrews and Boyle (2003) suggested some critical clinical questions that an evaluator can use to support his or her reasoning around evaluation with elderly people:

- What is the physiological status of the person?
- What social and cultural factors influence the type of care the person will need?
- What cultural values may influence the person's expectations for care by other family members?
- What resources are available to meet those needs?
- What are the locations for residence and care that the person finds most acceptable?

Caplan and Shechter (2008) also suggested several critical points that a therapist should consider when deliberating whether and how to make testing accommodations for elderly people. For example, a therapist can consider the client's level of experience with standardized testing situations. A therapist should reflect on the feelings of test anxiety the client may have had at some point. An elderly person may feel as if he or she is under a microscope and may feel anxious or humiliated, especially if a test requires him or her to fail repeatedly before the exam ends (Caplan & Shechter, 2008). Time spent building rapport with the client and his or her family can help the client ease into the testing situation. It is also useful to ensure that the client is clear about why the tests are being done, what the tests will entail, and how the results will be useful to the client and his or her family. Finally, if a therapist is administering several tests, he or she needs to consider the client's energy level and stagger the pattern of tests so the client is not faced with a succession of difficult, discouraging tests (Caplan & Schechter, 2008).

The gradual decline in functional capacities in vision, hearing, and the other senses as people age is a well-established fact (Bass-Haugen, Henderson, Larson, & Matuska, 2005). Consideration of these declines associated with aging during the evaluation process might include reminding older clients to bring glasses or hearing aides to the evaluation and to consider the acoustic features of the testing environment (Koltai & Bohmer, 2000). Ensuring that the testing environment is well lit and a comfortable temperature may also support older clients in demonstrating their best performances during testing.

A person-centered approach to evaluation and the subsequent intervention planning must give more consideration to the values and decisions of the client and his or her family (Dunn, 2000). Evaluating the needs of the older client and his or her family or caregiver requires respectful collaboration that takes into account the client's strengths and limitations while respecting his or her rights and wishes (Hasselkus, 1994; Levine, 1999). Effective evaluation is a more likely outcome when the evaluator uses respectful interpersonal approaches, such as

- Addressing the person by his or her last name and appropriate title;
- Making conscious attempts to elicit the client's life experiences and previous health care experiences;
- Listening attentively to the client's health concerns and health practice regimes; and
- Eliciting directly the client's preferences for care, including diet and the use of self-care remedies or cultural healers.

It is also important to keep in mind that many older people tire easily and an evaluation may need to be completed in two or more sessions. When planning the evaluation, the therapist needs to allow time for life review, but refocus the conversation if the life review begins to dominate the assessment. Finally, a therapist needs to triangulate evaluation data by eliciting collaborative information from multiple sources, including varied assessment methods and tools and data from significant others and caregivers.

Culture

A final set of person-related issues that can influence the evaluation process are issues that may occur when testing clients whose cultural backgrounds may be dissimilar to the therapist's. There are a number of ways that cultural differences may influence a client's performance on a test. Cultural factors that might influence testing include the client's socioeconomic status, language, educational level, ethnicity, migration history, generational level, reading and health literacy level, and comfort in a test-taking situation.

One of the most obvious influences is a difference in language. In the United States, nearly 45 million people over the age of 5 do not speak English in their home (U.S. Census Bureau, 2000). If the assessment a therapist chooses uses language, then at some level the test is a measure of the client's language skills. If a client's dominant language is different from that used in the test, these cultural differences need to be taken into account when interpreting test results. For example, a therapist who is not conversant in a client's dominant language and lacks cultural knowledge of the nuances or nonverbal mannerisms of the culture is likely to misinterpret the client's meaning (Marcos, 1994). Culturally and linguistically appropriate services include evaluation processes that ensure that the therapist assesses a person in an effective, understandable, and respectful manner that is consistent with the client's health beliefs and practices and that is provided in the client's preferred language (U.S. Department of Health and Human Services, 2001).

Even clients who are bilingual are likely to have a dominant language, which should be ascertained in order to ensure accurate and fair test results (Confresi & Gorman, 2004). In the case story presented earlier, Mr. Ortega had conversational English skills, but his native language was Spanish. At minimum, the occupational therapist treating Mr. Ortega should ascertain which language he prefers to use and assess him in that language. Language skills and maintenance can vary considerably, and a bilingual client's performance on an assessment is considerably influenced by his or her command of either language. Bilingual Latino children may use English words in Spanish phrases, often demonstrate pronunciation problems in either language, and may misorder words when communicating (Sattler, 2001). Such behaviors could be interpreted as a deficit in cognition, not limitations often seen in English-language learners (Helms, 2004). An evaluator can use some simple, straightforward questions to determine the most appropriate language for assessment. Some questions that could help an evaluator determine what languages should be used to assess a bilingual client are

- What language was spoken at home when you were a child?
- How old were you when you learned your second language?
- In what language are you most comfortable speaking and thinking? (Confresi & Groman, 2004, p. 102)

When a therapist is not proficient in the person's preferred language, effective evaluation of a non-English-speaking client requires a bilingual interpreter. A testing situation can be unfamiliar and uncomfortable for anyone. Clients who speak English as a second language, like Mr. Ortega, may be in more need of an interpreter when placed in anxiety-provoking situations like being in a new health care setting, dealing with troubling symptoms, being asked to discuss life situations, or being tested (Andrews & Boyle, 2003). The ideal situation is to use a medically trained interpreter who is proficient in the client's language and is knowledgeable about beliefs and practices in the client's cultural group. A trained interpreter should have a health care background, be trained in interpreting techniques, and have a clear understanding of patient rights.

If possible, it is recommended that the therapist arrange for the interpreter to meet with the client prior to the occupational therapy evaluation to obtain basic demographic information so that the client and interpreter have a chance to meet, discuss relatively nonthreatening topics, and become comfortable with one another. If a trained interpreter is not available, then a bilingual member of the health team is the next best choice. As a last resort, a relative, friend, or even another client might interpret. Such people often are eager to help and are readily available; however, there are a number of drawbacks to this line of action. Specifically, the therapist must consider the very important issue of confidentiality. The evaluator also must recognize that such an interpreter may share the client's culture and language but may be unfamiliar with medical terminology, hospital or clinic procedures, or issues of patient rights and health care ethics. Special attention must be given even to trained medical interpreters regarding occupational therapy because they are not familiar with our intentions or why certain information is needed from a client.

Other cultural differences may include the client's motivation for or attitudes toward testing—for example, a cultural value that emphasizes or deemphasizes competitiveness and speed in test-taking—and whether or not the client has had previous opportunities to learn the knowledge or the skills that the test measures (Linn & Gronlund, 1999). In their review of culture-fair testing measures in psychology, Linn and Gronlund concluded that "most attempts to remove cultural influences from tests have fallen short of their goal" (p. 455). They suggested a variety of strategies that a therapist might consider to support culture-fair testing. These include

- Using materials that are primarily nonverbal,
- Ensuring that pictures and diagrams that are used are familiar to the cultural group being tested,
- Selecting materials and methods that are interesting to the client,
- Liberalizing time limits and deemphasizing speed, and
- Simplifying the test-taking procedures to accommodate those clients who may have less experience in test-taking situations (Linn & Gronlund, 1999).

Assessment-Related Issues

Assessment-related issues most germane to the occupational therapy evaluation process include errors in clinical reasoning that can arise in the selection of an assessment, the application of the assessment, or the interpretation of assessment results. Assessments are tools that are designed with a particular task in mind, but as Anastasi (1992) said, "Whether a tool is an instrument of good or harm depends on how the tool is used" (p. 610). In a pinch, a screwdriver can be used as a poor excuse for a hammer, but the results are usually substandard and irreparable harm often is done to the materials. Similarly, assessments are misused when an occupational therapist does not give adequate attention to what is being evaluated, does not place the results of any one assessment in the context of an overall evaluation plan, places unquestioning faith in the results of a test, or uses an assessment for a client who is markedly different from the group for whom the assessment was intended (Goh, 2004; Hayes, 2008).

When selecting an assessment tool, the therapist might ask which is more important: knowing how a client's performance compares with others who have taken the same test or being able to discuss the person's performance in terms of speed, precision, or number of items correct, without referring to the performance of others. In the former situation, a norm-referenced test would be the best choice, and in the latter situation, the best choice is a criterion-referenced test. If a norm-referenced assessment is selected, the evaluator must recognize that norm samples vary and can be drawn nationally, regionally, or even from a population of incoming college freshmen; thus, the therapist must consider whether the norms for the selected assessment are relevant to the client being evaluated. The therapist can study the norm sample or norm tables in an assessment manual to help make this determination. The more closely the client approximates those in the norm group, the greater the confidence that the test is an appropriate choice and that the norms provide a meaningful basis of comparison.

For example, when designing items for the School Functional Assessment (SFA; Coster, Deeney, Haltiwanger, & Haley, 1998), the authors intentionally sought to use a multilevel definition of function and disability. Coster and her colleagues clearly wrote in the SFA user manual that "items were carefully worded to apply to students with a wide variety of functional disabilities and to recognize the capabilities of students who perform functional tasks in an alternative manner, either because of impairments or differences in cultural practices" (p. 46). A therapist can easily find data on the demographic characteristics of the standardization sample used in the development of the SFA and will notice that the developers were careful to draw a sample from both urban and rural settings, a variety of disabling conditions, a gender distribution that matched the nationwide demographic of students with disabilities (e.g., more males), and a racial and ethnic distribution that mirrored the population demographics of the U.S. Census.

A therapist also can ask himself or herself whether the norms are representative. What procedures were used to define the norm sample? Was the group randomly selected? If not, are significant subgroups of the population (e.g., gender, geographic areas, socioeconomic, racial and ethnic groups) represented in the sample? The authors of the Pediatric Evaluation of Disability Inventory (PEDI; Haley, Coster, Ludlow, Halitwanger, & Andrellos, 1992) specifically warned that occupational therapists

> using the PEDI to assess children from minority subgroups or at socioeconomic extremes should use caution in applying the normative standards until further data are obtained. Interpretation of the child's performance must be accompanied by careful consideration of the family and community practices and standards. (p. 6)

A therapist should read carefully the technical manual of the assessment to understand how norm-referenced scores were derived and the characteristics of the normative sample. It also is important to determine whether the norms are up-to-date and applicable in contemporary clinical situations. The copyright date on the user's manual often does not coincide with the date the norm sample was established, and an evaluator must read carefully to discern this information. It is important to note that the test manuals of some assessments may not provide adequate answers to these questions. In such cases, it becomes even more imperative for the therapist to consider reflectively the suitability of the measure.

Clinical reasoning around issues of application and interpretation can be supported by thoughtfully considering whether selected assessments may have a bias in content, criterion, or construct validity. Any assessment may have some degree of bias. Obvious sources of bias include bias grounded in culture, gender, geographic, or socioeconomic variables. Bias on the part of the therapist is another potential confounding variable, but this type of bias will be considered in the following section. A reflective therapist will ask whether the items in the test are perceived in the same way across cultures. For example, test items may have names or pictures of objects that are unfamiliar to clients from a particular cultural milieu. Thus, the Somali Bantu client who is being assessed may have no idea what a hockey puck is, a Hmong client may have never prepared a grilled cheese sandwich, and the client who is gay may not be sure how to respond to assessment items that perpetuate a heterosexual perspective or gender stereotypes. Such assessment tools would be inappropriate for these clients.

A reflective therapist can challenge his or her clinical reasoning by considering whether there is equivalence in the way that constructs in the test are conceptualized and defined cross-culturally. Even in assessments that have been translated from one language to another, it is important to recognize that the assessment still may contain items that can be misinterpreted because of a lack of equivalency in the translation process or to geographic variations in the language. An assessment also may contain language that a gay, lesbian, bisexual, or transgender client may find offensive, exclusionary, or stigmatizing (Prince, 1997). Assessments that contain such language may lead a client to offer constricted responses, particularly when engaged in interview and self-report instruments. Such assessments may contain items that do not reflect the life experiences of non-heterosexual clients. A client may offer constricted responses or closely monitor descriptions of experiences, values, or interests, particularly if he or she perceives that responses may lead to negative consequences from exposing his or her sexual orientation (Prince, 1997). Heterosexuals are rarely anxious about disclosing their sexuality because heterosexuality is assumed. When using interviews, health care providers often proceed within a heterosexual frame of reference, and the choice of language an evaluator uses may limit the therapist's ability to develop a helping relationship with a gay, lesbian, or transgendered client (Neville & Henrickson, 2006).

In tests that are criterion-referenced, the therapist should question whether the criteria used reflect sensitivity to cultural differences. For example, the Kohlman Evaluation of Living Skills (KELS; Thompson, 1992) is a self-care evaluation used in mental health practice settings. However, self-care rituals can vary cross-culturally (Andrews & Boyle, 2003). A client who reports a culturally influenced self-care routine that deviates from those listed in the scoring criteria of the KELS would be rated as needing assistance unless the therapist considers the potential for test bias in the KELS self-care criteria.

Evaluator-Related Issues

The therapist's clinical reasoning process is influenced by multiple factors: the therapist's perspective on evaluation, knowledge of and competence in administering a variety of assessments, interpretation of the data, choice of assessment, and openness to finding creative ways to understand the client and his or her family, to name a few. Some of the therapist-related issues that can influence testing of special populations include ethnocentrism, ethnorelativism, and evaluator proficiency in cultural assessment.

Ethnocentrism can be defined as a universal tendency of people to believe that their ways of thinking, acting, and believing are the only right, proper, and normal ways (Andrews & Boyle, 2003). This can become a significant problem in the evaluation process if a client's performance and responses are seen as a deficit, inferior, or bizarre. Ethnocentrism can lead to stereotyping, prejudice, and bias, which can be serious impediments to accurate evaluation. Therapist bias can be both conscious and unconscious, and an evaluator may make judgments or assumptions about the client on the basis of how the client dresses, talks, or presents himself or herself. For example, in traditional Latino families, children are raised to show *respeto* (respect) to elders and authorities. In a testing situation, such a child may respond to the therapist with brief answers and look to the floor when the therapist is speaking. If these behaviors are not interpreted in a cultural context, the therapist may erroneously conclude that the child shows signs of depression or lacks interpersonal communication skills.

Ethnorelativism is the opposite of ethnocentrism. It is a multicultural ideology that reflects a therapist's ability to integrate aspects of other cultures into his or her own (Brems, 1998). Ethnorelativism requires not only a realization of the inherent multiculturalism in the world but also that a therapist adapt his or her own cultural perspectives to accept a multicultural ideology (Wurzel, 2004). Adopting a multicultural ideology is particularly important to evaluation because it helps the therapist frame a client's occupational performance patterns within the context of the norms and expectations of the client's culture. A therapist often can hold values about health and healing that are at variance with the values held by people from non-Western cultures (Iwama, 2006; Phipps, 1995). Practices based on Western, middle-class values, such as an emphasis on activism as a response to disability, routinely working toward autonomy in activities of daily living, and predicating intervention on future-oriented time perspectives often disregard non-Western cultural mores (Kinébanian & Stomph, 1992). Iwama (2006) argued that occupational therapy models often present assumptions about occupational functioning that place considerable focus on the person; the person's social and physical environments are secondary or tertiary considerations. For individuals and groups who value interdependence over autonomy and who consider the collective needs before the needs of the person, evaluation processes focused on the person may miss the mark (Iwama, 2006).

A therapist has the responsibility to examine and avoid ethnocentrism and develop an ethnorelative perspective. One strategy to achieve this is by obtaining a sound educational foundation about the worldviews of different cultures (Campinha-Bacote, 2001). Sue and Zane (1987) described this process of expanding one's cultural knowledge as "developing cultural literacy" (p. 38). The development of cultural literacy is reflected in the way that a therapist studies the available scholarship about a client's culture and actively constructs a personal knowledge base for culturally responsive caring (Muñoz, 2007). In a testing situation, the therapist must judiciously use culture-specific knowledge, acknowledge within-group variations in cultural groups, and make a conscious effort to determine whether culture-specific information is applicable to his or her client. This is an approach to reasoning that Sue (1998) described as "dynamic sizing" (p. 448). Returning once again to Mr. Ortega's case story, clearly Mr. Ortega lived in El Salvador until very recently. He lives with his son and has contacts within a small community of Guatemalan immigrants, which may allow him some opportunities to maintain his cultural heritage. However, a culturally responsive therapist with good knowledge of Guatemalan culture would not assume Mr. Ortega follows the traditional life-ways of his culture. It is likely that Mr. Ortega's son, who has lived in the United States for nearly 2 decades, has become more acculturated to U.S. society. Dynamic sizing requires that the therapist apply what he or she knows about the culture and the client and determine the fit. In this case, when the therapist applies what he or she knows about Guatemalan culture to these two men in the same family, he or she would likely come to different understandings of each man.

Although it is important to work toward an increased understanding of others, the therapist also can develop an ethnorelative stance by developing awareness of his or her own cultural identity and by exploring his or her cultural heritage (Muñoz, 2007; Tervalon & Murray-Garcia, 1998). Cultural awareness is developed through a conscious process of examining one's own biases. Dyche and Zayas (2001) described this type of sensitivity and a willingness to stay open as "cultural empathy" (p. 246). This commitment to examine one's own prejudices and remain open to the experience of diversity and multiculturalism mirrors what Tervalon and Murray-Garcia (1998) described as "cultural humility" (p. 118). A therapist who demonstrates cultural humility recognizes and accepts that people and their ways of life are as varied as the trees in the forest. The strength and sturdiness of the oak make it no better or worse than the willow, the birch, or the larch. It simply is different.

An occupational therapist might practice cultural humility by taking an interpersonal stance of "informed not knowing" to help him or her remain open to cultural understanding (Laird, 1998). *Not-knowing* is an advanced level of therapeutic artistry manifest in an interpersonal approach featuring active listening, intentional respect, and a questioning process that conscientiously recognizes the client as the expert of his or her own experience (Anderson & Goolishian, 1992).

Another evaluator-related issue that can influence the evaluation process is examiner competency. A primary aspect of this competency includes the cultural awareness, knowledge, and skill set to perform a cultural assessment. Leininger (1978) defined *cultural assessment* as "a systematic appraisal or examination of individuals, groups, and communities as to their cultural beliefs, values, and practices to determine explicit needs and intervention practices within the context of the people being evaluated" (p. 850). Every clinical encounter is a cross-cultural encounter (Muñoz, 2007); therefore, cultural assessment must be an intentional effort on the part of the therapist to use evaluation processes that help him or her better understand what shapes a client's ideas about health, illness, and disease. Although nearly all contemporary models of occupational therapy practice identify culture as an essential component of the person and his or her environment, assessments in occupational therapy are rarely designed to elicit data that help a therapist complete a systematic appraisal of culture. Try to think of an assessment that intentionally directs the therapist to elicit data on the following areas that affect occupational functioning:

- Preferred language and communication styles
- Ethnic, racial, and sexual identity
- Views and concerns about discrimination and institutional racism as they relate to the client's health
- Structure and use of a client's informal network of support
- Migration experiences
- Cultural health beliefs and practices.

Multiple models of cultural competence suggest that self-awareness is a critical component of cultural competence (Campinha-Bacote, 2001; Leininger, 1978; Muñoz, 2007). A culturally responsive therapist can develop self-awareness by reflecting on his or her evaluation processes. Some questions to guide this reflective process include

- Do I routinely seek to develop my knowledge of cultural values and belief systems related to health and disease? What sources do I use?
- Can I effectively elicit a client's perception of what he or she believes caused the illness or disability? How did I accomplish this with recent clients?
- Can I elicit culturally relevant information from family members? What approaches work best?
- Do I intentionally consider culture when taking a history or intake interview so that I can develop a culturally sensitive occupational profile?

People also have the right to expect that the therapist is competent in the use of the assessment. The therapist has an ethical responsibility to achieve a minimal level of competency prior to administering an assessment. Minimal competency includes an expectation that the therapist can articulate his or her reasons for choosing an assessment, has studied the test manual, has observed administration of the test, has practiced the mechanics of administration, has had an observer check interrater reliability, is adept at selecting and preparing the test environment in accordance with test administration procedures, and is knowledgeable about methods for evaluating the usefulness of the assessment (Richardson, 2001). Some assessments, such as the Assessment of Motor and Process Skills (AMPS; Fisher, 1995), have clearly been designed for use by more-experienced evaluators and may require certification or post-professional continuing education. In a similar vein, if the therapist chooses to use an assessment that is frequently used by professionals in other disciplines, it is the responsibility of the therapist to demonstrate competency with such assessments to colleagues, clients, and client's families and to ensure that the rationales for selection and interpretation are grounded in an occupational therapy perspective.

Conclusion

This chapter explored person-related, assessment-related, and evaluator-related issues that may arise when testing special populations. It focused on adaptations to the evaluation process that may be required because of a client's age or developmental level, physical disability, or sociocultural context, with an emphasis on defining critical questions that can help support a therapist's clinical reasoning processes. Prior to conducting an evaluation, the therapist should consider how factors such as the client's age, language preference, level of acculturation, disability, or sexual orientation might influence the evaluation process. The evaluator must reflect on whether the available tools are culture-fair assessments that will offer a valid measurement of the client, thoughtfully consider whether accommodations are appropriate, and determine what effect such accommodations may have on the interpretation of the test results. Finally, the therapist should examine and avoid any personal ethnocentrism and recognize the possibility that the instruments available may not be effective measures for clients from all cultural subgroups.

Questions

1. Identify types of accommodations that can be made to testing situations.
2. Think about a situation that you have observed during fieldwork. Can you identify potential areas of bias that occurred during an evaluation?
3. Choose two assessment tools. Review them to determine areas of the tools that may exhibit cultural bias.
4. Describe the difference between ethnocentrism and ethnorelativism.
5. Review assessment tools that you have learned. Can you identify a culture-fair assessment?

References

American Psychological Association. (1999). *Standards for educational and psychological testing.* Washington, DC: Author.

Americans With Disabilities Act of 1990, Pub. L. 101–336, 42 U.S.C. § 12101.

Anastasi, A. (1992). What counselors should know about the use and interpretation of psychological tests. *Journal of Counseling and Development, 70*(5), 610–615.

Anastasi, A., & Urbina, S. (1997). *Psychological testing* (7th ed.). Upper Saddle River, NJ: Prentice Hall.

Anderson, H., & Goolishian, H. (1992). The client is the expert: A not-knowing approach to therapy. In S. McNamee & K. Gergen (Eds.), *Therapy as social construction* (pp. 25–39). Newbury Park, CA: Sage.

Andrews, M. M., & Boyle, J. S. (2003). *Transcultural concepts in nursing care.* Philadelphia: Lippincott Williams & Wilkins.

Bass-Haugen, J., Henderson, M. L., Larson, B. A., & Matuska, K. (2005). Occupational issues of concern in populations. In C. Christiansen, C. M. Baum, & J. Bass-Haugen (Eds.), *Occupational therapy: Performance, participation, and well-being* (pp. 167–187). Thorofare, NJ: Slack.

Bolt, S. E., & Thurlow, M. L. (2004). Five of the most frequently allowed testing accommodations in state policy. *Remedial and Special Education, 25,* 141–152.

Braden, J. P. (1994). *Deafness, deprivation, and IQ*. New York: Plenum Press.

Brems, C. (1998). Cultural issues in psychological assessment: Problems and possible solutions. *Journal of Psychological Practice, 4,* 88–117.

Brooks-Gunn, J., & Duncan, G. J. (1997). The effects of poverty on children and youth. *The Future of Children, 7*(2), 55–71.

Campinha-Bacote, J. (2001). A model of practice to address cultural competence in rehabilitation nursing. *Rehabilitation Nursing, 26*(1), 8–11.

Caplan, B., & Shechter J. (2008). Testing accommodations for the geriatric patient. *NeuroRehabilitation, 23,* 395–402.

Case-Smith, J. (2005). An overview of occupational therapy for children. In J. Case-Smith (Ed.), *Occupational therapy for children* (5th ed., pp. 2–29). St. Louis, MO: Mosby Elsevier.

Confresi, N. I., & Gorman, A. A. (2004). Testing and assessment issues with Spanish–English bilingual Latinos. *Journal of Counseling Development, 82*(1), 99–106.

Coster, W. J., Deeney, T., Haltiwanger, J., & Haley, S. M. (1998). *The School Functional Assessment: Standardized version*. Boston: Boston University.

Cox, M. L., Herner, J. G., Demczyk, M. J., & Nieberding, J. J. (2006). Provision of testing accommodations for students with disabilities on statewide assessments. *Remedial and Special Education, 27,* 346–354.

CTB/McGraw-Hill. (2005). *Guidelines for inclusive test administration*. Monterey, CA: Author. Retrieved October 30, 2009, from http://www.ctb.com/media/articles/pdfs/general/guidelines_inclusive.pdf

Duncan, G. J., & Brooks-Gunn, J. (2000). Family poverty, welfare reform, and child development. *Child Development, 71,* 188–196.

Dunn, W. (2000). *Best practice occupational therapy in community service with children and families*. Thorofare, NJ: Slack.

Dyche, L., & Zayas, L. H. (2001). Cross-cultural empathy and training the contemporary psychotherapist. *Clinical Social Work Journal, 29*(3), 245–258.

Ekstrom, R. B., & Smith, D. K. (2002). *Assessing individuals with disabilities in educational, employment, and counseling settings*. Washington, DC: American Psychological Association.

Fisher, A. (1995). *Assessment of Motor and Process Skills*. Fort Collins, CO: Three Star Press.

Fuchs, L. S., Fuchs, D., Eaton, S. B., Hamlett, C., & Karns, K. (2000). Supplementing teacher judgments of mathematics test accommodations with objective data sources. *School Psychology Review, 29*(1), 65–85.

Goh, D. S. (2004). *Assessment accommodations for diverse learners*. Boston: Pearson Education.

Haley, S. M., Coster, W. J., Ludlow, L. H., Haltiwanger, J. T., & Andrellos, P. J. (1992). *Pediatric Evaluation of Disability Inventory (PEDI)*. San Antonio, TX: Psychological Corporation.

Harnis, M., Amtmann, D., Cook, D., & Johnson, K. (2007). Considerations for developing interfaces for collecting patient-reported outcomes that allow that inclusion of individuals with disabilities. *Medical Care, 45,* 48–54.

Hasselkus, B. R. (1994). Working with family caregivers: A therapeutic alliance. In B. R. Bonder & M. B. Wagner (Eds.), *Functional performance in older adults* (pp. 339–351). Philadelphia: F. A. Davis.

Hayes, P. A. (2008). *Addressing cultural complexities in practice*. Washington, DC: American Psychological Association.

Helms, J. E. (2004). Fair and valid use of educational testing in grades K–12. In J. E. Wall & G. R. Walz (Eds.), *Measuring up: Assessment issues for teachers, counselors, and administrators* (pp. 81–88). Austin, TX: CAPS Press.

Hills, G. A., & Bernstein, S. R. (1997). Assessment of elders and caregivers. In J. Van Deusen & D. Brunt (Eds.), *Assessment in occupational and physical therapy* (pp. 401–417). Philadelphia: Saunders.

Hollenbeck, K., Tindal, G., & Almond, P. (1998). Teacher's knowledge of accommodations as a validity issue in high-stakes testing. *Journal of Special Education, 32,* 175–183.

Individuals With Disabilities Education Act Amendments of 1997, Pub. L. 105–17, 20 U.S.C. Chapter 33.

Individuals With Disabilities Education Improvement Act of 2004, Pub. L. 108–446, 20 U.S.C. §1400 et seq.

Iwama, M. (2006). *The Kawa Model: Culturally relevant occupational therapy*. Philadelphia: Elsevier/Churchill Livingstone.

Kinébanian A., & Stomph, M. (1992). Cross-cultural occupational therapy: A critical reflection. *American Journal of Occupational Therapy, 46*(8), 751–757.

Koltai, D., & Bohmer, K. W. (2000). Geriatric neuropsychological assessment. In R. Vanderploeg (Ed.), *Clinician's guide to neuropsychological assessment* (2nd ed., pp. 383–415). Mahwah, NJ: Lawrence Erlbaum.

Laird, J. (1998). Theorizing culture: Narrative ideas and practice principles. In M. McGoldrick (Ed.), *Re-visioning family therapy: Race, culture, and gender in clinical practice* (pp. 20–36). New York: Guilford.

Leininger, M. (1978). *Transcultural nursing: Theories, research, and practice* (2nd ed.). New York: Wiley.

Levine, C. (1999). The loneliness of the long-term caregiver. *New England Journal of Medicine, 340,* 1587–1590.

Linn, R. L., & Gronlund, N. E. (1999). *Measurement and assessment in teaching* (8th ed.). Upper Saddle River, NJ: Prentice Hall.

Marcos, L. R. (1994). The psychiatric examination of Hispanics: Across the language barrier. In R. G. Malgady & O. Rodriguez (Eds.), *Theoretical and conceptual issues in Hispanic mental health* (pp. 144–154). Melbourne, FL: Kreiger.

McEwen, J., & McKenna, S. P. (1996). Nottingham Health Profile. In B. Spilker (Ed.), *Quality of life and pharmacoeconomics in clinical trials* (2nd ed., pp. 281–286). Philadelphia: Lippincott-Raven.

Muñoz, J. P. (2007). Culturally responsive caring in occupational therapy: A grounded theory. *Occupational Therapy International, 14*(4), 256–280.

Neville, S., & Henrickson, M. (2006). Perceptions of lesbian, gay, and bisexual people of primary healthcare services. *Journal of Advanced Nursing, 55*(4), 407–415.

No Child Left Behind Act of 2001, Pub. L. 107–110, 115 Stat. 1425 (2002).

Padilla, A. M., & Borsato, G. N. (2008). Issues in culturally appropriate psychoeducational assessment. In L. A. Sukuki & J. G. Ponterotto (Eds.), *Handbook of multicultural assessment: Clinical, psychological, and educational applications* (3rd ed., pp. 5–21). New York: Wiley.

Phipps, D. (1995). Occupational therapy practice with clients from non–English speaking backgrounds: A survey. *Australian Occupational Therapy Journal, 42,* 151–160.

Pitoniak, M. J., & Royer J. M. (2001). Testing accommodations for examinees with disabilities: A review of psychometric, legal, and social policy issues. *Review of Educational Research, 71,* 53–104.

Post, M. W. M., Gerritsen, J., van Leusen, N. D. M., Paping, M. A., & Prevo, J. H. (2001). Adapting the Nottingham Health Profile for use in people with severe physical disabilities. *Clinical Rehabilitation, 15,* 103–110.

Prince, J. P. (1997). Assessment bias affecting lesbian, gay male, and bisexual individuals. *Measurement and Evaluation in Counseling and Development, 30,* 82–87.

Richardson, P. K. (2001). Use of standardized tests in pediatric practice. In J. Case-Smith (Ed.), *Occupational therapy for children* (pp. 217–245). St. Louis, MO: Mosby.

Sattler, M. (2001). *Assessment of children: Cognitive applications* (4th ed.). San Diego: Author.

Stewart, K. B. (2001). Purposes, processes, and methods of evaluation. In J. Case-Smith (Ed.), *Occupational therapy for children* (4th ed., pp. 190–213). St. Louis, MO: Mosby.

Sue, S. (1998). In search of cultural competence in psychotherapy and counseling. *American Psychologist, 53*(4), 440–448.

Sue, S., & Zane, N. (1987). The role of culture and cultural techniques in psychotherapy: A critique and reformulation. *American Psychologist, 42,* 37–45.

Swinth, Y. L. (2009). Occupational therapy evaluation and intervention related to education. In E. B. Crepeau, E. S. Cohn, & B. A. B. Schell (Eds.), *Willard and Spackman's occupational therapy* (11th ed., pp. 592–614). Philadelphia: Lippincott Williams & Wilkins.

Tervalon, M., & Murray-Garcia, J. (1998). Cultural humility versus cultural competence: A critical distinction in defining physician training outcomes in multicultural education. *Journal of Health Care for the Poor and Underserved, 9*(2), 117–125.

Thompson, L. K. (1992). *The Kohlman Evaluation of Living Skills* (3rd ed.). Bethesda, MD: American Occupational Therapy Association.

Thurlow, M., & Thompson, S. J. (2004). Inclusion of students with disabilities in state and district assessments. In J. E. Wall & G. R. Walz (Eds.), *Measuring up: Assessment issues for teachers, counselors, and administrators* (pp. 161–176). Austin, TX: CAPS Press.

U.S. Census Bureau. (2000). *United States 2000: Summary population and housing characteristics.* Washington, DC: U. S. Government Printing Office. Retrieved October 14, 2009, from http://www.census.gov/prod/cen2000/phc-1-1-pt1.pdf

U.S. Department of Health and Human Services. (2001). *Office of Minority Health: National standards for culturally and linguistically appropriate standards in health care* (Final Report). Washington, DC: U.S. Government Printing Office.

Weinstock-Zlotnick, G., & Hinojosa, J. (2004). The Issue Is—Bottom-up or top-down evaluation: Is one better than the other? *American Journal of Occupational Therapy 58*(5), 594–599.

Wurzel, J. (Ed.). (2004). *Toward multiculturalism: A reader in multicultural education* (2nd ed.). Newton, MA: Intercultural Resource Corporation.

Zins, J. E., Weissberg, R. P., Wang, M. C., & Walberg, H. J. (2004). *Building academic success on social and emotional learning: What does the research say?* New York: Teachers College Press.

Ethical Issues in Evaluation

Penny L. Kyler, ScD, OT, FAOTA

Overview

This chapter discusses the ethical responsibilities of the occupational therapist as a professional who is an evaluator and assessor of occupational performance. The chapter begins with a discussion of the history of ethics, personal values, and professional values. Next, the chapter discusses the professional codes of ethics and current issues that may cause the therapist ethical distress. Within the chapter, cases are presented to help readers consider their values and determine how these values coincide with or differ from the profession's core values and code of ethics. The chapter ends with an outline of some of the ethical issues that therapists need to consider when conducting an evaluation or assessment, identifying and analyzing ethical dilemmas that arise in the evaluation process.

Introduction

In the second edition of *Occupational Therapy Evaluation: Obtaining and Interpreting Data*, Hansen (2005) began her chapter with a discussion of Joan Rogers's 1983 Eleanor Clarke Slagle Lecture. She posed the following questions that a therapist needs to answer during the evaluation:

- What is the patient's status? (Science)
- What are the available options? (Art)
- What ought to be done? (Ethics)

According to Hansen (2005), Rogers's focus on ethics was at the clinical reasoning stage of planning and implementing portions of the therapeutic process. Evaluation is the foundation of clinical reasoning. This chapter examines how occupational therapy has moved forward in articulating the ethical considerations involved in evaluation.

Historical Arguments: The Hippocratic Tradition

Over many years, health care ethics or bioethics has been associated with the Hippocratic tradition. Hippocrates *(ca.* 460 B.C.–*ca.* 370 B.C.), considered the father of medicine, is credited with advancing the systematic study of medicine and improving the prescribing practices for physicians. Traditionally, physicians swearing to practice ethical medicine take the Hippocratic Oath (Edelstein, 1943). Early physicians taking the oath swore to the gods, promised to consider those who taught them the art, and agreed to abide by the rules of the profession. Today, physicians pledge to prescribe for the good of their patients, never do harm, leave certain procedures to specialists, and keep information confidential:

> I will prescribe regimen for the good of my patients according to my ability and my judgment and never do harm to anyone. . . . I will not cut for stone, even for patients in whom the disease is manifest; I will leave this operation to be performed by practitioners (specialists in this art). . . . All that may come to my knowledge in the exercise of my profession or outside of my profession or in daily commerce with men, whom ought not to be spread abroad, I will keep secret and will never reveal. If I keep this oath faithfully, may I enjoy my life and practice my art. (Thompson, 1987, p. 1462)

It is interesting to note that physicians begin by swearing in the names of the god of the physicians (Apollo), the god of the surgeons (Aesculapius), and the goddesses of prevention (Hygeia) and cure all (Panacea). From the very beginning, there was tension in medicine between the exoteric character of medicine as a scientific discipline and the esoteric or mysterious character of the profession based upon magic (science and art). The ethical prescriptions of the code are grouped under the three principles of beneficence, justice, and respect for people. The duty of those taking the oath is to do good and avoid doing harm (beneficence and nonmaleficence):

> I will prescribe regimen for the good of my patients according to my ability and judgment and never do harm to anyone. . . . In every house where I come I will enter only for the good of my patients, keeping myself far from all intentional ill-doing. (Thompson, 1987, p. 1463)

These principles and duties of ethics have carried over to modern times and are the bases for many of health professionals' codes of ethics, including the American Occupational Therapy Association's (AOTA's) Code. One distinctive component of a profession is having a code of ethics to which members of that profession are expected to adhere. The profession's ethics code stipulates certain kinds of conduct and affirms that members are accountable for their actions.

Occupational Therapy Code of Ethics

The *Occupational Therapy Code of Ethics* (AOTA, 2005a) has evolved over the past 60-plus years. The first *Code of Ethics* was proposed in 1976 and was meant to be action oriented, guiding and preventive rather than negative or merely disciplinary (AOTA, 1976). This 1976 proposed Code specifically addressed evaluation and research. Principle VIII noted, "Occupational therapists shall accept the responsibility for evaluating; developing and refining services... [and] at all times protect the rights of subjects, clients, institutions, and collaborators. The work of others shall be acknowledged" (p. 4). This version of the Code provided guidelines for each of the principles. For example, Principle VIII focused on evaluation and indicated through the guidelines that the "client's families have the right to have and occupational therapists have the responsibility to provide explanations of the nature, the purpose, and results of the occupational therapy services" (p. 4). These guidelines further stated that when the occupational therapist reports test results, he or she has the obligation to indicate any reservations regarding validity or reliability resulting from testing and circumstances or inappropriateness of the test norms for the person who was tested.

The *Occupational Therapy Code of Ethics* was revised in 1988, 1994, and 2005 and is currently under revision (http://www.aota.org/Consumers/Ethics.aspx). The 1994 *Occupational Therapy Code of Ethics* (AOTA, 1994) defined a principle based on an ethics approach. *Principle-based ethics,* a branch of applied philosophy, focuses on theories of the importance of general principles such as respect for autonomy, nonmaleficence, and justice (Beauchamp & Childress, 2009; Veatch & Flack, 1997). Over the course of years, AOTA moved away from the ephemeral realm of theory and abstract speculation to addressing practical questions and concerns raised by real problems and everyday practice that one may see during evaluation and assessments.

The 2005 *Occupational Therapy Code of Ethics* (AOTA, 2005a) articulates principles, provides a general approach to terminology, and proposes a framework for a systematic ethical stance. The 2005 Code also educates members and the general public and helps occupational therapists and occupational therapy assistants recognize and resolve ethical distress or dilemmas. The Code uses the principles of beneficence, nonmaleficence, autonomy and confidentiality, duty, procedural justice, veracity, and fidelity. The *Occupational Therapy Code of Ethics* (AOTA, 2005a) provides enough information to enable occupational therapists, occupational therapy assistants, and the general public to understand professional values. Further, the Code states the duties, rights, and responsibilities of all parties engaged in the occupational therapy process. Sometimes the language is expressed in terms that are not necessarily literal or direct (*nonmaleficence*—refrain from any undue influences that may compromise provision of service), and sometimes the language is very direct (*beneficence*—provide services in a fair and equitable manner). Nonmaleficence and beneficence deal with preventing harm and doing good, respectively. The *Occupational Therapy Code of Ethics* (AOTA, 2005a) is also a rule-based code, indicating that occupational therapists and occupational therapy assistants must comply with laws, moving away from an aspirational code (procedural justice). Previous AOTA Codes did not directly link ethical behavior with legal behavior. As more states licensed occupational therapy professionals, the *Occupational Therapy Code of Ethics* (AOTA, 2005a) became the basis for many state practice acts' disciplinary actions. Thus, the AOTA Code can be viewed as an aspirational document and a guideline for legally expected clinical practice behaviors.

The concept of justice is much broader and nuanced than what appears in the *Occupational Therapy Code of Ethics* (AOTA, 2005a). The principle of *justice* is concerned about the ways good and harm are distributed. The ethics of justice, or distribution of resources, must deal with the fact that some clients need health care because their voluntary lifestyle choices create medical problems. Some justice issues deal with commitments that create inconsistency and pull the occupational therapist into conflict between justice and fidelity. For example, the commitment to justice would mean that each person, regardless of standing, is seen by the therapist at his or her appointment time; however, the concept of fidelity may override this when a client that a therapist has been treating is suddenly transferred and needs a summary to take to the new facility. The Code describes *fidelity* as respect for colleagues and other professionals, yet does not speak to fidelity from the contractual relationship formed between the occupational therapist and his or her client.

In evaluation and assessment, the ethical principle of fidelity refers to the obligation (or duty) to the client based on a real or implied promise. This real or implied promise is part of the therapeutic relationship that an occupational therapist develops with his or her client. Fidelity directs the therapist to balance on a case-by-case basis duties and conflicts in order to maximize the possible benefits to those clients receiving intervention. Fidelity is keeping a promise and does relate to scheduling appointments, agreeing to fee schedules, and keeping records. Fidelity is also reciprocal in that each party offers something to the other and agrees to be bound by the mutual agreement—hence the fundamental relationship between a therapist and client is based on fidelity (Veatch & Flack, 1997).

Core Values

Another important document developed by AOTA is the *Core Values and Attitudes of Occupational Therapy Practice* (1993). The *Core Values* describes the beliefs that have been the foundation of the profession since its inception. The seven core concepts are

1. *Altruism,* or concern for the welfare of others;
2. *Equality,* or the belief that all people should have the same fundamental human rights and opportunities;
3. *Freedom to exercise choice and be independent;*
4. *Justice,* or the importance of upholding the moral and legal principles of fairness, equity, truthfulness, and objectivity;
5. *Dignity,* or the importance of valuing the inherent worth and uniqueness of each;

6. *Truth,* or faithfulness to the facts and reality; and
7. *Prudence,* or the ability to govern and discipline oneself through reasoning (AOTA, 1993).

Occupational Therapy Pledge and Creed

Prior to the *Occupational Therapy Code of Ethics* (AOTA, 2005a) and the *Core Values and Attitudes in Occupational Therapy Practice* (AOTA, 1993) were the occupational therapy pledge and creed. The creed was bought to the the AOTA's Executive Board by Myra McDaniel for action in 1970 (AOTA, 1970). The director of the occupational therapy program of the Boston School of Occupational Therapy wrote the creed. The pledge and creed, similar to medicine's Hippocratic Oath, were to be taken by occupational therapists. Among the five statements, the pledge and creed asked occupational therapists to "reverently and earnestly" care for those crippled in mind and body (beneficence) and "keep inviolate whatever I may learn of the lives of the sick" (confidentiality). The pledge and creed for occupational therapists never became an official document of AOTA.

Legal and Ethical Constructs

Moving away from ethics and values, official documents of AOTA are a series of statements in the form of laws that govern practice and the actions of occupational therapists and occupational therapy assistants. Some laws directly influence the occupational therapist's evaluation of clients. Laws may determine when a client is evaluated, what evaluation tools a therapist is qualified to use, and what information is provided and to whom.

The ethical concept of justice is based on the legal sense of fairness and following rules. Legal issues are interwoven with ethical considerations. For example, the right to due process (a legal construct) is a basic consideration when the ethical principles associated with autonomy and informed consent are followed by a therapist. Laws and ensuing regulations are one type of consideration or perspective that must be remembered when providing any occupational therapy service. An occupational therapist must also follow the *Occupational Therapy Code of Ethics* (AOTA, 2005a) and the profession's other official documents, including *Standards of Practice for Occupational Therapy* (AOTA, 2005b), *Standards for Continuing Competence* (AOTA, 2005c), and practice guidelines. These official documents and publications of AOTA provide a therapist with a framework for clinical reasoning and an approach to practice. When conflicts occur between what is legal and what is ethical, the therapist faces an ethical dilemma that must be resolved before proceeding with the evaluation process.

Legal precedents for a client's civil rights stem from legislation and resulting government regulations. In keeping with federal law, a therapist must not use evaluations or assessments that discriminate based on age, race, gender, economic status, medical condition, or behavioral or physical disability. For example, the practice of occupational therapy in educational settings is governed by federal laws and regulations such as the Education of the Handicapped Act Amendments of 1983 (Pub. L. 98–199), the Education for All Handicapped Children Amendments of 1986 (Pub. L. 99–457), and the Amendments to Education for All Children with Handicaps (Pub. L. 101–476), which changed its name to the Individuals With Disabilities Education Act (IDEA) and was recently reauthorized as the Individuals With Disabilities Education Improvement Act (Pub. L. 108–446). Other federal laws that must be adhered to include the Health Insurance Portability and Accountability Act (HIPAA; Pub. L. 104–191), the Family Educational Rights and Privacy Act (FERPA; Pub. L. 93–380), and regulations such as Title VI of the Civil Rights Act of 1964 for people with limited English proficiency and the U.S. Office of Minority Health's Cultural and Linguistically Appropriate Standards (CLAS) for health facilities that have been embraced by the Joint Commission (formerly JCAHO).

Legal positions and rules are upheld by the courts, and a therapist must follow the laws and interpretations of law. For an occupational therapist, the aspirational ethical concepts detailed in the *Occupational Therapy Code of Ethics* (AOTA, 2005a) address the expected conduct of those within the profession of occupational therapy.

Ethical Decision Making

How are evaluation dilemmas different from other types of ethical dilemmas characteristic of providing intervention? A simple response to the question is that there is no difference. An ethical dilemma is characterized by competing issues that may not have clear right or wrong answers. By definition, an ethical dilemma involves the need to choose from among two or more morally acceptable courses of action. At times, a therapist's choice may prevent selecting the other, or there may be a need to choose between equally unacceptable alternatives (Hansen, 2005). As a therapist works with other clinicians to care for a client with complex needs, he or she may come face-to-face with varying expectations and values from coworkers, employers, health care industry representatives, and even the client. These events will challenge the therapist's personal sense of ethical correctness and may cause him or her to rethink his or her approach.

Evaluation is the beginning component of occupational therapy intervention. As noted by Hansen (2005), ethical considerations are extremely important during the evaluation process, and decisions about what is the "right" action in a given situation are an integral part of the occupational therapist's daily life. The planning and implementation of the assessment process must be congruent with the consumer's or surrogate's interests and goals. On completion of the evaluation, the final recommendations and goals must be congruent with any goals that the client or surrogate have identified (Hasselkus as cited in Hansen, 2005). A client or surrogate must be given the opportunity to acknowledge that the goals are both acceptable and desirable.

A therapist makes decisions on the basis of what he or she learned in school, what ethnocultural traditions he or she may have absorbed, and general life experiences. This tripod is the basis of ethical decision making because these three areas reflect a person's values and beliefs. Aside from religious and spiritual beliefs, familiar patterns may serve as the root of one's personal beliefs about right and wrong. Hence, ethical behavior includes

- Family traditions, standards, and interactions;
- Culture and norms of the society in which people live;
- Influence of friends, colleagues, and teachers;
- Writings and speeches (teachings or conveyed beliefs) of people who are important or influential in our lives (e.g., grandparents, friends);
- Wild card events that we do not control but that change the dynamics of our lives and our civilization (war, technology, economy, sociological changes); and
- Professional culture of occupational therapy.

Given the above list—and there are certainly more areas that could be added—it is important that the occupational therapist know and understand his or her own values. The therapist must be aware of the values he or she brings to the interaction. In addition, the therapist must examine interactions to assess whether what he or she believes is ethically right and wrong is reflected in the interaction. The determination of right action in a given situation is complex and multidimensional. In some cases, there are no good choices, nor are there clear winners and losers. Deciding the best solution under specific circumstances is not simple.

An occupational therapist makes determinations of right and wrong on the basis of his or her personal and professional values. Ethical dilemmas exist because there are no clear-cut answers in many practice situations. There may be two or more options available that a therapist could consider acceptable, but in most cases, there should be one resolution that is the best solution (Hansen, 1990, p. 4).

Decision making is a personal concept, and although there are ways to approach making a decision, each person brings to the thought process his or her own biases. Each person is a mixture of some good qualities (strengths) and some not-so-good qualities (weaknesses). This is what makes us unique and is part of how we approach making decisions. There are no right or wrong approaches to making a decision as long as that decision is based on fact. A therapist responds to facts at his or her personal core. Does the fact bring forth anger, disbelief, calmness, and so on? A therapist must be aware of a fact that creates emotion or perception/response in a situation. With each fact surrounding the ethical concern, a therapist must decide whether to explore or overlook the emotional reaction.

An analogy to approaching an ethical decision is similar to making a meal for friends. A person must first consider the mixture of menu, place, time, and people. This mixture can change depending on the circumstances. A person must make sure the food is cooked and presented in such a way as to be pleasing to the eye, taste buds, and digestion. Throwing in too much spice or salt, serving a bad glass of wine, or dining with an overly perfumed or demanding person will disrupt the meal and lead to indigestion. In planning the meal, a person considers the many forces and types of interest that come forward. In considering an ethical decision, a therapist thinks of the parts that may go together in order to find a resolution to the dilemma. In the process, the therapist asks questions and considers several options. The mixture of choices and the characteristics of ethical evaluation require the integration of all aspects of decision making.

Whenever an assessment takes place, the occupational therapist has to begin at the personal level and ask whether he or she is competent to administer and interpret the assessment. This basic question derives from the ethical principles of duty and nonmaleficence. Without competence to perform the assessment, harm may take place. Beyond competency as an evaluator, the two critical questions to ask are

1. To whom does the occupational therapist have a primary duty when making decisions about which evaluations to use?
2. How should the data from the evaluation be reported, and to whom?

Most occupational therapists view the client as their priority. When evaluating a child, the client also can mean the client's family. The occupational therapist has to consider the client's family and significant others, along with his or her own employer and the facility for which he or she works, his or her fellow professionals, and the agency or person who is paying for the evaluation. Conflicts can and do arise, because the priorities, goals, and values of the different people and groups may clash or at least not coincide in a harmonious manner (Hansen, 2005).

A therapist asks questions concerned with discerning the facts prior to resolving an ethical dilemma. What are the facts and what do the facts mean to the outcome of the assessment? Aside from the first question of "Am I competent to perform the assessments?" other questions to consider include the following:

- Has there been collaboration between myself and the client?
- Have I considered occupational performance areas from the client's perspective of participation?
- Have I considered the ethnocultural components of the client?
- Have I considered the family in a family-centered context?
- Have I considered the subjective (emotional and psychological) and objective (physically observable) aspects of performance?
- Have I accurately performed and documented the assessment?
- Most importantly, is the summary a true reflection of what I have seen and heard from the client and his or her family? (See Appendix 14.A, "Questionnaire for Identifying Potential Conflicts in Assessment.")

Table 14.1. Resolving Ethical Issues When Choosing Evaluation Tools and Interventions

Resolving an Ethical Issue	Choosing Evaluation Assessments
Identify the ethical concern or problem	Identify client problems or assets
Develop questions about the ethical concern	Develop questions regarding client problems or assets
Choose an approach to resolve the ethical concern	Choose an assessment/evaluation tool
Ask the questions; get the facts	Gather data to develop an intervention approach
Analyze the answers	Project (predict) outcomes after intervention Monitor client progress
Make a decision	Make recommendations about further services

Steps in Ethical Decision Making

A therapist might take simple steps in discerning ethical issues. However, once a therapist begins with simple steps, he or she may find himself or herself led down a path of further quandary. To mitigate larger quandaries, the occupational therapist needs to develop some basic ethical analysis skills. Ethical analysis skills are finding the facts, understanding the circumstances, listening to the therapist's own voice, and using other resources as needed. The thought processes used in resolving ethical issues are the same as those used in selecting an assessment tool and developing an intervention approach.

Conceptual frameworks influence how the therapist explores ethical dilemmas and client problems. Conceptual frameworks also influence the types of assessments and interventions (Neistadt, 2000). The therapist may resolve an ethical concern by looking at the profession's *Code of Ethics* and guidelines in conjunction with his or her background and sense of ethics. The therapist might determine the appropriate assessment on the basis of the frame of reference he or she selects. Just as ethical discernment may be based on a lifetime of experiences and formal education, an occupational therapist has approaches to evaluation that are drawn from a frame of reference not explicitly articulated but based on clinical practice experience (Rogers, 1983). Table 14.1 outlines resolving ethical issues when choosing assessments and interventions.

● ● ● ● ● ●

Case Example 14.1. Case Intervention Based on Evaluations Done by Others

Sue, an occupational therapist, has been seeing **Franklin, age 10,** in her private practice for more than 1 month. He comes twice a week. His mother tells

Sue that her major concern is that Franklin reacts to things in an extremely poor way. Prior to coming to Sue, Franklin's mother went to a psychiatrist who told her Franklin probably had attention deficit hyperactivity disorder. Previously, Franklin's mother had him evaluated at a well-respected multidisciplinary clinic that included an occupational therapist, a developmental psychologist, and others. Franklin's mother has come to Sue's clinic because she likes Sue's philosophy: "Just collaborate with the parents and do what the parents want to work on." At this time, Sue does not have a formal treatment plan and did not do an evaluation because the parents did not want to pay for it. On the basis of the results of the copy of the evaluation given to her, Sue is focusing on motor performance problems because that is what Franklin's mother wants her to focus on. Sue, however, has noticed several behavioral issues that the multidisciplinary clinic had addressed in the information she received from them.

Sue begins the steps in an ethical decision-making process:

Step 1. Decide what the central question is and what are the known facts.
Step 2. Seek additional information if needed to answer these questions:

- Are there some financial concerns driving the family?
- Is Sue observing something that needs further evaluation?
- Is Sue seeking further evaluation to increase her reimbursement?
- Does Sue have the expertise to do an evaluation battery?
- What does Franklin's mother say are her goals for her child?
- What does Franklin say are his goals for himself?

Step 3. Decide on an action, and understand your justification of the selected action.
Step 4. If needed, decide on alternative actions.
Step 5. Implement your decision. When implementing your decision, think about these questions:

- Is the action legal? (Have you reflected on the legal consequences?)
- Is it balanced? Is it fair to all concerned? (Not all actions have to result in a win–win situation.)
- Does it set up a situation that produces the most good or provides the least-harmful outcome for all involved? (Does your response help create a positive environment?)
- How does the decision make you feel about yourself? (Hansen, Kyler-Hutchison, & Trompetter, 1994)?

● ● ● ● ● ●

In thinking about the five steps, there are two schools of thought. The first claims that acts are right to the extent that they produce good consequences and wrong to the extent that they produce bad consequences. The key terms here are *good* and *bad*. When thinking about good and bad, one must consider the benefits and harms of particular actions. The second looks at ethical decision making from the societal perspective. What are the norms of the society? This perspective recognizes that different societies reach different conclusions regarding the rightness or wrongness, goodness or badness of an action

Table 14.2. Sue's Alternative Actions To Decide What To Do Next

Action	Consequence	Ethical Principle Involved (Based on 2005 *Occupational Therapy Code of Ethics;* AOTA, 2005a)
Decide to approach the mother about the need for an evaluation	Child continues in occupational therapy without proper evaluation Mother feels uncomfortable	Fidelity to client Obligation of competence—Concept of justice by adherence to *Framework–II* (AOTA, 2008) Concept of autonomy Family vs. individual power Informed consent
Decide not to do a formal evaluation and go with the assessment done by another source	Goes against the *Framework–II,* because an occupational therapist must observe and analyze performance skills personally (could/should this be done without formal evaluation?)	Procedural justice—Possible violation of state regulations
Meet with the family and child to explain the limitations imposed on you because of the lack of formal evaluation on-site	Family has reasons for selecting current program and does not wish to discuss their finances	Duty of veracity to client, professional code of ethics Possible violation of occupational therapy practice act and regulations about service provision
Decide not to continue treating the child	Child does not get needed services Missed opportunity for family education about the scope of occupational therapy services Family gets turned off regarding occupational therapy and does not seek further services	Duty of veracity Duty of fidelity

(Veatch & Haddad, 2008). The occupational therapist must choose from among a number of alternative actions in deciding what to do next (see Table 14.2).

This case example provides an illustration of how to review a case. The primary ethical principles involved are beneficence, fidelity, and nonmaleficence. However, you should remember that differences in judgment about the actions in this case could occur. Differences are the result of dissimilar views of the facts, matters of personal preference, and differences in the view of rightness or wrongness.

Lessons From Others

The process of evaluating is not the sole domain of occupational therapy. Many health professionals focused on emphasizing evaluation as a specific clinical area for much longer periods than occupational therapy. Evaluation emphasizes building relationships and partnerships among clients and professionals and providing a clear view to the provider of what needs to be done.

In fields such as psychology, medicine, nursing, and social work, or in the arenas of education and mental health, professions have established critical definitions and expectations of evaluations. One example developed by the American Psychological Association (APA) defines evaluation by the evaluation format used. The organization notes in its code of ethics that services should be provided regardless of age, gender, gender identity, race, ethnicity, culture, national origin, religion, sexual orientation, disability, language, or socioeconomic status. The American Psychological Association's current code (2002) devotes an entire section to assessment and evaluation (see http://www.apa.org/ethics/code2002.html#9_01). In particular, the APA's code of ethics addresses the use of current and obsolete evaluative tools, cost, training in administering the tools, and explaining the test results.

The occupational therapist should be concerned with fairness, veracity, and equity when collecting data. The National Academy of Engineering, a group not generally associated with health, provides clear guidance on the ethics of evaluation and appropriate records management. It discusses the ethical duties of professionals regarding fabrication or falsification of data and general norms for the responsible management of data that can be carried over to evaluation records (see Box 14.1). Other matters touched upon by the National

---

Box 14.1. Excerpts From the National Academy of Engineering's *Code of Ethics*

The primary data, the methods used to obtain them, and the procedures applied to the primary data to create compilations of them, or derivations from them must be accurately reported.

If the primary data are based on human observation, those observations should be recorded promptly and accurately and in sufficient detail to preserve the record of factors that might turn out to be significant, and in a way that minimizes doubt about the time of the occurrence or the time at which it was recorded.

Necessary research materials should be made available to others who attempt to replicate your work.

Institutions that are the recipients of research grants own the data from those research projects. The Principal Investigator (PI) for a project has custody of that data and primary responsibility for maintenance of the data record and such matters as preserving the confidentiality of sensitive information about human subjects, if any, in the data record. Collaborators on the research project for which the data was collected, including trainee collaborators, have the right of access to the data.

Source. National Academy of Engineering. (2006). *The responsible collection, retention, sharing, and interpretation of data.* Available online at http://www.onlineethics.org/CMS/research/modindex/moddata.aspx

Academy of Engineering that directly translate to occupational therapy are responsible data collection, retention, and sharing and interpretation of data that bear on the integrity of data.

The American Psychological Association, National Academy of Engineering, and other professional organizations also clearly discuss fair treatment of collaborators, including fair apportionment of funds and preservation of confidentiality of research subjects or proprietary knowledge of sponsors and collaborators. It is interesting to note that the current *Occupational Therapy Code of Ethics* (AOTA, 2005a) does not explicitly discuss either evaluation or assessment, or ownership of data, or fabrication of data.

As more occupational therapists move toward participating in research, several areas need to be considered because they are open to ethical concerns. The *Occupational Therapy Code of Ethics* (AOTA, 2005a) discusses veracity and fabrication and falsification of data and borrowing from others without acknowledgment that these areas are part of truth-telling. Fabrication is, in a sense, lying, and our moral system usually treats lying as wrong. However, the Code clearly indicates that a member should "Refrain from using or participating in the use of any form of communication that contains false, fraudulent, deceptive, or unfair statements or claims" (p. 641). Lastly, remember that clients, employers, research funders, and insurance companies do have rights and obligations associated with accessing the client's record. The information that an occupational therapist puts into the record must be truthful.

The next case discussion highlights the ethical implications of modifying standardized assessments. Harry, an occupational therapist, has been in practice for more than 30 years and always has worked with the same client population. He has seen formal evaluations come and go and has watched as the profession has championed various assessments. During these years, Harry has developed excellent clinical intuition for knowing in which areas his clients will have demonstrated occupational performance deficits. Over the years, Harry has taken parts of multiple formal standardized evaluation tools and made up his own. For example, Harry's homemade evaluation tool provides an understanding of the client's occupational history and experiences, including his or her interests, values, and needs. Harry says, "Why pay money for these formal tools when I have taken the best from each of them and constructed a quicker, and more comprehensive, economical, and useful tool?" Consider the following questions:

- What are the rights of the clients receiving these evaluations?
- What are the implications for borrowing from other sources?
- Who owns the revised evaluation tool?
- What are the potential concerns when a client moves to another facility and a copy of Harry's occupational therapy evaluation is requested?
- If outcomes from the evaluation are excellent, is it appropriate for a therapist to take certain liberties?

Special Issues in Evaluation

Many ethical issues relate to administering evaluations, interpreting data, and interacting with a client. This section covers related topics, including electronic health records, culture, copyright, dissenting ethical concerns, and confidentiality.

Ethical Consequences of Electronic Health Records

A new area that many occupational therapists are just beginning to face is working with an electronic format for data keeping. Although the vast majority of health information transactions are still in a paper format, there is a move toward electronic health records. It is believed that electronic health records will improve record keeping, facilitate communication among professionals, drive down health care costs, and decrease medical errors. The Health Information Technology for Economic and Clinical Health Act (HITECH Act), part of the 2009 economic stimulus package, was developed to give physicians more incentive to adopt electronic health records. The HITECH Act promises incentive payments to those who adopt and meaningfully use "certified electronic health records" and, eventually, will reduce Medicare payments to those who do not use an electronic health record (Moore, 2009). Some facilities and practices already use electronic health records.

As society moves toward electronically formatted record keeping and fully integrated electronic health records, concerns have arisen about data sets, registries for research, and electronic evaluations. There are several ethical principles associated with electronic health records concerns. Although electronic health records may represent beneficence because of the increased access to health care and potentially improve the quality of care and health, they have not demonstrated access for disadvantaged people. Disadvantaged people may not have equal access to health information because of their socioeconomic class or age. A disadvantaged person may suffer a breach of justice because of his or her lack of access to health information resources.

Electronic health records also may jeopardize a person's autonomy when a client's health data are shared or linked without the client's knowledge. A therapist needs to be aware of who has access to evaluation and assessment data. A client's fidelity may be breached by the exposure of health data through mistakes or theft. Lack of trust in the security of health data may persuade a client to conceal critical health information, thus compromising his or her treatment. A therapist needs to be aware of who will have access to the client's records (Layman, 2008). Moreover, a therapist needs to protect the confidentiality of a client's record by password protecting files and must use procedures and programs that thwart identity theft and protect private information from computer hackers. When a therapist works in an environment that requires the use of a port to provide timely information regarding patient evaluations and assessments and progress and to expedite billing, he or she needs to be aware of who will have access to that information. This is especially important when the therapist is required to file evaluation and assessment reports in the electronic file.

In December 1995, the American Nurses Association's Board of Directors approved the establishment of the Nursing Information & Data Set Evaluation Center (NIDSEC). NIDSEC has defined review criteria to evaluate and recognize information systems from developers and manufacturers that support documentation of nursing care within automated Nursing Information Systems (NIS) or within Computer-based Patient Record (CPR) systems. This is something that the *Occupational Therapy Code of Ethics* (AOTA, 2005a) has not yet addressed.

Culture and Ethics

The *Occupational Therapy Practice Framework: Domain and Process, 2nd Edition (Framework–II*; AOTA, 2008) addresses culture by saying, "The expectations, beliefs, and customs of various cultures can affect a client's identity and activity choices and need to be considered when determining how and when services may be delivered" (p. 651). Evaluation of a person from a different culture also may have an ethical component. To begin with, many of the assessments occupational therapists use to evaluate or assess clients are based on Western medicine and American norms. Therefore, because dysfunction is culturally specific, an evaluation may identify a disability based on Western medicine and American norms. The *Occupational Therapy Code of Ethics* (2005a) addresses culture in Principle 1, under the concept of beneficence. The Code notes that the occupational therapist recognizes and appreciates a variety of cultural components and provides services in a fair and equitable manner.

An occupational therapist must be aware of and concerned with the real or perceived coercion inherent in the imbalance of power between the occupational therapist and the client. Occupational therapy can look to the American Medical Association (AMA) for guidance in the area of culture and evaluation. The AMA, using the methods developed by Berlin and Fowkes (1983), suggests a mnemonic for remembering how to engage people from other cultures. In their work, *How Do Physicians-In-Training Become Culturally Competent?* Berlin and Fowkes suggested the LEARN model guidelines:

- Listen with sympathy and understanding to the patient's perception of the problem.
- Explain your perceptions of the problem and your strategy for treatment.
- Acknowledge and discuss the differences and similarities between these perceptions.
- Recommend treatment while remembering the patient's cultural parameters.
- Negotiate agreement.

It is important to understand the client's views of the world and his or her health issues so that medical treatment fits in his or her cultural framework.

Another example is by Anne Fadiman, the author of *The Spirit Catches You and You Fall Down,* who describes two cultural perspectives as differing views of what is ethically correct treatment rather than as one viewpoint that is ethical and the other nonethical (Fadiman, 1997). Although Berlin and Fowkes's (1983) approach focuses on use of the LEARN acronym during treatment, it is also useful during the evaluation process.

The American College of Physicians (Forrow, 2008) provided some enlightening discussion of the pulls of ethics and culture, noting ethical barriers to culturally competent evaluation. It observed that an ethical conundrum requires the person to do something that may violate his or her fundamental personal values in order to maintain standards of scientific practice. The American Medical Association (AMA) approached this topic by what it called *cultural dissidence* (AMA, 2002). Cultural dissidence may be a widely misunderstood concept because it involves personal feelings and prejudices that have the potential for misuse of power by professionals. As an example, since 9/11, people of Middle Eastern descent have been pulled aside in airports for wearing religious headwear. An occupational therapist may have developed some prejudged perceptions and values about people of Middle Eastern descent without ever having met such a person. A therapist must be aware of his or her prejudices, consider what he or she does to ensure that he or she does not misuse power, and provide intervention within the values and cultural framework of the client.

In some cases, it may be difficult to resolve an ethical dilemma. For example, a therapist attempts to evaluate an Indo-Asian female client who seeks approval from her spouse for everything she says and does. The therapist may consider this behavior incorrect and inappropriate. However, this behavior may be the cultural imperative for this ethnic group. A therapist can resolve these feelings by remembering that the client must be regarded as having equally important ethical concerns in making decisions.

One specific aspect of culture is language. The following example illustrates ethical concerns a therapist must address when confronted with a language barrier. An occupational therapist evaluates a previously healthy 10-year-old girl because of a fractured radius and generalized weakness. The girl and her parents speak only Russian, and the facility does not have any Russian-speaking staff or interpreters. One of the housekeeping staff speaks broken Russian and is able to explain to the parents that the occupational therapist wants to do an evaluation of their child. The occupational therapist does an evaluation including active and passive range of motion, muscle tone, and eye–hand coordination. The girl uses scissors, ties her shoe, and plays a variety of games. The parents are thankful for the attention and nod in understanding. The therapist provides a written home program in English with expectations that the parents will actively engage their daughter in play. Three weeks later, the family returns and the girl has lost considerable function in all areas of occupational performance. Consider the following ethical questions:

- What would be proper preparation for working with this family?
- Are there any issues of autonomy that need to be considered?
- Can a therapist make sound clinical judgments and reach conclusions when a client is using an interpreter or translator with the same degree of certainty/effectiveness as when an interpreter is not needed?
- Was informed consent for treatment given?
- Is there a difference in working with clients of limited English proficiency versus non-English speakers?

Ethics of Copyright

With the rapid advancement of information technology, copyright has become more complex and challenging. Neither the current *Occupational Therapy Code of Ethics* (AOTA, 2005a) nor the *Framework–II* (AOTA, 2008), *Accreditation Standards for a Master's-Degree-Level Educational Program for the Occupational Therapist* (Accreditation Council for Occupational Therapy Education [ACOTE], 2007b), or *Accreditation Standards for a Doctoral-Degree-Level Educational Program for the Occupational Therapist* (ACOTE, 2007a) addresses copyright in sufficient detail. Copyright poses a series of concerns for ethical professional behaviors. As noted in the *Framework–II*, evaluation includes information about the client and the client's needs, problems, and concerns about performance in areas of occupation. The analysis of occupational performance focuses on collecting and interpreting information using assessments designed to observe, measure, and inquire about factors that support or hinder occupational performance. Many occupational therapy professionals use standardized or copyrighted tools, and occupational therapy educators use these same tools in teaching students how to perform a particular assessment. Copyright standards address how frequently a therapist can use a photocopy of the evaluation booklet or score sheet, and for what purposes, without paying for the original evaluation and score sheet.

A work is copyrighted when that work has been created in a tangible form, like writing or recording. In the case of a single creator, it is protected for the creator's life plus 70 years. If the work is created as a work for hire or in conjunction with one or more people, the work is copyrighted for 95 years after the first publication or 120 years from creation, whichever comes first.

The Digital Millennium Copyright Act of 1998 (Pub. L. 105–304) amended several areas of the U.S. copyright law. Section 108, "Limitations on Exclusive Rights: Reproduction by Libraries and Archives," allows libraries and archives to reproduce and distribute one copy of a work under certain circumstances. For example, libraries may photocopy journal articles, book chapters, and so on, and send these copies to other libraries through interlibrary loan. Copies of materials from libraries given to therapists or students should have printed on them: "Notice: This material may be protected by Copyright Law (Title 17 U.S.C.)." Faculty and students have the ethical duty to abide by copyright laws. Guidelines for what a person can or cannot copy are widely available and should be sought out and reviewed prior to copying information for clients and other professionals. Answer the following questions to determine whether a person can use copyrighted material:

- Are there fees that the therapist must pay to use this assessment? If so, has the therapist paid the fees?
- Does the therapist need additional permission to use the assessment materials? Some assessments are available without charge (e.g., Behavioral and Emotional Screening System [Reynolds & Kamphaus, 2009]), but a therapist must obtain permission from the author before using them.
- Does use of the assessment require that the evaluator undergo any training and supervision to administer the evaluation? For example, a therapist should not administer the Sensory Integration and Praxis Tests (Ayres, 1989) unless he or she has received training from the publisher.
- Does the therapist who is administering the evaluation hold the appropriate credentials to conduct this evaluation? For example, some evaluations, like the Vineland Adaptive Behavior Scales, Second Edition (Sparrow, Cichetti, & Balla, 2005), require that the evaluator be a licensed psychologist.

In addition, the occupational therapist must be sure to use the correct forms and procedures when conducting the assessment and reporting the results. If the assessment is standardized, the therapist must follow the administration procedures as stipulated in the test manual.

Many assessments that occupational therapists use are not copyrighted. Evaluators must properly acknowledge the developer or publisher whenever they use an assessment; otherwise, readers of the evaluation report assume that the assessment is original to the occupational therapist doing the evaluation, which is rarely the case. Although there is a great deal of information about copyright on the Internet, an occupational therapist must seek out and ask an expert such as a librarian about copyright. Lack of knowledge is not an acceptable excuse for copyright infringement and not being in compliance with federal and state laws.

The following is a case example of an ethical dilemma regarding copyright laws. Harry and Louise are a husband-and-wife occupational therapy team. They own a large practice in a metropolitan area. Their clinic rent has increased. Due to HIPAA and other regulations governing their practice, they have to complete and store extra paperwork. Their records for those clients with occupational injuries and workers' compensation insurance claims include drug tests, radiographic notes, physician notes, and physician's leave certification. Lately, Harry and Louise have been discussing how to lower their overhead costs. Louise said that they should photocopy the evaluation booklet and score sheet for an assessment they frequently use that they had been purchasing from the evaluation company. (Each booklet costs $50, and the score sheets are $50 for a packet of 25.) Harry is willing to try it. His primary concern is that the photocopying cost will exceed the negotiated rate with the photocopy company. Consider the following questions:

- What was the original purchase arrangement?
- What are the benefits and burdens associated with this case? How are they assessed?
- What information do Harry and Louise have that they might not need? Is there any liability with Harry and Louise having such extensive records?
- Are there any rules, regulations, guidelines, or laws that come into play in this situation?
- Is there any harm associated with the actions of Harry and Louise?

Dissenting as an Ethical Concern

There are situations when an occupational therapist will follow his or her ethical decision, but in doing so, clash with employer rules or legal regulations. These ethical judgments stem from the therapist's concern for others. In addition to personal moral philosophies, contextual factors such as rewards, rules, and codes also influence ethical decisions. In these cases, ethical distress occurs. In resolving dilemmas, the focus cannot be only on the therapist's subjective ethical convictions; instead, the therapist must focus on the context of the ethical dilemmas.

Ethical dissent is a multistep process that involves feeling apart from one's organization and that is driven by the recognition of wrongdoing, the need for intervention, perceived responsibility, and the screening of alternatives. Ethical dissent is essentially a person's expression of disagreement with an organization's practices, policies, and operations (Kassing, 1998). *Whistleblowing* is an extreme case of ethical dissent involving the disclosure of unethical practices to people both inside and outside the organization who possess the ability to initiate a change in the outcome of a dilemma (Kassing, 1998). Ethical dissent in the form of whistle-blowing may present a threat to the formal chain of command, but can improve long-term organizational effectiveness.

Ethical dissent is broader than whistle-blowing. Ethical dissent is considered to be an antecedent to whistle-blowing because whistle-blowers tend to express disagreements within the organizations initially and turn to public, external sources only when organizations are unresponsive to their concerns (Stewart, 1980). External sources are people outside the normal departmental chain of command, such as the human resources department of a facility or the agency administrator. An occupational therapist should assess available strategies for expressing ethical dissent in response to personal, relational, and organizational influences that other people will not perceive as adversarial or unconstructive.

Confidentiality

Last, but certainly not least, are issues associated with evaluation and confidentiality. Since the passage of HIPAA, an occupational therapist has to consider how, with whom, and when to share information regarding client care, including evaluations. The purpose of HIPAA is to give clients control of their medical information when moving between locations.

In essence, HIPAA states that high levels of privacy and confidentiality need to be maintained and information must be handled with the utmost care and security. Only people or groups with a clear need to have the information should receive it, and all privileged information—oral, written, and electronic—must be protected from unnecessary or casual access. Under HIPAA, a client

- Must be told (in writing) how his or her health care information may be used,
- Has a right to see his or her health records,
- Has a right to amend (change) incorrect/incomplete information in the records,
- Must give authorization before information is released (with a few exceptions), and
- Has a right to complain formally if he or she feels his or her privacy was not protected.

The privacy rule applies only to covered entities, which include individuals such as occupational therapists, organizations, and agencies that are covered entities. These groups must comply with the privacy rule's requirements to protect the privacy of health information and provide people with certain rights with respect to their health information. If an entity is not a covered entity, it does not have to comply with the privacy rule. More information about HIPAA is available from the official government Web site at http://www.hhs.gov/ocr/privacy/index.htm.

The issue of confidentiality and evaluation is also important in the educational arena. FERPA provides parents the right to inspect and review their child's education records, the right to make amendments to education records, and the right to have some degree of control over information that can be disclosed from education records. This statute extends to the records maintained by an educational agency of all children who receive services under Part B of IDEA. Additionally, any student's medical or health records maintained in an educational agency or institution are viewed as "education records" and are subject to FERPA (Oregon Department of Education, 2006).

It is the responsibility of therapists practicing in school systems to be aware of FERPA regulations and provide opportunities for parents to review evaluation reports. Parents also must be given the right to make amendments to reports. Finally, therapists have to abide by the parents' wishes as to what information can be given out from the evaluation records and to whom that information may be given out.

Conclusion

As with other aspects of the intervention process, evaluation and assessment require attention to the professional requirements and the ethical and legal guidelines for good practice. This chapter contains a description of the development of an occupational therapist's professional values and ethical discernment and how they relate. An occupational therapist should be familiar with the list of ethical considerations regarding evaluation and assessment from the perspective of the key players in the process. Using the analysis system provided in this chapter and remaining cognizant of the differences and similarities between ethics and the law will help an occupational therapist resolve the ethical dilemmas encountered in practice.

Questions

1. Create a list of your own personal values. (They can be different from the AOTA *Core Values*.) Identify ways that each value might influence your practice decisions regarding evaluation or assessment. Provide examples.
2. List how the seven core values and attitudes may influence your professional behavior in regard to how you conduct an assessment or evaluation.
3. We make decisions on the basis of what we learned in school, our ethnocultural traditions, and life experiences. Wild cards are events that we do not control that change the dynamics of our lives. What are the wild cards that have changed your life? How have the wild cards of technology changed how you view evaluation?
4. Technologies today use very small, relatively inexpensive, wireless-enabled computers that have resulted in the near omnipresence of information gathering and that can analyze, store, and share data via the Internet. Some of these technologies will also be autonomous, making decisions about what data to gather and share and what actions to take. Given this, how should an occupational therapist protect client confidentiality?
5. You receive a referral from another professional for an evaluation. You do not think that this evaluation is necessary or beneficial to the client. Are you obligated to perform this evaluation? How can you handle this situation?
6. The facility where you work copies all assessment forms rather than purchasing this copyrighted material. What should you do in this situation?
7. An occupational therapist has evaluated a client and, on the basis of clinical observations, documents that this client needs services even though the assessment data do not support the need for intervention. If you were the treating therapist, what action would be appropriate?

Acknowledgment

I acknowledge Ruth A. Hansen, PhD, OT, for her support and encouragement. The content of this chapter builds upon the previous version of this chapter, which was revised with permission.

Disclaimer

The views expressed in this publication are solely the opinions of the author and do not necessarily reflect the official policies of the U.S. Department of Health and Human Services or the Health Resources and Services Administration, nor does mention of the department or agency names imply endorsement by the U.S. government.

References

Accreditation Council for Occupational Therapy Education. (2007a). Accreditation standards for a doctoral-degree-level educational program for the occupational therapist. *American Journal of Occupational Therapy, 61,* 641–651.

Accreditation Council for Occupational Therapy Education. (2007b). Accreditation standards for a master's-degree-level educational program for the occupational therapist. *American Journal of Occupational Therapy, 61,* 652–661.

American Medical Association. (2002). *Racial and ethnic disparities in health care.* (Report from the Council on Scientific Affairs). Available online at http://www.ama-assn.org/ama/no-index/about-ama/13602.shtml

American Occupational Therapy Association. (1970). *Occupational Therapy Creed and Pledge: Executive Board minutes* (Executive Board Meeting, November 5–6, 1970).

American Occupational Therapy Association. (1976). Draft principles of occupational therapy ethics. *OT News, 30*(12), 4.

American Occupational Therapy Association. (1988). Occupational therapy code of ethics. *American Journal of Occupational Therapy, 42,* 795–796.

American Occupational Therapy Association. (1993). Core values and attitudes of occupational therapy practice. *American Journal of Occupational Therapy, 47,* 1085–1086.

American Occupational Therapy Association. (1994). Occupational therapy code of ethics. *American Journal of Occupational Therapy, 48,* 1037–1038.

American Occupational Therapy Association. (2005a). Occupational therapy code of ethics (2005). *American Journal of Occupational Therapy, 59,* 639–642.

American Occupational Therapy Association. (2005b). Standards of practice for occupational therapy. *American Journal of Occupational Therapy, 59,* 663–665.

American Occupational Therapy Association. (2005c). Standards for continuing competence. *American Journal of Occupational Therapy, 59,* 661–662.

American Occupational Therapy Association. (2008). Occupational therapy practice framework: Domain and process (2nd ed.). *American Journal of Occupational Therapy, 62,* 625–683.

American Psychological Association. (2002). *Ethical principles of psychologists and code of conduct.* Retrieved January 13, 2010, from http://www.apa.org/ethics/code/index.aspx

Ayres, A. J. (1989). *The Sensory Integration and Praxis Tests.* Los Angeles: Western Psychological Services.

Beauchamp, T. L., & Childress, J. F. (2009). *Principles of biomedical ethics* (6th ed.). New York: Oxford University Press.

Berlin, E. A., & Fowkes, W. C. (1983). A teaching framework for cross-cultural health care. *Western Journal of Medicine, 139,* 934–938.

Digital Millennium Copyright Act of 1998, Pub. L. 105–304, 17 U.S.C. §§ 512, 1201–1205, 1301–1332.

Edelstein, L. (1943). *The Hippocratic Oath: Text, translation, and interpretation.* Baltimore: Johns Hopkins Press.

Education for All Handicapped Children Amendments of 1986, Pub. L. 99–457.

Education of the Handicapped Act Amendments of 1983, Pub. L. 98–199.

Fadiman, A. (1997). *The spirit catches you and you fall down: A Hmong child, her American doctors, and the collision of two cultures.* New York: Farrar, Straus & Giroux.

Family Educational Rights and Privacy Act of 1974, Pub. L. 93–380, 20 U.S.C. §1232g *et seq.*; 34 C.F.R. §99.

Forrow, L. (2008). *Cultural differences in complicated cancer patients.* Retrieved January 13, 2010, from http://www.acpinternist.org/archives/2008/03/four.htm

Hansen, R. A. (1990). Lesson 10: Ethical considerations. In C. B. Royeen (Ed.), *AOTA Self-Paced Clinical Course—Assessing function.* Rockville, MD: American Occupational Therapy Association.

Hansen, R. (2005). Ethical implications in evaluation. In J. Hinojosa, P. Kramer, & P. Crist (Eds.), *Occupational therapy evaluation: Obtaining and interpreting data* (2nd ed., pp. 245–261). Bethesda, MD: AOTA Press.

Hansen, R. A., Kyler-Hutchison, P. L., & Trompetter, L. (1994, October). Ethical issues and the health professions. In *1994 Special Lecture Series*. College Misericordia, Dallas, PA.

Health Information Technology for Economic and Clinical Health Act, Title XIII of the American Recovery and Reinvestment Act of 2009 §13405(c).

Health Insurance Portability and Accountability Act of 1996, Pub. L. 104–191, 45 C.F.R. §§160, 164.

Individuals With Disabilities Education Act Amendments of 1997, Pub. L. 105–117, 20 U.S.C. §1400 *et seq.*

Individuals With Disabilities Education Act of 1990, Pub. L. 101–476.

Individuals With Disabilities Education Improvement Act of 2004, Pub. L. 108–446.

Kassing, J. W. (1998). Development and validation of the organizational dissent scale. *Management Communication Quarterly, 12*(2), 183–229.

Layman, E. J. (2008). Ethical issues and the electronic health record. *The Health Care Manager, 27*(2), 165–176.

Moore, P. (2009). What's in the stimulus for you? *Physicians Practice, 17*(5), 32–42. Available from http://www.physicianspractice.com/index/fuseaction/articles.details/articleID/1311.htm

National Academy of Engineering. (2006). *The responsible collection, retention, sharing, and interpretation of data.* Retrieved January 13, 2010, from http://www.onlineethics.org/CMS/research/modindex/moddata.aspx

Neidstadt, M. E. (2000). *Occupational therapy evaluation for adults.* Baltimore: Lippincott Williams & Wilkins.

Oregon Department of Education. (2006). *FERPA and IDEA Part B: Confidentiality provisions.* Retrieved January 13, 2010, from http://www.ode.state.or.us/teachlearn/conference-materials/sped/ferpa.ppt

Reynolds, C., & Kamphaus, R. (2009). *BASC–2 Behavioral and Emotional Screening System.* Retrieved August 20, 2009, from http://www.pearsonassessments.com/HAIWEB/Cultures/en-us/Productdetail.htm?Pid=PAaBASC2bess

Rogers, J. C. (1983). Clinical reasoning: The ethics, science, and art (Eleanor Clarke Slagle Lecture). *American Journal of Occupational Therapy, 37*(9), 601–616.

Sparrow, S., Cichetti, D., & Balla, D. (2005). *Vineland Adaptive Behavior Scales* (2nd ed.). Circle Pines, MN: AGS Publishing.

Stewart, L. P. (1980). Whistle blowing: Implications for organizational communication. *Journal of Communication, 30*(4), 90–101.

Thompson, I. (1987). Fundamental ethical principles in health care. *British Medical Journal, 295*(5), 1461–1465.

Title VI of the Civil Rights Act of 1964, 42 U.S.C. §2000d *et seq.*

Veatch, R. M., & Flack, H. E. (1997). *Case studies in allied health ethics.* Upper Saddle River, NJ: Prentice Hall.

Veatch, R. M., & Haddad, A. M. (2008). *Case studies in pharmacy ethics* (2nd ed.). New York: Oxford University Press.

Appendix 14.A. Questionnaire for Identifying Potential Conflicts in Assessment

Occupational Therapist

— Am I competent enough to do this assessment?

— Do I have the necessary knowledge, skills, and attitudes to select, administer, and interpret the results of each evaluation?

— Am I competent enough to supervise other occupational therapy personnel in the collection of data for this assessment? Am I sure that competent individuals are carrying out all delegated tasks properly?

— Have I accurately documented the services provided? Is the summary assessment an accurate reflection of the separate evaluations?

Occupational Therapy Assistant

— Am I competent enough to carry out the data collection and evaluations that I am expected to perform?

— Am I receiving adequate training and supervision to carry out the assigned portions of the assessment process?

— Have I accurately reported the data and contributed to the overall assessment process?

Client Being Assessed (Family, Significant Others, Guardian)

— Has the client been informed about the purpose of the assessment and about how it will be administered and by whom? Does this client understand how the results of the assessment will be used?

— Has the client been informed about how this service will be billed?

— Has the client been given the opportunity to decide if the assessment should be done?

— Are the client's goals the basis for developing and carrying out the assessment process?

Employer (Facility, Agency, Company)

— Is the assessment consistent with the mission of the facility?

— Will there be accurate billing for services?

— How will the interpretations and recommendations of the occupational therapist be used?

Payer

— Is the assessment a necessary and billable service?

— If there is no third-party reimbursement, does the client know this? Has the client given consent before the initiation of the evaluation?

— Will the occupational therapist and the billing office request fair compensation for the services and request payment only for services provided?

Professional Colleagues

— Is the referral consistent with the client's goals and needs?
— Is this assessment necessary?
— Has the occupational therapist communicated the results of the assessment clearly, so that other members of the service delivery team have useful information?
— Have copyrighted evaluation materials been used according to the laws regulating their use?
— Is it necessary to pay fees to use the assessment tool? If so, have the fees been paid?
— Must the occupational therapist obtain permission to use the materials?
— Are specific training and supervision required to conduct the evaluation?
— Does the evaluator hold the appropriate credentials to do so?
— Has the occupational therapist used the correct forms and procedures in conducting the evaluation and reporting the results?
— If it is a standardized evaluation, has the evaluator followed the procedures exactly?

Community and Society

— Is this assessment consistent with the concepts of due process, reparation for wrongs that have been done (physical or emotional), and the fair and equitable distribution of occupational therapy services to individuals needing those services?

Source. Adapted with permission from Hansen, R. (2005). Ethical implications in evaluation. In J. Hinojosa, P. Kramer, & P. Crist (Eds.), *Occupational therapy evaluation: Obtaining and interpreting data* (2nd ed., pp. 245–261). Bethesda, MD: AOTA Press. Copyright © 2005 by the American Occupational Therapy Association.

15

● ● ● ● ●

Use of Evaluation Data To Support Evidence-Based Practice

●

Michelle E. Cohen, PhD
Pamalyn J. Kearney, MS, OTR/L

Overview

This chapter discusses how evidence-based practice within occupational therapy influences the evaluation of clients. It begins with a history and description of traditional evidence-based practice. From that base, the chapter presents ways to use data from evaluation and reevaluation to document practice and offers examples of evidence-based practice literature. Using evaluation data, an occupational therapist can develop the evidence needed to support his or her practice. The chapter concludes with a discussion on how to disseminate the evidence to promote evidence-based practice.

What Is *Evidence-Based Practice?*

Before one can consider the relationship between evaluation and evidence-based practice, it is first necessary to understand what evidence-based practice is and how an occupational therapist can practice from an evidence-based perspective. *Evidence-based practice* in health care is a process that combines the current best-published evidence with practitioner expertise and client preferences when determining appropriate therapeutic interventions (Ilott, 2003; Law & Baum, 1998; Sackett, Rosenberg, Muir Gray, Haynes, & Richardson, 1996; Sackett, Straus, Richardson, Rosenberg, & Haynes, 2000). There are a variety of definitions of evidence-based practice in the literature, and most reflect this interaction among evidence; expertise; and client values, beliefs, and preferences. Sackett and his colleagues (1996) advised that the best evidence comes from combining clinical expertise and knowledge gained through practice with pertinent published clinical research.

The underlying concepts for evidence-based practice have evolved from the concept of "evidence-based medicine," a phrase first coined during the 1980s at McMaster Medical School in Canada (Rosenberg & Donald, 1995). Supporters of evidence-based practice recognize that the ability to provide best care requires the integration of current best evidence, practitioner expertise, and client preferences (Law & MacDermid, 2008a; Lee & Miller, 2003; Sackett et al., 2000). The occupational therapy process is a dynamic one that can vary, not only for each client–therapist partnership but also over the course of an individual intervention (Lee & Miller, 2003). The occupational therapist who wishes to incorporate evidence-based practice into his or her clinical practice must be inquisitive; engage in self-directed, lifelong learning; be willing to consider evidence that conflicts with his or her current knowledge and beliefs; and be able to communicate research findings to clients and their families. This therapist needs to be able to critically analyze existing research findings to determine whether he or she can translate those findings into his or her practice. Moreover, the therapist needs to examine the best available evidence in the form of published reviews or expert opinions.

The occupational therapist begins engaging in evidence-based practice in the evaluation of a client by developing a clear and searchable question related to client needs or the assessment he or she plans to use. Once the therapist decides on the questions, he or she must search the literature for the most current and relevant evidence (Ilott, 2003; Rosenberg & Donald, 1995; Taylor, 1997). Evidence-based practice requires that a therapist be able to locate evidence quickly and easily (Dysart & Tomlin, 2002; Ilott, 2003; Lloyd-Smith, 1997). Searching databases for literature, however, is a skill that becomes easier with practice. A therapist is encouraged to use resources such as the reference librarians at public or university libraries and online tutorials.

After locating current and relevant literature, the therapist carefully reads the material. While reading the published summaries, the therapist notes the information about the assessments and their use. The therapist combines the evidence reported and documented with his or her own clinical expertise. While reading, the therapist examines the assessments and strategies along with other information. One area to focus on is the information provided about the particular client issues and the client's (and family's) particular values, beliefs, and preferences (Ilott, 2003; Taylor, 1997). The therapist should evaluate the outcomes of the changes implemented with evidence in practice (Ilott, 2003). These outcomes may be in such areas as client performance, quality of life, cost of delivery of services, or therapist effectiveness. The therapist should consider how effective the assessments were in determining treatment effectiveness.

There are many advantages to practicing occupational therapy from an evidence-based perspective. Perhaps the most significant advantage is that evidence-based practice allows the therapist to upgrade his or her knowledge of current best practice (Taylor, 1997). Evidence-based practice helps health care providers justify and demonstrate the effectiveness of their interventions to clients, families, and payers of health care services (Lloyd-Smith, 1997).

Evidence-based practice allows for effective use of resources by enabling the occupational therapist and the client to focus efforts on interventions that have a greater likelihood of success (Taylor, 1997). The use of evidence-based practice can help an occupational therapist identify assessment procedures and interventions that have become standard practice but that have not yet been recognized as best practice (Law & MacDermid, 2008b).

Tickle-Degnen (2002) identified several ways a therapist can use evidence-based practices during the early rapport-building stages of a therapist–client interaction. Early rapport building is ongoing in the initial evaluation of a client. As described earlier, it is important that a therapist explore the literature to identify the most appropriate, valid, and reliable assessments and methods to gather pertinent client information. During this exploration, the therapist focuses on the specific assessments used and how the therapist used them. A therapist also might explore more descriptive or qualitative literature that provides information about the occupational desires, needs, and lifestyles of other people with similar diagnoses or characteristics as his or her clients. The therapist may find this information useful when using qualitative or nonstandardized methods of collecting data for the client's occupational profile. Information obtained in the descriptive or qualitative literature may be helpful as a point of discussion with the client to identify similarities and differences with the client's situation and allow the therapist an opportunity to show interest, knowledge, and awareness of others in similar situations. The therapist may choose to share current understanding regarding the efficacy of therapeutic interventions as part of his or her education in the occupational therapy process.

How To Engage in Evidence-Based Practice

In the traditional use of evidence-based practice, an occupational therapist bases decisions for evaluations, interventions, and outcomes on the best available published evidence and his or her clinical reasoning abilities. This section discusses what evidence is pertinent to occupational therapy practice and how best to evaluate and use that evidence.

The best evidence for practice is information obtained from peer-reviewed journals. Peer-reviewed publications provide for expert evaluation of the material before dissemination; therefore, readers know that experts have evaluated the manuscript to determine that it has sufficient validity for publication. Within the realm of peer-reviewed publications, the best evidence for practice is supported by valid scientific research. This research can use either quantitative or qualitative methods.

A therapist needs research to establish validity for evaluation and treatment decisions in practice. The relevance of research to practice depends on the direct applicability of the study, the design of the study, the method of intervention used within the study, and the number of subjects studied. Common sense indicates that the closer a study is to the practice situation under question, the more applicable it will be. Studies that have the same population as the client or group in question will be more applicable than those with populations with different diagnoses. Often the best available evidence may be in the literature of a related population or field, so a therapist needs to interpolate the evidence from related studies that best fit the situation under consideration.

The more rigorous the design of the study, the more likely it is to support the validity of practice decisions. Experimental studies with appropriate controls, interventions, and measures may provide more valid support for practice decisions than studies without controls. However, a therapist needs to consider the artificiality of controlled experiments against the reality of practice; therefore, he or she needs to understand the various research methods and the strengths and weaknesses of each.

All evidence is obtained from empirical observation. This can range from clinical observations made in practice settings to tightly controlled observations in experimental research. Each type of observation has its own limitations. Generally, clinical observations are limited by small sample sizes and, more importantly, by the observer's biases. On the other hand, a limitation of observations in experimental research can be the controlled environment of the research study.

The literature presents many hierarchies that rank the rigor of the various research methods and their applicability to practice (Helewa & Walker, 2000; Law & Philp, 2002; Lloyd-Smith, 1997; Sackett, 1989). The majority of these hierarchies are based in quantitative research methods. Figure 15.1 portrays a commonly used hierarchy.

One characteristic that all hierarchies share is the basic structure of putting the most valid research evidence at the top and the less stringent or less applicable evidence below. Hierarchies for evidence-based medicine often start with laboratory studies conducted by scientists, usually within a highly controlled laboratory setting. These *in vitro studies* (those that take place in artificial environments) often use tissue samples or animals as subjects. Although these studies have the most rigor in terms of experimental validity, laboratory studies are rarely applicable to occupational therapy. Therefore, the hierarchy presented in this chapter considers only *in vivo studies* (involving human beings). The hierarchy of evidence presented in Figure 15.1, adapted from Lloyd-Smith (1997), puts meta-analyses at the top and respected opinion at the base. The following paragraphs describe in more detail the levels of evidence included in this hierarchy and strategies for evaluation of quantitative data.

How To Evaluate Quantitative Evidence

The first level on the quantitative research hierarchy of evidence presented in Figure 15.1 is *respected opinion*. Respected opinions from knowledgeable people within a field can be a good start for clinical decision making when they are supported with appropriate scientific evidence to provide trustworthiness. In

Meta-analysis of randomized controlled trials
(Analyses combine studies to increase power)

Experimental studies
(Random assignment of subjects to groups,
one of which acts as a control group)

Quasi-experimental studies
(Nonrandom assignment of subjects,
may not have control group)

Nonexperimental studies
(Descriptive research,
case studies)

Respected opinion
(Review articles)

Figure 15.1. Hierarchy of support for evidence-based practice in which the form designates that the evidence moves down from the most rigorous type of evidence or research to the least rigorous types. *Source.* Adapted from Lloyd-Smith (1997).

applied fields such as occupational therapy and psychology, research publication commonly lags behind the publication of theory and opinion. A therapist needs to be aware of the information published in assessment manuals. More significantly, a therapist needs to read reviews of assessments that may be in journals and periodicals, because they may be more critical. When research studies about evaluations are not available, the best available evidence is that of published opinion, including published reviews. An example is a recent review article in the *American Journal of Occupational Therapy* that presented an in-depth analysis of driving assessments for use in evidence-based practice (Classen et al., 2009). Common places for finding reviews of assessments are the *Mental Measurement Yearbook* Web site (www.unl.edu/buros), the *Educational Testing Service* Web site (http://ets.org/tests/), and the *Health & Psychosocial Instruments* (HaPI) database (most easily found at a library).

Moving up the hierarchy, the next level of evidence comprises studies characterized as *nonexperimental*, which are research studies that have no manipulation or intervention or in which the researcher does not control intervention. Such studies describe an already occurring or ongoing event. There are generally three types of studies classified as nonexperimental: *descriptive studies, case studies*, and *correlation research*. Descriptive or observational studies describe an event or characteristic of a group. When examining these studies relative to evaluation, the therapist needs to consider the specific assessments used to determine outcomes.

Case studies, another type of nonexperimental research, are used to develop clinical knowledge. Case studies are in-depth studies of one client and his or her disease course and response to treatment. They are directly applicable to client care. However, because case studies use only one or a few subjects, their generalizability to other clients or other environments is limited. When reading a case study, the therapist needs to review the occupational therapy process, including the assessment used and how the treating therapist measured outcomes. Due to the nature of case studies, the therapist should be attentive to the methodology and interpretations of the author, and the reliability and validity of the assessments and process used. A good example of a case study is Kardos and White's (2006) case study demonstrating the use of assessments for the development of transition planning of a secondary student with cognitive disabilities.

The third level from the base of the hierarchy is *quasi-experimental* research. Quasi-experimental studies involve manipulation of an independent variable and measurement of a dependent variable that is under the control of the researcher. Quasi-experimental studies do not randomly assign subjects to groups; these studies may have only one group under study, or they may involve multiple groups. If more than one group is used, the groups are nonequivalent, because subjects within the groups are not randomly assigned. With respect to evaluation, again the therapist needs to attend to the specific assessments used and the measurement of the dependent variable. The results of quasi-experimental studies have less internal validity, but because they study preexisting groups, may have greater external validity (Portney & Watkins, 2009). These types of studies may have great applicability to practice. For example, Baum and colleagues (2008) studied the validity and reliability of the Executive Function Performance Test (Baum, Morrison, Hahn, & Edwards, 2003) in a matched-control designed study. In this quasi-experimental study, they demonstrated the use of an assessment for occupational therapy practice.

The fourth level from the base of the hierarchy of evidence contains studies that use true *experimental* designs, commonly referred to as *randomized controlled trials*. These studies are designed within experimental parameters; subjects are randomly assigned to treatment or no-treatment groups, and independent and dependent variables are under the researcher's control. As with quasi-experimental design, the therapist needs to focus on the assessments being used. Gutman, Kerner, Zombek, Dulek, and Ramsey (2009) presented a randomized control trial demonstrating the effectiveness of an occupational therapy intervention for adults with psychiatric disabilities in which they used a number of assessments to evaluate subjects before and after intervention.

The top level in the quantitative research hierarchy consists of studies that use *meta-analysis*, a statistical procedure for combining data from multiple single-subject studies to determine the effect of the intervention. Unlike a review article, the meta-analysis does not merely summarize the results from individual studies. By combining individual randomized controlled trials, the meta-analysis increases the power of a single study, improving both the estimate of the effect size the intervention provides and the ability to generalize the results (Portney & Watkins, 2009). Meta-analyses usually involve studies with the same target population and intervention, providing greater certainty of the effect of an intervention. Because meta-analyses pool data from a number of randomized controlled trials, they also increase the external validity of the results. The results are generalized more readily to multiple settings. Unfortunately, there are relatively few meta-analyses in the health profession literature. Often in meta-analysis, because the concern lies with the variables of interest, the authors do not identify or discuss assessments in great depth. Although meta-analytic studies are important pieces of evidence, they usually do not have much relevance to evidence-based practice in evaluation.

Often the therapist will not find published quantitative evidence to directly support his or her specific concerns. Another area from which to find evidence is the field of qualitative research. The following section covers evaluation of qualitative studies for evidence-based practice. Again, when reviewing qualitative literature, the therapist should review the assessments used to determine their appropriateness for the topic, reliability and validity, and the manner in which they are being used.

How To Evaluate Qualitative Evidence

Qualitative research can help a therapist by providing information that helps him or her with clients and relationships and provides understanding of how clients live their lives and what they value. This understanding can guide the occupational therapist in how to evaluate a client to obtain the most pertinent information to guide client-centered practice (Hammell, 2004). It is important to note that information about specific qualitative assessments and their reliability and validity is often not covered extensively.

Just as for quantitative research, the occupational therapist needs to evaluate the various types of qualitative research for validity. Unlike quantitative research, qualitative research does not have a hierarchy that ranks the rigor of the research. However, many publications suggest how to evaluate qualitative research for evidence-based practice (Cohen & Crabtree, 2008; Devers, 1999; Dixon-Woods, Shaw, Agarwal, & Smith, 2004; Giacomini & Cook, 2000; Greenhalgh & Taylor, 1997; Henderson & Rheault, 2004; Popay & Williams, 1998). The therapist needs to determine whether the research article addresses the therapist's clinical question about evaluation in some meaningful way. Often, qualitative research studies will address a broad query without extensive detail on evaluation. However, in the process of addressing the query, the authors may present ideas on how they gained access to the participants and built trust and rapport, which may be important when initiating or carrying out an evaluation. Often, a therapist can translate these examples and use them to improve his or her evaluation of a client.

A major issue with qualitative research is the issue of bias. Qualitative researchers are the data collection tool for their studies (Toma, 2006). They determine what data are relevant and what data to collect and drive the analysis of data. Therefore, qualitative researchers must reflect upon their own personal perspectives, values, and interests and the way in which these influence the research process (Patton, 2002; Toma, 2006). Ideally, bias is addressed directly in the methods section with a discussion on reflexivity that demonstrates how researcher bias was handled in data collection and data analyses. Regardless, the therapist, when reviewing the article, should note the potential influence of bias.

In a qualitative study, Doig, Fleming, Cornwell, and Kuipers (2009) examined the use of a client-centered goal-directed therapy from the perspective of adults with traumatic brain injury receiving care in a community-based setting. In their analysis, the researchers identified the importance of significant others and the treating occupational therapist. Further, Doig and colleagues described the use of the Canadian Occupational Performance Measure (COPM; Law et al., 2005) and goal-attainment scaling in the evaluation and goal-setting process. The researchers described several positive themes that emerged from semistructured interviews with the participant groups (clients, significant others, occupational therapists), including benefits resulting from the structure that was provided by goal-directed therapy, positive impact of clear goals on motivation, and a sense of goal ownership by clients. The article described a process to ensure quality and rigor, with a specified number of interviews that the researcher and a research assistant independently coded and the use of colleague checks to ensure that new codes and categories were appropriately defined and described. Missing from the research report, however, was a description of a reflective process wherein the researcher identified his or her perspectives and critically analyzed the impact these may have had on the data analysis process. An occupational therapist working with a similar population may choose to explore further the applicability of the COPM and goal-attainment scaling in his or her practice but should seek out additional literature to learn a variety of perspectives on each of these tools.

A therapist also should evaluate the conclusions section in an article presenting qualitative research. The authors should present evidence from the outcomes and the literature to support the conclusions they have drawn. Therefore, the presentation of the data should adequately describe each theme. The researcher also should describe how the theme was developed. Moreover, when reading such articles through the lens of evaluation, the therapist should examine carefully the assessments used and their appropriateness given the study. Although qualitative studies may not use formal assessments, they provide rich data for the therapist to determine how to evaluate clients.

In general, an occupational therapist will find that qualitative research is more accessible and perhaps more directly related to practice. A therapist needs to remember, however, the very individual nature of the reality addressed through qualitative research and the ways that assessments are used within such studies.

What Are the Data of Occupational Therapy Practice?

When neither quantitative nor qualitative evidence is available to support a therapist's practice, the best support for practice is practice itself. To use individual practice data as support for subsequent decisions, the therapist needs to know what data are available that support practice, how to evaluate the source of the data, how to compile the data, and how to disseminate his or her findings so others can benefit from them.

An evidence-based perspective on occupational therapy practice as it relates to evaluation can lead the occupational therapist to think about the data he or she generates through practice. The therapist must decide how to document outcomes and the efficacy of occupational therapy interventions. The therapist may begin to seek evidence that a particular intervention strategy, whether an old favorite or a new approach, is most effective in helping clients regain occupational performance. When designing new programs, the therapist may conscientiously include evaluative outcome measures that will assist in the creation of clinical evidence to support practice. Administrators and third-party payers may have the therapist justify the effectiveness of his or her interventions. Answering these calls requires that the occupational therapist begin to identify the data that support practice and consider carefully what other data he or she should collect and analyze.

Occupational therapy practice is rich with potential areas of data collection to support occupational therapy intervention, explore the therapeutic process, and understand better the lived experience of clients receiving occupational therapy services. This information can be relevant when analyzing the impact of occupational therapy intervention to help determine whether changes resulted specifically from occupational therapy intervention or from a combination of factors. It is also important in determining the impact of intervention and applicability of outcomes data. Thoughtful consideration of evaluation and reevaluation data can help the therapist produce outcomes data either in a prospective analysis of practice or in a retrospective chart review. Some evidence-based questions a therapist can use to guide selection of assessments and development of strategies to document evaluation findings include

- What data are treatment decisions based on?
- Are those data based on standardized assessments that have been determined to be valid and reliable?
- Can nonstandardized assessment data be generalized to other clients who the therapist sees or to other practice settings?
- Do evaluation and reevaluation results demonstrate that occupational therapy intervention was effective for a particular client or population?

Efficacy of intervention requires that the therapist look at the measurement of intervention strategies. Depending on the goal of outcomes assessment, the occupational therapist may choose to collect data based on a specific guideline for intervention. For example, if the therapist uses the person–environment–occupation approach (Law et al., 1996), he or she may set out to collect specific data on the person's skills, abilities, experiences, or roles; environmental setup, cues, barriers, or supports; the occupations the client engages in or wishes to engage in; and the relationship of all these components to occupational performance and occupational therapy intervention. The occupational therapist then can relate the results of his or her research back to the theoretical approach, further validating that approach as an appropriate guide to practice (Ottenbacher & Hinderer, 2001).

Using Data Generated From Practice

It is often difficult to apply the findings of studies to practice settings. It may be difficult to find any published literature that provides direct evidence for practice decisions. However, practice itself offers a rich opportunity to accumulate the data necessary to make informed decisions. Although it is difficult to conduct randomized controlled trials within the confines of clinical practice, two types of studies are feasible within the clinical setting and offer clinicians the ability to gather data through practice: case studies and single-subject designs. Case studies are a form of nonexperimental research and single-subject designs qualify as quasi-experimental research.

A typical *single-subject design* starts with the measurement of baseline data. Baseline data represent the state of the outcome variable, or target behavior, prior to any intervention. A therapist can obtain baseline data as part of the initial evaluation process. Then the therapist compares the baseline state of the target behavior to new data following phases in the study during which interventions are presented or withdrawn. The therapist collects data over all phases of the study; data collection can be incorporated into reassessment practices. Data collection usually results from objective, quantitative evaluations. Data often address the frequency of occurrence of the target behavior in the presence or absence of the interventions.

Qualitative evidence from evaluation and reevaluation also can provide data. These qualitative data can describe the roles a person has, how they are valued, and whether this changes over the course of intervention. One strategy to collect this type of data may be through use of the COPM (Law et al., 2005) during evaluation and reevaluation. Qualitative data also can describe the process of an intervention and whether the client values it, thereby providing information on the likelihood of carryover of recommendations. Qualitative data also can provide important information about cultural values and beliefs that can affect occupational therapy outcomes, including those related to illness, disability, and role performance.

Case studies often start with an interesting clinical problem. Unlike a single-subject study, there is typically no systematic collection of baseline data prior to the implementation of intervention. Often, a case study is retrospective; the therapist recognizes later that a case is interesting or unique or that a unique intervention produced optimal outcomes. Case studies arise out of the general course of practice. Unlike research that the therapist undertakes for the sake of gaining new knowledge, case studies are the documentation of new knowledge that the therapist gained serendipitously through practice. For example, Carver (2009) presented a case study that described the process of assisting a client with multiple brain injuries to learn to self-catheterize and the development of a custom piece of adaptive equipment for this task.

Case studies offer therapists a unique opportunity to provide evidence to the clinical community. A well-documented case study can provide evidence for practice and contribute to the generation of hypotheses for more formal research endeavors. By documenting cases in a systematic manner, a therapist can begin to amass the data necessary for larger, more experimentally valid research.

Gathering Data

An occupational therapist generates large volumes of data in day-to-day evaluation, treatment, reassessment, and reevaluation of clients, as well as through case studies and single-subject studies. To use these data to demonstrate outcomes and provide evidence for practice, a therapist needs to organize the data and ensure that the information obtained on individual clients is available for later use. The easiest and most efficient method of compiling data is to develop a database. With the use of readily available commercial software packages, setting up a database is relatively easy to do.

The first step in setting up a database is determining what data are important to compile. In general, a database should start with the variables that describe the clients. The first descriptor should be a unique identification number for each individual in the database. It is important to adhere to Health Insurance Portability and Accountability Act of 1996 (Pub. L. 104–191) regulations and protect the anonymity of individuals when assigning identifiers. The use of patient numbers and Social Security numbers is inappropriate because these numbers can be connected easily to a client's private information. Therefore, the numbers used for a database should be unique and not connected to the client other than for the purpose of the database. Security-protected listings of medical record numbers, Social Security numbers, and other unique identifiers should be kept separate from the overall database.

Once identifiers are determined, the next category of descriptive information is demographic data, such as age, race, gender, diagnosis, and medical history. The therapist needs to collect demographic data to describe the characteristics of the individuals in a given group. Demographic data are also important sources of potential confounding variables when attempting to determine the effectiveness of a treatment. Access to these data allows for analysis of the impact of these variables on the outcome of interest.

The second source of data available to clinicians is information generated from assessments used in the evaluation and reevaluation of individual clients. It is important that a therapist collect all the pertinent outcome information during evaluations and reevaluations. These data also need to be coded and re-corded in the database. Use of standardized assessments can be very beneficial in creating the database because they help to ensure that the data collected are both valid and reliable. This strengthens the conclusions drawn from the data and aids in replication of the interventions.

When setting up a database, it is best to collect as much data as possible. It is better to have data available and not need it than to need the data and not have it. Therefore, a therapist should include all information possible pertain-ing to diagnosis and treatment—not just treatment provided by the occupa-tional therapist, but concomitant treatments as well, including all medication. This information will be helpful in future analyses when explaining other pos-sible causes for the outcomes.

Databases provide valuable archival information. It is important to take sufficient time to set up a comprehensive and well-documented database; oth-erwise, the therapist will find himself or herself with data that are not clearly defined, not adequately documented, or too difficult to compile after the fact. Taking the time to plan and set up a well-thought-out database will ensure that when it comes time to analyze and disseminate the data, the data will be in a usable form. Moreover, there will be a clear record of exactly what informa-tion the therapist collected for each variable without having to rely on human memory or information from other sources.

Disseminating Data

The knowledge base in any field is highly dependent on the dissemination of information in a public forum. In general, scientific knowledge progresses through the sharing of results, the critical evaluation of the results over time, and the replication of results in other settings. Without this cycle, therapists and researchers are forced to rely on outdated or erroneous information. Evidence-based practice is dependent on the public sharing of the newest and best available information for practice.

There are many levels in the dissemination of information. The first level consists of colleagues within the therapist's own institution or immediate com-munity. This informal sharing of information can provide an initial level of criticism that helps a therapist refine ideas and processes. Journal clubs, brown bag lunches, and newsletters are ideal and low-pressure methods for bringing ideas into a public forum. However, the therapist should not stop at this level; the information will most likely not receive the critical feedback that is needed to ensure its validity.

Once assured by colleagues that results are interesting, the therapist has a professional and moral obligation to disseminate them to a wider forum. Publications and conference presentations are the two major avenues for dis-seminating new information. Conference presentations may be particularly ef-fective if the proceedings of the conference are published. Although conference presentations move information to the public more quickly, they are not optimal; the audience is usually still limited and often biased toward a particular venue. More importantly, conference presentations often provide interesting opportunities to discuss outcomes with colleagues and their experiences with specific assessments.

Publication is the primary way of disseminating information throughout the public domain and ensuring that the information will be retrievable in the future. Publication can take the form of journal articles, books and book chapters, and magazines and newsletters. In general, journals serve the purpose of presenting new and interesting information, books and book chapters present reviews, and magazines and newsletters present new ideas and theories that generally have not been thoroughly tested. Journals are of two types: peer-reviewed and non–peer-reviewed. *Peer-reviewed journals* require that manuscripts undergo a process of evaluation by experts in the discipline who evaluate the manuscript on the basis of the current level of knowledge in the field. Peer review ensures that the presented information has sufficient rigor, interest, and uniqueness to warrant dissemination. *Non–peer-reviewed journals* generally do not have the same rigor because other experts do not generally critically evaluate manuscripts.

Conclusion

It is critical that an occupational therapist engage in evidence-based practice, with a particular focus on evaluation and assessment. As the therapist gathers data on the client and chooses appropriate assessments, the therapist can collect and provide information about the evidence of practice. The information gathered during effective practice can become the data for evidence-based practice. When the therapist uses the data from practice to provide evidence for practice, he or she not only aids practice, but also, when disseminating findings, provides evidence to support the field of occupational therapy in general.

Questions

1. Describe the relationship between evidence-based practice and evaluation. How can a therapist evaluate data to support evidence-based practice?
2. Choose one assessment and support your decision to use this tool through available evidence.
3. Choose one practice area. Identify the assessments commonly used in this practice area. In your opinion, does evidence support the use of these tools?
4. Think about a practice site where you have been. What data have you seen there that a therapist could collect to use for future evidence for practice?
5. Search an online database for evidence-based practice. Identify information in that database that might be useful to you in evaluation or assessment.

References

Baum, C. M., Connor, L. T., Morrison, T., Hahn, M., Dromerick, A. W., & Edwards, D. F. (2008). Reliability, validity, and clinical utility of the Executive Performance Test: A measure of executive function in a sample of people with stroke. *American Journal of Occupational Therapy, 62,* 446–455.

Baum, C. M., Morrison, T., Hahn, M., & Edwards, D. F. (2003). *Test manual: Executive Function Performance Test.* St. Louis, MO: Washington University.

Carver, M. D. (2009). Adaptive equipment to assist with one-handed intermittent self-catheterization: A case study of a patient with multiple brain injuries. *American Journal of Occupational Therapy, 63,* 333–336.

Classen, S., Levy, C., McCarthy, D., Mann, W. C., Lanford, D., & Waid-Ebbs, J. K. (2009). Traumatic brain injury and driving assessment: An evidence-based literature review. *American Journal of Occupational Therapy, 63,* 580–591.

Cohen, D. J., & Crabtree, B. F. (2008). Evaluative criteria for qualitative research in health care: Controversies and recommendations. *Annals of Family Medicine, 6,* 331–339.

Devers, K. J. (1999). How will we know "good" qualitative research when we see it? Beginning the dialogue in health services research. *Health Services Research, 34,* 1153–1188.

Dixon-Woods, M., Shaw, R. L., Agarwal, S., & Smith, S. (2004). The problem of appraising qualitative research. *Quality and Safety in Health Care, 13,* 223–225.

Doig, E., Fleming, J., Cornwell, P. L., & Kuipers, P. (2009). Qualitative exploration of a client-centered, goal-directed approach to community-based occupational therapy for adults with traumatic brain injury. *American Journal of Occupational Therapy, 64,* 559–568.

Dysart, A. M., & Tomlin, G. S. (2002). Factors related to evidence-based practice among U.S. occupational therapy clinicians. *American Journal of Occupational Therapy, 56,* 275–284.

Giacomini, M. K., & Cook, D. J., for the Evidence-Based Medicine Working Group. (2000). Users' Guides to the Medical Literature XXIII. Qualitative research in Health Care B. What are the results and how do they help me care for my patients? *Journal of the American Medical Association, 284,* 357–362.

Greenhalgh, T., & Taylor, R. (1997). How to read a paper: Papers that go beyond numbers (qualitative research). *British Medical Journal, 315,* 740–743.

Gutman, S. A., Kerner, R., Zombek, I., Dulek, J., & Ramsey, C. A. (2009). Supported education for adults with psychiatric disabilities: Effectiveness of an occupational therapy program. *American Journal of Occupational Therapy, 63,* 245–254.

Hammell, K. W. (2004). Dimensions of meaning in the occupations of daily life. *Canadian Journal of Occupational Therapy, 71*(5), 296–305.

Health Insurance Portability and Accountability Act of 1996, Pub. L. 104–191, 45 C.F.R. §§160, 164. Retrieved October 27, 2004, from http://www.hhs.gov/ocr/hipaa/

Helewa, A., & Walker, J. M. (2000). *Critical evaluation of research in physical rehabilitation: Towards evidence-based practice.* Philadelphia: Saunders.

Henderson, R., & Rheault, W. (2004). Appraising and incorporating qualitative research in evidence-based practice. *Journal of Physical Therapy Education, 18,* 35–40.

Ilott, I. (2003). Challenging the rhetoric and reality: Only an individual and systematic approach will work for evidence-based occupational therapy. *American Journal of Occupational Therapy, 57,* 351–354.

Kardos, M. R., & White B. P. (2006). Evaluation options for secondary transition planning. *American Journal of Occupational Therapy, 60,* 333–339.

Law, M., Baptiste, S., Carswell, A., McColl, M. A., Polatajko, H., & Pollock, N. (2005). *The Canadian Occupational Performance Measure* (4th ed.). Ottawa, Ontario, Canada: CAOT Publications.

Law, M., & Baum, C. (1998). Evidence-based occupational therapy. *Canadian Journal of Occupational Therapy, 65,* 131–135.

Law, M., Cooper, B., Strong, S., Stewart, D., Rigby, P., & Letts, L. (1996). The person–environment–occupation model: A transactive approach to occupational performance. *Canadian Journal of Occupational Therapy, 63,* 9–22.

Law, M., & MacDermid, J. (Eds.). (2008a). *Evidence-based rehabilitation: A guide to practice* (2nd ed.). Thorofare, NJ: Slack.

Law, M., & MacDermid, J. (2008b). Introduction to evidence-based practice. In M. Law & J. MacDermid (Eds.), *Evidence-based rehabilitation: A guide to practice* (pp. 3–14). Thorofare, NJ: Slack.

Law, M., & Philp, I. (2002). Evaluating the evidence. In M. Law (Ed.), *Evidence-based rehabilitation* (pp. 97–107). Thorofare, NJ: Slack.

Lee, C. J., & Miller, L. T. (2003). The process of evidence-based clinical decision making in occupational therapy. *American Journal of Occupational Therapy, 57,* 473–477.

Lloyd-Smith, W. (1997). Evidence-based practice and occupational therapy. *British Journal of Occupational Therapy, 60,* 474–479.

Ottenbacher, K. J., & Hinderer, S. R. (2001). Evidence-based practice: Methods to evaluate individual patient improvement. *American Journal of Physical Medicine and Rehabilitation, 80,* 786–796.

Patton, M. Q. (2002). *Qualitative research and evaluation methods* (3rd ed.). Thousand Oaks, CA: Sage.

Popay, J., & Williams, G. (1998). Qualitative research and evidence-based healthcare. *Journal of the Royal Society of Medicine, 91,* 32–37.

Portney, L. G., & Watkins, M. P. (2009). *Foundations of clinical research: Applications to practice* (3rd ed.). Upper Saddle River, NJ: Prentice Hall Health.

Rosenberg, W., & Donald, A. (1995). Evidence-based medicine: An approach to clinical problem-solving. *British Medical Journal, 310,* 1122–1126.

Sackett, D. L. (1989). Rules of evidence and clinical recommendations on the use of antithrombotics agents. *Chest, 25,* 25–35.

Sackett, D. L., Rosenberg, W., Muir Gray, J., Haynes, R., & Richardson, W. (1996). Editorial—Evidence-based medicine: What it is and what it isn't. *British Medical Journal, 312*(7023), 71–72.

Sackett, D. L., Straus, S. E., Richardson, W. S., Rosenberg, W., & Haynes, R. B. (2000). *Evidence-based medicine: How to practice and teach EBM* (2nd ed.). New York: Churchill Livingstone.

Taylor, M. C. (1997). What is evidence-based practice? *British Journal of Occupational Therapy, 60,* 470–474.

Tickle-Degnen, L. (2002). Client-centered practice, therapeutic relationship, and the use of research evidence. *American Journal of Occupational Therapy, 56,* 470–474.

Toma, J. D. (2006). Approaching rigor in applied qualitative research. In C. F. Conrad & R. C. Serlin (Eds.), *The SAGE handbook for research in education* (pp. 405–423). Thousand Oaks, CA: Sage.

16

● ● ● ● ●

Use of Evaluation Data in an Outcomes-Oriented Approach

●

Carol Haertlein Sells, PhD, OT, FAOTA
Virginia Carroll Stoffel, PhD, OT, BCMH, FAOTA

Overview

This chapter considers uses of evaluation data beyond those specific to clinical practice. In day-to-day clinical practice, the focus is on the individual client needs and the processes used, including screening, determination of level of functional performance based on the results of specific assessments, intervention planning, and so forth. Beyond meeting clinical practice needs, evaluation data provide critical information for the occupational therapist in the roles of program administrator and researcher. These applications of data then relate directly back to clinical practice as occupational therapists use the data to develop, improve, or even discontinue specific intervention programs and provide the evidence that guides clinical decision making.

This chapter provides an overview of the use of evaluation data for three purposes. First, the chapter discusses the use of evaluation data for outcomes measurement, including evidence that supports standardized and systematic assessments in clinical use. In this section, the use of data shows how data can guide practice, including data-based retrospective chart reviews and systematic reviews of the literature. Second, the chapter summarizes the use of small clinical research studies that support evaluation processes, specifically single-subject designs. Third, the chapter presents how data can be used in program development and evaluation.

Promoting the Profession

Earlier chapters in this text provide substantial information to provide the new therapist or update the seasoned therapist with the skills needed to conduct evaluations using a variety of assessments. These assessments should reflect theoretical premises and should be psychometrically sound, administered in uniform or standardized formats, and interpreted accurately. Knowledge obtained using these assessments is key to the profession's continued efforts to improve evaluation procedures to provide the best information to clients and their families, colleagues, and health care payers and regulators. The occupational therapist's efforts to be a conscientious and competent therapist can extend to the development and promotion of the profession. This can be done when evaluation data are recorded in a way that not only benefits the individual recipients of services but also clearly and succinctly communicates the outcomes of interventions. Further, the therapist advances the profession when he or she evaluates the effectiveness of intervention programs for those outside the profession. Given the demands of accountability in the health care environment of the 21st century, an occupational therapist must embrace the systematic use of sound evaluation data to report outcomes and evaluate programs.

Outcomes Measurement for Occupational Therapy

It is the goal of health care to extend life and "ensure optimal quality of life" (Oldridge, 1996, p. 95). If these are the desired outcomes of health care, then *outcomes measurement* is "a comprehensive and integrated system of assessments to measure the efficiency and effectiveness of health care services and interventions" (Barr, Schumacher, & Ohman, 2003, p. 1) to reach those goals. Barr and colleagues posed four questions in outcomes assessment:

1. Are the services and therapies provided improving the client's status, at least preventing or slowing further deterioration of the client's condition?
2. Are our treatments effective (do they work?) and efficient (are they produced using only the necessary resources?)?
3. Are clients *better* because they receive these services?
4. Have we made a difference in clients' end results or "outcomes"? (p. 1)

The occupational therapist should ask these questions of himself or herself when providing services. In outcomes measurement, the therapist's interest extends to groups of clients or populations. Because health care outcomes are increasingly defined by functional indicators (Clifton, 2005a), that is, what the client defines as *better,* the contributions from the occupational therapist can be significant because occupational therapy addresses the aspects of living that improve quality of life.

Predictably determining the outcomes of occupational therapy services, often to maintain credibility in the competitive health care marketplace, has been discussed in the literature since the 1980s. The American Occupational Therapy Association (AOTA), in partnership with the American Occupational Therapy Foundation, embraced this as a mandate when it provided funds to create the Center for Outcomes Research and Education at the University of Illinois at Chicago (Kielhofner, Hammel, Finlayson, Helfrich, & Taylor, 2004). The development of an entity devoted to outcomes research and education was an important step toward establishing a tradition of outcomes research in the profession. More recently, the AOTA *Centennial Vision* (AOTA, 2009a) adopted an outcomes-driven professional "road map" for the future that includes the development of a national database for occupational therapy clinical outcomes by 2011. The first step toward achieving this goal is the adoption of the Boston University Activity Measure for Post Acute Care (AM–PAC) as the primary tool to gather functional improvement data for the measurement of occupational therapy outcomes (AOTA, 2009b). Another clinical outcomes–related goal from the AOTA *Centennial Vision* is that the preparation of all future occupational therapists include "competencies in using outcome measures and interpreting/applying outcomes data" by 2013 (AOTA, 2009a). It is clear that occupational therapy shares the goal of sound outcomes measurement with colleagues across the spectrum of health professions, including medicine, dentistry, nursing, physical therapy, and psychology.

An Outcomes-Oriented Approach

Occupational therapists agree that clinical outcomes research is significant to present and future practice, but they seldom engage in such efforts, primarily because of insufficient knowledge of research methods and institutional barriers to do so (Bowman & Llewellyn, 2002). It is important to clarify the nature of outcomes research as compared to clinical trials research. Ellek (1996) describes *outcomes research* as examining "the effectiveness of treatment as it is administered under real-life circumstances, where patients as well as the treatment itself are likely to have some variances" (p. 886), versus *clinical trials,* which are conducted under strict protocols and ideal conditions with little variation. A thorough discussion of the structure and processes of outcomes research is beyond the scope of this chapter. A therapist is encouraged to gain additional graduate, post-professional education to develop research skills. However, each therapist can adopt an outcomes-oriented approach to clinical practice by drawing on the best available practice evidence, including standardized assessments in evaluation, and using consistent methods for reporting data. The increased emphasis on intervention outcomes in the profession in the past decade reflects issues and trends in all of health care for the past 20 years (Coster, 2008; Ellek, 1996; Law, Baum, & Dunn, 2005). The involvement of each therapist in acquiring the information necessary to determine the outcomes of occupational therapy interventions is key to building the body of evidence to support practice.

What Are Occupational Therapy Outcomes?

It is worth considering at this point what might be measured as occupational therapy outcomes. The *Occupational Therapy Practice Framework: Domain and Process, 2nd Edition (Framework–II;* AOTA, 2008) defines *outcomes* as "important dimensions of health, attributed to interventions, [including] the ability to function, health perceptions, and satisfaction with care" (p. 660). The primary outcome of the profession, "supporting health and participation in life through engagement in occupation" (p. 626), includes two outcomes that are common across the provision of health care—health and participation (World Health Organization [WHO], 2001)—and one that is unique to occupational therapy—engagement in occupation. The *Framework–II* lists nine categories of outcomes as examples of "how the broad outcome of engagement in occupation may be operationalized" (p. 662):

1. Occupational performance in areas of occupation (activities of daily living [ADLs], instrumental activities of daily living [IADLs], rest and sleep, education, work, play, leisure, and social participation) that are measured as improved or enhanced
2. Adaptation
3. Health and wellness
4. Participation
5. Prevention
6. Quality of life
7. Role competence
8. Self-advocacy
9. Occupational justice.

Other aspects of the domain of occupational therapy as described in the *Framework–II,* particularly performance skills and client factors, suggest more outcomes to be measured. Examples of *performance skills* include motor skills such as posture, coordination, and bending; sensory–perceptual skills specific to tasks, such as locating, visualizing, and discerning sensory input; and communication and social skills such as gesturing, maintaining physical space with others, and taking turns. Examples of *client factors* that might be measured as outcomes include values such as honesty and fairness; the mental functions of orientation, memory, motivation, and attention; sensory functions and pain; and neuromusculoskeletal and movement-related functions. The *Framework–II* provides specific definitions to operationalize the outcomes of most occupational therapy interventions.

The emphasis on function and participation implicit in occupational therapy outcomes within the *areas of occupation* is consistent with models of outcomes measurement found in the rehabilitation literature. The focus in rehabilitation has moved away from pathology and impairment models toward models that emphasize function and well-being (Clifton, 2005b). Barr and colleagues (2003) provided an overview of the history of outcomes measurement, including the Nagi disability model, the *International Classification of Functioning, Disability and Health (ICF)* from the WHO (2001), and the Wilson–Cleary outcomes model. All models move from the measurement of outcomes at the level of pathology to measurement of function and performance in society. The concepts addressed by these models, broadly used in medical rehabilitation, are consistent with desired outcomes in the domain of occupational therapy service.

Implementing an Outcomes-Oriented Approach

An outcomes-oriented approach begins with the belief that data are important to guiding clinical practice and that a therapist is well suited to gather, record, and report data. An outcomes-oriented approach is a dynamic system in which data give feedback about the impact (outcome) of an individual intervention, as well as information about the process and effect of the intervention (program evaluation). A therapist can model an outcomes-oriented approach after the process of outcomes research. Kielhofner, Hammel, and colleagues (2004) suggested that the first step in doing outcomes research is identifying client needs.

IDENTIFYING NEEDS OF CLIENT POPULATIONS

Assessing an individual client's needs is the focus of much of this text; in an outcomes-oriented approach to client needs, the evaluation process is population-focused as well as individually focused. Not only are evaluation data gathered and maintained for an individual client, they are stored in a database (commercial or facility specific) for the purpose of determining and documenting the needs of the population of which the individual client is a part (e.g., older adults with hip fractures with impairment in dressing, fourth graders with handwriting deficits, adults with mental illness with employment needs). The identification of outcomes measures can be daunting; a PubMed search of "outcomes assessment in healthcare" yielded almost 50,000 refereed publications that used standardized outcome assessments. When this search was restricted to occupational therapy, there were more than 2,100 journal citations. Some familiar standardized measures for reporting individual and population evaluation data in occupation-based outcomes include the following:

- The Functional Independence Measure™ (FIM; Uniform Data System for Medical Rehabilitation [UDSMR], 1997) has been used in dozens of studies to report the status of daily living activities for people with disabilities in rehabilitation programs. The Functional Independence Measure for Children (WeeFIM; UDSMR, 1993) was used to describe outcomes of 814 pediatric patients in inpatient rehabilitation (Chen, Heinemann, Bode, Granger, & Mallinson, 2004). The FIM and WeeFIM maintain databases through the UDSMR, located at the Center for Functional Assessment Research at the State University of New York at Buffalo, to which subscribers submit information and have access to large pools of data for outcomes prediction, communication, information, and management.
- The Canadian Occupational Performance Measure (COPM; Law et al., 1998) has been reviewed for its contribution to outcomes research in 33 different studies (Carswell et al., 2004).

Several assessments that have been used to measure outcomes in pediatrics and school-based practice include

- Pediatric Evaluation of Disability Inventory (PEDI; Haley, Coster, Ludlow, Haltiwanger, & Andrellos, 1992),
- Beery–Buktenica Developmental Test of Visual–Motor Integration (5th ed., BEERY™ VMI; Beery, Buktenica, & Beery, 2004),
- Peabody Developmental Motor Scales–2 (PDMS–2; Folio & Fewell, 2000), and
- School Function Assessment (Coster, Deeney, Haley, & Haltiwinger, 1998).

Fortunately, there are sources available with compilations of occupation-based outcomes measures. Law and colleagues (2005) organized more than 100 outcomes measures according to the categories of the current *ICF* (WHO, 2001), including measurement of participation; play, work, ADL, IADL, and leisure performance; occupational roles and balance; community integration and social support; and environmental factors. Earlier, Unsworth (2001) compiled resources for occupation-based outcomes assessments. She identified 24 assessments that measure outcomes linked to the levels of the 1997 predecessor to the *ICF,* the *International Classification of Impairments, Disabilities and Handicaps.* There is considerable overlap between these two classification systems, making Unsworth's list of assessments still useful for identifying outcomes measures.

USING STANDARDIZED MEASURES OF OUTCOMES

In an outcomes-oriented approach, the use of standardized measures of outcomes is critical both to the process of individual evaluation (identifying the client's needs) and to the systematic accumulation of evaluation data for information about client populations. The following are examples of studies that use standardized measures to record occupation-based outcomes for individuals; the data can be applied to similar client groups, and the instruments can be considered for clinical applications:

- The impact of occupational therapy services on 37 kindergarteners; fine motor and emergent literacy outcomes (Bazyk et al., 2009) were measured using the VMI, PDMS–2, and three subtests of the Observation Survey of Early Literacy Achievement (Clay, 1993) and Approximations to Text (Pappas, 1993).
- The outcome of individualized occupational therapy intervention for people with psychotic conditions was compared to usual care for 44 adults in a United Kingdom city (Cook, Chambers, & Coleman, 2009). Outcomes measures included the Social Functioning Scale (Birchwood, Smith, Cochrane, Wetton, & Copestake, 1990) and the Scale for the Assessment of Negative Symptoms (Andreasen, 1989).
- The relationships among sensory processing and classroom behavior and educational outcomes were examined for 28 children with autism spectrum disorders using the Short Sensory Profile (Ashburner, Ziviani, & Rodger, 2008; McIntosh, Miller, Shyu, & Dunn, 1999).

- Ross and colleagues reported on the outcomes of augmenting a traditional occupational therapy and physical therapy treatment program in occupational health service clinics in Vermont using the Worker-Based Outcomes Assessment System tool (Ross, Callas, Sargent, Amick, & Rooney, 2006) on 136 participants with work-related musculoskeletal disorders.
- The outcomes of rehabilitation were identified for 125 inner-city older women (Lysack, Neufeld, Mast, MacNeill, & Lichtenberg, 2003) using the FIM (UDSMR, 1997), the Geriatric Depression Scale (Sheikh & Yesavage, 1986), the Mattis Dementia Rating Scale (Mattis, 1988), and the Charlson Index of Co-Morbidity (Charlson, Pompei, Ales, & MacKenzie, 1987).
- The progress made by 44 preschool children in fine motor skills and related functional outcomes was assessed in a multisite study (Case-Smith, 1998) using standardized instruments, including subtests from the Sensory Integration and Praxis Tests (Ayres, 1989) and the Southern California Sensory Integration Tests (Ayres, 1972), the Developmental Test of Visual Perception (Hammill, Pearson, & Voress, 1993), the Sensory Profile (Dunn & Westman, 1997), the Peabody Developmental Motor Scales–2 (Folio & Fewell, 2000), and the PEDI (Haley et al., 1992).
- The effectiveness of a rehabilitation program on quality of life and symptom severity for 47 participants with chronic fatigue syndrome (Taylor, 2004) was examined using the Chronic Fatigue Syndrome Symptom Rating Form (Jason et al., 1997) and the Quality of Life Index (Ferrans & Powers, 1985).

These studies are examples of studies that used standardized outcomes measures, whose results can be interpreted and generalized to the same clinical populations. The instruments used can provide the evaluation data necessary to plan interventions unique to an individual client and to contribute to a body of evidence that guides practice with an identified clinical population. This process—the generating of evidence about the impact of services in a particular area of practice—is the third step in outcomes research (Kielhofner, Hammel, et al., 2004). Readers can consult the articles describing these studies for more information about how they can use these standardized instruments in their own practice with the same clinical populations.

To follow an outcomes-oriented approach, the use of standardized measurement instruments to gather evaluation data is critical. The quality of the assessments and methods used, both qualitative and quantitative, determines the success of a program in making a difference in client outcomes. Qualities of standardized assessments are reviewed elsewhere in this text. Moreover, the occupational therapy and rehabilitation literature report ongoing development of instruments and measurement techniques (Baker, Jacobs, & Tickle-Degnen, 2003; Baum et al., 2008; Baum & Edwards, 2008; Carswell et al., 2004; Cup, Scholte op Reimer, Thijssen, & van Kuyk-Minis, 2003; Fang, Hsiung, Yu, Chen, & Wang, 2002; Goverover

& Hinojosa, 2004; Hartman-Maeir, Harel, & Katz, 2009; Hotchkiss et al., 2004; Huebner, Custer, Freudenberger, & Nichols, 2006; Jang, Chern, & Lin, 2009; Katz, Golstand, Traub Bar-Ilan, & Parush, 2007; Lindstrom-Hazel, Kratt, & Bix, 2009; Passmore, 2004; Reker et al., 2005; Simmons, Crepeau, & White, 2000; Stagnitti & Unsworth, 2004). Authors have discussed the development of functional assessments and the outcomes of occupational therapy interventions since the 1980s. Gutman (2008), editor-in-chief of the *American Journal of Occupational Therapy*, recently wrote that the development of assessments is a research priority for the profession, noting that it is consistent with the AOTA *Centennial Vision* (AOTA, 2009a).

With the explosion of new standardized assessments in the past decade, the selection of appropriate measures for one's clinical situation can be daunting. Criteria for the selection of outcomes measures have been suggested (Barr et al., 2003; Clifton, 2005b; MacDermid & Michlovitz, 2008). These sources recommend against using instruments that are locally developed (i.e., institution-based) because they do not meet standards for validity, reliability, and consistent administration. Criteria for selection of outcomes measures include the following:

- The therapist must define the scope of the clinical population receiving services. The clinical population must match the population for whom an assessment was developed.
- The scores of the population are distributed across the full range of the assessment so that the therapist can differentiate among them and detect improvement or deterioration.
- The scoring system must be sensitive enough to detect changes.
- The domains or concepts that the therapist wants to measure should be included in the assessment, whether they are reported as separate domains or a summary score.
- The assessment must report appropriate indicators of intrarater, interrater, and internal reliability.
- The assessment must report appropriate indicators of content, convergent, discriminate, and construct validity.
- The assessment must be feasible to administer (in terms of time and cost), with clear directions for administration.
- The assessment must be acceptable to the client population, with minimal discomfort.
- The assessment must help guide clinical practice for the client and aid in goal setting (MacDermid & Michlovitz, 2008).
- The assessment must measure the outcomes of interest to the groups or stakeholders interested in the outcomes data, including measure of program effectiveness.

Law and colleagues (2005) offered a selection process for the identification of suitable outcomes measures. Their "decision-making process that occupational therapists can use to guide the measurement of occupational performance" (p. 33) is as follows:

1. Identification of occupational performance issues by the client, often gained by means of an interview or other self-report method
2. Identification of occupational performance issues for this client by another individual or group who may be involved in caregiving or other critical support roles
3. Further assessment of specific occupational performance areas (e.g., IADLs, work) using appropriate measures
4. Assessment of environmental conditions and occupational performance attributes such as client factors, performance skills, and performance patterns
5. Selection of specific outcomes measures that meet the criteria listed above, with an emphasis on clinical utility and compilation of other useful data (i.e., will contribute to evaluation of the program or services)
6. Implementation of the assessment process and interpretation of the results (Law et al., 2005).

Identifying Who Is Interested in Outcomes Data

The data that result from outcomes measurement are of interest to at least three constituent groups or stakeholders: clients, providers, and payers or regulators. Clients include people who receive occupational therapy services and their families or caregivers, facilities and agencies that offer occupational therapy services, and other communities who receive or may benefit from occupational therapy services. Providers are therapists and other health professionals. Payers or regulators include public and private insurance programs and state and federal regulatory groups that set standards and policies for practice and reimbursement. Table 16.1 identifies these constituents and provides examples of the uses of outcomes measurement by each.

Role of Qualitative Data in Outcomes

Many of the standardized assessment instruments noted earlier provide quantitative information necessary for uses identified by providers and payers/regulators. Qualitative evaluation data also provide important information that initially can identify client needs and expectations. Following intervention services, qualitative measures can provide the evaluation data for subjective outcomes such as satisfaction and quality of life from the client's perspective. Clients value the interpersonal and communication skills of providers, and the impact of these skills on a client's compliance and motivation in therapy cannot be underestimated (Clifton, 2005b). For providers, the subjective outcomes of client satisfaction with intervention services and quality of life following services can be important predictors of the success of an intervention.

Examples of studies that used qualitative approaches to gather information about client needs include an ethnography of the occupational needs of patients in a hospice program (Jacques & Hasselkus, 2004), narrative interviews about the influence of chronic lower back pain on the motives for occupational performance (Satink, Winding, & Jonsson, 2004), phenomenological

Table 16.1. Constituents of Outcomes Measurement

Constituent Group	Description	Uses of Evaluation Data
Clients	Individuals (e.g., patients, clients, residents, students, consumers) Families and caregivers Groups (e.g., agencies, facilities, communities, neighborhoods) who are affected by occupational therapy services	Monitoring success of interventions Making predictions for status at discharge, return home, relocation to another facility or program Illustrating need for continuation of services Providing program development and evaluation (groups)
Providers	Occupational therapists and occupational therapy assistants Other health care professionals (e.g., physical therapists, psychologists, nurses, doctors, speech therapists) Facilities and agencies (e.g., hospitals, skilled nursing facilities, outpatient rehabilitation programs, schools)	Monitoring success of interventions Making qualitative and quantitative comparison of clinical performance by individual providers, programs, departments, facilities (quality assurance) Providing risk management assessment Monitoring cost-effectiveness and cost containment measures Providing program development and evaluation
Payers and Regulators	Public health programs (e.g., Medicare, Medicaid) Private insurance companies Federal, state, and local regulatory boards (e.g., Agency for Healthcare Quality and Research, state licensing boards)	Developing policies and professional standards by regulatory boards Establishing reimbursement guidelines and policies Determining reimbursable services

interviews and observation to uncover how people with dementia respond to the problems and changes they experience in everyday occupations (Nygard & Ohman, 2002), and phenomenological interviews with older adults with multiple sclerosis (Finlayson, 2004). The study by Finlayson illustrates application of a theoretical framework—the determinants of health framework—to explore and understand factors that may influence a client's health-related concerns. By applying a theoretical framework in the evaluation process, a therapist can collect data on important outcomes of services from the client's perspective. The therapist can use qualitative techniques alongside standardized quantitative measures to get more comprehensive and accurate information from a client group. In the Finlayson study, each participant was interviewed twice, the first time from a phenomenological perspective and the second to clarify information from the first interview and administer standardized quantitative instruments. The qualitative results identified areas of health concern—outcomes important to the client group (e.g., staying mobile and independent) that may not have emerged from quantitative instruments.

Other qualitative studies provide outcome expectations from the perspective of clients and family members and typically include participation in meaningful occupations and participation in society (well-being and quality of life). A study by Cohn, Miller, and Tickle-Degnen (2000) identified parents' priorities for therapy for children with sensory modulation disorders. Interviews revealed child-focused and parent-focused "hopes for therapy outcomes" (p. 36) that resulted in proposed interventions to meet those outcome expectations. Another study used a longitudinal qualitative design to describe the outcomes of an individualized adaptation-based intervention for low-income older adults with multiple chronic illnesses returning to the community (Spencer, Hersch, Eschenfelder, Fournet, & Murray-Gerzik, 1999). Outcome expectations were obtained from the older adult participants, family members, and occupational therapists providing services. The authors noted the importance of recognizing multiple outcome expectations in planning interventions. Qualitative data collection techniques have much to offer in terms of identifying client needs and in outcomes related to well-being and quality of life.

Qualitative data also have been useful in predicting intervention outcomes. Simmons and colleagues (2000) found that narrative information from the COPM (Law et al., 1998) used in combination with the FIM (UDSMR, 1997) "enhances accuracy in prediction of outcomes for rehabilitative services for persons in adult physical disabilities settings" (Simmons et al., 2000, p. 471). Kielhofner, Braveman, et al. (2004) reported the outcomes of a vocational program for people with AIDS. They found that evaluative data from an occupation-based narrative interview, the Occupational Performance History Interview–II (Kielhofner, Mallinson, Forsyth, & Lai, 2001), were closely associated with outcomes and helped predict future behaviors regarding successful and unsuccessful outcomes related to employment, return to school, and volunteerism.

Databases as Resources of Outcomes-Related Data

In addition to the evaluation data that occupational therapists can acquire in clinical settings, there is information beyond the immediate clinical environment that is crucial to the success of our clients, programs, and agencies and facilities—nonclinical knowledge (Clifton, 2005a). Government agencies, nonprofit agencies, educational institutions, and professional associations are excellent resources for health care goals, standards of practice, outcome expectations, and other information that is useful in outcomes measurement and management. Some government agencies and other resources are listed here as examples of those available. All have Web sites that are easy to locate using popular search engines.

- The *U.S. Department of Health and Human Services,* located at www.hhs.gov, has established strategic objectives for the health of the country for the past 30 years with initiatives focused on "Healthy People."

"Healthy People 2020" is currently under development and will include current and extensive databases and statistics when it is released in 2010.

- The *Centers for Disease Control and Prevention* houses the National Center for Health Statistics, which promotes the development of prevention and intervention programs for a wide range of health conditions and provides extensive educational resources. It can be found at www.cdc.gov.
- The *National Institutes of Health (NIH)* establishes funding priorities for health-related research and administers federal funds. The many agencies under the NIH umbrella maintain extensive databases of health information resources. Check www.nih.gov for more information.
- The *National Institute on Disability and Rehabilitation Research (NIDRR),* under the umbrella of the U.S. Department of Education, Office of Special Education and Rehabilitation Services, funds rehabilitation research, advocates for people with disabilities, and houses disability databases through the National Rehabilitation Information Clearinghouse (NARIC). Information can be located at www.ed.gov/about/offices/list/osers/nidrr/index.html.
- The *Agency for Healthcare Research and Quality,* which is found at www.ahrq.gov, oversees quality-of-care research, provides clinical practice guidelines, and has extensive policy statements and databases related to outcomes.
- The *Substance Abuse and Mental Health Services Administration* focuses on programs and services for people of all ages who are at risk for mental illness or substance use disorders. Its Office of Applied Studies houses an extensive database, the *National Survey on Drug Use and Health,* which is conducted annually to determine national behavioral health practices and issues. For more information, go to www.samhsa.gov.
- The *Institute of Medicine,* located at www.iom.edu, develops information, policy statements, and recommendations on various health issues.
- The *American Heart Association,* found at www.americanheart.org, provides public education and research funding and promotes hospital-based quality improvement guidelines for cardiovascular care.
- The *State University of New York at Buffalo Center for Functional Assessment Research* houses the UDSMR, which maintains the FIM (UDSMR, 1997) and WeeFIM (UDSMR, 1993) databases. See www.udsmr.org/WebModules/UDSMR/Com_CFAR.aspx for more information.
- The *Virginia Commonwealth University Traumatic Brain Injury Model System* supports education, reports research on traumatic brain injury, and provides links to databases at www.tbi.pmr.vcu.edu.
- *AOTA* establishes standards of practice, hosts an evidence-based resource directory including databases, and provides links to related Internet sites. See www.aota.org.
- The *American Physical Therapy Association* establishes standards of practice and productivity standards and provides links to research-related sites. See www.apta.org.

Mental Health Outcomes

Measurement of mental and behavioral health services outcomes deserves its own discussion. An occupational therapist who works in a mental health program will work toward the same desired occupational therapy services outcomes as his or her colleagues in rehabilitation and other practice areas as noted throughout this chapter—occupational performance, satisfaction, role competence, and so forth, as articulated in the *Framework–II* (AOTA, 2008). The mental health professionals with whom an occupational therapist works—psychologists, social workers, counselors, psychiatrists—use primarily verbal methods of intervention (in addition to psychotropic medications) and have identified changes in everyday life or function as an important outcome of counseling, psychotherapy, and related verbal therapies in the past decade (Kazdin, 1999; Lyons, Howard, Mahoney, & Lish, 1997).

The psychology and counseling literature has discussed the efficacy and effectiveness of medications and psychotherapy (Howard, Moras, Brill, Martinovich, & Lutz, 1996). *Efficacy* is whether an intervention works under experimental conditions; *effectiveness* is whether the intervention works in practice. A third concept, *progress,* asks whether an intervention works for a particular patient. Howard and colleagues (1996) suggested that researchers and payers or regulators are concerned with efficacy and effectiveness, clinical providers with effectiveness, and clients with progress. The measurement of therapeutic outcomes in psychology and treatment has historically emphasized the statistical significance of outcomes (i.e., whether a client's post-intervention score on an outcomes measure was statistically different from a pre-intervention score as established by a normative group; Howard et al., 1996; Kazdin, 1999; Thompson, 2002).

In the 1980s, Jacobson and colleagues developed an approach—a metric called the Reliable Change Index (RCI)—deemed to have both clinical relevance and sound psychometrics for determining whether the magnitude of change from treatment effects was statistically reliable (Jacobson, Roberts, Berns, & McGlinchey, 1999). The RCI has received considerable attention and modification since its original inception (Ogles, Lunnen, & Bonesteel, 2001), including the development and comparison of different RCI indexes (Maassen, Bossema, & Brand, 2009; Waldorf, Wjedl, & Schottke, 2009). Although described as measuring "clinical significance," the significance refers to a cutoff score that "can be used to categorize clients as recovered or not recovered" (Jacobson et al., 1999, p. 301) and that "does not include information regarding the clinical importance of the change" (Ottenbacher, Hsu, Granger, & Fiedler, 1996, p. 1231). The concept of *practical significance* refers to the statistical magnitude of the *effect* of an intervention outcome on a population; this concept should not be confused with the effect of therapy on outcomes related to daily life skills that have practical value.

The concept of *clinical significance* in psychotherapy and counseling, as elucidated by Kazdin (2001), seems most closely related to the outcomes that one might expect from occupational therapy intervention—"differences in the everyday lives of the clients" (p. 456). Kazdin suggested that the current outcomes measures used in psychotherapy and counseling measure symptoms rather than impairment, do not include the client's perspectives on what is important to be successful in therapy, and do not address the relationship between "clinical significance" as defined by a metric such as the RCI and client functioning in everyday life. Kazdin proposed that psychology and the other counseling professions identify the constructs that "capture the impact of treatment" (p. 458) and how that impact might be "evident in everyday life" (p. 458). He went on to suggest a need for a measure or measures that assess these constructs.

An occupational therapist who practices in a mental health setting might offer the paradigm of the domain of occupational therapy to counseling and psychology colleagues as an excellent starting point for defining the constructs of everyday life. Outcomes measures identified in this chapter—for example, the COPM (Law et al., 1998), which has a large body of literature supporting its application across clinical populations—could be used to launch a discussion about occupational therapy professionals as functional specialists. An occupational therapist has much to teach his or her mental health colleagues about the conceptualization of daily functioning and measuring the outcomes of mental health intervention.

Retrospective Chart Reviews and Systematic Reviews of the Literature

The amount of evaluation data stored in medical and educational records potentially can yield millions of pieces of information about occupational therapy services. The fourth step in the outcomes research process proposed by Kielhofner and colleagues (2004)—accumulating and evaluating evidence about specific occupational therapy services for the purposes of understanding clinical practice and outcomes measurement—can be accomplished with retrospective chart reviews.

Retrospective cohort studies occasionally appear in the occupational therapy literature, with more seen in recent years. The advantage of retrospective reviews is the availability of large sample sizes for data analysis—sample sizes that would be unfeasible to secure in prospective studies. Fulks and Harris (1995) analyzed the scores on the Miller Assessment for Preschoolers (Miller, 1993) of 54 children who were prenatally exposed to drugs to determine whether a distinct clinical profile existed. The authors noted that prospective studies of this population of children, although more desirable if multiple outcomes measures could be used, are difficult, given the drug addiction and unreliability of the mothers. Gathering the information retrospectively provides at least a glimpse into the needs and potential interventions for this clinical population.

Ivarsson, Söderback, and Stein (2000) reported a retrospective content analysis of 64 occupational therapy records documenting services for people with psychoses in Sweden. This analysis provided insights into treatment goals, the content of occupational therapy interventions, and the client-centered approach of the therapists. The findings demonstrated a need for a standardized measure of therapy outcomes; fewer than 5% of the items analyzed addressed the outcomes of occupational therapy. Retrospective chart reviews thus not only provide a better understanding of a practice area but also identify gaps in documentation of services and the need for standardized measures in a practice area.

Researchers evaluated the Cognitive Orientation to Daily Occupational Performance, an intervention for children, during the final phase of its development (Polatajko, Mandich, Miller, & Macnab, 2001). Data from the outcomes of earlier studies of the intervention were compiled in a retrospective chart audit to see whether the intervention did, in fact, have "clinical replicability" (consistency) in terms of treatment effects. This compilation of data provided valuable information about the replicability of the intervention without the complexities associated with multisite research.

The large number of cases that researchers can analyze in retrospective chart reviews is illustrated in two studies (Chen et al., 2004; Ottenbacher et al., 2004). Chen and colleagues analyzed the records of therapy services and functional assessments of 814 pediatric patients who received inpatient rehabilitation over 3 years at 12 facilities using the admission and discharge ratings of the WeeFim (UDSMR, 1993). This study had the advantages of a large sample size and a standardized assessment that yields consistent data. Large retrospective studies are feasible only if data have been reported in this manner. This is further illustrated by the report by Ottenbacher and colleagues (2004), in which data were analyzed from 744 inpatient medical rehabilitation hospitals and centers on 148,807 patient records across 5 impairment groups over 7 years in a retrospective cohort study. This volume of data is available for review only when consistent data reporting measures are used; in this case, the FIM (UDSMR, 1997) was the primary functional outcomes measure, along with length of stay, living setting after discharge, and mortality. The most remarkable result from this study—an increase in mortality rates over 7 years from 1% to 4.7%—has considerable credibility because of the volume of cases analyzed, a criterion that could be met only with retrospective review.

More recent studies using retrospective data analysis include identification of the sensory-processing and behavioral problems of young children with fetal alcohol spectrum disorders (Franklin, Deitz, Jirikowic, & Astley, 2008) and the identification of the primary use of "prefunctional" activities (65.77%) compared to functional activities by occupational therapists during inpatient stroke rehabilitation (Smallfield & Karges, 2009). Retrospective data can provide insights into client characteristics and assessment and intervention protocols, provided that data are collected in a systematic manner that lends itself to further analysis.

Qualitative data also can be analyzed retrospectively, as illustrated by the following three studies. Retrospective analysis of data from the COPM on 38 mothers of children with disabilities (Donovan, VanLeit, Crowe, & Keefe,

2005) found that their occupational performance was challenging emotionally and lacked sufficient social contact. A retrospective analysis of naturalistic home video of infants with disabilities demonstrated the first categorization of levels of object play in the home environment (Baranek et al., 2005). Support for the theory underlying a sensory integrative approach was determined after a retrospective analysis of parent interview data and assessment data for a child with sensory-processing problems (Schaaf & Nightlinger, 2007). Other types of reviews that use evaluation data and contribute to our understanding of occupational therapy practice include meta-analysis and systematic reviews of the literature. Researchers have used both of these strategies in the past decade to provide more resources for evidence-based practice in many clinical arenas.

Meta-analysis is a systematic review of research evidence that uses statistical procedures for combining data from several studies to analyze the effectiveness of specific treatment interventions (Clifton, 2005b). Operational definitions and procedures for inclusion of studies are explicit to ensure that the same interventions are being reviewed, and analysis is typically done on comparison studies (experimental designs). Meta-analyses are important procedures in the fourth step of the outcomes research process (Kielhofner et al., 2004)—analyzing evidence for a specific occupational therapy practice area. They are important because they provide the evidence needed for practice and fulfill the expectations of an outcomes-oriented approach in handling data. They also are restricted to areas of practice that have generated enough research studies of sufficient quality to be analyzed. Examples of meta-analysis studies reported in the occupational therapy literature include a review of the effect of alternative keyboard designs on the acquisition of upper-extremity musculoskeletal disorders (Baker & Cidboy, 2006); analysis of the co-occurrence of communication disorders with motor impairments in children with language disorders (Rechetnikov & Maitra, 2009); the effectiveness of physical, psychological, and functional interventions in treatment of multiple sclerosis (Baker & Tickle-Degnen, 2001); the effectiveness of occupational therapy–related treatments for people with Parkinson's disease (Murphy & Tickle-Degnen, 2001); and a review of research on sensory integration treatment (Vargas & Camilli, 1999).

When insufficient numbers of research studies exist to apply the statistical procedures of a meta-analysis, a systematic review that completes a comprehensive literature search for relevant studies on a specific topic can be done (Brown & Burns, 2001; Murphy, Robinson, & Lin, 2009). A systematic literature review has a clear clinical topic of interest and selection standards for the relevant literature, evaluates the quality of the studies using predetermined criteria, and yields conclusions to guide clinical practice decisions. This is another helpful approach in evaluating intervention outcomes and providing evidence for practice. The Systematic Process for Investigating and Describing Evidence-Based Research, or SPIDER (Classen et al., 2008), is a tool that helps researchers assess the value of primary studies for potential use in systematic literature reviews. The tool was determined to have strong content and criterion validity and significant correlations between quality indicators and the overall quality score. The SPIDER can be found as an appendix in the above reference. Some systematic literature reviews of interest to an occupational therapist are a review of assessments that predict driving performance of people with traumatic brain injury (Classen et al., 2009), an analysis of the research to support the use of splinting for people with carpometacarpal osteoarthritis (Egan & Brousseau, 2007), a review of the impact of high- and low-technology modifications to automobiles on the driving performance of older adults (Arbesman & Pellerito, 2008), a review of outcomes of interventions for people with substance-use disorders (Stoffel & Moyers, 2004), and a review of the effects of botulinum toxin-A on the functional use of upper extremities for children with cerebral palsy (Hoare & Imms, 2004).

AOTA has developed resources to address the profession's need to have access to research to support clinical decision making. The steps of identifying evidence to support practice have been articulated in journal articles, and AOTA has developed a site (www.aota.org/Educate/Research.aspx) for evidence-based practice (EBP) and research on the AOTA Web site that includes articles, an *EBP Resource Directory,* evidence bytes, critically appraised topics and papers, "Evidence Perks" (a quarterly column in *OT Practice*), and an evidence brief series on a wide range of topics. Another resource to identify evidence for occupational therapy practice comes from Australia, where a team of occupational therapists has developed a Web-based evidence resource called OTseeker (Bennett et al., 2003). OTseeker, located at www.otseeker.com and available at no cost to users, is a database that contains abstracts of systematic reviews and randomized controlled trials relevant to occupational therapy. In the database, trials are critically appraised and rated to assist the occupational therapist in evaluating validity and interpretability. These ratings will help the therapist judge the quality and usefulness of trials for informing clinical interventions. In one database, OTseeker provides occupational therapists with fast and easy access to trials from a wide range of sources (Bennett et al., 2003).

Some other evidence-focused resources with helpful information for occupational therapists include the four databases of the Cochrane Library, which are available through institutional subscription; OTDBASE (www.otdbase.org), available with individual and institutional subscriptions; PEDro, located at www.pedro.org.au, and RehabDATA, www.naric.com/research, which are both available for free on the Web; and OT CATS (www.otcats.com) and Critically Appraised Topics in Rehabilitation Therapy (https://qspace.library.queensu.ca/handle/1974/213), which also are both available for free on the Web. These evidence-focused resources, among many others, make access to the information needed to understand and support best practice increasingly accessible and understandable. Opportunities are limited for the typical occupational therapist to participate in the efforts needed to do retrospective reviews of charts and evaluation data, systematic reviews of the literature, meta-analyses, outcomes research, and so forth. However, occupational therapists need to recognize the value of the evaluation data that are acquired every day and the methods necessary to make that data available to advance the profession's knowledge base, so that each occupational therapist can be part of the ongoing efforts of the profession to provide the highest-quality services with the most-desired outcomes to our clients.

Clinical Research Methods Using Small Numbers of Participants

The strategies described in this chapter for using evaluation data to build evidence and knowledge about occupational therapy services—retrospective chart reviews, meta-analysis, and systematic reviews of the literature—depend upon the availability of large bodies of data and literature to be successful. However, some research methodologies can be applied in the clinical setting and are within the range of accomplishment for most occupational therapists and, if used, could make significant contributions to the profession's knowledge base. Single-subject research methods, in particular, provide the "opportunity for the therapist to evaluate treatment procedures within the context of clinical care, and to share insights about patient behavior and response that are typically ignored or indiscernible using traditional group research approaches" (Portney & Watkins, 2009, p. 271).

Single-subject research studies have appeared in the occupational therapy literature on a regular basis, with some examples from recent years, including a study of the effects of an occupational therapy intervention emphasizing sensory integration with 5 preschool children with autism (Case-Smith & Bryan, 1999), an examination of the effectiveness of using a weighted vest for increasing attention to a fine motor task and decreasing self-stimulatory behaviors in preschool children with pervasive developmental disorders (Fertel-Daly, Bedell, & Hinojosa, 2001), and a study on the effects of traditional and computer-aided instruction on promoting independent skin care in adults with paraplegia (Pellerito, 2003).

Patrick, Mozzoni, and Patrick (2000) suggested that single-subject designs are the best approach to use when "confronted with questions of effectiveness and clinical decision making in the absence of sufficient development of standards of care" (p. 60) that are based on research and empirical findings. This view concurs with the position of Portney and Watkins (2009), who suggested that "the clinician, working in the practice setting, is uniquely qualified to perform these [single-subject] studies. This is especially true in terms of the importance of clinical replication" (p. 271). This observation reinforces the important role of the typical occupational therapist in contributing to the knowledge base of the profession through systematic and careful documentation of occupational therapy services. Both of the references presented in this paragraph are good resources for more information about single-subject research methods and determining their suitability for implementation in one's practice setting.

Program Development and Evaluation

Another important use of evaluation data is the development and evaluation of occupational therapy service programs. In the competitive health care marketplace of the 21st century, all occupational therapists and occupational therapy assistants need to consider potential new service areas of practice. New practice areas emerge in occupational therapy because a therapist sees the need for occupation-based prevention and intervention services across wide spectrums of the population. Examples of new service areas that have emerged in the past decade are backpack awareness education programs, older adult driver awareness campaigns and driver rehabilitation programs, low-vision services, and technology and assistive device development and consulting. Efforts have been directed toward the development of service programs in the community including hospice care, horticultural programs for people with psychiatric disabilities, and violence prevention in the schools.

Ideas for new programs can be operationalized only with data to support the need for a new initiative. Two texts on occupational therapy services in community settings (Fazio, 2001; Scaffa, 2001) provide detailed outlines for planning, implementation, and evaluation of new programs. They are invaluable resources for expanding occupational therapy services in familiar practice arenas as well as in new areas of practice that previously had not been considered. In addition to these texts, articles about innovative programs with new and familiar clinical populations can serve as models for program development and evaluation. Some examples are the implementation and evaluation of an online program to manage fatigue, which was developed from a standard face-to-face format (Ghahari, Packer, & Passmore, 2009); development of a program to manage stress for people living in impoverished conditions in South Africa (Crouch, 2008); the conversion of a face-to-face group energy conservation program to a group teleconference format for people with multiple sclerosis (Finlayson, 2005); a social participation program for children with Asperger syndrome (Carter et al., 2004); the development of programs for underserved clinical populations using participatory action research (Taylor, Braveman, & Hammel, 2004); and new programs for people with chronic rheumatic disease by Samuelson and Ahlmén (2000) and Bailey, Starr, Alderson, and Moreland (1999).

The application of systematic screening and evaluation procedures for a risk appraisal for older adults (identified through the research literature on evidence for practice) allowed one therapist to educate older adults about fitness and promote a community wellness program (Toto, 2001). This occupational therapist adopted an outcomes-oriented approach, used resources for evidence to support practice, implemented use of a standardized assessment protocol in her program, met the needs of older adults in her community, and promoted the value of occupations and the profession of occupational therapy. In this example, the evaluation data helped to provide the best possible occupational therapy services to the clients.

Conclusion

Can evaluation data change practice? The use of evaluation data in a systematic manner can be used to shape and change the profession. Evaluation data can be used for outcomes measurement to support the use of standardized assessments in clinical use. Data-based retrospective chart reviews and systematic reviews of the literature can be used to guide practice. Small clinical research studies, such as single-subject designs, can support evaluation processes. Finally, the collection of evaluation data can be effectively used in program development and evaluation. The collection and use of evaluation data can effectively be used to improve practice.

Questions

1. How does the use of standardized assessment tools relate to the determination of outcomes measures?
2. Choose an occupational therapy topic and research it using three of the databases discussed in this chapter. What did you find? Did it change your understanding of your chosen topic?
3. How do quantitative outcomes data differ from qualitative outcomes data? Give an example of a topic that would be appropriate for each type of data.
4. Think about areas of practice that you have been exposed to or in which you have worked. Identify a topic that would be appropriate for a single-case study.
5. Explain how program development and evaluation relate to outcomes data.
6. Explain how the development of new arenas of practice relates to outcomes data.
7. Overall, how do you think the proliferation of increased outcomes data will affect the profession of occupational therapy?

References

American Occupational Therapy Association. (2008). Occupational therapy practice framework: Domain and process (2nd ed.). *American Journal of Occupational Therapy, 62,* 625–683.

American Occupational Therapy Association. (2009a). *AOTA's Centennial Vision: What it is, why it's right.* Retrieved October 26, 2009, from http://www.aota.org/News/Centennial/Updates.aspx

American Occupational Therapy Association. (2009b). *Q&A: AOTA's endorsement of outcomes measurement tool.* Retrieved October 26, 2009, from http://www.aota.org/News/AOTANews/QA.aspx

Andreasen, N. C. (1989). Scale for the Assessment of Negative Symptoms. *British Journal of Psychiatry, 155,* 53–58.

Arbesman, M., & Pellerito, J. M., Jr. (2008). Evidence-based perspective on the effect of automobile-related modifications on the driving ability, performance, and safety of older adults. *American Journal of Occupational Therapy, 62,* 173–186.

Ashburner, J., Ziviani, J., & Rodger, S. (2008). Sensory processing and classroom emotional, behavioral, and educational outcomes in children with autism spectrum disorder. *American Journal of Occupational Therapy, 62,* 564–573.

Ayres, J. (1972). *Southern California Sensory Integration Tests manual.* Los Angeles: Western Psychological Services.

Ayres, J. (1989). *Sensory Integration and Praxis Tests*. Los Angeles: Western Psychological Services.

Bailey, A., Starr, L., Alderson, M., & Moreland J. (1999). A comparative evaluation of a fibromyalgia rehabilitation program. *Arthritis Care and Research, 12*, 336–340.

Baker, N. A., & Cidboy, E. L. (2006). The effect of three alternative keyboard designs on forearm pronation, wrist extension, and ulnar deviation: A meta-analysis. *American Journal of Occupational Therapy, 60*, 40–49.

Baker, N. A., Jacobs, K., & Tickle-Degnen, L. (2003). A methodology for developing evidence about meaning in occupation: Exploring the meaning of working. *OTJR: Occupation, Participation and Health, 23*, 5–66.

Baker, N. A., & Tickle-Degnen, L. (2001). The effectiveness of physical, psychological, and functional interventions in treating clients with multiple sclerosis: A meta-analysis. *American Journal of Occupational Therapy, 55*, 324–331.

Baranek, G. T., Barnett, C. R., Adams, E. M., Wolcott, N. A., Watson, L. R., & Crais, E. R. (2005). Object play in infants with autism: Methodological issues in retrospective video analysis. *American Journal of Occupational Therapy, 59*, 20–30.

Barr, J., Schumacher, G., & Ohman, S. (2003). *Outcomes Assessment and Health-Related Quality of Life Measurement*. Boston: National Education and Research Center for Outcomes Assessment in Healthcare (NERCOA), Northeastern University.

Baum, C. M., Connor, L. T., Morrison, T., Hahn, M., Dromerick, A. W., & Edwards, D. F. (2008). Reliability, validity, and clinical utility of the Executive Function Performance Test: A measure of executive function in a sample of people with stroke. *American Journal of Occupational Therapy, 62*, 446–455.

Baum, C. M., & Edwards, D. (2008). *Activity Card Sort* (2nd ed.). Bethesda, MD: AOTA Press.

Bazyk, S., Michaud, P., Goodman, G., Papp, P., Hawkins, E., & Welch, M. A. (2009). Integrating occupational therapy services in a kindergarten curriculum: A look at the outcomes. *American Journal of Occupational Therapy, 63*, 160–171.

Beery, K. E., Buktenica, N. A., & Beery, N. A. (2004). *The Beery–Buktenica Developmental Test of Visual–Motor Integration* (5th ed.). Minneapolis, MN: Pearson.

Bennett, S., Hoffmann, T., McCluskey, A., McKenna, K., Strong, J., & Tooth, L. (2003). Introducing OTseeker (Occupational Therapy Systematic Evaluation of Evidence): A new evidence database for occupational therapists. *American Journal of Occupational Therapy, 557*, 635–638.

Birchwood, M., Smith, J., Cochrane, R., Wetton, S., & Copestake, S. (1990). The Social Functioning Scale: The development and validation of a new scale of social adjustment for use in the family intervention programme with schizophrenic patients. *British Journal of Psychiatry, 157*, 853–859.

Bowman, J., & Llewellyn, G. (2002). Clinical outcomes research from the occupational therapist's perspective. *Occupational Therapy International, 9*, 145–166.

Brown, G. T., & Burns, S. A. (2001). The efficacy of neurodevelopmental treatment in paedeatrics: A systematic review. *British Journal of Occupational Therapy, 64*, 235–244.

Carswell, A., McColl, M. A., Baptiste, S., Law, M., Polatajko, H., & Pollock, N. (2004). The Canadian Occupational Performance Measure: A research and clinical literature review. *Canadian Journal of Occupational Therapy, 71*, 210–222.

Carter, C., Meckes, L., Pritchard, L., Swensen, S., Wittman, P. P., & Velde, B. (2004). The Friendship Club: An after-school program for children with Asperger syndrome. *Family and Community Health, 27*, 143–150.

Case-Smith, J. (1998). Outcomes research using a collaborative, multi-site model. *Journal of Rehabilitation Outcomes Measurement, 2*(6), 9–17.

Case-Smith, J., & Bryan, T. (1999). The effects of occupational therapy with sensory integration emphasis on preschool-age children with autism. *American Journal of Occupational Therapy, 53*, 489–497.

Charlson, M. E., Pompei, P., Ales, K. L., & MacKenzie, C. R. (1987). A new method of clas-
sifying prognostic comorbidity in longitudinal studies: Development and validation. *Journal
of Chronic Diseases, 40,* 373–383.

Chen, C. C., Heinemann, A. W., Bode, R. K., Granger, C. V., & Mallinson, R. (2004). Impact
of pediatric rehabilitation services on children's functional outcomes. *American Journal of
Occupational Therapy, 58,* 44–53.

Classen, S., Levy, C., McCarthy, D., Mann, W. C., Lanford, D., & Waid-Ebbs, J. K. (2009).
Traumatic brain injury and driving assessment: An evidence-based literature review. *American Journal of Occupational Therapy, 63,* 580–591.

Classen, S., Winter, S., Awadzi, K. D., Garvan, C. W., Lopez, E. D., & Sundaram, S. (2008).
Psychometric testing of SPIDER: Data capture tool for systematic literature reviews. *American Journal of Occupational Therapy, 62,* 335–348.

Clay, M. M. (1993). *Observation Survey of Early Literacy Achievement.* Portsmouth, NH:
Heinemann Educational.

Clifton, D. W., Jr. (2005a). Outcomes management. In D. W. Clifton, Jr. (Ed.), *Physical rehabilitation's role in disability management: Unique perspectives for success* (pp. 207–228). St.
Louis, MO: Elsevier/Saunders.

Clifton, D. W., Jr. (2005b). How to locate sources of disability-related data. In D. W. Clifton,
Jr. (Ed), *Physical rehabilitation's role in disability management: Unique perspectives for success* (pp. 229–238). St. Louis, MO: Elsevier/Saunders.

Cohn, E., Miller, L. J., & Tickle-Degnen, L. (2000). Parental hopes for therapy outcomes: Children
with sensory modulation disorders. *American Journal of Occupational Therapy, 54,* 36–43.

Cook, S., Chambers, E., & Coleman, J. H. (2009). Occupational therapy for people with psychotic conditions in community settings: A pilot randomized controlled trial. *Clinical Rehabilitation, 23,* 40–52.

Coster, W. J. (2008). Embracing ambiguity: Facing the challenge of measurement (Eleanor
Clarke Slagle Lecture). *American Journal of Occupational Therapy, 62,* 743–752.

Coster, W. J., Deeney, T., Haley, S. M., & Haltiwanger, J. (1998). *School Function Assessment.*
San Antonio, TX: Psychological Corporation.

Crouch, R. B. (2008). A community-based stress management programme for an impoverished
population in South Africa. *Occupational Therapy International, 15*(2), 71–86.

Cup, E. H. C., Scholte op Reimer, W. J. M, Thijssen, M. C. E., & van Kuyk-Minis, M. A. H.
(2003). Reliability and validity of the Canadian Occupational Performance Measure in
stroke patients. *Clinical Rehabilitation, 17,* 401–409.

Donovan, J. M., VanLeit, B. J., Crowe, T. K., & Keefe, E. B. (2005). Occupational goals of
mothers of children with disabilities: Influence of temporal, social, and emotional contexts.
American Journal of Occupational Therapy, 59, 249–261.

Dunn, W., & Westman, K. (1997). The Sensory Profile: The performance of a national sample
of children without disabilities. *American Journal of Occupational Therapy, 51,* 25–34.

Egan, M. Y., & Brousseau, L. (2007). Splinting for osteoarthritis of the carpometacarpal joint:
A review of the evidence. *American Journal of Occupational Therapy, 61,* 70–78.

Ellek, D. (1996). Health policy: Policy implications of outcomes research. *American Journal of
Occupational Therapy, 50,* 886–889.

Fang, C. T., Hsiung, P. C., Yu, C. F., Chen, M. Y., & Wang, J. D. (2002). Validation of the
World Health Organization quality of life instrument in patients with HIV infection. *Quality of Life Research, 11,* 753–762.

Fazio, L. S. (2001). *Developing occupation-centered programs for the community: A workbook for students and professionals.* Upper Saddle River, NJ: Prentice Hall.

Ferrans, C. E., & Powers, M. J. (1985). Quality of Life Index: Development and psychometric
properties. *Advances in Nursing Science, 8,* 15–24.

Fertel-Daly, D., Bedell, G., & Hinojosa, J. (2001). Effects of a weighted vest on attention to
task and self-stimulatory behaviors in preschoolers with pervasive developmental disorders.
American Journal of Occupational Therapy, 55, 629–640.

Finlayson, M. (2004). Concerns about the future among older adults with multiple sclerosis. *American Journal of Occupational Therapy, 58,* 54–63.

Finlayson, M. (2005). Pilot study of an energy conservation education program delivered by telephone conference call to people with multiple sclerosis. *NeuroRehabilitation, 20,* 267–277.

Folio, M., & Fewell, R. R. (2000). *Peabody Developmental Motor Scales* (2nd ed.). Austin, TX: Pro-Ed.

Franklin, L., Deitz, J., Jirikowic, T., & Astley, S. (2008). Children with fetal alcohol spectrum disorders: Problem behaviors and sensory processing. *American Journal of Occupational Therapy, 62,* 265–273.

Fulks, M. L., & Harris, S. R. (1995). Children exposed to drugs in utero: Their scores on the Miller Assessment for Preschoolers. *Canadian Journal of Occupational Therapy, 62,* 7–15.

Ghahari, S., Packer, T. L., & Passmore, A. E. (2009). Development, standardization, and pilot testing of an online fatigue self-management program. *Disability and Rehabilitation, 19,* 1–11.

Goverover, Y., & Hinojosa, J. (2004). Brief Report—Interrater reliability and discriminant validity of the deductive reasoning test. *American Journal of Occupational Therapy, 58,* 104–108.

Gutman, S. (2008). From the Desk of the Editor—Research priorities of the profession. *American Journal of Occupational Therapy, 62,* 499–501.

Haley, S. M., Coster, W. J., Ludlow, L., Haltiwanger, J., & Andrellos, P. (1992). *Pediatric Evaluation of Disability Inventory (PEDI)*. San Antonio, TX: Psychological Corporation.

Hammill, D. D., Pearson, N. A., & Voress, J. K. (1993). *Developmental Test of Visual Perception* (2nd ed.). Austin, TX: Pro-Ed.

Hartman-Maeir, A., Harel, H., & Katz, N. (2009). Kettle Test—A brief measure of cognitive functional performance: Reliability and validity in stroke rehabilitation. *American Journal of Occupational Therapy, 64,* 592–599.

Hoare, B. J., & Imms, C. (2004). Upper-limb injections of botulinum toxin-A in children with cerebral palsy: A critical review of the literature and clinical implications for occupational therapists. *American Journal of Occupational Therapy, 58,* 389–397.

Hotchkiss, A., Fisher, A., Robertson, R., Ruttencutter, A., Schuffert, J., & Barker, D. B. (2004). Brief Report—Convergent and predictive validity of three scales related to falls in the elderly. *American Journal of Occupational Therapy, 58,* 100–103.

Howard, K. I., Moras, K., Brill, P. L., Martinovich, Z., & Lutz, W. (1996). Evaluation of psychotherapy: Efficacy, effectiveness, and patient progress. *American Psychologist, 51,* 1059–1064.

Huebner, R. A., Custer, M. G., Freudenberger, L., & Nichols, L. (2006). The Occupational Therapy Practice Checklist for adult physical rehabilitation. *American Journal of Occupational Therapy, 60,* 388–396.

Ivarsson, A., Söderback, I., & Stein, F. (2000). Goal, intervention, and outcome of occupational therapy in individuals with psychoses: Content analysis through chart review. *Occupational Therapy International, 7,* 21–41.

Jacobson, N. S., Roberts, L. J., Berns, S. B., & McGlinchey, J. B. (1999). Methods for defining and determining the clinical significance of treatment effects: Description, application, and alternatives. *Journal of Consulting and Clinical Psychology, 67,* 300–307.

Jacques, N. D., & Hasselkus, B. R. (2004). The nature of occupation surrounding dying and death. *OTJR: Occupation, Participation and Health, 24,* 44–53.

Jang, Y., Chern, J.-S., & Lin, K.-C. (2009). Validity of the Loewenstein Occupational Therapy Cognitive Assessment in people with intellectual disabilities. *American Journal of Occupational Therapy, 63,* 414–422.

Jason, L. A., Ropacki, M. T., Santoro, N. B., Richman, J. A., Heatherly, W., Taylor, R., et al. (1997). A screening scale for chronic fatigue syndrome: Reliability and validity. *Journal of Chronic Fatigue Syndrome, 3,* 39–59.

Katz, N., Golstand, S., Traub Bar-Ilan, R., & Parush, S. (2007). The Dynamic Occupational Therapy Cognitive Assessment for Children (DOTCA–Ch): A new instrument for assessing learning potential. *American Journal of Occupational Therapy, 61,* 41–52.

Kazdin, A. E. (1999). The meanings and measurement of clinical significance. *Journal of Consulting and Clinical Psychology, 67,* 332–339.

Kazdin, A. E. (2001). Almost clinically significant (*p* < .10): Current measures may only approach clinical significance. *Clinical Psychology: Science and Practice, 8,* 455–462.

Kielhofner, G., Braveman, B., Finlayson, M., Paul-Ward, A., Goldbaum, L., & Goldstein, K. (2004). Outcomes of a vocational program for persons with AIDS. *American Journal of Occupational Therapy, 58,* 64–72.

Kielhofner, G., Hammel, J., Finlayson, M., Helfrich, C., & Taylor, R. (2004). Documenting outcomes of occupational therapy: The Center for Outcomes Research and Education. *American Journal of Occupational Therapy, 58,* 15–23.

Kielhofner, G., Mallinson, T., Forsyth, K., & Lai, J. S. (2001). Psychometric properties of the second version of the Occupational Performance History Interview (OPHI–II). *American Journal of Occupational Therapy, 55,* 260–267.

Law, M., Baptiste, S., Carswell, A., McColl, M. A., Polatajko, H., & Pollock, N. (1998). *Canadian Occupational Performance Measure* (3rd ed.). Ottawa, Ontario, Canada: CAOT Publications.

Law, M., Baum, C., & Dunn, W. (2005). *Measuring occupational performance: Supporting best practice in occupational therapy* (2nd ed.). Thorofare, NJ: Slack.

Lindstrom-Hazel, D., Kratt, A., & Bix, L. (2009). Interrater reliability of students using hand and pinch dynamometers. *American Journal of Occupational Therapy, 63,* 193–197.

Lyons, J. S., Howard, K. I., Mahoney, M. T., & Lish, J. D. (1997). *The measurement and management of clinical outcomes in mental health.* New York: Wiley.

Lysack, C. L., Neufeld, S., Mast, B. T., MacNeill, S. E., & Lichtenberg, P. A. (2003). After rehabilitation: An 18-month follow-up of elderly inner-city women. *American Journal of Occupational Therapy, 57,* 298–306.

Maassen, G. H., Bossema, E., & Brand, N. (2009). Reliable change and practice effects: Outcomes of various indices compared. *Journal of Clinical and Experimental Neuropsychology, 3,* 339–352.

MacDermid, J., & Michlovitz, S. (2008). Incorporating outcomes measures in evidence-based practice. In M. Law & J. MacDermid (Eds.), *Evidence-based rehabilitation: A guide to practice* (2nd ed., pp. 63–94). Thorofare, NJ: Slack.

Mattis, S. (1988). *Dementia Rating Scale: Professional manual.* Odessa, FL: Psychological Assessment Resources.

McIntosh, D., Miller, L., Shyu, V., & Dunn, W. (1999). Development and validation of the Short Sensory Profile. In W. Dunn (Ed.), *The Sensory Profile examiner's manual* (pp. 59–73). San Antonio, TX: Psychological Corporation.

Miller, L. J. (1993). *Miller Assessment for Preschoolers.* San Antonio, TX: Psychological Corporation.

Murphy, S. L., Robinson, J. C., & Lin, S. H. (2009). Conducting systematic reviews to inform occupational therapy practice. *American Journal of Occupational Therapy, 63,* 363–368.

Murphy, S., & Tickle-Degnen, L. (2001). The effectiveness of occupational therapy-related treatments for persons with Parkinson's disease: A meta-analytic review. *American Journal of Occupational Therapy, 55,* 385–392.

Nygard, L., & Ohman, A. (2002). Managing changes in everyday occupations: The experience of persons with Alzheimer's disease. *OTJR: Occupation, Participation and Health, 22,* 70–81.

Ogles, B. M., Lunnen, K. M., & Bonesteel, K. (2001). Clinical significance: History, application, and current practice. *Clinical Psychology Review, 21,* 421–446.

Oldridge, N. B. (1996). Outcomes measurement: Health state preferences and economic evaluation. *Assistive Technology, 8,* 94–102.

Ottenbacher, K. J., Hsu, Y., Granger, C. V., & Fiedler, R. C. (1996). The reliability of the Functional Independence Measure: A quantitative review. *Archives of Physical Medicine and Rehabilitation, 77,* 1226–1232.

Ottenbacher, K. J., Smith, P. M., Illig, S. B., Linn, R. T., Ostir, G. V., & Granger, C. V. (2004). Trends in length of stay, living setting, functional outcome, and mortality following medical rehabilitation. *Journal of the American Medical Association, 292,* 1687–1695.

Pappas, C. (1993). Is narrative "primary"? Some insights from kindergarteners' pretend readings of stories and information books. *Journal of Reading Behavior, 25,* 97–129.

Passmore, A. (2004). A measure of perceptions of generalized self-efficacy adapted for adolescents. *OTJR: Occupation, Participation and Health, 24,* 64–71.

Patrick, P. D., Mozzoni, M., & Patrick, S. T. (2000). Evidence-based care and the single-subject design. *Infants and Young Children, 13*(1), 60–73.

Pellerito, J. M., Jr. (2003). The effects of traditional and computer-aided instruction on promoting independent skin care in adults with paraplegia. *Occupational Therapy International, 10,* 1–19.

Polatajko, H. J., Mandich, A. D., Miller, L. T., & Macnab, J. J. (2001). Cognitive Orientation to Daily Occupational Performance (CO-OP): Part II—The evidence. *Physical and Occupational Therapy in Pediatrics, 20*(2/3), 83–106.

Portney, L. G., & Watkins, M. P. (2009). *Foundations of clinical research: Applications to practice* (3rd ed.). Upper Saddle River, NJ: Prentice Hall.

Rechetnikov, R. P., & Maitra, K. (2009). Motor impairments in children associated with impairments of speech or language: A meta-analytic review of research literature. *American Journal of Occupational Therapy, 63,* 255–263.

Reker, D. M., Reid, K., Duncan, P. W., Marshall, C., Cowper, D., Stansbury, J., et al. (2005). Development of an integrated stroke outcomes database within Veterans Health Administration. *Journal of Rehabilitation Research and Development, 42,* 77–92.

Ross, R. H., Callas, P. W., Sargent, J. Q., Amick, B. C., & Rooney, T. (2006). Incorporating injured employee outcomes into physical and occupational therapists' practice: A controlled trial of the Worker-Based Outcomes Assessment System. *Journal of Occupational Rehabilitation, 16,* 607–629.

Samuelson, U. K., & Ahlmén, E. M. (2000). Development and evaluation of a patient education program for persons with systemic sclerosis (scleroderma). *Arthritis Care and Research, 13,* 141–148.

Satink, T., Winding, K., & Jonsson, H. (2004). Daily occupations with or without pain: Dilemmas in occupational performance. *OTJR: Occupation, Participation and Health, 24,* 144–150.

Scaffa, M. (Ed.). (2001). *Occupational therapy in community-based practice settings.* Philadelphia: F. A. Davis.

Schaaf, R. C., & Nightlinger, K. M. (2007). Occupational therapy using a sensory integrative approach: A case study of effectiveness. *American Journal of Occupational Therapy, 61*(2), 239–246.

Sheikh, J. I., & Yesavage, J. A. (1986). Geriatric Depression Scale (GDS): Recent evidence and development of a shorter version. *Clinical Gerontologist, 5,* 165–173.

Simmons, D. C., Crepeau, E. B., & White, B. P. (2000). The predictive power of narrative data in occupational therapy evaluation. *American Journal of Occupational Therapy, 54,* 471–476.

Smallfield, S., & Karges, J. (2009). Classification of occupational therapy intervention for inpatient stroke rehabilitation. *American Journal of Occupational Therapy, 63,* 408–413.

Spencer, J., Hersch, G., Eschenfelder, V., Fournet, J., & Murray-Gerzik, M. (1999). Outcomes of protocol-based and adaptation-based occupational therapy interventions for low-income elderly persons on a transitional unit. *American Journal of Occupational Therapy, 53,* 159–170.

Stagnitti, K., & Unsworth, C. (2004). The test–retest reliability of the child-initiated pretend play assessment. *American Journal of Occupational Therapy, 58,* 93–99.

Stoffel, V., & Moyers, P. (2004). An evidence-based and occupational perspective of interventions for persons with substance-use disorders. *American Journal of Occupational Therapy, 58*, 570–586.

Taylor, R. R. (2004). Quality of life and symptom severity for individuals with chronic fatigue syndrome: Findings from a randomized clinical trial. *American Journal of Occupational Therapy, 58*, 35–43.

Taylor, R. R., Braveman, B., & Hammel, J. (2004). Developing and evaluating community-based services through participatory action research: Two case examples. *American Journal of Occupational Therapy, 58*, 73–82.

Thompson, B. (2002). "Statistical", "practical" and "clinical": How many kinds of significance do counselors need to consider? *Journal of Counseling and Development, 80*, 64–71.

Toto, P. E. (2001, December). Moving toward evidence-based practice. *Gerontology Special Interest Section Quarterly, 24*, 4.

Uniform Data System for Medical Rehabilitation. (1993). *Guide for the Uniform Data Set for Medical Rehabilitation for Children* (WeeFIM) (Version 4.0). Buffalo: State University of New York.

Uniform Data System for Medical Rehabilitation. (1997). *Guide for the Uniform Data Set for Medical Rehabilitation* (Adult FIM™) (Version 5.1). Buffalo: State University of New York.

Unsworth, C. (2001). Measuring the outcome of occupational therapy: Tools and resources. *Australian Occupational Therapy Journal, 47*, 147–158.

Vargas, S., & Camilli, G. (1999). A meta-analysis of research on sensory integration treatment. *American Journal of Occupational Therapy, 53*, 189–198.

Waldorf, M., Wjedl, K. H., & Schottke, H. (2009). In the concordance of three reliable change indexes: An analysis applying the dynamic Wisconsin Card Sorting Test. *Journal of Cognitive Education and Psychology, 8*, 63–80.

World Health Organization. (2001). *International classification of functioning, disability and health*. Geneva: Author.

Index

Page numbers in *italic* type indicate tables and figures.

A

Accommodations
  for physical disabilities, 278–279
  purpose, 276–277
Accountability, 69–71
Accountable evaluation, 15
Accreditation standards, 11–12
Accuracy, of assessments, 180
Activity Card Sort (ACS), 137–138
Activity configurations, 106
Administration of assessments, 109–110
Adult environments, measures for, 143–145
Adult participation scales, 137–142
Age-equivalent scores, *221*, 223
Alternate, parallel forms of reliability or
    equivalence, *189*, 190–191
  see also reliability
Ambiguity error, 226
Anxiety, 117–118
AOTA, 72–73
Assessment of Motor and Process Skills
    (AMPS), 218
Assessments
  administration, 109–110
  analyzing, 48–50, *50*, 58
  biases, 25–26
  client, 25
  defined, 3
  environments, 111–113, 143–150
  errors in, 115–118
  ethical issues, 51–52
  formats of, 60
  identifying, 42
  implementation, 59–61, 110–114
  influence of contextual factors, 26

  information resources, 46–48
  information resources for, *47*
  intended purposes, 44–45
  learning, 94–95
  participation, 134–143
  practical considerations, 45–46, 57–58
  psychometric integrity, 60
  selecting, 42–48, 59, 114–115
  special populations, 284–286
  techniques, 107–109
  types of data, 86–91
  user qualifications, 45
  see also test scores; validity

B

Behavioral health outcomes, 349–350
Beneficence, ethical principle of, 9–10
Biases
  accounting for, 233
  controlling, 159–160
  item bias, 115–116
  personal, 25–26, 116–117, 225–226
  in qualitative evidence, 328
  special populations, 285–286
Bilingual clients, 282–284, 310–311
Bottom-up approach, 33

C

Canadian Occupational Performance
    Measure (COPM), 128–129, 173,
    174–175, 341
Capacity vs. performance, 118
Caregiver reports, 132
  see also reports
Ceiling scores, 199, 211

363

About the Editors

Jim Hinojosa, PhD, OT, FAOTA, is a professor in the Department of Occupational Therapy in the School of Culture, Education, and Human Development at New York University. Dr. Hinojosa has an extensive record of publications, including more than 130 articles and chapters and eight textbooks. He has served as chairperson of the Commission on Practice of the American Occupational Therapy Association (AOTA), on the Board of Directors of AOTA, and on the Board of Directors of the American Occupational Therapy Foundation (AOTF). Dr. Hinojosa served as member-at-large on AOTA's Commission on Continuing Competence and Professional Development. In recognition of his leadership, AOTA presented him with their highest honor, the Award of Merit, and the Eleanor Clarke Slagle Lectureship Award in 2007. He is a Fellow of AOTA.

Paula Kramer, PhD, OTR, FAOTA, is professor and chairperson of the Department of Occupational Therapy at University of the Sciences in Philadelphia. She has published numerous scholarly articles and chapters and has co-authored six textbooks. She has been the editor of the *AOTA Education Special Interest Section Quarterly Newsletter* and has chaired the Essentials Review Committee for the Accreditation Council for Occupational Therapy Education® (ACOTE®). Dr. Kramer was a former chairperson of ACOTE and currently serves on the AOTA Board of Directors. She received the A. Jean Ayres Award from AOTF for her contributions relating theory to practice and is a Fellow of AOTA.

Patricia Crist, PhD, OTR, FAOTA, is founding chairperson and professor of the Department of Occupational Therapy at Duquesne University in Pittsburgh. Dr. Crist has completed numerous scholarly works, presentations, and workshops regarding fieldwork education, mental health interventions, parents with disabilities, and the practice–scholar role. She has co-edited five invited publications on occupational therapy education and one on the scholarship of practice. Dr. Crist currently is on the AOTA Board of Directors and is past-president of the Board of

Directors of the National Board for Certification in Occupational Therapy (NB-COT). She chaired the 2002–2003 NBCOT National Study of Practice, which is the basis of the blueprint for the national certification examination. Dr. Crist is a Fellow of AOTA.